La Grande

Mademoiselle

at the Court

of France

La Grande

Mademoiselle

at the Court

of France

1627–1693

VINCENT J. PITTS

THE JOHNS HOPKINS UNIVERSITY PRESS
BALTIMORE AND LONDON

FRONTISPIECE: Detail from an engraving of Mademoiselle in her middle years, probably 1666.

The Johns Hopkins University Press
2715 North Charles Street
Baltimore, Maryland 21218-4363
www.press.jhu.edu

Library of Congress Cataloging-in-Publication Data will be found at the end of this book.

A catalog record for this book is available from the British Library.

ISBN 0-8018-6466-6

Contents

Illustrations are on pages 88–98

Acknowledgments

MY DEBT TO PEOPLE AND TO INSTITUTIONS ON BOTH SIDES OF THE Atlantic in the preparation of this study is immense and freely acknowledged. I am unable to express adequately my gratitude to M. François Avril of the Département des Manuscrits of the Bibliothèque Nationale de France and his colleagues for the many courtesies shown to me in the course of my research. I am also most appreciative of the special efforts made to assist me by M. Henri Zuber, M. Emil Rousseau, and their colleagues at the Archives Nationales de France. I would like to mention as well M. J.-C. Garetta of the Bibliothèque de l'Arsenal; M. Louis Amigues of the Archives of the Ministère des Affaires Etrangères; M. Daniel Guérin of the Archives Départementales de l'Yonne, Auxerre; Mme Micheline Durand of the Musée Municipale of Auxerre;

the late Msgr. le Comte de Paris and the Fondation Saint Louis for access to the Fonds de Dreux; Messrs. Jacques and Michel Guyot, the current proprietors of Saint-Fargeau; M. Daniel Allix of Brinon-sur-Beuvron; and Dr. Frances Harris, of the British Library, London.

The vast resources of the Yale University library system have facilitated much of my secondary research. I would also like to thank the staff of Houghton Library, Harvard University, and the curators of the Morgan Library, New York, for permission to examine materials found in their respective collections.

A number of academic readers have given generously of their time and talent to comment on the manuscript. Elborg Forster has shared with me her insights into the world of seventeenth-century France and has made several helpful suggestions on various translation problems. Ray Kierstead has provided many a useful caution. Jacques Guicharnaud has done his best to broaden my understanding of the literature and language of Mademoiselle's France. Patricia Ranum has graciously shared transcriptions of Mademoiselle's letters to Cosimo III de Medici with me, and Orest Ranum, whose erudition is matched only by his kindness, has been of inestimable help and encouragement at every stage of this project.

A number of lay readers have done their best to keep the text both readable and comprehensible to nonspecialists. Let me thank them here: John Carey, Raymond Kosinski, Connie Mortensen, John Metz, Mary Pasti, Charles Quigley, and Br. Joseph Zutelis, CSC. Alex Rostocki was of great help with the photographs. I would also like to thank the staff of the Johns Hopkins University Press for their very professional efforts to transform my manuscript into a book worthy of Mademoiselle.

I can only hope that none of these will be disappointed with the outcome.

Finally, a word of thanks to my good friend Anne Develay, of Nevers, France, whose suggestion one rainy October afternoon some years ago that we visit Saint-Fargeau provided my introduction to the subject of this book.

I am incapable of any base action or dark deeds: I am more likely to show mercy than to render justice. I am melancholy, and like to read good solid books. . . . I enjoy society and the conversation of well-bred persons. . . . Above all others, I like soldiers and to hear them talk about their craft. . . . I confess that I talk willingly about war; I know that I am brave, with much courage and ambition. . . . I enjoy violins above all other music, and dancing more than I can say. . . . No one has ever had any power over me. . . . The great sorrows I have known would have killed other people.

MADEMOISELLE

She didn't like anyone, and hated to be constrained in any way. One had to go to great lengths to get around her whenever one wished her to follow one's advice, trying to persuade her that she had the same thoughts. Since she would never decide something on the spot, she would return a little later and propose what one had suggested as if it came from herself. She understood herself well, and would say sometimes, "My God, why have you given me such a disposition?"

She had, however, some very good qualities, because she was gentle and good and hospitable to everyone; she had an enormous amount of wit and a nobility of spirit; in these areas, her sisters were well beneath her level.

JEAN REGNAULT DE SEGRAIS

Introduction

THREE HUNDRED YEARS AFTER HER DEATH, A GANGLY SPINSTER cousin of Louis XIV still attracts many admirers. Anne-Marie-Louise d'Orléans, duchess de Montpensier, always called "La Grande Mademoiselle," is a stock figure in French textbooks. She was born to great wealth and dynastic position, and her vast fortune and royal rank made her a perennial candidate for every vacant throne in Europe, beginning with

that of France. But none of the many proposals to place a "crown matrimonial" on her head ever came to fruition, and Mademoiselle was destined to live and die as the dutiful, unmarried daughter of one prince,
and the somewhat superfluous, if colorful, satellite of another. She can
still be found in this last role at Versailles, in the salon of the Oeil de
Boeuf in Nocret's allegorical portrait of the royal family, as pale Diana in
the train of radiant Apollo.

She survives in popular memory as the heroine of the Fronde who
turned the cannon of the Bastille on the royal troops and saved a rebel
army to fight another day. Connoisseurs of *petites histoires* and readers of
Madame de Sévigné recognize her as the princess whose attempted misalliance with a captain of the king's guard sent shock waves through
polite society and inspired one of Sévigné's most famous letters.

None of these events can explain the fascination with Mademoiselle
by students of French history in every generation since the first printing
of her *Mémoires* in 1718. Yet this interest is not surprising. Mademoiselle's
lifetime, 1627–1693, spanned the classic "age of absolutism." She was a
witness to the ministries of Richelieu and Mazarin, a participant in the
Fronde, and an observer of Louis XIV's most successful years. Her
Mémoires capture much of what she saw, and, as in Saint-Simon, some of
the set pieces, such as the death agonies of Anne of Austria, and the
wedding of Louis XIV to the infanta Maria Theresa, are dramatic and
memorable re-creations. Unlike Saint-Simon, who was simply a spectator at the theater of royalty, Mademoiselle was a member of the cast, and
brought to her recollections the insights of a participant.

It is a tribute to the power of her *Mémoires* that its first publication
was suppressed in France. Succeeding decades saw numerous editions,
both in Paris and Amsterdam, based on a manuscript entrusted by the
princess to a prominent member of the parlement of Paris, Achille de
Harlay. The nineteenth century saw the reissue of this version, as well as a
newer edition prepared by Adolphe Chéruel. Chéruel's edition, based on
a manuscript in Mademoiselle's own hand, eliminated many eighteenth-
century stylistic "corrections" that had masked the vigor of the original.
Mademoiselle's other writings include literary portraits, satirical short
stories, an exchange of letters with Madame de Motteville on the virtues
of the unmarried state and the role of women in public life, and two
religious tracts written late in life and recovered from near oblivion.
When used in conjunction with the *Mémoires*, they permit us to engage a
strong and forceful seventeenth-century personality.

Since the beginning of the twentieth century, innumerable biographies or studies of La Grande Mademoiselle have been published in France, three since 1985. In the last generation, moreover, the works of literary scholars such as Marc Fumaroli, Jean Garapon, Emmanuèle Lesne, and Faith Beasley, probing Mademoiselle's writings, have offered fresh insights and suggested new ways to approach a familiar historical personality. These specialized and detailed studies have coincided with attempts by historians to use the memoir literature of the period to explore contemporary values and perceptions of political and social change in sixteenth- and seventeenth-century France. All of this helps us to see Mademoiselle in a different light.

Not the least of such modes of inquiry is the appearance of women's studies in the past two decades. A generation or more of scholarship has been enriched by the attempts of feminist scholars to explore and reinterpret the role of women in the early modern period. Some scholars in the field have preferred general studies of groups or classes, or have concentrated on the rediscovery of hitherto obscure persons who deserve better from Clio. One can hardly quarrel with this. But there is also a need to examine the lives of prominent women with as much care as is accorded to their male counterparts. In an excellent biography of Lady Rachel Russell, Lois G. Schwoerer reminds us that until we undertake such studies, "our understanding of the past will remain incomplete and one-sided."[1]

In the case of La Grande Mademoiselle, the world of Anglo-American scholarship has been especially remiss. The only two English-language biographies of the princess to appear in this century date from the 1950s, and suffer from certain obvious limitations. Francis Steegmuller's *The Grand Mademoiselle* (1956) is a graceful, if condescending, study that concentrates on the matrimonial aspirations of the princess. Vita Sackville-West's *Daughter of France* (1959) draws a more nuanced picture. As the daughter of a landed family of the English nobility, raised in country-house circles, Sackville-West seems to have had an instinctive appreciation of her subject. In the end, however, her own strong personality intrudes, and the reader is left wondering whether the *personnage* encountered is more Sackville-West than Anne-Marie-Louise d'Orléans.

In another study of Mademoiselle, Christian Bouyer cautions us on the need to make use of all available sources in any approach to Mademoiselle.[2] One cannot disagree with this commonplace; still, in this book the emphasis will be on Mademoiselle's perceptions of the world as evidenced by her *Mémoires* and other writings. To that degree, this work will not be "objective." It attempts to see matters as Mademoiselle saw them, giving people and events the importance Mademoiselle assigned them, and to "intervene" to offer appropriate background, suggest a modern insight, or correct any glaring errors of chronology in Mademoiselle's recollections. The emphasis at all times will be on the *Mémoires*. The reasoning here is very simple: they are a most unusual product of Mademoiselle's gender and class. The bulk of memoir literature of Mademoiselle's time was written by men. In addition to Mademoiselle, the only other women of her generation to leave memoirs of note were Marie de Longueville, duchess de Nemours, who wrote a short account of her involvement in the Fronde; Madame de Motteville, whose extensive work is, in fact, a chronicle of Anne of Austria's life and ends with that queen's death; and the considerably less prominent Madame de la Guette. None of the others is "inner-directed," and none offers any opportunity to study a personality over time.

Memoirs covering the events of many years, like those of Motteville or Saint-Simon, were typically written at the end of a lifetime, polished and edited in a way that provides a coherent and final view of the matters in question.

Mademoiselle's *Mémoires* follow a very different path. They were written in parts, separated by decades. The first part, written before 1660, records Mademoiselle's memories of Richelieu and the court of Louis XIII, chronicles her actions during the Fronde, and describes in dramatic terms her deep disillusionment with her father, Gaston d'Orléans, and the psychological costs of her break with paternal authority. The second part of her *Mémoires*, begun in 1677, contains her account of the famous failed engagement to Antonin de Lauzun. This was the only great romance of Mademoiselle's life, one in which she sought to break with social convention by choosing her own husband, and, in a defiance of dynastic principle, finding a commoner to wed. It is a story of betrayal at the hands of Louis XIV, and a portrayal of the hypocrisy of court life. The last part, written in 1689–90, chronicles the greatest disillusionment of all: Mademoiselle's discovery that Lauzun was only an ambitious courtier and that his affection, such as it was, had not survived a decade of solitary confinement in a remote fortress in the Alps. The conclusions drawn and the lessons offered are developed gradually, out of a mix of more ordinary experience, as would be the case as a life unfolded over the decades. The reader can follow the development and emergence of a personality, and test assumptions by reference to other works of Mademoiselle—literary portraits, satirical short stories, letters, and religious reflections—which can be dated precisely.

The most frequently occurring themes in Mademoiselle's *Mémoires* are confrontation and betrayal: confrontation with authority and betrayal by those she trusted. Her narrative is in large part an exploration of the limits of public and private authority in the France of her time and the distortions of the "natural order" that occurred when these two modes of authority came into conflict with one another. As Robert Muchembled reminds us, royal authority in seventeenth-century France was largely modeled on the dominant concept of patriarchal authority in the private sphere, which conceded to fathers or their surrogates (husbands or eldest brothers) almost absolute power to regulate the destinies of wives and children. For males, the subordination was usually temporary. In time, they would succeed to the role of *pater familias.* But for wives and daughters, subordination and satellite status were assumed to be permanent conditions of life. In the public sphere, the king and, by extension, his ministers and officers, expected the same deference and obedience from subjects that family members owed to the head of the household. In theory, the two modes of authority were supposed to act in concert to assure the simultaneous well-being of state and society.[3]

For Mademoiselle, a member of the reigning dynasty, the convergence of paternal and royal authority ought to have been all the more crushing. But for most of Mademoiselle's first thirty years, her father, Gaston d'Orléans, was a prominent rebel and critic of royal and ministerial authority. This conflict of authorities, which came to a head during the Fronde, provided Mademoiselle and a handful of other aristocratic women the opportunity to expand, at least temporarily, the permissible sphere of activities allocated to women. Mademoiselle was to argue that duty to her father excused disobedience to the king. This window closed with the reconciliation of Gaston and the court during Mademoiselle's years in exile (1652–57). With the poles of authority again in alignment, Mademoiselle found herself relegated once more to a secondary and subordinate position.

But the experience of those years, and her sense of betrayal at the hands of Gaston, altered Mademoiselle's perceptions of the limits of authority and the degree of independence permissible to a princess of the royal house. Her attempts to control her own destiny, so vividly illustrated by the *affaire Lauzun,* were doomed to failure. This last episode, which poisoned much of her later life, made the limits of the possible only too evident. Royal authority, social convention, and simple greed all played a part in the final tragedy of Mademoiselle's life. But Mademoiselle did not go quietly; her *Mémoires* chronicle the events and portray her tormentors—Louis XIV, Condé, Madame de Montespan—with a pitiless realism that was to attract the attention of royal censors of a later generation. Her appeal for vindication was to posterity, and in writing well Mademoiselle was to have the best revenge.

In the end, what holds one's attention is the strong personality that emerges from those pages, a personality whose stages of development are reflected in the *Mémoires* and whose voice, even when muted with grief and disillusionment, speaks loudly of the time and place of its origin.

La Grande

Mademoiselle

at the Court

of France

These Mémoires *are only for me, so it doesn't matter that they are neither polished nor short. They are only to amuse me when I grow old, as I hope to do, by reminding me of my youth. . . . The lesson I take from them is to despise the world more and more and to understand how little certainty it offers . . . born with everything one could have and with all the advantages God has given me, I have been unhappy all my life.*

MADEMOISELLE

The late Mademoiselle could have been the happiest princess in the world if she had wanted to . . . under the pretext of not wanting a master over her, she would not accept or follow any good advice; she was never able to find a suitable husband.

JEAN REGNAULT DE SEGRAIS

1 The Daughter of France

TO THE GRANDEES OF THE REALM GATHERED AT THE LOUVRE, THE birth of a princess on May 27, 1627, brought mixed emotions. For Louis XIII and his queen, Anne of Austria, still childless after twelve years of marriage, the birth of this royal niece provided unmitigated relief, a sentiment shared by the king's chief minister, cardinal de Richelieu. Had she been a male, the infant in the crib would have stood second in the line of succession, junior only to her father, Gaston, the king's younger brother and heir presumptive.

Already the focus of every plot directed against the king and Richelieu, Gaston would have gained immeasurably from the birth of an heir to the Bourbon dynasty. But the Salic law, which regulated the succession to the crown, barred females from the throne. A princess, however talented or wealthy, had no independent political standing. When the time came, she could be used as a pawn to advance the interests of state and dynasty as the king saw fit. So for Gaston and his entourage, the birth of a daughter was, if not a catastrophe, a major disappointment and a serious political setback.

Indeed, the baby owed her very existence to the dynamics of power within the ruling family. Scarcely a year earlier, Gaston, a discontented adolescent of eighteen, had been drawn into a plot by members of the high aristocracy to seize power through the removal, and probable assassination, of Richelieu, who had already begun to consolidate his position by means of his uncanny psychological dominance of the twenty-six-year-old king. The plot was uncovered, and the punishments were severe. Gaston's governor, the maréchal d'Ornano, was arrested, as were Alexandre and César de Vendôme, two half brothers of the king and Gaston. A royal cousin, the comte de Soissons, fled the country to avoid interrogation, and the duchess de Chevreuse, a close friend of the queen, was banished to her estates. Ornano and Alexandre de Vendôme were to die in prison; an even more terrible punishment befell the young and well-connected Henri de Talleyrand, comte de Chalais, who suffered a public beheading for his part in the conspiracy.

In the case of Gaston, *raison d'état* tempered official wrath. There was little, after all, that could be done to punish the heir to the crown without risking even more upheaval. At the urging of the queen mother, Marie de Medici, the king and Richelieu confined themselves to an admission of complicity by Gaston. In addition, Gaston was forced to honor his long-standing betrothal to the richest heiress in the kingdom, his distant cousin Marie de Bourbon-Montpensier. Although this proposal dated from the time of Gaston's late father, Henri IV, by the mid 1620s the arrangement had taken on an additional political coloration. Marie de Montpensier's widowed mother had remarried Charles, duc de Guise, and the union of Gaston with Marie de Montpensier was viewed by many at court as a political alliance between the throne and the Guise family, to the detriment of other aristocratic court factions. Some historians argue that the "conspiracy of Chalais" may have had its origins in an attempt to block the marriage, rather than in any more fundamental opposition to Richelieu.[1]

Gaston, however, had little choice under the circumstances. On August 6, 1626, the young couple were married by Richelieu at Nantes, in a simple ceremony in a local church. Although by royal standards the celebrations were meager, the bridegroom was well paid for his consent. Hitherto he had borne the titular style "duke of Anjou," without the estates or pensions that an adult brother of a king of France normally enjoyed. Now he was created duc d'Orléans and Chartres, and comte de Blois, with an ordinary annual income of 100,000 livres from these domains. In addition, the king bestowed on his brother 660,000 livres in pensions, as well as other emoluments, for a total annual income of 1,000,000 livres, an enormous provision by the standards of the time. Gaston's household was put on a footing scarcely inferior to the king's, with a bishop as grand almoner and the duc de Bellegarde as superintendent of his household, more than forty gentlemen-in-waiting, a legion of other servants, noble and commoner, and, as befitted his high status, an *introducteur des ambassadeurs*. His person was to be guarded by detachments of the French and Swiss Guards, who were to wear his livery and to march at the head of his entourage with drums beating (except, it was added, in the king's presence). The wealth and independence thus conveyed made Gaston a worthy match for Marie de Montpensier.[2]

The sole heiress of several great landed fortunes accumulated in the previous century by the Montpensiers, Marie brought to her nuptial bed three ducal titles, a sovereign principality (Dombes, a part of the Holy Roman Empire), an infinity of lesser distinctions, counties, marquisates, and baronies, with pensions and other annual revenues aggregating 330,000 livres, and a large diamond, reputedly worth 240,000 livres as a wedding present from her mother.[3]

By her marriage to Gaston, Marie de Montpensier, already a princess of the blood, ascended the small step that separated her from the very summit of the French and European social structures. By virtue of her marriage vows, she had become the third woman in France, junior only to the queen and the queen mother. Her new standing brought about a remarkable transformation in the behavior of a princess hitherto considered passive and almost sheeplike in personality. As an in-law of the queens of England and Spain, Gaston's sisters, and of the haughty queen of France, Anne of Austria, she frequently exercised her prerogative to address them as "sister," to the consternation in particular of Anne of Austria. Nor was she above snubbing lesser members of the extended Bourbon clan, such as the princess de Condé, in the assertion of her status.[4]

Characterized by one contemporary observer as "proud as a dragon," the duchess d'Orléans enjoyed yet another triumph in the fall of 1626, when it became evident that she was pregnant. The queen, after twelve years of a bitter and unhappy marriage and several miscarriages, had not been able to provide her royal husband with a dauphin, her primary dynastic duty. There was therefore a very good chance that the unborn infant in the womb of Marie de Montpensier would someday be king of France—that is, if it was a boy, and the duchess had little difficulty convincing herself that this was indeed the case. As she strolled down the corridors of the Louvre, she accepted the homage of sycophantic courtiers who congratulated her on the impending birth of the heir to the throne of Henri IV.[5]

The rejoicing proved to be especially premature for Marie de Montpensier. The birth of the little princess was not simply a dynastic misfortune and a personal failure: it was a death sentence. The pregnancy had not been easy; the delivery was difficult. The third lady of France, like many other women of her time, succumbed to the complications of childbirth, dying scarcely a week after the delivery of the child whose conception had brought her such joy.

She left her infant daughter a healthy dose of Bourbon pride and a purse to match, but not any given names. As was customary in the French royal house, princes and princesses were privately baptized at birth but not given any Christian names until a later, public baptism, held when they were between seven and ten years of age. The little princess in question was to undergo this ritual in 1636, when she received the name Anne-Marie-Louise.

Even without a set of given names, the infant hardly wanted for nomenclature. As her mother's heiress, she could be called by any of her mother's senior titles; as her father's daughter, she was also Mademoiselle d'Orléans. Yet for most of her life, almost none of her many names was used routinely. Within court circles, senior members of the royal house were referred to by certain special designations. The prince de Condé, first prince of the blood, was normally styled "Monsieur le Prince," while the comte de Soissons, head of another branch of the family, was "Monsieur le Comte." The king's brother, or the most senior if there were several, was known as "Monsieur," and the wife of "Monsieur," quite logically, was "Madame." Thus, virtually all contemporary references to Gaston omit his titles and speak simply of "Monsieur."

Daughters of the king were usually called "Madame" followed by a given name, for example, "Madame Elisabeth" or "Madame Henriette." The case of a royal niece, daughter of "Monsieur," now arose for the first time since the use of such titles began. According to Saint-Simon, writing many years later, the infant princess at first was simply called "Mademoiselle d'Orléans" or "Mademoiselle de Montpensier." But members of Gaston's household and her own attendants often spoke of the child as "Mademoiselle," without the surname, since the reference was obvious. The habit soon spread, and a new court title evolved to designate the daughter, or sometimes eldest daughter, of Monsieur. Thus, the princess came to be known almost exclusively as "Mademoiselle," both in her own lifetime and in the history books of later generations.[6]

Shortly after her mother's death, the infant was removed from her mother's apartments at the Louvre and installed at the neighboring palace of the Tuileries. Unlike the Louvre, an ancient dwelling still in transformation, the Tuileries was a new palace, begun by Catherine de Medici scarcely a half century earlier and continued by Mademoiselle's grandfather Henri IV, who commissioned a series of galleries and pavilions to join the two structures. The results were dazzling. The Pavilion of Flora, with its distinctive chimneys, set off one end of the Tuileries. Beyond it, facing the Seine, stretched the Grand Gallery, which joined the Gallery of Kings, today the Gallery of Apollo, at the extremity of the Louvre. The symmetries and harmonies of this sequence of buildings were much appreciated by contemporaries. Like all royal residences of the period, Mademoiselle's apartments were open to the public. A visitor gained access to them by mounting the great oval staircase under the high dome that marked the entrance to the Tuileries. Both the Tuileries and the Louvre were famous for their rich decorations: paintings from the royal collections, gilt ceilings, carved doorways, and furniture gathered by Marie de Medici.

The gardens of the Tuileries, laid out in rectangular segments, were already a favorite Parisian promenade. The formal garden between the Tuileries and the Louvre came to be known as the *parterre de Mademoiselle*. On the opposite side of the building lay a park that ran down to the city wall. There were fountains, fishponds, and an aviary for visitors to enjoy as they strolled along long avenues of elms alternating with cypresses and mulberries. At the end of the garden, the city walls framed a gate known as the Porte de la Conférence. Beyond lay the open countryside. This provided a useful escape route from the palace complex in times of trouble and an easy exit for excursions in calmer times. One might take a carriage drive along the banks of the Seine on the newly built Cours-la-Reine, which intersected the road to Versailles, where

Mademoiselle's uncle Louis XIII had recently acquired a small country estate.[7]

To minister to the needs of this infant princess, her guardians assembled a vast household. Nearly forty senior staff members, including a personal physician, a surgeon, and an apothecary, looked after Mademoiselle's physical well-being. She had a chaplain and two almoners to minister to her spiritual needs and supervise her charitable duties. Jacques Le Coigneux, one of Gaston's inner circle, aided by two assistants and a treasurer, managed her estates and financial affairs. The intellectual development and moral education of the royal child fell to a governess, an undergoverness, and a preceptress. In addition to these high servants, who were entitled to a salary or pension and, in most cases, lodging, there were pages, valets, squires, and ushers to uphold the dignity of the noble household, and servants to minister to the wants of Mademoiselle's attendants. Her governess, for example, received a special allowance to pay for a page, two lackeys, two chambermaids, and a valet of her own; the undergoverness claimed similar prerogatives. To permit the infant to enjoy a drive through Paris or in the country, there were coaches, a coachman, and a postilion. There were also detachments of the Swiss and French Guards, who were entitled to a daily ration of bread and wine: four loaves a day for the French guards, two for the Swiss. The total staff, somewhere in excess of seventy persons, consumed a vast amount of food and drink, prepared by the household's own cooks and bakers; there was also a constant need for candles to light the vast rooms of the palace, straw for the horses, and linen for the table, bedchambers, and persons of the house. In 1630, a typical year, the cost of all this grandeur came to nearly 83,000 livres. Even by royal standards, this was extravagant. Her household, Mademoiselle noted afterward, was larger than those her various royal aunts had enjoyed as unmarried princesses.[8]

From Mademoiselle's point of view, the most important member of her staff in her early years was her governess, Jeanne de Harlay, marquise de Saint-Georges. Madame de Saint-Georges was the daughter of Madame de Montglat, who had been the governess of Louis XIII, Gaston, and the other royal children of the preceding generation. Madame de Saint-Georges had been the personal choice of the queen mother for the post, and her appointment as Mademoiselle's governess was viewed as a natural extension of a long-standing tie.

Madame de Saint-Georges was responsible for the child's overall formation, that is, her preparation for her role in life as a royal princess, one who might even some day wear the crown of a queen consort. To this end, Madame de Saint-Georges devoted much time to the princess's education in the minutiae of court etiquette, to her acquisition of the essential social graces, and to her development of the poise expected of a woman of high rank. Above all, Madame de Saint-Georges imparted to her charge an exalted sense of her own importance as a member of the ruling house and a great heiress in her own right.

Madame de Saint-Georges does not seem to have spent much time on academic exercises. Admittedly, the education of royalty was uneven in the period, especially for princesses. Whereas Mademoiselle's cousin Louis de Bourbon, the future Grand Condé, benefited from an unusually thorough schooling at a Jesuit academy, his sister, Anne-Geneviève de Bourbon, received as little formal education as Mademoiselle, and his future wife, the niece of Richelieu, did not know how to read or write at the time of her marriage. A generation later, Fénelon was still complaining about the neglect of women's education. In this respect, Mademoiselle might have served as his model. Mademoiselle's appalling handwriting became a family joke. Her spelling was no better, leaving modern scholars to work out the intended meaning of near-phonetic constructions. Mademoiselle had little or no training in the fashionable languages of the period, Italian and Spanish, and her attempts to learn these as an adult were not particularly successful. She was to dismiss this shortcoming, somewhat defensively, by insisting that there were so many good books in her own language that she had no need of those in other tongues.[9]

In retrospect, Mademoiselle had many reservations about her upbringing. Her recollections of Madame de Saint-Georges mix affection with the contempt children often display toward overly indulgent parents or teachers. She roundly criticizes her governess for encouraging an exaggerated sense of her own importance and for doing little to counteract the flattery of attendants and courtiers. The result was a headstrong and somewhat spoiled child. It should be added that Mademoiselle did not blame Madame de Saint-Georges alone for this outcome. Part of the problem, she insisted, was the absence of any higher authority to reinforce the efforts of her governess. The allusion was to her absent father and grandmothers, who were not available to supervise the princess's education.[10]

We owe the details of Mademoiselle's childhood and her perception of them to Mademoiselle herself, who devotes an unusual amount of time to them in the first part of her *Mémoires*. In doing so, she breaks a convention of the period. Few sixteenth- or seventeenth-century memoir writers spend more than a few pages on their early years. Mademoiselle, who picked up her pen for the first time in her late twenties, saw the importance of the events of those years from her later perspective and chose to do otherwise.

The first image that Mademoiselle's *Mémoires* provides is one of loneliness in the midst of her vast array of servants. She opens her narrative with a lament for her dead mother, "the beginning of the misfortune of my house." To her mind, the absence of a mother to look out for her interests largely explained her meager education and the failure of the rest of her family to see to her later "establishment," that is, a suitable marriage. A few pages later she connects the results of this upbringing to the coolness between herself and her grandmother Guise. As a result of the overbearing arrogance she had developed, the child treated her grandmother Guise with disdain: the "faraway grandmother" was not sufficiently royal for Mademoiselle. In fact, Catherine-Henriette de Guise, busy with seven living children by her second marriage, many of whom were close in age to Mademoiselle, had no time for this exalted grandchild, in spite of the political ties between the Guises and Gaston.[11]

Mademoiselle accepted her mother's loss as an act of divine providence and her grandmother Guise's coolness as the result of her own childhood behavior. But when she describes her relationship with the rest of the royal family, the explanations become more complicated. Unlike her grandmother Guise, Mademoiselle's royal grandmother, Marie de Medici, took a real interest in the child. The queen mother chose Madame de Saint-Georges as her granddaughter's mentor and spent a good deal of time supervising the princess's household. Mademoiselle attributed this preference to the old queen's special affection for Gaston and for her dead mother. But all of this was hearsay; it is what others told Mademoiselle later. As Mademoiselle complains, she could not remember ever seeing her grandmother.[12]

When Mademoiselle was scarcely four years old, in the summer of 1631, Marie de Medici left France forever. Some months earlier, she had tried to persuade Louis XIII to dismiss Richelieu as his chief minister. After several dramatic days, during which it seemed that Louis might do so, the king chose otherwise. Louis confirmed the cardinal in his functions, and Richelieu's opponents, ministerial and aristocratic, were crushed instead, in an episode known as the Day of Dupes (November 11,

1630). Louis XIII initially concealed his anger toward his mother. A superficial reconciliation in the winter of 1630–31 was followed by an extraordinary piece of theater. While the court was staying at Compiègne in February 1631, Louis slipped away early one morning, leaving orders to place his mother under arrest and transfer her to Moulins. Marie refused to budge and remained at Compiègne under guard until the following July, when she evaded her guards and crossed the frontier into the Spanish Netherlands. This was the beginning of a long exile: she was to die in poverty in Cologne in 1642 without ever seeing France or her granddaughter again. Mademoiselle claimed to feel the loss as keenly as that of her mother.[13]

Even more overwhelming for Mademoiselle was the absence of her father. Until his death in 1660, Gaston was to remain the center of Mademoiselle's emotional universe, and the *Mémoires* detail the evolution over time of a complex father-daughter relationship. In her early years, she perceived her father as heroic. Shortly after Marie de Medici had fled into exile, Gaston also left France as a result of the breach between the king and the queen mother.[14] Beyond this simple explanation by the princess lay a far more tangled story.

Until recently, Gaston d'Orléans has been treated by historians with almost universal contempt. The 1925 *Larousse Histoire de France Illustrée*, for example, summing up an almost official position by the corps of French historians, called him "a man of mediocre intelligence . . . . frivolous . . . . selfish and very ambitious," who was associated "unsuccessfully and ingloriously" in all the troubles experienced by France during the reign of Louis XIII and the minority of Louis XIV. Carl Burckhardt echoed this judgment, calling Gaston "thoroughly spoiled, thoroughly weak, thoroughly despicable." It is a point of view that runs in tandem with the official canonization of Richelieu and his work. Only in recent years have scholars begun to reexamine the opposition to Richelieu in a somewhat more comprehensive fashion. Although scarcely exonerating Gaston, they do suggest that the opposition to Richelieu's policies had its roots deep in French social and constitutional history, however self-serving or personally despicable individual opponents might have been. In short, Gaston has been placed in a long line of champions of mixed or limited monarchy, as opposed to the Bourbon centralism that was gathering momentum under Richelieu. Mademoiselle and her contemporaries certainly did not articulate the argument in this form, but much evidence has come to light to support this interpretation.[15]

Gaston, always at the center of the innumerable plots against Richelieu, used his status as heir to the crown to rally his aristocratic backers, and his family position to embarrass the king. In 1629, he went briefly into exile after a harsh exchange of accusations with the king; he was lured back with the gift of an additional duchy, a large sum of money to pay his debts, and official appointments for some key followers. Shortly thereafter, he aligned himself with Marie de Medici in the intrigues that culminated in the Day of Dupes. After some hesitation, Gaston broke openly with the minister just before his mother's arrest. Upon receiving the news of the queen mother's detention, Gaston fled the court. He took with him the Montpensier jewelry, his daughter's property, to finance his efforts to unseat Richelieu.

From the relative safety of Burgundy, Gaston tried to persuade his aristocratic admirers and provincial authorities to rise against the régime. When the king retaliated with punitive decrees, the parlement of Paris refused to register them, forcing Louis and Richelieu to take measures against jurists sympathetic to Gaston in order to intimidate the rest into compliance. Gaston retaliated with another broadside directed at both king and minister, taking care to lay the blame at Richelieu's door for the collapse of traditional liberties and the misery and poverty of the population. If the king did not know the truth, said Gaston, it was because Richelieu controlled access to the royal person and prevented others from speaking openly. With this flourish, Gaston slipped over the border into Lorraine and exile, followed by a royal decree outlawing his supporters and seizing his property. This episode climaxed with the ill-fated uprising of the duc de Montmorency, governor of Languedoc, and ended with Montmorency's ignominious death on the scaffold in October 1632.[16]

Mademoiselle was deeply affected by Gaston's departure, although, as she notes, she was too little to understand the circumstances. She was, however, dimly aware that Monsieur, who was "away with the army," was in some danger. The thought upset her so much that she refused for some time to appear at court. Mademoiselle adds in passing that the king appointed a new set of custodians to oversee her financial affairs in the absence of Monsieur. Since Le Coigneux and a number of Gaston's other appointees had followed him into exile, this was a necessary measure; it also had the effect of denying Gaston access to Mademoiselle's money to finance his activities. Indeed, as Mademoiselle observes somewhat naïvely, her new guardians did so thorough a job that when Gaston returned several years later, they presented him with a large sum they had accumulated during his exile.[17]

Mademoiselle's most vivid memory of that period is of the solemn ceremonies of installation for knights of the royal Order of the Holy Spirit held at Fontainebleau in May 1633. This was coupled with an unusual ritual of degradation, which stripped two members of the order of their rank for having followed Gaston into rebellion and exile. Since they were not present, their disgrace was symbolized by the defacing of their armorial bearings. When the meaning of this activity was explained to the little princess, she became extremely distraught. "I soon began to cry, and felt so upset that I wanted to leave, and said that it was unseemly for me to watch." It was not proper, in her eyes, to compel her attendance at a public affront to her father.[18]

Mademoiselle rounds out her picture of the royal family in those years by discussing her relationship with the king and queen. She assures her readers that in spite of the strain between Louis XIII and Gaston, the king and queen always treated her with great affection, so much so that she commonly referred to the king as her *petit papa* and the queen as her *petite maman*. The king, she believed, was especially kind to her because of the pain caused by his brother's absence. Sensing this, the little princess took advantage of intimate moments to mention her father to the king, timid advances that the king evidently ignored or gently turned aside. As for the queen, with hindsight Mademoiselle came to be somewhat suspicious of her expressions of affection. She believed that these were largely motivated by the queen's supposed interest in a possible marriage with Gaston in the event of Louis's death, a suggestion not original to Mademoiselle. Its inclusion in the *Mémoires* was possibly intended to remind the reader that even at the very heart of the royal family there was deep discord. Indeed, had Louis and his Spanish queen, so often accused of plotting against her royal husband, agreed on anything, even something as simple as a liking for their small niece, it would have been remarkable.[19]

Overall, the picture Mademoiselle presents is one of dissension and disarray within the royal family. But how can she explain the phenomenon of the heirs of the great Henri IV tearing themselves and the kingdom to pieces? Mademoiselle found her answer, as did many of her contemporaries, in the actions of the king's chief minister. Like her father, Mademoiselle saw little to admire in Richelieu, whom she saw as the true source of the unhappiness in her own young life. Richelieu makes his first appearance in her *Mémoires* in 1634, when Gaston was engaged in negotiations with the court for his return. It is Richelieu, rather than the king, who drives the process, attempting to impose a humiliating set of conditions on Monsieur. Chief among these was a requirement that Gaston repudiate his second wife, Marguerite de Lorraine, the sister of duke Charles IV of Lorraine, whom he had married in 1632 while in exile. The marriage of the heir to the crown was an affair of state, and Louis XIII refused to recognize a union he had not sanctioned. By the fall of 1634, Gaston had obtained a number of important concessions, including permission to reside within his own domains (a precaution against a summary arrest), a large sum of money to pay his debts, and amnesty for his followers. But with respect to his marriage, he obtained only a promise that he would not be compelled to marry another until the question was resolved.[20]

Gaston returned to France in October 1634, but his wife remained in exile. It is difficult to determine precisely what the objection to Marguerite de Lorraine was, except that her family was traditionally allied with the Habsburg enemy. Louis and Richelieu may have had domestic considerations in mind. As long as Gaston's marital situation remained unsettled, he was not in a position to strengthen his hand by siring a son to take the place of a dauphin, and thereby recreating the threat posed by Marie de Montpensier's pregnancy seven years earlier. If so, Mademoiselle saw none of this, accusing Richelieu of a far baser motive. Her entourage convinced her that Richelieu was determined to break the Lorraine marriage in order to force Gaston to marry his own niece, Madame d'Aiguillon. The very idea of such a misalliance struck the little princess, so full of dynastic pride, as "shameful" and brought tears of rage to her eyes. She took a child's revenge by singing aloud all the street songs she had heard directed against the minister and his niece.[21]

Her father, she notes proudly, returned to France without agreeing to this "ridiculous" condition. The princess, now seven, was taken to Limours for a reunion with Gaston. Although he had long abandoned Mademoiselle to the care of her attendants and valued her chiefly for the vast income he was free to use during her minority, Gaston was capable of an occasional affectionate gesture toward the little girl. Shortly before the two came into view of one another, Gaston slipped off the blue ribbon of the Order of the Holy Spirit he ordinarily wore, and passed it to one of his companions to see if his daughter would recognize him without it. When the moment came, Mademoiselle did not hesitate an instant; the "force of nature" (perhaps supplemented by Gaston's resemblance to Louis XIII) substituted for any recollection of Monsieur's features, and she threw herself into Gaston's arms. Gaston was delighted and for a few days showered her with the charm for which he was famous in court circles.

The fun climaxed with a *ballet de cour* that Gaston arranged to allow his daughter to show off her mastery of the art; she had, it seems, been too small to dance at a recent one at court. For this one, dubbed the "dance of the pygmies" by Mademoiselle, a troop of little girls of the high aristocracy were paired with young gentlemen of the same size. The dance went well; the lights and costumes created a wonderful effect. A small mishap heightened Mademoiselle's happy recollection of the event: a tiny bird escaped from a cage and managed to frighten the young Mademoiselle de Brézé, one of Richelieu's nieces. The little girl became hysterical, to the undisguised merriment of the company, especially Mademoiselle.[22]

Mademoiselle groups this small triumph with a more serious and telling defeat. As a symbol of reconciliation between Gaston and Richelieu, one of Gaston's intimates, Antoine de Puylaurens, married a cousin of the cardinal in November 1634. But several months later, in February 1635, as the new duke attended a royal ballet at the Louvre, he was arrested on the cardinal's orders and imprisoned at Vincennes, where he died under mysterious circumstances the following summer. His arrest and, simultaneously, that of two other servants of Gaston, was intended to put pressure on Gaston to renounce his marriage to Marguerite de Lorraine. Puylaurens, in the afterglow of his own marriage to Richelieu's cousin, had been expected to secure Gaston's consent to a repudiation of the Lorraine princess. Gaston, however, had remained defiant: Puylaurens's disgrace was the price of failure. Gaston, aware of Puylaurens's ambiguous role, abandoned him to his fate.

At the time, Mademoiselle knew nothing of the background of this event. Puylaurens had cultivated the young Mademoiselle. He visited her whenever he was in Paris. He would bring her sweets and, as the confidant of the beloved if distant Gaston (now installed at Blois), treat her with the deference and attention due his master's daughter. His arrest and unexplained death shook the child. In it, she saw one more instance of the "vengeance and bad faith" of Richelieu.[23]

The recollection of these events may explain Mademoiselle's silence on the next major event of her young life, her baptism in September 1636 at the Louvre, where she finally received her given names. Her god-parents were Anne of Austria and Richelieu. According to cardinal de Retz, some of Gaston's entourage plotted to assassinate Richelieu at the ceremony, but the plot failed because the service had to be postponed due to the illness of one of the principals. The story, although not other-wise verifiable, has the ring of truth. A similar plan some weeks earlier by followers of Gaston and the comte de Soissons, known as the "conspiracy of Amiens," had collapsed because of the reluctance of the two princes to assassinate a churchman of Richelieu's high rank and risk the king's probable reaction to his "liberation" from his hated chief minister.[24]

In the late summer of the following year, 1637, Mademoiselle paid an extended visit to her father's domains on the Loire. Within the context of her *Mémoires*, the trip is a kind of extended metaphor, which brings together Mademoiselle's impressions of the court and French society under Richelieu. Mademoiselle began her trip with a visit to Chantilly to take leave of her royal aunt and uncle. She arrived at a moment of high drama. The previous day, August 17, Richelieu had interrogated the queen on her secret correspondence with her brother, the king of Spain, other members of the Habsburg family, and the duke of Lorraine. She had been forced to sign a written confession of her treasonable activities, including a confirmation that she had been aware of aristocratic schemes to marry her to Gaston in the event of Louis's death, and had received a written pardon from the king. The court speculated on the queen's fate: repudiation, imprisonment in a convent, even a return to Spain.

Mademoiselle believed that her arrival helped dispel the gloomy mood. More likely, the presence of Madame de Saint-Georges provided Anne of Austria with a friendly face. Madame de Saint-Georges had served as a conduit for communications between Gaston and his sister-in-law in the past, and her presence was fortuitous for Anne. Mademoiselle's role was to disguise the substance of the talk, on the presumption that the two would refrain from discussing any matter of importance before a child who might be induced to repeat what she had heard. After making Mademoiselle promise to forget anything she overheard, the two adults fell into a deep discussion. Mademoiselle kept her promise and does not reveal what she heard, although the implication is that Anne wished to warn Gaston of the results of her interrogation.[25]

Shortly thereafter, Mademoiselle departed for the Loire. Bursting with joy and anticipation, she wrote to her "good papa" to assure him of her eagerness to obey his summons.[26] At Pithiviers, where they entered

Monsieur's domains, Mademoiselle's party was met by officers of Gaston's household, who would serve as her escort. From this point, the trip became a kind of triumphal tour. Mademoiselle was greeted at various stops by the local officials and warmly welcomed in the great houses along the route. Like any modern tourist, Mademoiselle was enchanted by the beauty of the "garden of France," with its many souvenirs of the Valois kings of earlier centuries.

Gaston rode out to Chambord to meet his daughter, who was fascinated by the great château built by François I. The two amused themselves on the famous double staircase that enabled them to ascend and descend simultaneously without ever seeing one another. After playing at this for a little while, they climbed into a carriage and set out for Blois, where Mademoiselle was once more greeted by the local authorities massed in robed splendor to pay homage to the ten-year-old girl.

Since his return to France, Gaston had preferred to remain safely within his own appanage, with the château of Blois as his primary residence. He installed his daughter and her entourage in a wing of the building across the courtyard from the one containing his own apartments. This arrangement facilitated frequent and impromptu visits. Monsieur took particular pleasure in playing cards with Mademoiselle, taking care to see that she won most of the time. Her prizes were locally made watches and bits and pieces of jewelry that Gaston had procured in town. After the heavy mood at Chantilly, the contrast with that of Blois is striking.

Much of Mademoiselle's time was spent visiting with her Vendôme cousins, the children of Gaston's half brother and fellow conspirator, César de Vendôme. The Vendômes, like Gaston, saw themselves as victims of Richelieu and had aligned themselves with Gaston in opposition to the minister. Toward the end of her stay, the princess paid a visit to their château of Chenonceaux on the Cher. There, Mademoiselle was fascinated with the old-fashioned furnishings from the previous century, and by the château's association with the memory of Henri III, the last Valois, and of his queen, Louise de Lorraine, from whom the Vendômes had inherited the property.

Mademoiselle also spent a few days at Fontevrault as the guest of the abbess, another one of Henri IV's bastard children and therefore Mademoiselle's aunt. The young princess was much taken by the scale and grandeur of the foundation, and Mademoiselle notes approvingly that its abbesses, often daughters of the royal house, had jurisdiction over the auxiliary communities of monks on the grounds and answered only to Rome. The visit also allowed her to exercise one of her own royal prerogatives: the laymen of her escort, normally forbidden to enter the grounds of the abbey, were admitted as members of her suite.

The sight of Blois and Chenonceaux, their connections with the great events and personalities of the previous century, and the presence of the Vendômes and the abbess of Fontevrault, all descendants of Henri IV, led naturally to Mademoiselle's evocation of the founder of the dynasty. The cult of Henri IV, whose statue on the Pont Neuf was already a Parisian landmark, was at its peak in the half century after his assassination in 1610. Several biographies had already appeared; the memoirs of his chief minister, the duc de Sully, were published in 1638, shortly after Mademoiselle's visit to the Loire. Writing in the 1650s about her early years, Mademoiselle was very aware of the image of her grandfather as the warrior king who had validated his right to the succession at sword's point, but whose reign had brought peace and harmony to a country torn by civil strife.

During the course of her visit to the Loire, Mademoiselle was often in the company of the comtesse de Béthune, whose husband, Philippe de Béthune, the brother of the duc de Sully, had also served under the great Henri. Mademoiselle visited the Béthunes at their beautiful château of Selles, where the couple regaled her with their recollections of her royal grandfather. Mademoiselle was much taken with the dignified old man who had been her grandfather's ambassador to Rome and later a governor to one of Henri's sons. The fact that Henri held him in such high esteem, she asserts, made Béthune respected by all. There could be no better judgment of a man than selection for high office by a king whose ability and heroic virtues had earned him the title of "Henri the Great." For Mademoiselle, Henri IV provided the yardstick for measuring other crowned heads, and Henri's ministers the measure for evaluating their official successors.[27]

Lest her readers miss the point, Mademoiselle brings Richelieu back directly into the picture by means of an account of visits to Champigny-sur-Veude, a former property of her Montpensier ancestors, and to the nearby town and duchy of Richelieu. Mademoiselle devotes nearly six pages of text to the excursion, considerably more space than she devotes to any other episode of her trip. Champigny had been one of the principal country residences of Mademoiselle's Montpensier ancestors since the beginning of the sixteenth century. Most of the family was buried in its beautiful chapel, and its treasures included a reliquary supposedly containing a piece of the true cross and stained glass windows that are still a tourist attraction.

Richelieu's family was among the gentry of the region who had looked to the Montpensiers for patronage in the sixteenth century. Richelieu's grandfather had been a lieutenant of the guard in the Montpensier household, and Richelieu's father, who had held minor office under Henri III, probably owed his introduction at court to the Montpensiers. Richelieu's ancestral properties, including the estate of that name, were exceedingly modest in scale. In the 1630s, the cardinal began to acquire a number of adjacent properties in the area to serve as the landed base for the ducal status he had acquired. Part of his plan called for the expansion of the modest manor house at Richelieu into an impressive country seat and the construction of an entirely new and artificial town to serve as its companion piece.

Champigny was one of the properties Richelieu required to complete his grand design. In 1635, shortly after the arrest of Puylaurens, the cardinal bullied Gaston, the custodian of Mademoiselle's property, into exchanging this estate for that of Blois-le-Vicomte, near Paris. To add insult to injury, Gaston was also forced to pay the cardinal more than 50,000 livres for the furniture at Blois-le-Vicomte and to bear the expenses of the demolition of the château at Champigny; the stones were to be used in the construction of the new town of Richelieu. The details of this sordid story have been confirmed by a modern study of Richelieu's finances and are not a distortion of Mademoiselle's. Gaston explained years later to Mademoiselle that he had been intimidated by the arrest of Puylaurens and that the exchange so obviously exceeded his authority as custodian that he believed Mademoiselle would be able to overturn the transaction in the courts after she attained her majority. Mademoiselle found all of this quite credible, since Richelieu was able to exercise his power, which Mademoiselle denounces as "tyranny," even over members of the royal family. Gaston omitted to mention to Mademoiselle, at least in her early version, that the cardinal had taken the precaution of having Gaston attest in writing that he had validly exercised his power as Mademoiselle's guardian, and indemnify Richelieu and his heirs for any damages should this prove otherwise.[28]

Richelieu moved quickly, and by the time of Mademoiselle's visit, the bulk of the château had been pulled down, except for a few scattered outbuildings, a wing used to house the pages of the household, and the chapel. The chapel itself had survived only because the pope, Urban VIII, had refused Richelieu permission to desanctify the building, a necessary prelude to its demolition. Mademoiselle believed that Urban acted out of respect for her Montpensier ancestors, who had been prominent Catholic partisans during the religious wars of the sixteenth century and who had many living descendants. In fact, Urban's objections were probably bound up with his ongoing struggle with Richelieu about the extent and disposition of the cardinal's ecclesiastical benefices.[29]

At Champigny, Mademoiselle was much moved by the demonstrations of loyalty and affection of the inhabitants, many of whom claimed to remember her grandfather Montpensier, who had died in 1608. Mademoiselle lingered at the chapel, the sepulcher of her Montpensier ancestors and the visible evidence of one of Richelieu's rare defeats. This display of filial piety was performed in the presence of Richelieu's niece Madame d'Aiguillon, who had journeyed to Champigny to greet Mademoiselle and who was obviously annoyed at the use Mademoiselle was making of her visit. The presence of Madame d'Aiguillon was not a coincidence. Although Mademoiselle disdains to mention the subject, the idea of a marriage between her and Gaston had surfaced again, and Madame d'Aiguillon's visit was supposedly in connection with this project.[30]

Accompanied by Madame d'Aiguillon, Mademoiselle left Champigny for the town of Richelieu, which lay nearby. It consisted entirely of new buildings, replacing what might with exaggeration have been called a village. It was intended to serve as a backdrop to the château, characterized by Mademoiselle as "the work of the vainest and most ambitious man in the world." The scale of the pile that rose before her eyes astonished the resident of the Tuileries. A huge courtyard opened onto a vast central building crowned with a dome and flanked by pavilions that led to additional wings and more pavilions. A great terrace linked the various wings and imposed an overall unity on the complex. Niches in the walls of the central building housed sculptures, many in bronze, gathered from all over Europe by the cardinal. Mademoiselle was especially taken by the masterpieces that decorated the balcony overlooking the courtyard: two "slaves" by Michelangelo originally intended for the tomb of Julius II. These had been a gift of François I to the constable Anne de Montmorency; Richelieu had appropriated these items from the family after the execution of Henri de Montmorency in 1632.

If the exterior of the château owed its splendor to the pillaged treasures of other buildings (including the stones of Champigny), the interior betrayed its origins as an insignificant country manor. Richelieu had wished to preserve as much of the original house as possible. To avoid overwhelming the original rooms, the architects had designed the newer apartments and reception rooms on a relatively small scale. While this preserved the internal proportions of the edifice, it created, in the eyes of Mademoiselle, a striking imbalance between the grandeur of the exterior and the mediocrity of the interior. To compensate, Mademoiselle adds, Richelieu arranged to have the interior decorated and furnished in the most extravagant manner. She notes that she had never seen anything like the immense profusion of "beautiful things" in the mansion, which included paintings and objets d'art that had belonged to the fabled Isabella d'Este a century earlier. The walls and ceilings were heavily gilded and further embellished with works by the most fashionable contemporary Italian painters.

To complete the picture of parvenu grandeur tinged with rapacity and insecurity, Mademoiselle adds a telling detail. In the midst of all this overdecoration, Richelieu had preserved intact a fireplace mantel with his father's coat of arms. He had done so because the heraldic achievement in question included the collar of the Order of the Holy Spirit. To be admitted, a member had to be able to prove at least three generations of noble descent: this was the cardinal's answer to those who questioned his family background. On this point, Mademoiselle was prepared to defend the cardinal. He was in fact a gentleman of good family: her grandfather Montpensier's servants assured her that the duke had always treated the senior Richelieu as a gentleman, and this in a generation when princes were more rigorous about such distinctions than Mademoiselle's contemporaries.[31]

Throughout the visit, Mademoiselle and her entourage did their best to exasperate Madame d'Aiguillon. Among the men in Mademoiselle's escort was the baron du Vigean, one of Gaston's suite. His presence caused a great deal of dismay to his estranged wife, one of Madame d'Aiguillon's companions. There was a sharp exchange on the matter between the cardinal's niece and the little princess (or, more probably, Madame de Saint-Georges). This brought forth protestations of innocence and incomprehension: Vigean was little better than a flunky, a pensioner of sorts of Gaston's secretary, Léonard Goulas, not a person of enough importance for Mademoiselle to be aware of his identity. The discomfiture of Madame d'Aiguillon and her entourage caused no end of private merriment to Mademoiselle and her ladies; even the normally somber Madame de Saint-Georges joined in the laughter.[32]

Other than more mockery, there was little left to do at Richelieu except to enjoy walks in the gardens. But Mademoiselle did not find them appealing. They did not measure up to the splendor of the buildings, because nature had denied that place a "charm to match" the handiwork of the architects.[33]

With this final comment, which sums up Mademoiselle's entire verdict on Richelieu's efforts, the party set out for Fontevrault and Chenonceaux, with their properly royal antecedents. At Chavigny, Madame d'Aiguillon managed to free herself from her increasingly onerous duties as Mademoiselle's escort. While at lunch the poor woman became faint; Madame du Vigean pronounced her feverish. Mademoiselle joined in the theatrics, insisting that Madame d'Aiguillon return home to convalesce. With relief on both sides, the parties took leave of each other. The episode caused as much laughter in private as did the earlier flap over baron du Vigean.[34]

In the course of her wanderings, Mademoiselle had several other encounters with Gaston. The image conveyed is one of growing trust and affection between the two, often in ways that might seem surprising given Mademoiselle's age. Once, while at Tours, Gaston insisted on introducing his mistress of the hour, Louison Roger, to his daughter. The proposal to do so gave rise to some spirited discussions involving Gaston, Madame de Saint-Georges, and the princess. Mademoiselle Roger was only sixteen but well bred and of good bourgeois stock. In the end, the presentation came off well; Mademoiselle liked the young woman, and the two saw each other frequently.

On another occasion, again at Tours, Mademoiselle and Gaston shared lodgings at the episcopal palace. As at Blois earlier in the trip, Gaston would visit unexpectedly, sometimes late in the evening. He would have Mademoiselle awakened, and pass the time entertaining her with tales of his adventures in exile. His favorite story, told repeatedly, was a romantic version of the events surrounding his elopement with Marguerite de Lorraine. Its connection to his continuing estrangement from the court gave the story an additional allure. Mademoiselle became a partisan, sight unseen, of this absent stepmother. She even accepted Monsieur's explanation that the surprising opposition of the duke of Lorraine to this marriage had stemmed from the duke's commitment to an eventual marriage between Gaston and a widowed Anne of Austria. Gaston assured his daughter that such a proposition was entirely a fantasy of the queen's.[35]

Mademoiselle returned to Paris in the fall of 1637. In spite of her youth, the princess began now to be more intimately involved with the court and its activities, and her *Mémoires* reflect more directly the political events of the later part of the reign of Louis XIII.

Shortly after her return, France was astounded by the news that the queen was pregnant. In her joy, Mademoiselle overlooked the obvious consequences for Gaston: after the birth of the future Louis XIV in September 1638, her father was no longer the king's likely successor.[36] The queen asked that Mademoiselle stay with her at Saint-Germain during her pregnancy. Richelieu, albeit reluctantly, agreed. For Mademoiselle, this extended visit provided her first real glimpse of the inner workings of the court.

Louis XIII was an avid hunter, and Mademoiselle often followed the royal hunt in her carriage. One of her companions, Marie de Hautefort, had become close to the king in recent months. Louis often climbed into Mademoiselle's coach for the ride home, sitting between the princess and Madame de Hautefort. If the king was in the right mood, he would amuse the ladies with small talk. If the party stopped for a roadside picnic, the king would insist on serving all the ladies himself, even though the object of his attention was clearly Madame de Hautefort. He even permitted the company to speak in disparaging terms of Richelieu and sometimes joined in the fun.[37]

But the king's moods were volatile. When things went well, the king would entertain the ladies in his own apartments, where the royal musicians would often play small pieces composed or arranged by Louis in honor of Madame de Hautefort. But if there had been some spat between Louis and Hautefort, the king would plunge into melancholy and anger. He would brood for hours behind closed doors, unapproachable even by his intimates, and would write lengthy accounts of his exchanges with Madame de Hautefort, which, Mademoiselle adds, were found among his papers after his death. Louis was also very awkward with people he did not see frequently. Mademoiselle thought such shyness inappropriate in a king of France, where, she maintained, the tradition of the monarchy was one of familiarity, in contrast to the austere and distant manner of their Habsburg rivals.[38]

The birth of the future Louis XIV in September 1638 occasioned a brief reunion with Gaston, summoned to court to witness the event, and the unhappy end of Mademoiselle's idyll at court. Once more, the villain was Richelieu, who took exception to Mademoiselle's characterization of the newborn dauphin as "my little husband." The phrase originated in a suggestion by Anne of Austria that Mademoiselle seems to have taken a bit too seriously. Louis XIII found the expression amusing, but Richelieu saw many implications in this childish conceit and ordered Mademoiselle sent back to Paris. En route, she was forced to stop at the cardinal's residence at Rueil for a scolding that reduced her to tears. Richelieu may not have intended to upset her so much, and he tried to make amends with a good meal before sending her on her way.[39]

Mademoiselle continued to see the queen and Madame de Hautefort, making day trips to Saint-Germain from time to time and basking in the sympathy of her fellow victims of Richelieu's harshness. The queen soothed her ruffled feelings with the thought that perhaps the infant dauphin was too little to be her husband; instead, she could wed the queen's younger brother, Ferdinand of Spain, at that time the Spanish commander in the Lowlands.[40]

Mademoiselle soon put any idea of marriage out of her head. She was scarcely eleven, but the Paris season beckoned. A great deal of activity revolved around the balls given in the winter months by rival branches of the Bourbons, the families of Soissons and Condé. There was more than a social rivalry here. Louis de Bourbon, comte de Soissons, was a long-time ally of Gaston's, a bitter and relentless foe of Richelieu's, and a perpetual candidate for the hand of Mademoiselle. Henri de Bourbon, prince de Condé, had made his peace with Richelieu in the late 1620s, and had benefited greatly from ministerial favor, obtaining a number of important and lucrative offices and pensions. After the execution of his brother-in-law the duc de Montmorency, he had even secured the reversion of much of the Montmorency fortune for his wife. The bond between Richelieu and the Condés was sealed in February 1641 with the marriage of Richelieu's niece Claire-Clémence de Brézé and Condé's heir, the young duc d'Enghien, with ceremonies on a scale that befitted the princely status of the groom and the ministerial importance of the bride's uncle. Mademoiselle thoroughly disapproved of the match as a misalliance, a sentiment shared by the young bridegroom. She was especially offended by the conduct of Henri de Condé, who, she felt, had debased himself by soliciting the union of the two families "on his knees."

The bride was the Mademoiselle de Brézé of the "dance of the pygmies" of 1634, and Mademoiselle was to preserve for her a lifelong mixture of contempt and pity: contempt for her lack of accomplishments and pity for the ill treatment she was to endure at the hands of the Condés after the cardinal's death. There was also a certain amount of jealousy: the duc d'Enghien, who would succeed his father someday as first prince of the blood, was an entirely suitable match, politics aside, for Mademoiselle herself, a thought that would recur in later years. Surprisingly, Mademoiselle actually approved of one of Richelieu's actions, a refusal to countenance a second marriage with the Condés, in this case that of Condé's daughter to Richelieu's nephew. Whereas the marriage of Mademoiselle de Brézé elevated her to the rank of a princess of the blood, the marriage of Mademoiselle de Bourbon to a mere nobleman would have had the opposite effect, reducing the princess to her husband's rank, and Richelieu refused to permit this.[41]

The social rivalry between Anne de Montafié, comtesse de Soissons, the mother of Louis de Bourbon-Soissons, and Charlotte de Montmorency, princess de Condé, reflected the political rivalries between Richelieu's clients and Richelieu's foes. If guests favorable to the Condés put in an appearance at a Soissons ball, the ladies of the Soissons faction would refuse to dance with them. Mademoiselle and her good friend Marie de Longueville, the niece of the comte de Soissons, spent a great deal of time surveying the battlefield and recording the small victories and defeats of the day. When Mademoiselle was forced to appear at one of Madame de Condé's functions, the tables were turned and she would find herself the object of comments by the Condés. Mademoiselle's enthusiasm for the Soissons faction may have been stimulated by the suggestions that Soissons, who had been a candidate for the hand of Mademoiselle's mother decades earlier, would be just as suitable a match for her.[42] These bloodless variations on the theme of Montague and Capulet were, said Mademoiselle, "our affairs of state."[43]

If the balls were bloodless, the politics were not. At court, Mademoiselle ruefully recalled, "there were more important plots than those we undertook at our balls." In 1641, Soissons organized yet another uprising against Richelieu, using as his base of operations the principality of Sedan, an imperial territory belonging to the duc de Bouillon, another of Richelieu's determined enemies. Although Henri de Guise, Gaston's former brother-in-law, supported Soissons, a wary Gaston held aloof from this latest conspiracy against the cardinal. Gaston also turned aside a suggestion by Soissons that he seal the bonds between them by a marriage with Mademoiselle. To conceal the fact of an alliance, Soissons even suggested that Mademoiselle be abducted and brought across the frontier for a hasty ceremony. Gaston had the sense to decline. Shortly thereafter, in July 1641, Soissons, supported by Spanish troops, defeated a royal army under the maréchal de Châtillon at La Marfée. But in his moment of triumph, Soissons fell dead, the victim, it would seem, of a stray shot or the misfiring of his own pistol.[44]

The king, shaken by Châtillon's defeat, made no effort to hide his joy at the news of Soissons's death, and forbade anyone at court to wear mourning for this wayward prince of the blood. For Mademoiselle, the death of Soissons gave rise to some reflections on fate and to sincere grief, occasioned by the visible distress of the Soissons family and, in particular, her friend Marie de Longueville, who, parenthetically, became a great heiress by virtue of the event.[45]

Although Gaston was not seriously implicated in this plot, he was deeply angered by the death of Soissons. Within weeks of the collapse of Soissons's rebellion, Gaston joined in the last great effort to remove Richelieu from power. At the center of the conspiracy was a handsome young courtier, Henri d'Effiat, marquis de Cinq-Mars, who had been placed in the king's household by Richelieu in an attempt to supplant Madame de Hautefort as the king's favorite. The effort had succeeded only too well, and Cinq-Mars, newly appointed *grand écuyer de France*, evidenced little gratitude to Richelieu for his good fortune, but instead made the fatal mistake of taking the king's carping about Richelieu literally.

Cinq-Mars seems to have had at least some contact with Soissons and his supporters. Fearing exposure, he launched a far-ranging scheme to remove Richelieu, by assassination if necessary, and to reverse much of the foreign policy of the cardinal. In effect, this meant abandoning the anti-Habsburg princes in Germany and their various Protestant allies in favor of a peace with the Catholic Habsburgs of Spain and Austria. Emissaries of Cinq-Mars negotiated a treaty of alliance with Spain that provided for the use of Spanish troops in the event of an uprising. The duc de Bouillon, commanding the royal armies in Italy, promised to make Sedan available as a place of refuge if the plot failed.

Within the royal family, Cinq-Mars received secret encouragement from the queen and from Gaston. The queen's reasons for entangling herself in the plot were not hard to understand. In spite of the birth of a dauphin in 1638 and of a second son, Philippe, in 1640, which relieved king and cardinal of the nightmare of Gaston's succession, Anne continued to live in semidisgrace, on the suspicion that she, like Gaston, was the automatic beneficiary of the endless schemes directed against Richelieu. At the time of the conspiracies of Soissons and Cinq-Mars, there was discussion of removing her sons from her custody, and the queen of France was reduced to begging the minister's intervention to avoid this public humiliation.[46]

For Gaston, opposition to Richelieu had become instinctive. On relatively good terms with his brother at the time of the Soissons rebellion, Gaston, like Cinq-Mars and many others in the king's inner circle, including Mademoiselle, had heard Louis's occasional carping about the cardinal. Like his brother, Gaston seemed to be charmed by Cinq-Mars, and though initially skeptical, finally accepted Cinq-Mars's arguments that Louis would countenance, after the fact, Richelieu's disappearance. By allowing his young favorite to snipe at Richelieu and even seeming to encourage it, Louis may have contributed to the widespread impression that the bond between king and minister was sufficiently frayed to permit an attempt on the latter.

But the cardinal struck first. In June 1642, Cinq-Mars was arrested. Under interrogation, he refused to implicate the queen, so little could be done against her. But others were not so lucky. A number of aristocrats fled into exile to avoid the headsman, while the duc de Bouillon, arrested in the field, saved his life by agreeing to submit his hitherto independent stronghold of Sedan to French authority. In addition, Richelieu forced the dismissal of a number of officers who commanded the king's household troops, including Tilladet, the captain general of the regiment of French Guards, and Henri de Tréville, the captain of the Musketeers. Gaston barely escaped the fate of Bouillon. Several members of his entourage were arrested and interrogated, including his *premier écuyer*, François de Brion. Gaston denied his involvement until Richelieu confronted Gaston's emissary, Louis Barbier, abbé de la Rivière, with a copy of the conspirators' treaty with Spain. Cornered but hoping to avoid the worst, Gaston signed a humiliating confession in early July. There was talk in court circles of exile to Venice and even of the possibility of somehow depriving him of his rights to the succession. Fearing arrest, Gaston fled across the border once more, this time taking refuge at the court of his sister Christine, duchess of Savoy. From the safety of his sister's domains, Gaston negotiated his return by confirming his guilt in a statement sworn before the chancellor of France, Pierre Séguier. By the time Cinq-Mars and his good friend François de Thou were delivered over to the headsman in early September, Gaston was home again, comfortably installed in his great château at Blois.[47]

King and cardinal were not, however, finished with Gaston. Richelieu was dying, and Louis XIII's health was visibly failing. The next reign could not be too far over the horizon. The dauphin was a child of four. There was every likelihood of a regency, and Gaston would have strong claims to the post. Indeed, the only conceivable alternative was Anne of Austria. For Richelieu and Louis XIII, this was indeed a Hobson's choice.

The two proceeded step by step. On December 1, 1642, Louis stripped Gaston of his governorship of Auvergne, disbanded the prince's household troops, and barred him from any office of state, specifically that of regent in the event of the king's death. Three days later, the cardinal was dead, but Louis was determined to follow through. Gaston sent La Rivière to protest these measures, but Louis refused to budge, stating publicly that his affection for Gaston was outweighed by his duty to his children and the state.[48]

These events had a profound effect on the young Mademoiselle. She had been embarrassed by Gaston's behavior during the investigation of the Cinq-Mars affair and by the widespread criticism in aristocratic circles of his abandonment of Cinq-Mars and Thou. The death of her exiled grandmother, Marie de Medici, occurred during Gaston's flight to Savoy. The strict mourning required by court etiquette provided Mademoiselle with a suitable pretext to remain shut up in the Tuileries and avoid social gatherings. She noticed that very few visitors called to offer their condolences, an indication of Gaston's momentary disfavor in aristocratic circles.[49]

Mademoiselle shrewdly observed that the severity of Richelieu's response to the conspiracy of Cinq-Mars was due in part to a need to reassert an authority that many believed to have been seriously weakened. Although the cardinal was her godfather, Mademoiselle avoided any personal contact with the dying prelate, commenting on his final grasp at power and reporting his death in an entirely impersonal fashion. She could not refrain, however, from a tribute to Richelieu's ability to retain his hold on the affairs of state. So well did he succeed, she noted, that his advice was followed after his death, and his memory was respected even by his enemies.[50]

In an effort to help Gaston, Mademoiselle became directly involved in political matters for the first time. Misreading the mood of Louis XIII after Richelieu's death, she attempted to second La Rivière's efforts to obtain the repeal of the declaration of December 1. The king intended to appear before the parlement of Paris on December 9 to command the registration of his decree. The previous day, Mademoiselle went to her uncle to beg him to reconsider, but Louis was inflexible. In desperation, Mademoiselle considered throwing herself in front of Louis as he made his way into the parlement. But the king, who had been forewarned, sent word to her not to attempt any such public action. On December 9, the decree was duly registered.[51]

This was not, however, the end of the matter. The six months that separated the death of Richelieu from that of the king in May 1643 were clearly a time of transition. Without the inflexible Richelieu at his side, Louis began to temper his earlier decisions. Many of the great aristocrats in exile received permission to return home. Gaston was permitted to return to court, and established his residence at the hôtel de Guise. Mademoiselle entertained him at the Tuileries, where the royal violins played and Gaston was his usual vivacious and charming self. For all her joy, Mademoiselle could not refrain from thinking of Cinq-Mars and Thou, lying "by the wayside," already forgotten by Gaston and her guests in the happiness of the moment.[52]

Gaston spent much of his time trying to persuade Louis to reverse the edict of December 1. Eventually, the king's resistance weakened. The alternative to Gaston, after all, was Anne of Austria, whom Louis had no more reason to trust; there was also the possibility that Gaston would spark a civil war by asserting his rights to the regency after the king's death. To mollify his brother, Louis issued a decree in late April 1643, setting up a structure for the governance of the kingdom during his son's minority. Anne was nominated as regent, but was to be constrained by the appointment of a ministerial council, whose members, chiefly pro-tégés of Richelieu, were not removable, and were to control the levers of power. Foremost among them was cardinal Jules Mazarin, whom Richelieu had designated as his successor. Gaston was to preside over this council, with the title "lieutenant general of the kingdom." Gaston and Anne swore that they would respect these wishes, a promise that neither intended to keep.[53]

For Mademoiselle, late February 1643 brought another major departure, that of Madame de Saint-Georges, who died after an illness of some months' duration. This was the first loss of someone who had played a major part in her life, and it affected her deeply. There was a classic deathbed scene: after blessing her own children, Madame de Saint-Georges asked for Mademoiselle's permission to offer her the same; the benediction and farewell left Mademoiselle in tears. Gaston, hoping to distract her, brought her to stay temporarily with him at the hôtel de Guise.[54]

Mademoiselle does not record any tears for the death of her uncle, who finally succumbed on May 14, 1643. For Mademoiselle, the mantle of royalty successfully covered the weakness of the man, and her account of Louis's last weeks is one of majesty and Christian resignation in the face of death. From his windows at Saint-Germain, the king could see the distant abbey church of Saint-Denis, which housed the tombs of French kings. This sight gives rise to reflections on eternity. He organizes the necessary formalities for his funeral, orders the roads between the two places repaired so that the funeral carriage could pass safely, and arranges the music of the *De Profundis* that would be sung in the royal chamber immediately after his death. His instructions for the administration of the kingdom after his death are given with the same "tranquillity of spirit."[55]

For Mademoiselle and her contemporaries, the king's death was to set in motion events of profound and unforeseen consequences.

News arrived that Madame had given birth to a son; this gave me the greatest, most infinite joy I have known in my whole life. The entire court rejoiced, and I ordered displays of fireworks; I forgot nothing to show my happiness, which I felt in my heart as well as in appearances. I wrote to Their Royal Highnesses in terms that would melt rocks.

MADEMOISELLE

Mademoiselle said to me once that she really wished there had never been a Salic law in France. Mademoiselle, I replied, you would not be who you are if there had not been a Salic law; that is what makes you a princess of the blood.

JEAN REGNAULT DE SEGRAIS

2 A Most Eligible Princess

TO MADEMOISELLE AND HER CONTEMPORARIES, THE SPRING OF 1643 seemed to herald a rebirth of the high aristocracy. These early months of the regency of Anne of Austria, characterized by Mademoiselle as the "most beautiful imaginable," saw the rapid expansion of the court.[1] Paris was crowded with newly returned exiles, survivors of the many purges of Louis XIII and his chief minister. None of this was a surprise to contemporaries: these were, after all, the former opponents of Richelieu, and it was to be expected that Anne of Austria, the most prominent victim of all, would welcome and reward those who had shared her many years of disgrace.

Not the least of these old allies of the queen was Gaston d'Orléans, who took up residence at the Luxembourg, where he welcomed his long-suffering wife, Marguerite de Lorraine, after a decade of separation. It was too late to do anything for Marie de Medici, whose remains were brought back to France to lie at Saint-Denis with those of her predecessors, but Mademoiselle's living grandmother, the duchess de Guise, returned from her Italian refuge. Mademoiselle's Vendôme cousins also benefited from the change of régime. The younger son of the family, François, duc de Beaufort, seemed to be a particular confidant of the queen, entrusted with the guarding of the little Louis XIV in the days immediately after the death of Louis XIII.

For Gaston d'Orléans, the dawn of this new day was radiant. His position as uncle and closest male relative of the little king gave him enormous standing. This was reinforced by his popularity among the officers of the city government and most importantly, the judges of the parlement, who would be asked to break the provisions of the late king's will as contrary to the fundamental laws of the kingdom. His support was essential to Anne of Austria's attempts to void the strictures imposed on her by Louis XIII. For the right price, Gaston and his chief rival, Henri de Condé, were only too willing to oblige. These two senior members of the Bourbon family stood with Anne before the assembled *parlementaires* on May 18, 1643, while the chancellor of France, Pierre Séguier, successfully argued for the nullification of the late king's testament. Condé's reward was the private assurance by the queen that his son Louis de Bourbon-Condé would continue to command the armies of France in Flanders. Gaston retained the second position, after the queen, on the council of regency and the presidency of the council of war, that is, the nominal overall command of France's armies in the field, with the title of lieutenant general. Anne named him governor of Languedoc, a position that carried twice the income of his lost governorship of Auvergne. She also increased his state pension and showered him with special grants, all of which served to maintain the spendthrift Gaston in ruinously extravagant splendor. Like many other noble mendicants in the early years of the regency, Gaston had reason to say "the queen is so good."[2]

The shifting alliances and alignments of the various noble clans need not be detailed here; suffice it to say that underlying the frequent twists and turns was the bedrock rivalry of the families of Condé and Vendôme, with Gaston generally aligned with the Vendômes. This competition for power and influence often manifested itself through surrogates. In 1643, for example, Madame de Montbazon, wife of a Rohan, quarreled with Madame de Longueville, the daughter of the prince de Condé. Accused of disrespect to Longueville and her mother, the princess de Condé, Montbazon was forced to offer a public apology for her behavior. This episode was followed several months later by a duel between the duc de Guise (Mademoiselle's uncle) and Gaspard de Coligny, the son and heir of the maréchal de Châtillon. To observers of the time, the connections between these events were obvious. Madame de Montbazon and her famous stepdaughter, the duchess de Chevreuse, were allied with the Guises, the Vendômes, and the Orléans, while Coligny's family were long-standing clients of their Condé kin.[3]

These rivalries provided room for maneuver by the regent and her chief minister, Jules Cardinal Mazarin, who might otherwise have found themselves entirely at the mercy of these aristocratic wolves. Initially, none of the factions saw the soft-spoken and accommodating minister as a player in the game of power. But the queen recognized the talent and the devotion to the Crown of this creature of Richelieu's. Much sooner than the high nobility realized, Mazarin came to dominate the queen's council and government. In retrospect, Mademoiselle saw this prefer-ence as a great mistake on the part of Anne of Austria, repeating, as it were, Louis XIII's error of entrusting all power to a single minister.[4] But in September 1643, Mademoiselle was as surprised as anyone by the first manifestation of the cardinal's authority, the imprisonment of the duc de Beaufort on the charge of plotting to assassinate Mazarin and seize control of the state. Beaufort's arrest, which had the support of the Condés, was followed by the exile of his aristocratic fellow intriguers, collectively known as the *Importants*.[5]

Gaston had avoided any involvement in Beaufort's plot, in spite of his many ties to the Vendômes. For the moment, he was a pillar of state, dividing his time between domestic bliss at the Luxembourg and fre-quent appearances at the Louvre. His chief counselor, the abbé de la Rivière, continued to advocate a policy of conciliation and cooperation with the regent—in return, of course, for patronage and influence. For the time being, Gaston saw the wisdom of this course of action.[6]

One reward for his good behavior was the independent command of armies in the field, something that Richelieu and Louis XIII had never permitted.[7] In the saddle, Gaston proved himself to be a more than competent general. In late July 1644, he crowned a successful campaign in Flanders with the capture of the important fortress city of Gravelines. The fall of Gravelines was followed within weeks by word of Louis de Bourbon-Condé's great triumph at Freiburg (August 1644).[8] Mazarin's policy of harnessing the rivalry of the princely houses and balancing Condé with Orléans, to the benefit of the state, seemed, indeed, to be effective.[9]

Mademoiselle was, by her own admission, a spectator to all of these great events, but not one who was especially interested in the politics of the moment.[10] Her guiding star remained Gaston, and as long as he was for the regent, so was Mademoiselle. In the early days of the regency, as the queen worked to break the late king's will, Mademoiselle was often asked to amuse the young king and his brother Philippe—in effect, to baby-sit—while the elders of the clan tended to the affairs of state.[11] She also spent many hours accompanying Anne of Austria on routine visits to the churches and convents of Paris, an act of family solidarity on her part that, in Mademoiselle's eyes, was not appreciated at its true worth.[12]

Just sixteen at the time of Louis XIII's death, Mademoiselle had grown into a tall, large-boned young woman, with plain but regular features. Her eyes were blue, her hair ash-blonde; her limbs, if not elegant, were at least straight, a boast in an age of congenital deformity among high aristocrats too closely inbred. Her facial features were of the classic heavyset Bourbon variety, complete with the prominent nose that Mademoiselle was honest enough to characterize as "large and aquiline" in a self-description written in 1657.[13]

In spite of her hero worship of Gaston, Mademoiselle's relationship with her father was strained by differences in temperament and character. Unlike Gaston, who had made a career of equivocation, Mademoiselle was rapidly acquiring a reputation for headstrong behavior, particularly in defense of what she perceived to be her prerogatives of rank. This was a common enough characteristic of aristocrats of the period, but in Mademoiselle's case it was exacerbated by the slight ambiguity of her position within the royal family as the granddaughter, rather than daughter, of a king.

In other matters, her stubbornness often drove her staff to distraction. The poet Jean de Segrais, who served in Mademoiselle's household, recalled that she did not take advice willingly and that the easiest way to persuade her to do something was to insinuate that the idea had originally been hers. He added that in calmer moments she understood her weakness and would wonder why God had "given me such a disposition." Her new governess, Anne Le Veneur, comtesse de Fiesque, the successor to Madame de Saint-Georges, pronounced her completely unmanageable. Although a surrogate for paternal authority, Madame de

Fiesque was frequently at loggerheads with her young charge, necessitating appeals to Gaston and his direct involvement. If Mademoiselle saw Fiesque as a petty tyrant, her adversary was quick to paint Mademoiselle as too outspoken, in ways that were bound to irritate the court and in particular the Italian-born chief minister, "Monsignore Giulio."[14]

Like many before her, Mademoiselle discovered that it was not easy to determine her father's position on the plots and cabals of the moment. At the time of Beaufort's downfall, which she witnessed "with indifference," the abbé de la Rivière warned her that her ties to Elisabeth de Vendôme, Beaufort's sister, were not in Gaston's best interest. But Mademoiselle was adamant and remained on friendly terms with her cousin, thereby causing unanticipated friction with her father.[15]

Notwithstanding these strains, Mademoiselle continued to use social functions and official engagements to champion the primacy of the house of Orléans. The news of Gaston's military success at Gravelines brought her "unbelievable joy." Mademoiselle, secretly offended that Anne of Austria kept a plan of the battle of Rocroi in her study, covered the walls of her apartments with maps of Gaston's campaign.[16] As was traditional, Gaston's victory was celebrated with a *Te Deum* at Notre Dame and a public holiday. Mademoiselle's stepmother hosted a ball and a reception at the Luxembourg. Mademoiselle followed this two days later with another ball at the Tuileries, at the end of which she sent the musicians to the Palais-Royal to serenade the queen.[17]

An incident in late 1644 seemed to substantiate Madame de Fiesque's criticism of the princess. In October of that year, the court received word of the death of the queen of Spain, Elisabeth de France, sister of Gaston d'Orléans and wife of Philip IV, the brother of Anne of Austria. In spite of the war between Spain and France, then in its tenth year, dynastic pride and the etiquette of the time prescribed official mourning. A memorial service was scheduled for December at the cathedral of Notre Dame. Louis de Bourbon-Condé, fresh from his battlefield triumphs, asked that his mother, wife, and sister be accorded the same prerogatives at the ceremony as Mademoiselle, who, the Condés argued, was the first princess of the blood, but no more. Mademoiselle, on the other hand, insisted upon her position as a "granddaughter of France," that is, a member of the immediate royal family, who therefore outranked the Condés. There were no obvious precedents, because there had not been a legitimate niece or nephew in the male line of a sovereign for several centuries.[18] Anne of Austria, seeking to please the victorious young prince, agreed to Condé's request. This brought forth a storm of protest on the part of Mademoiselle. At the last minute she claimed she was ill and would not attend. An enraged Anne of Austria complained to Gaston, who forced Mademoiselle to go.

Once there, Mademoiselle arranged to have her train carried by two gentlemen pages, a privilege reserved for members of the royal family; princesses of the blood made do with one bearer. The young Condé countered by drafting members of his entourage to perform the same duty for the Condé ladies. But Mademoiselle was still not ready to yield. Inside the cathedral, she tried to leave a vacant seat between herself and the Condés, to indicate a separate rank. The duchess de Longueville would have none of it, pushing her sister-in-law (Richelieu's niece, whom Mademoiselle so disliked) into the vacant place. Mademoiselle sat through the service thoroughly mortified. The aftermath was a monumental scene as Mademoiselle repeated for all and sundry her claims to a superior status. Her elders did not take kindly to this behavior. Anne of Austria threatened to confine her to a convent, and Gaston, intimidated by the fury of the queen, forced his daughter to spend several days shut up in her rooms at the Tuileries.[19]

Not everyone thought Mademoiselle was completely in the wrong. Madame de Motteville, the faithful friend of Anne of Austria, disapproved of Mademoiselle's defiance of the queen but believed that Mademoiselle's claim to superiority over the Condés was well-founded. She, like many of her contemporaries, saw Mademoiselle's actions as an assertion of her father's high rank.[20] Perhaps swayed by this argument, Gaston, somewhat belatedly, changed his mind. After all, he had always insisted on his superior position, adopting the style "royal highness," while leaving to the Condés and to Soissons the simple "highness" normally accorded princes of the blood.[21] Now it was Gaston's turn to complain to Anne of Austria and to Mazarin about the usurpation by the Condés of distinctions to which they were not entitled. The uproar now engulfed the senior members of the royal family, including the queen regent and the queen's chief minister. In the hopes of appeasing both sides, Anne took the responsibility for permitting the Condés to act as they had, and the incident closed with an exchange of polite banalities between Gaston, the queen, Mazarin, and the young Condé.[22]

At best, this was a Pyrrhic victory for Mademoiselle, and it is worth noting that she makes no mention of the episode in her *Mémoires*. In her own eyes she had been subjected to public humiliation at the hands of the Condés. Worst of all, she had been abandoned by the father whose own claim to a special standing was the basis for her actions.

Mademoiselle made use of her aunt's death for another purpose in her *Mémoires*: to illustrate her growing disillusionment with the regent and with Mazarin. The death of the queen of Spain had left a void within the circle of European crowned heads, and Mademoiselle's age and high rank made her an obvious candidate to replace her aunt. Anne of Austria and Mazarin raised the subject with Mademoiselle and Gaston on several occasions. Mademoiselle's hopes soared, but the matter was dropped. In Mademoiselle's eyes the reasons were transparent: bad faith on the part of Anne and Mazarin, and gullibility born of good faith on her part and that of her father.[23] There was another reason, perhaps equally evident to contemporaries, namely, the state of war between the two countries that precluded such a marriage except as a gage of peace; and in 1644 that peace was nowhere on the horizon.[24]

It is not surprising that marriage and her future establishment were very much on the mind of Mademoiselle in the years before the Fronde. Paris in the 1640s was full of young aristocrats of both sexes pursuing affairs of the heart. Although Mademoiselle frequently asserted that she had a dislike for "gallantry," her *Mémoires* recount many of the most famous episodes of the period. Mademoiselle was evidently enthralled by the adventures of the young Condé and his friends, who were commonly referred to as the *petits maîtres*. In addition, there were the antics of Mademoiselle's Guise uncles, various Vendôme cousins, and Gaston himself, whose affection for his wife did not preclude occasional diversions.[25]

In an age when matrimony was seen more as an alliance of families than as a union of individuals, some of these liaisons nevertheless led to marriage. The most spectacular case was the wedding in 1645 of Marguerite de Rohan, daughter of the duc de Rohan and heiress to the vast Rohan fortune, to a penniless gentleman named Henri Chabot. Although Chabot held a minor post in Gaston's household, he was numbered among Condé's aristocratic protégés. Chabot had caught the eye of Rohan in the early 1640s. In spite of the direct and formal opposition of her mother, the dowager duchess, Marguerite succeeded in eloping with her beau. This outcome had been stage-managed by Condé, who even secured from the regent a ducal title for Chabot in order to spare the heiress the loss of her high status.[26]

Mademoiselle passes no judgment on the Rohan misalliance that many at court, including Condé's mother, found shocking. Mademoiselle was far more affected by a more conventional marriage that took place in the same year, that of Louise-Marie de Gonzague to Ladislaus IV, king of Poland. Louise-Marie was the daughter of the duke of Nevers, of a junior branch of the Gonzaga rulers of Mantua. The duke of Nevers, whose claim to Mantua was supported by France in opposition to a rival supported by the Habsburgs, was a useful pawn in French diplomacy. The marriage of Nevers's daughter to the Polish king was an important affair of state and had been encouraged by Mazarin. In early October, a large delegation of Polish noblemen and clergy arrived in Paris to claim the royal bride. With a great Polish aristocrat serving as proxy for the bridegroom, and with the bishop of Warsaw presiding, the wedding was held in the chapel of the Palais-Royal, in the presence of most of the royal family.

In an effort to avoid yet another wrangle over precedence, the regent had decided that she alone would share the bride's table at the wedding dinner (the king and the male members of the family were to be seated separately). But she reckoned without Mademoiselle, who refused to attend wedding, dinner, or after-dinner festivities. Not only was she banished from the royal table, but etiquette decreed that in the presence of the queen of Poland, a princess was entitled to sit only on an uncomfortable armless stool known as a *tabouret*. This was too much for Mademoiselle who had always taken precedence over Louise-Marie de Gonzague, that "queen for a day." For the whole of the next week, devoted to formal calls and presentations, Mademoiselle avoided the court on one pretext or another, even after Mazarin asked her to reconsider. This was in marked contrast to the position taken by the Condés. To Mademoiselle's dismay, the princess de Condé, "vain as she was," was conspicuous in her attendance on the newly minted queen.[27]

Mademoiselle was not the only family member to react this way; her stepmother and the comtesse de Soissons also managed to avoid encounters with the queen bride. But Mademoiselle, with her outspoken ways, had drawn the attention of the regent to her behavior. Given the political background of the marriage, Mademoiselle's attitude did not promote the interests of state as the regent perceived them. After the usual reproaches by Gaston, Mademoiselle finally agreed to call at the Palais-Royal. She found the two queens together, about to attend a play at the palace theater. To Mademoiselle's astonishment, she was not invited to sit in the royal box but was directed to the gallery below, to join the rest of the audience. Mademoiselle refused to take a place without "any other princesses," in the midst of the Polish delegation. She stormed out and returned home to the Tuileries. Anne of Austria was furious. Gaston came by that same evening to scold her, and La Rivière was dispatched to pacify the regent, an effort that required Mazarin's intervention as well. At La Rivière's insistence, Mademoiselle called on the cardinal at his apartment in the Palais-Royal to thank him in person for his help, the only time, Mademoiselle assures her readers, that she ever so honored Mazarin.[28]

Determined to have the last word, Mademoiselle considered herself well avenged when Queen Louise-Marie called on Gaston at the Luxembourg. Gaston was busy with his barber, leaving her to cool her heels in an anteroom until she finally left in a huff. By the time she quit Paris, the rest of the Orléans family as well as the Guises had turned away from her, having had enough of "this royalty."[29]

But what of Mademoiselle herself? Mademoiselle at long last introduces the first serious suitor for her hand, none other than Charles Stuart, prince of Wales, son of Charles I and Mademoiselle's aunt Henrietta Maria. At the time of the memorial service for the queen of Spain, Henrietta Maria had taken refuge in France from the civil strife across the Channel. She was received with all the honors due a queen consort of England and a daughter of Henri IV and installed in a suite of apartments at the Louvre. Mademoiselle and the rest of the royal family were sympathetic to her plight and included her as a matter of course in the social calendar of the French court.

Henrietta Maria, always in dire financial circumstances, spent much of her time following events in England and worrying about the future of her children. In 1646, her eldest son, Charles, joined his mother in exile. Mademoiselle met her English cousin for the first time while the court was at Fontainebleau. Her initial impression was mixed: she thought him tall, dark, and "passably agreeable in his person." What she found less acceptable was his inability to speak or understand a word of French.[30] Under the circumstances, Mademoiselle had to accept Henrietta Maria's assurances that the prince had fallen madly in love with her, that he spoke about her constantly, and that he would have been on her doorstep at all hours had his mother not intervened in the name of propriety. Charles, it would seem, was in despair at the rumors that Mademoiselle might marry the newly widowed Emperor Ferdinand III.[31]

Although Mademoiselle asserted that she knew the value of these theatrics, she nevertheless made good use of her royal suitor in the months ahead.[32] Whenever Mademoiselle visited her aunt, Charles was there. He made a point of escorting her to and from her carriage, hat in hand. If she went to the theater at the Palais-Royal, Charles would sit by her side and shower her with compliments.

Henrietta Maria, her hopes swelling, played the part of an indulgent future mother-in-law. Once, when Mademoiselle was to attend a reception at the home of Madame de Choisy, the wife of Gaston's chancellor, Henrietta Maria came to the Tuileries to help Mademoiselle arrange her coiffure and jewelry, while young Charles held a candle nearby to illuminate the dressing table. Anne of Austria, who did not discourage the prince's courtship, had a final look at the outcome and sent her niece on her way. When Mademoiselle arrived at the Choisy residence, Charles was waiting at the door. When she retired briefly for a few final adjustments to her costume before making her entrance, Charles was there again to hold up a candle before the mirror. He spent the rest of the evening following Mademoiselle around the floor. At the end, he was there to see her home, not leaving until she was safely through the gates of the Tuileries. A mutual cousin, Ruprecht of the Palatine acted as Charles's interpreter. Through this medium, the young Stuart assured his lady that he understood everything she said. Mademoiselle left it to her readers "to believe this if they want to."[33]

Charles's attentions were the talk of Paris that winter. The courtship climaxed with a festival at the Palais-Royal, an Italian musical followed by a ball. For this occasion, Anne of Austria herself supervised Mademoiselle's costume. The crown jewels of France and those of England still in the possession of Henrietta Maria set off Mademoiselle's fresh features. There were many, Mademoiselle recalled, who found her adolescent good looks a fit match for the richness of her dress.

The theater had been modified with benches scattered about to accommodate the ladies, and with a temporary dais holding a single throne. When it came time to be seated, the young king, Louis XIV, declined to take the throne in the presence of his guest the prince of Wales. The prince reciprocated with a comparable refusal. The solution was for Mademoiselle to occupy the seat, with Louis and Charles Stuart taking places on the steps of the dais. Below them the other princes and princesses present made themselves comfortable. Courtiers assured her later that she seemed made to grace that throne. The experience was a heady one, and its narration forms one of the set pieces of Mademoiselle's *Mémoires*. It also served to clarify her thoughts about Charles

Stuart. From the height of her temporary throne, Mademoiselle looked down upon the dispossessed prince "with my heart as much as my eyes." Charles was nothing but "an object of pity."[34]

For Mademoiselle had instead become mesmerized by the possibility of a marriage to Emperor Ferdinand III, widowed by the death of his empress, Maria Anna, the sister of Anne of Austria. Despite the state of war between France and the Habsburgs, the French court had sent a special envoy, one Mondevergue, to Vienna to present formal condolences to the emperor. Mondevergue returned to France with a report that Ferdinand and several of his ministers had mentioned Mademoiselle as a replacement for Maria Anna. Mademoiselle had good reason to believe that such a match was possible and even politically desirable. When the news of the empress's death had reached the court, La Rivière, the voice of Gaston, had raised the matter with Mademoiselle.[35] On the day of the ball at the Palais-Royal, the regent had talked to her about such an alliance and had promised to do whatever she could to bring it about. There were further discussions with Mazarin and La Rivière, both of whom assured Mademoiselle that they favored the proposal.[36]

Having made up her mind, Mademoiselle was impervious to the misgivings of others, including Gaston, who had second thoughts about the proposal. The emperor, he argued, was too old, older than Gaston, and the Spanish etiquette of the court of Vienna would not be to his daughter's taste. A match with Charles Stuart, or with the young duke of Savoy, would make her far happier. To this, Mademoiselle retorted that the establishment was more important than the person and that the emperor was her true choice.[37]

Having heard that the emperor was very religious, Mademoiselle flung herself into a round of devotions. As a pupil of Anne of Austria, she was well acquainted with all of the fashionable churches and convents of greater Paris, but this time her fervor led to an unexpected consequence. In a burst of piety, she resolved to renounce the imperial crown in favor of a Carmelite veil. Mademoiselle's description of her state of exaltation suggests some form of adolescent hysteria, and Gaston saw it for what it was. He forbade Mademoiselle to consider it further, denounced the devout ladies around the regent for planting the idea, and asked the queen not to take Mademoiselle on any more convent visits. The shock of paternal authority had the desired effect; Mademoiselle put the matter out of her mind and returned to her quest for an imperial marriage.[38]

Unfortunately for Mademoiselle, who continued to mistreat her

Stuart suitor during this period, the imperial match turned out to be a mirage. Word eventually reached France that the emperor had settled on a Habsburg cousin, Maria Leopoldine of the Tyrol, as his new empress. This turn of events was a severe humiliation for Mademoiselle, who had paraded her hopes in public for months. She blamed La Rivière and Mazarin for the outcome: they had urged her on with false assurances but had done nothing to bring the matter to closure.[39]

The emperor Ferdinand was not the only Habsburg candidate for Mademoiselle's hand. When La Rivière had broached the subject with Mademoiselle in 1646, he had also suggested an alternative candidate, the emperor's brother, the archduke Leopold, governor of the Spanish Netherlands.[40] While awaiting word from Vienna, Mademoiselle put the idea out of her mind. There matters might have rested except for the intervention of an impecunious officer of Gaston's guards named Compet de Saujon. Saujon, a gentleman "with cape and sword," stood high in Gaston's favor, in part because his sister was Gaston's mistress of the moment.[41] Mademoiselle, who had placed Saujon's sister in her stepmother's household, considered him a dreamer and a teller of tall tales and found his company amusing.

In the course of 1647, a friend and fellow officer of Saujon's, one Vilermont, was taken prisoner while on campaign in Flanders. He was treated with much courtesy by the enemy and eventually released on parole. At a dinner in his honor hosted by a senior Spanish commander, Ottavio Piccolomini, duke of Amalfi, the conversation turned to personalities at the court of France. The duke mentioned Mademoiselle as a princess whose qualities would make her welcome in the Spanish Netherlands as a fit consort to the archduke.

Vilermont reported this conversation to Saujon, who relayed it to Mademoiselle and urged Mademoiselle to receive Vilermont after he returned to Paris. Under her questioning, Vilermont amplified and embellished Piccolomini's statements. The general, it seemed, had been gratified to learn that a marriage between Mademoiselle and Charles Stuart was not likely. In her version of events, Mademoiselle found the supposed remarks of the Spanish general flattering but of no special consequence. She dismissed Vilermont with thanks, but took no action on his report.

Saujon, however, returned to the charge, encouraging her to make the most of the opportunity. Together with Vilermont, who had become acquainted with members of the archduke's staff during his brief captivity, Saujon initiated a series of contacts with these officials to discuss the possibility of a marriage between Mademoiselle and the archduke. Saujon began his overtures while Mademoiselle was still furious at the court for its failure to follow through on a match with Ferdinand III. In spite of her later protestations to the contrary, she seems to have encouraged Saujon. He brought Mademoiselle correspondence suggesting that such a match was very much on the minds of officials on the other side of the frontier. As part of the arrangement, the archduke was to receive the Spanish Netherlands as an independent principality from the king of Spain. There was a recent precedent for this: from 1596 to 1633 the provinces in question had been nominally independent under the rule of the infanta Isabella and her husband, the archduke Albert.

The proposal appealed to Mademoiselle's imagination in that it combined the elements of a prestigious establishment, a sovereign status, and a link with the infanta Isabella, who had sheltered Gaston d'Orléans in exile, and whom Mademoiselle eulogizes elsewhere as "the greatest princess who ever lived."[42] Although dismissing Saujon's initiative as a "fantasy," which she listened to only as a diversion—the expression "building castles in Spain" comes to mind—Mademoiselle did nothing to discourage Saujon. Inevitably, these actions came to the attention of Mazarin and the regent. In April 1648, one of Saujon's couriers was intercepted. Saujon was arrested at the beginning of May and interrogated by Mazarin himself. What Mademoiselle had dismissed as a fantasy was taken far more seriously by Mazarin and by the regent. Mademoiselle was not a private person but a member of the royal family; beyond Mademoiselle lay Gaston d'Orléans, and Saujon was in his service. The court wondered if Gaston, who in fact was unaware of these activities, was implicated in the affair.[43]

Mademoiselle reacted to Saujon's arrest by feigning astonishment: what could be the reason for such a measure? But the reason, or at least the rumored explanation, a treasonable correspondence with the enemy implicating the princess, spread like wildfire through Paris. Alarmed, Mademoiselle sought out La Rivière to ask about Saujon. But La Rivière would say little, except that Saujon was a "criminal."[44]

For several days, Mademoiselle braved the gathering storm. Through members of his family, Saujon succeeded in getting word to Mademoiselle of what he had said to Mazarin. Mademoiselle applied again to La Rivière for information but was turned away politely. A lady of the court, one of Mademoiselle's friends, told her that Saujon was accused of plotting to carry her off to marry the archduke. Mademoiselle had no choice but to ridicule the idea. A visit to the Luxembourg proved fruitless: Gaston was having dinner at Mazarin's and not expected until late.

The tempest broke the next day at the Palais-Royal when Mademoiselle, determined to confront the whispered accusations, made an appearance. The regent's council was just rising. La Rivière, who had been in attendance, was one of the first to emerge. Seeing Mademoiselle in the anteroom, he warned her to expect a reprimand from the queen and from Gaston. While they were standing there, Gaston appeared in the doorway and called for his daughter. Mademoiselle advanced through the open door, followed by her aunt, Mademoiselle de Guise. But Gaston would not permit Guise to enter, pushing her back and, in Mademoiselle's words, "slamming the door in her nose" with enough force to frighten his daughter.[45]

Once in the room, Mademoiselle found herself alone with the regent, Gaston, and Mazarin. Anne of Austria told Mademoiselle that they knew about Saujon and his schemes. When Mademoiselle, all innocence, inquired what the queen meant, Anne replied that they were aware of the proposal to marry her to the archduke, who would have the sovereignty of the Netherlands. When Mademoiselle was silent, Anne, out of patience, blurted a curt "Answer!" To this, Mademoiselle responded that the queen did Saujon too much honor by putting him in prison; a madhouse would have been a more fitting place of detention. Mademoiselle knew better than to rely on Saujon to find her a place in the world; that responsibility belonged to the regent, and she had no doubt that Anne would find her something suitable, given the court's many obligations to Gaston. She had before her the example of Louise-Marie de Gonzague. If Anne had gone to such lengths to secure a crown for someone so vastly inferior in rank to Mademoiselle, why should Mademoiselle expect any less from the regent?

Anne of Austria was not accustomed to sarcasm. For once, however, the haughty Habsburg had met a worthy foe; the granddaughter of Henri IV was not to be intimidated, at least in her telling of it. When the furious regent accused Mademoiselle of sending a faithful servant to the block, Mademoiselle stared at her and Gaston and retorted that at least in her case it would be for the first time, thereby conjuring up the ghosts of Richelieu's victims, many of whom had perished in the service of these two accusers. The import of the remark was not lost on her audience, as the tone deteriorated still further. When Anne, exasperated at the counterattack, ordered Mademoiselle to answer the questions she was asked, the princess offered a backhanded apology: never having been interrogated before, she did not know how to reply. The insulting allusion was to the infamous interrogations of Anne in 1637 by Richelieu and chancellor Séguier. After a few more volleys, Mademoiselle, sensing a stalemate, brought the matter to a close by asking the queen if she had anything more to ask of her. When the reply was in the negative, Mademoiselle made her bow and swept out of the room "victorious" in combat but "furious."[46]

Mademoiselle portrays the entire scene as a confrontation between herself and the regent. Gaston is absolutely silent throughout, as is Mazarin, although the cardinal is unable to hide his amusement at her spirited rejoinders to the queen. Madame de Motteville, in her account, adds that Mademoiselle also turned on Gaston, demanding that he defend her since it was his own honor that was impugned by such accusations.[47] After all, if La Rivière had raised the subject of such a marriage more than a year earlier, as Mademoiselle took pains to chronicle, it is likely that Anne and Mazarin were also well aware of it. If so, the counterattack by Mademoiselle was effective, and may explain Gaston's evident discomfiture at the scene unfolding before his eyes. Permitting his daughter to be so exposed to the regent's anger, if perfectly in character, did his reputation little good. In aristocratic circles, some agreed with the suggestion that he had been the actual target of the inquiry and that he should have defended his daughter. Others argued that he bore the ultimate responsibility because of his failure to follow through on the proposed matches with either the emperor or the king of Spain. Still others suggested an even baser motive: that the entire episode had been orchestrated by La Rivière to derail Mademoiselle's ongoing attempts to gain control of her own property, which was still managed on her behalf by appointees of Gaston.[48]

The aftermath was considerably less dramatic than the scene that preceded it. Mademoiselle was confined to her rooms at the Tuileries for a few days. The queen, convinced that her brother-in-law was not implicated in a plot against the state, saw the affair for what it was, a foolish misstep by a headstrong young woman, and turned her attention to more serious matters. For her part, the princess managed a tearful reconciliation with Gaston and a cool and somewhat formal one with Anne of Austria. She took some comfort in a few words of encouragement from her young cousin Philippe, who intercepted her when she visited the queen to assure her that he was always on her side. Mademoiselle then made a point of spending time away from court, visiting various country estates of friends, on the pretext that her presence would be odious to her persecutors.

In August 1648, at the urging of Gaston, who feared the consequences of a permanent breach between the regent and his daughter, Mademoiselle attended a *Te Deum* at Notre Dame in honor of Condé's recent victory over the Spaniards at Lens. For Mademoiselle, who had wept tears of rage at the news of yet another triumph by the detested Condé and who still felt aggrieved by the regent's behavior toward her, this was a bitter pill to swallow. Nevertheless, she went, sat next to Mazarin, and used the opportunity to plead for Saujon's release. After the service, she returned home to dine alone. There she learned that the queen regent had used the ceremonies to cover the arrest of two prominent members of the parlement of Paris, Broussel and Blancmesnil, who had led the opposition to Mazarin's policies in judicial circles. The news had ignited passions throughout the city, and the populace was said to be on the verge of revolt.

That night, royal troops remained on duty around the Tuileries to prevent any attempt by the city militia, which had mobilized in support of the parlement, to seize the Porte de la Conférence, the city gate at the western end of the gardens of the Tuileries. To Mademoiselle's surprise, the rebels did not seem intimidated by the proximity of the royal forces. If the king's guards controlled the major crossroads, the militia were in control of the districts beyond. At the *barrière des sergents* on the Rue Saint-Honoré, militiamen took up posts within a few feet of royal sentries.

The next morning, Mademoiselle was awakened by the beat of drums and the rattle of gunfire. From her windows, she could see royal troops across the river storming the old Tour de Nesle, which had been occupied by rebels during the night. This was the first clash of arms, however one-sided, that Mademoiselle had ever seen. The sight of wounded soldiers as they passed under her windows frightened Mademoiselle. Later events, she remarked ruefully, were to harden her to the spectacle of wounded and dying men.[49]

Mademoiselle's forced reconciliation with the court thus coincided with the opening of the prolonged and episodic period of civic strife in France known as the Fronde. In its origins, as well as in its long-term consequences, the Fronde remains a subject of debate among specialists of the period. For our purposes, the Fronde may be viewed as a convergence of revolts by many different elements of French society against royal authority, each movement having its own causality and agenda, but all unfolding more or less simultaneously and drawing strength from each other.

The wellsprings of discontent were many. The Fronde took place against a background of a deepening agricultural depression that had begun a number of decades earlier, and that had resulted in a growing sense of misery and despair in the countryside. Royal taxation had grown exponentially since 1635, when Richelieu had brought France into open warfare against the Habsburgs, and was imposed on a faltering agricultural economy that directly or indirectly supported an overwhelming proportion of the population. In many segments of society, there was a festering discontent with this financial burden. Some of the expedients to raise revenues, such as the imposition of special levies within the city of Paris, affected large segments of the urban population. Other measures, such as the attempt by the crown to regain control over the appointment of high magistrates by the abolition of the *paulette*, a special payment that permitted a magistrate to pass his office to an heir, struck at the sense of caste that had developed within the parlement of Paris. For many in the high aristocracy, the early euphoria of the regency had given way to impatience as the regent's government continued Richelieu's policies in both the domestic and the foreign spheres, albeit without the frequent use of the ax to cow opponents. This meant in practice a centralization of power and patronage to the detriment of aristocratic factions at court and, it should be noted, at the expense of noblemen of substance in the provinces, who resented the intrusion of royal authority at much lower levels than had been traditional before Richelieu. The drawn-out war with the House of Austria, the champion of the Counter-Reformation in Europe, offended an influential segment of devout French Catholics, both noble and commoner, who considered the policy of Richelieu, now pursued by Mazarin, to be scandalous, if not outright sacrilegious.[50]

Whether any government could have avoided an explosion under these circumstances is open to discussion. What seems less debatable is that the shortcomings of Mazarin and the queen exacerbated the situation. Anne of Austria had had no schooling in government prior to her assumption of the regency. Once in power, her imperious temperament gave her little tolerance for dissenting opinions, even when voiced by former fellow victims of Richelieu. Her impatience with aristocratic critics, however, was dwarfed by her contempt for the institutional opposition she perceived in the parlement of Paris. During the early years of the regency, much of the criticism of royal measures, particularly those that dealt with the finances of the state, came from the parlement. For this, the haughty descendant of Charles V had no tolerance whatsoever. Mazarin, for all his diplomatic prowess, seemed equally at sea, without any sense of the long tradition of remonstrance cherished by the high magistrates of the parlement, and with no skills for dealing with it.

The fundamental error of Anne and Mazarin was the attempt to overawe their opponents with unambiguous assertions of royal supremacy coupled with displays of force. Within the political tradition of the monarchy was a strong belief that the plenitude of royal power was lodged in the king and could not, ultimately, be exercised by any surrogate. A regent was expected to exercise a caretaker role; matters of a grave constitutional nature were beyond the legitimate authority of any except the king in person exercising his plenary power. It followed that decisions on issues of such magnitude would have to be postponed until a minor king, such as Louis XIV in 1648, reached his majority. By extension, if a surrogate authority, such as a minister or regent, attempted measures that belonged within this reserved sphere, resistance was not rebellion against the king but a defense of the unwritten fundamental laws of the kingdom, the right, indeed the duty, of revolt.[51]

The ill-advised arrest of Broussel and Blancmesnil after a period of open dispute between the court and the parlement of Paris crystallized the revolt against the regency government and opened up the fault lines in French society. This relatively minor event, so much less dramatic than the famous arrests of powerful noblemen in the previous reign, sparked the uprising against royal authority that was to dominate the events of the next five years.

Mademoiselle later confessed that at first she did not recognize the gravity of the events she was witnessing. Her reaction to the early episodes of the Fronde was a wry satisfaction at the discomfiture of the regent, Mazarin, and Gaston, at the turn events had taken, coupled with amusement at the sight of citizen militiamen, unused to carrying arms, trying not to trip over their scabbards.[52] Mademoiselle was at the Palais-Royal when the entire parlement of Paris marched in procession to the palace to demand the release of their two colleagues, and witnessed the humiliation of the regent and Mazarin, forced to submit when faced with the city under arms. This show of weakness, so soon after their assertion of royal authority, convinced the parlement to continue its own deliberations on the *paulette* and other matters touching on royal authority. In this early blunder on the part of the royal government, Mademoiselle saw the explanation for the ensuing years of turmoil.[53]

The first phase of the Fronde, sometimes called the Fronde of the parlement, or the Old Fronde (1648–49), was essentially a struggle between the parlement of Paris and certain aristocratic factions in alliance with it, and the government of Anne of Austria. The queen benefited from the support of both Gaston and the prince de Condé, a fact that decided Mademoiselle's allegiance during the opening episodes: if Gaston was loyal, so, despite her reservations, was Mademoiselle.

After the release of the *parlementaires*, the court withdrew to Rueil, thus putting some distance between itself and the Paris militia. Gaston and his family remained in Paris, although Gaston, playing the intermediary, was a frequent visitor to Rueil. Shortly thereafter, he moved his pregnant wife and two small daughters, Mademoiselle's half sisters, to Rueil. They were soon joined by the Condé family, probably at the urging of Anne of Austria. Mademoiselle found herself the only member of the royal family in residence in Paris. She put the best face she could on the apparent indifference of the court to her movements and, unbidden, joined the rest of the royal family at Rueil. She told the queen she had felt it was her duty to come, but let Gaston and La Rivière know of her resentment that she had been so singularly snubbed.[54]

In late September, Condé, no longer required in the field, arrived at Rueil. Surprisingly, he and Gaston joined in urging a conciliatory policy on the regent. For Gaston, who, as a peer of the realm, often took his seat in parlement to listen to its debates, this was not unusual. Condé's motives are more difficult to explain, but may have been due to a wish to upstage Mazarin. Unable to count on either Condé's sword or Gaston's prestige, Mazarin and Anne were forced into an unwanted peace. An agreement between the regent and the magistrates confirmed the jurisdiction of parlement, asserted in July, over the finances of the state, abolished a number of extraordinary commissions created earlier over the protests of parlement, lowered the *taille* for 1648, and repealed certain taxes on foodstuffs. In addition, the final article of the agreement created a right of habeas corpus for members of parlement, who were not to be troubled in the exercise of their function by extraparlementary measures such as royal *lettres de cachet*.[55]

These measures were registered in parlement on October 24 and a week later, the court returned to Paris as a sign of reconciliation. This was a complete defeat for the government, and neither Mazarin nor the regent had any intention of honoring the terms forced upon them. In the months that followed, the four actors at the center of power, Mazarin, Anne of Austria, Gaston, and Condé, debated the best means to nullify the parlementary triumph. The approach of winter would bring with it the cessation of military activities in the field and the withdrawal of the troops to their winter quarters. This meant that troops would be available to intimidate the parlement and the population of Paris. Shortly before Christmas, the four had agreed on this course of action, which would be preceded by the court's departure from Paris.[56] Mazarin and the queen settled on the night of January 5 for the court's withdrawal to Saint-Germain, hoping to slip away unnoticed as Paris celebrated the eve of the feast of the Three Kings. Other than the principals, only a handful of officials knew the regent's intentions. Even so, rumors circulated at court, and Mademoiselle caught wind of them while visiting her father at the Luxembourg on the day of the flight. Mademoiselle found the story hard to believe because Gaston, who had been battling the gout for some days, did not seem in a condition to leave Paris. But when Mademoiselle put the question to him as a jest, Gaston was evasive. This convinced Mademoiselle and her stepmother, who was also in the dark, that the rumor was probably true.

Around three in the morning, the comte de Comminges, an officer of the queen's guard, appeared at the Tuileries with an order to join the queen's party, which was waiting at the Cours-la-Reine with the rest of the royal family. Once there, after the usual battle over precedence with the princess de Condé, Mademoiselle took her place in the queen's carriage. The regent was in an exultant mood: as Mademoiselle put it, she could not have been happier if she had "won a battle, taken Paris, and hanged all those who had displeased her."[57]

Saint-Germain was in chaos. The château had not been prepared for the court's stay for fear of arousing the suspicions of the parlement. Most of the courtiers, including Mademoiselle, found themselves without furnishings, food, or servants. Mademoiselle slept her first night in a room without glass in the windows to keep out the January cold, on a mattress sent by Madame de Fiesque from Paris, which she shared with her little half sister, Marguerite-Louise. The child was frightened, and Mademoiselle and the attendants had to sing her lullabies to get her back to sleep.

The inconvenience persisted for about a week, for the Parisians reacted to the flight by blocking the movement of household goods and furniture to Saint-Germain. Mademoiselle moved in with her stepmother, where she had the use of a bed and her stepmother's servants to help her dress. In the absence of a wardrobe, the servants washed her nightclothes during the day and her petticoats for day wear while she slept. The biggest hardship was the food: Mademoiselle did not think much of the cuisine served at her father's table, and she soon grew weary of her stepmother's complaints about "bagatelles."[58]

Shortly thereafter Mademoiselle obtained an apartment of her own. The parlement of Paris still refused to permit furnishings belonging to the royal household to leave Paris. Mademoiselle was able to help. She sent a page to the parlement to request permission to transport some of "her" belongings to Saint-Germain, which included articles intended for the queen. The magistrates, after receiving the fifteen-year-old boy in formal session, agreed to the request. Mademoiselle was convinced that this courtesy was due to her own popularity in the city; it does not seem to have crossed her mind that the judges probably intended a gesture to the daughter of Gaston d'Orléans, traditionally a friend of the parlement. Among the goods transported was a box full of the queen's heavily perfumed leather gloves. When these were inspected by the local authorities, who were not used to such refined smells, the strong scent caused a round of sneezing. The story caused much laughter at Saint-Germain, and the page, hero of the hour, was thereafter styled "the ambassador."[59]

The evident improvement in Mademoiselle's relationship with the court was underlined by an important concession. Saujon, who had already been released from prison at Gaston's request, was allowed to resume his position in the army. Mademoiselle, her pride thus salvaged, had no further cause of complaint against the government.[60] As for the renewed cordiality on the part of the queen and Mazarin, Mademoiselle was shrewd enough to guess the cause: the endless balancing act between Gaston and the Condés. The situation had become even more complicated by a split in the ranks of the Condés. The prince's younger brother, Armand de Bourbon, prince de Conti, and his ambitious sister, the duchess de Longueville, together with her husband, had slipped away from court, and had surfaced in Paris as allies of the parlement. This event created a breach between the regent and the dowager princess de Condé, Mademoiselle's old adversary in all questions of precedence. For Mademoiselle, the fact that the duchess de Longueville, whom she considered a natural rival, had joined the Fronde was decisive; Mademoiselle's allegiance would be to the court.[61]

The unanticipated rally of many great aristocrats to the parlementary side stunned the court and opened a new chapter in the tangled history of the rebellion. The Longuevilles and Conti were joined by others: the duc de Beaufort, who had escaped in May 1648 from his prison cell at Vincennes; the duc d'Elbeuf, a relative of the Guises; the duc de Bouillon, whose brother, the maréchal de Turenne, commanded the French forces on the Rhine; the prince de Marcillac, heir to the duc de la Rochefoucauld; and the duc de la Trémouille. In addition to these *grands seigneurs*, the coadjutor bishop of Paris, Paul de Gondi, had declared for the rebels. The apparent support of the Church and of such prominent noblemen seemed to legitimize the parlement's stance as the defender of the French constitutional order against a tyrannical, foreign-born prime minister.

In response to these developments, the government accused unnamed members of the parlement of sedition and ordered the parlement to remove itself to the small provincial town of Montargis. The judges replied by declaring Mazarin an enemy of the state and gave him a week to leave the country. In collusion with the city officials, it seized control of the available royal funds, began to raise troops, and appointed its aristocratic supporters as officers to lead them. The prince de Conti, by virtue of his standing as a prince of the blood, was named the titular commander-in-chief.

The duc de Longueville, who was governor of Normandy, left Paris with the announced intention of rallying that province to the Fronde. Shortly afterward, the regional parlement at Rouen declared its solidarity with its Parisian counterpart. About the same time, a smoldering revolt in Bordeaux erupted again, largely because of missteps by the local governor, the duc d'Epernon. Similarly, a quarrel between the parlement of Provence and the royal governor, the comte d'Alais, sparked riots at Aix, where Alais was besieged in his own residence.

For the moment, the government had to let local authorities loyal to the Crown deal with these regional disturbances. The attention of Mazarin and the regent remained on the far more dangerous situation in Paris, which the government was determined to master. Since the available troops, perhaps ten thousand at most, were not sufficient to control the streets of Paris, the royal plan was to starve the city into submission by cutting its supply routes. To this end, Condé and Gaston, nominally co-commanders, set up headquarters at Saint-Cloud and Saint-Denis.

The military engagements that followed were caused largely by royal attempts to block key roadways or to seize convoys of foodstuffs bound for Paris. In most instances, the royal forces gained the upper hand. In early February, the two princes, commanding jointly, easily defeated forces under the duc d'Elbeuf at Charenton, near the junction of the Seine and the Marne. Thereafter, the military balance seemed to turn increasingly against the Fronde. At the end of the month Turenne attempted to rally his troops to the Fronde but was unsuccessful. His army, almost entirely German mercenaries in the service of France, had no interest in following their chief. Turenne was forced to abandon his command to avoid arrest in the field. Outside Paris, the troops of the Fronde continued to lose ground to the royal army, and the price of food soared.

In spite of these royal successes, certain considerations led Mazarin to seek an accommodation with the parlement of Paris. The news of the execution of Charles I of England at the hands of his rebellious subjects gave pause to both sides. At the same time, the Spanish enemy, sensing an opportunity, had sent an "envoy" to discuss peace terms with the parlement of Paris. Over the objection of some magistrates, the representative of the archduke Leopold (Mademoiselle's would-be husband) was received and heard. Although this "negotiation" came to little, it lent weight to the criticism that Mazarin alone was responsible for the continuation of the war with Spain at a moment when the Peace of Westphalia (October 1648) had given rise to hopes for an end to all hostilities. In fact, the archduke's initiative was largely due to the old ties between the Spanish Crown and a number of the aristocratic Frondeurs, notably Bouillon and Madame de Chevreuse. This tacit alliance was underscored in early March when a Spanish army reinforced by Frondeur aristocrats invaded Picardy.

So the court, notwithstanding its victories, had reason to end the conflict with the parlement and to split the magistrates from their allies, the aristocratic extremists in league with Spain and the street mobs of Paris. Contacts between the parlement and the court had never been completely severed, and negotiations began in earnest in early March, with Gaston as an ardent proponent of conciliation. The resulting Peace of Saint-Germain, registered in parlement on April 1, was a compromise. Parlement and the Crown agreed on a level of royal borrowing for the next two years; the declarations of October 1648 were reaffirmed; and Mazarin remained in place. The aristocratic allies of the parlement were amnestied and bought off with large pensions and appointments to high office. Parlement agreed to disarm and dismiss its troops. More or less simultaneously, the Crown reached accommodation with the various local rebels in the provinces. By early April, the parlementary Fronde was at an end.[62]

During these months, Mademoiselle was mostly a spectator, reporting, without much enthusiasm or interest, on the various battles fought around Paris. She claims to have had little understanding of the issues involved in the Fronde. Her time at Saint-Germain, she insists, was spent in the pursuit of amusements thought suitable for a young princess, such as following the love affairs of others and passing time with the princess de Carignan, a sister of the rebel comte de Soissons who had been killed in battle in 1641.[63] Mademoiselle was amused by Carignan's tales of her years in exile in Spain and Italy. Carignan, said Mademoiselle, had "wit but no judgment"; her daughter, Louise-Christine de Savoie, had more sense. For amusement, Mademoiselle turned to the mother; for serious discussion, to the daughter.[64]

Mademoiselle admits to one political act during the period. As the fortunes of the Fronde faded and its noble supporters cast around for new allies, the duc de Beaufort attempted to persuade Gaston to join the rebellion. His proposals to Gaston were contained in a letter forwarded to Mademoiselle at Saint-Germain. After conferring with Beaufort's brother-in-law, the duc de Nemours, Mademoiselle decided that the better part of valor was to burn the letter and not convey its contents to Gaston.[65]

The court did not return to Paris after the establishment of peace, but remained at Saint-Germain until the end of April and then decamped to Compiègne. Needing a pretext for visiting Paris, Mademoiselle paid a visit of condolence to her aunt Henrietta Maria, whose husband, Charles I of England, had perished on the scaffold at Whitehall in January. Inevitably, the visit led to a resurrection of the proposal to marry Mademoiselle to the young Charles Stuart, now become, in title at least, Charles II. Henrietta Maria spared no effort to bring the matter to closure, sending her trusted adviser, Henry, Lord Jermyn, to ask for Mademoiselle's hand. When Mademoiselle rejoined the court at Compiègne, all the interested parties were there to discuss it. Anne of Austria encouraged her niece to accept; Mazarin promised that the government of France would help the exiled king regain his throne; and the abbé de la Rivière was there to represent Gaston. La Rivière argued that there was no other available candidate in Europe for Mademoiselle: the emperor had remarried; his heir was affianced to a Spanish infanta; the archduke Leopold would never become the independent ruler of the Netherlands; the king of France and his brother, Philippe, were too young; and Condé, the only other suitable match in France, was already married. Mademoiselle had already made it clear that she considered a marriage with the minor sovereigns of Germany or Italy beneath her. So Charles Stuart was the only possibility.

But Mademoiselle had not changed her opinion of Charles Stuart. In addition to her earlier reservations, some pragmatic considerations entered her calculations. Charles was in Holland, planning an expedition to Ireland as part of his plan to reconquer his domains. The current proposal called for a hasty trip to Paris to marry Mademoiselle before departing on the campaign. Mademoiselle would remain behind. Mademoiselle did not agree. If she could not accompany the king, which would be her preference, at the least she would feel obliged to use her wealth to support his efforts. This idea gave her pause. She had always lived in luxury. If she were to beggar herself for her husband's sake, presumably he would be suitably grateful if they regained his lost kingdom. But if Charles failed, Mademoiselle would be penniless.[66] Moreover, Mademoiselle had not forsworn the hope of a Habsburg marriage. While in Paris, she had visited with the Chevreuses, newly returned from a brief exile in the Spanish Netherlands, to get their opinion of that country and of the court of the archduke. As for the emperor, she reminded La Rivière that the empress was pregnant and might well die in childbirth.[67]

Mademoiselle was determined to avoid an English entanglement. To her readers, Mademoiselle explained that in matters matrimonial, using one's head was all important: "I had to consider my own interests before those of others, however close."[68] She knew that Gaston and Anne had advised Jermyn that they could not compel her and that he would have to win her consent. This gave her an unusual amount of freedom to negotiate directly with Jermyn. It did not take her long to find a roadblock. She would accept, she told Jermyn, if Charles converted to Catholicism. This was completely impossible. Mademoiselle turned a deaf ear to Jermyn's exasperated explanation of why this was out of the question, and Jermyn had to adjourn the discussions until the arrival of Charles Stuart.[69]

When Charles arrived some weeks later, Mademoiselle was still under pressure to agree to the proposal. Anne of Austria teased her mercilessly,

"Your cavalier has arrived."[70] Mademoiselle gave back as good as she got, remarking to La Rivière that she hoped Charles would whisper "sweet nothings" to her. No one had ever dared to do so before, on account, she added, of her disposition, not her rank, since others had had the temerity to flirt with "queens of our acquaintance."[71]

But the encounter was not a success. Charles had learned enough French since his last stay in France to chat with Louis XIV about dogs and hunting. But he could not find the vocabulary to reply to Anne of Austria's repeated questions about his political situation. From that moment, says Mademoiselle, she resolved not to marry Charles: she had a poor opinion of a king who did not know his own business, or at least could not articulate it. In this, she added, she recognized her own Bourbon blood in Charles, for the Bourbons were given to concentrating on "bagatelles" rather than on serious matters.[72]

From then on, Charles could do nothing right in Mademoiselle's eyes. She found his table manners atrocious and his charm nonexistent. After dinner one evening, Anne of Austria left them alone for a little while; there ensued an awkward silence that was broken only when Mademoiselle summoned the comte de Comminges to join them for some conversation. The visit ended with Charles appointing Jermyn as his spokesman and Mademoiselle turning to other matters.[73]

After the court returned to Paris in mid-August 1649, Mademoiselle saw little of her unwanted suitor. The empress, as Mademoiselle had guessed, did die in childbirth, and Mademoiselle resuscitated her dreams of an imperial marriage. Nicolas Goulas, another of Gaston's advisers, was to recall that nothing pleased Mademoiselle more than "the thought of being the first lady of Christendom."[74] When Mademoiselle stopped at Saint-Germain one afternoon, Henrietta Maria again argued that a king of eighteen was a better catch than a fifty-year-old emperor with four children, and she apologized for her son's open flaunting of his mistresses. Her words fell on deaf ears: Mademoiselle was polite, but not interested.[75]

Shortly thereafter, Mademoiselle endured a bout with smallpox, a common and often fatal malady of the time. Luckily for her, the case was mild, and the crisis soon passed. Its sole lasting effect was some damage to Mademoiselle's complexion; for one so plain, she noted, this was a small price to pay for survival.[76] Given the danger of contagion, she had remained shut up in her rooms at the Tuileries during her convalescence. She passed the time reading the polite inquiries that arrived every day

from members of the court. There was, however, one name conspic-
uously and shockingly absent from the list of inquirers and well-wishers:
that of the prince de Condé. Usage at court as well as ties of blood
mandated the formality of an inquiry, however insincere. But no missive
ever arrived from the hôtel de Condé, a boorishness that deepened Mademoiselle's long-standing aversion to the great warrior.[77]

The two were thrown into one another's company soon after Mademoiselle resumed her normal routine. In early December, Louis XIV and
his brother, Philippe, received the sacrament of confirmation in a ceremony at the Palais-Royal. As with baptism, the Catholic ritual requires
godparents for the recipient. Gaston and Mademoiselle represented the
king, while Condé and his mother performed this service for Philippe.
Condé spoiled the day for Mademoiselle by taunting her about her recent illness, even suggesting that she had not really been sick. Mademoiselle received this strange jest badly. Condé, she observed, had become
all-powerful at court, largely, she argued, because Gaston had allowed
the prince's pretensions to go unchallenged.[78]

Since the cessation of hostilities in April 1649, Condé had cast a large
shadow. His price for saving the regency from the parlement of Paris
seemed exorbitant. Even by the standards of his fellow aristocrats, his
demands for pensions, appointments to office, and other considerations
for himself and his followers were excessive. In the process, he managed
to offend many other powerful Frondeurs, notably the Vendômes, who
sought some of the same offices claimed by Condé; Paul de Gondi, who
commanded a following in the parlement and on the streets; and Madame de Chevreuse and other members of the Lorraine family. Mazarin
turned to these disgruntled aristocrats in search of a counterweight to
Condé and found willing allies. As part of this new alignment, the cardinal negotiated a marriage between his niece, Laura Mancini, and the duc
de Mercoeur, the Vendôme heir and older brother of Beaufort. To seal
the bargain, the Vendômes were to regain the lucrative post of admiral of
the seas, which had been confiscated under Richelieu and bestowed upon
a now deceased nephew of Richelieu. Condé had claimed the vacant
office in right of his wife, sister of that last holder.

Infuriated by the rapprochement between Mazarin and the Vendômes, Condé refused to sign the marriage contract between the Man-
cinis and the Vendômes. Some in Condé's entourage actually called for
an armed insurrection against the minister. This was avoided through a
"mediation" by Gaston that secured little better than a thinly disguised

capitulation by Mazarin. The cardinal had to promise in writing that the admiralty would not revert to the Vendômes; that he would seek Condé's approval for the marriages of his nieces and nephews; and even that Condé would have to approve all senior government appointments. In an atmosphere of intimidation and under threat of violence, with Condé openly contemptuous of the minister, Mazarin signed still another declaration on January 16, 1650, promising to defend the interests of the Condés as if they were his own. There seemed to be no doubt that Condé had come to dominate the machinery of state, to the consternation of all those who were not his clients.[79]

Mademoiselle shared these misgivings. Urged on by a friend, Madame de Guémené, a member of the Rohan family, Mademoiselle went to the Luxembourg on January 18 to urge her father to take a stand against Condé. She reminded Gaston that Marie de Medici, as regent, had arrested Condé's father, and she encouraged Gaston to seek Condé's arrest. To this, Gaston replied cryptically that she should be patient and she would soon be satisfied.[80]

Her curiosity aroused, Mademoiselle directed her carriage to the Palais-Royal. There it was evident that something unusual had taken place. The regent's council had been meeting behind closed doors for an inordinately long time. The entrances to the guardroom and a number of antechambers were closed; armed guards stood posted before the queen's apartments. Finally the queen appeared. She told her niece that Condé, his brother Conti, and his brother-in-law Longueville had been arrested while waiting for the council to convene and were already on their way to captivity at the royal fortress at Vincennes.[81] The decision to arrest the princes had been made in secrecy. Gaston was one of the few who had known, because his support, given reluctantly, had been essential to the plan's success. Even La Rivière had learned of the decision only a few hours before the plan was put into effect.

As for Mademoiselle, she could scarcely contain her glee at the fall of Condé.[82]

*When people of my rank are in a place, they are its mistresses, and
justly so. It is my duty to be here because it belongs to Monsieur.*

MADEMOISELLE

*But listen people of France
How Mademoiselle has told the
City of Orléans boldly
I am your Master.*

. . . . . .

*In a thousand years one will
Still recount the adventure of this
Brave Maiden
The Maid of Orléans.*

JEAN REGNAULT DE SEGRAIS

3   The Second Maid of Orléans

THE ARREST OF THE PRINCES DID NOT END THE STRUGGLE FOR
control of the state during the minority of Louis XIV. If Mazarin and the
regent believed that the imprisonment of Condé, Conti, and Longueville
would paralyze the Condé faction, they soon learned otherwise. In the
absence of the males of the clan, the women assumed the leadership
roles. The duchess de Longueville withdrew to Normandy, where she
tried to rally her husband's clients to resist the Crown; when this attempt
failed, she fled across the border to Stenay, where she and Turenne signed
a treaty of alliance with the Spanish foe. In April, the dowager princess
appeared before the parlement of Paris to urge that body to demand the
princes' freedom. At the end of May, Condé's wife, seconded by a number of his aristocratic friends, surfaced in Bordeaux to rekindle the revolt

sparked earlier by widespread resentment of the royal governor, the duc d'Epernon. Elsewhere, in Burgundy and in Champagne, Condé's partisans created additional disturbances.[1]

To deal with these uprisings and with the threat posed by Turenne and his Spanish allies, Mazarin and the regent spent most of 1650 away from the capital on a series of military expeditions and royal visitations intended to reassert the king's authority. To secure Paris, they had to depend on Gaston, who remained there as lieutenant general of the kingdom, and whose influence and popularity with the parlement and people of Paris had not diminished.

This reliance on Gaston's loyalty, and the need to bind him to the court, was reflected in the court's treatment of Mademoiselle, who was expected to join the royal expeditions. Mademoiselle would have preferred to stay at home, close to the Luxembourg and Gaston's government, which became ever more autonomous as the months passed, but she could not evade the will of the regent and the cardinal. After a short campaign in Normandy in February 1650, Mademoiselle feigned illness to avoid the next expedition, to Dijon to regain control of Burgundy. She was forced to accompany the court to Compiègne in June and to Bordeaux in early July, where she witnessed a long and inconclusive struggle between the royal forces and those of the Bordelais, led by Condé's partisans and financed in part with Spanish gold.

While there, Mademoiselle was treated as Gaston's representative, a questionable assumption at best, because Gaston did not confide in his daughter. Nevertheless, Mademoiselle reveled in the role. In her *Mémoires* she portrays herself as a participant in, and commentator on, the events in Bordeaux. Troubled by the spectacle of civil war and worried about the advance of Turenne's forces on Paris, Gaston had become the voice of the loyal opposition to Mazarin's policies. He sent the marquis du Coudray-Montpensier to help mediate the conflict in Bordeaux. The regent and Mazarin, who did not appreciate this interference, asked Mademoiselle to repeat their arguments that the Bordelais were not interested in a peaceful solution, and sent the marquis back to Paris with dispatches to that effect.[2]

The siege dragged on through a hot summer. Mademoiselle spent much of it in the queen's company, with a limited choice of pastimes: sewing with the queen and her ladies, writing letters to friends in Paris, or standing at the window to watch boats sailing up and down the Dordogne.[3]

Gaston, however, took a more active part in events. As the enemy troops neared Paris, his reproaches became more pointed, accusing Mazarin of a lack of judgment for denuding the north of troops and abandoning Paris to the enemy. Coudray-Montpensier returned to the court with a delegation from the parlement of Paris and orders from Gaston to intervene in the ongoing discussions between the court and the parlement of Bordeaux. Although the queen and the cardinal were resentful, they could not afford to antagonize Gaston or his Parisian allies, who were permitted to join in the negotiations. Once more, Mademoiselle found herself the surrogate for Gaston. She was staying at a house outside of Bordeaux belonging to one of the parlementary deputies from Bordeaux. As they usually assembled there to discuss the progress of the negotiations, Mademoiselle often joined the delegates to review the day's events.[4]

The lieutenant general of the kingdom did not confine his initiatives to the negotiations at Bordeaux. The archduke Leopold, whom Mademoiselle had once hoped to marry, was now operating on the Marne, not far from Paris. In the hopes of stirring up unrest in Paris, the archduke sent an offer to Gaston and the parlement to negotiate a general peace. Gaston, whether out of fear of an uprising should he refuse or out of ambition to be the peacemaker between France and Spain, accepted the proposal. He then notified the court at Bordeaux, and requested full powers to treat with the archduke.

Once more, Gaston's independent role alarmed the regent and Mazarin. But given the danger to Paris and the need to conciliate Gaston, they could hardly refuse his request, although Anne of Austria confided to Mademoiselle that she did not believe the Spanish were sincere. Mazarin went a step further, and faulted Gaston's acceptance of the archduke's offer before the court had given its consent. This provoked an explosion on the part of Mademoiselle. With Paris in danger, she argued, it was entirely appropriate for Gaston to negotiate with the archduke without waiting for word from the court. Had he refused, the Paris mob might have opened the gates to the invader. Should the negotiations fail, the blame would fall to the Spaniards; if they succeeded, the withdrawal of the enemy could only serve Mazarin's purposes. After all, the likelihood of keeping Condé locked up for years would improve dramatically if there was no need for his military services. In the end, Mazarin reluctantly agreed to permit Gaston to deal with the archduke, although the negotiations eventually proved futile.[5]

From this point, Mademoiselle portrays herself as an independent voice on political matters, even while perceived by the court as a surrogate for her father. Thus, she strongly urged the regent to come to terms with the rebels in Bordeaux. When the queen accused her of Frondeur leanings, she replied that she was simply speaking the truth and criticized Mazarin's policy of keeping the court away from Paris. As a result, she argued, the king's authority in his own capital was fast eroding as the court wasted its time moving from village to village in the provinces.[6]

When terms of the amnesty were accepted at the beginning of October, the queen received Condé's wife and son in private audience in a gesture of reconciliation and invited Mademoiselle to attend as Gaston's representative.[7] Mademoiselle began to wonder if some new shift in the political constellation was taking place. Her suspicions were reinforced by the alacrity with which both Condé's partisans and Mazarin sought her out. Pierre Lenet, a confidant of the Condés, met with her several times. With him, Mademoiselle was blunt: Mazarin could not be trusted, and without Gaston's help the Condés would never succeed in freeing the prince. In her discussions with Mazarin, Mademoiselle was equally direct. She was aware that the Condés were attempting to play Gaston against Mazarin, and Gaston had reason to be wary of a bargain at his expense. In replying to her, Mazarin spoke of his affection for Gaston and of his desire to be of service to his daughter: there was still the hope of an imperial marriage, and Mademoiselle should have control of her finances, not Gaston.[8]

As the court made its way back to Paris, the dialogue between the chief minister and the princess continued along the same lines. Mazarin told Mademoiselle that he was aware of Gaston's contacts with Condé's partisans, and he also knew the underlying cause of Gaston's unease. While the Spanish were within striking distance of Paris, Mazarin had feared that Turenne would attempt to rescue the princes. To forestall this, he had ordered the transfer of the captives from Vincennes to the fortress of Marcoussis, safely out of enemy range. In Mademoiselle's version of events, based on a conversation with Gaston shortly afterward, their transfer had violated the understanding between Gaston and the cardinal that any such order would require Gaston's countersignature. This arrangement was Gaston's protection against an accommodation between Condé and Mazarin at Gaston's expense. The transfer fed Gaston's fear that he would be the victim of a reversal of alliances, and invigorated his own negotiations with Condé's supporters.[9]

Mazarin exacerbated this atmosphere of suspicion with his decision to move the captive princes to Le Havre, whose governor, a member of the Richelieu family, was a faithful client of the cardinal's. Mazarin sent repeatedly to Paris to obtain Gaston's consent, but it was not forthcoming. Because the return of the court to Paris was delayed by a lingering illness of the queen, the cardinal entreated Mademoiselle to set out for the capital immediately with an invitation to Gaston to join the court at Orléans. If Gaston accepted, she was to use the time together on the road to convince her father of the cardinal's good intentions. But Mademoiselle, who took pains in her *Mémoires* to document the manifestations of public hostility toward Mazarin in Bordeaux and at various stops along the route, would have none of it. She refused to leave the court without the permission of Gaston.[10]

Mazarin then sent his invitation through less exalted channels, but to no avail. At Orléans, to Mazarin's disappointment, there was no Gaston, but there was news that the cardinal had been hanged in effigy by the Paris mob. At Pithiviers, Michel Le Tellier, one of the ministers who had remained with Gaston in Paris, brought word of Gaston's continued anger, but no assurance that he would join the court. After several anxious days, word arrived that Gaston would, after all, put in an appearance at Fontainebleau.

The long-awaited meeting between Gaston, the regent, and her chief minister did nothing to resolve matters. Even a personal appeal from Anne of Austria, so often a successful tactic in the past, failed, and the two parted on bad terms. Gaston, fearful of a betrayal that would leave him at the mercy of Condé, was appalled by Anne's final position: the transfer to Le Havre was in the king's best interests whether or not Gaston consented. To this Gaston could only reply that he did not agree, and he made preparations to return to Paris alone, rather than accompany the court.[11]

Before leaving, Gaston confided in his daughter. He saw Mazarin's measures as leading to catastrophe: in Paris many members of parlement were tempted to resurrect the Fronde. Gaston did not tell his daughter of his negotiations with Condé's partisans, because, says Mademoiselle, he knew of her aversion to the Condés. But Mademoiselle, thanks to Mazarin's revelations, was already aware of these overtures, and Gaston did hint that he was working with Condé's allies in parlement to secure his release. She declined another request by Mazarin to persuade her father to travel to Paris with the court to avoid the appearance of a breach.[12]

The court entered Paris on November 15, 1650. Exactly a month later, a royal army, with Mazarin present on the field, met and defeated a mixed force of Spaniards and partisans of Condé under the command of Turenne. The battle, named after Rethel, the nearest major town, was a dramatic victory for the cardinal: Turenne barely avoided capture or death, and his army no longer existed as an identifiable force. The power of the Condés should have been broken. This was certainly the belief at court, where news of the victory arrived on December 18, and a *Te Deum* in celebration of this triumph was sung at Notre Dame on December 20.[13]

But the events of the Fronde unfolded with a more complicated inner logic. The defeat of Turenne, if left unchallenged, was a mortal danger to all of the forces in opposition to Mazarin, no matter how disunited, including Gaston, who had gone too far to draw back. Even before the royal victory at Rethel, the parlement had taken up the question of the princes' imprisonment, citing as its authority the decrees of October 1648. These deliberations concluded at the end of December with a resolution calling for the release of the princes and the return of the duchess de Longueville from exile. The resolutions were coupled with demands for Mazarin's dismissal. All of this commotion served as a useful cover for negotiations between the leaders of the Old Fronde such as Gondi, Beaufort, and Madame de Chevreuse, and supporters of the Condés, led by Anne de Gonzague (known by her married title as the Princess Palatine) and François de la Rochefoucauld, with each side supported by parlementary allies. For his part, Mazarin was frantically negotiating simultaneously with both factions, hoping to cling to power by preventing a fatal union of the Old Fronde and the Fronde of the Princes.[14]

Gaston, as always, represented a third force, whose support would be critical in a confrontation. He made frequent appearances in the parlement to listen to its debates, and in early January, he agreed to serve as a mediator between the parlement and the regent. But his inclinations were evident. Mademoiselle, who followed these events closely, noted the public signs of a rapprochement between the Condés and Gaston. The younger comtesse de Fiesque, daughter-in-law of Mademoiselle's governess, gave a ball that January where supporters of the Condés and clients of Gaston mixed freely. Victory at Mazarin's expense was in the air, and Mademoiselle, always antipathetic to the Condés, was uncharacteristically gracious to her former foes.[15]

At the very end of January, a secret accord bound the elements of the opposition, including Gaston, to seek the liberation of the princes and the dismissal of Mazarin. Various offices of state, pensions, and other honors were to be distributed among the factions. Condé would not seek the vacant post of constable, that is, the rank of commander in chief of the French army, without Gaston's consent, and promised to marry his heir, the duc d'Enghien, to one of Gaston's younger daughters.[16]

The break between Gaston and Mazarin followed almost immediately. On February 1, Gondi appeared in the parlement to announce Gaston's support for the demand that the princes be freed. That evening, Gaston faced down Mazarin at the Palais-Royal. Mazarin, exasperated at the turn of events, lost his composure. While explaining matters to the boy king, he compared the parlement of Paris to its regicide namesake across the channel, and Beaufort and Gondi to Cromwell and Fairfax. Gaston flew into a rage at the comparison. He stormed out of the building after publicly vowing never to return to the council chamber as long as Mazarin remained in office.[17]

Mademoiselle learned of this exchange that same evening and hurried to the Luxembourg to congratulate her father. She approved of Gaston's stand but feared that Gaston, with his temperamental dislike of finality, would waver. But Gaston had gone too far to back away. His demands were seconded within days by assemblies of provincial noblemen meeting in Paris under his patronage and by an assembly of clergy dominated by Gondi.[18]

Gaston even took matters a step further. He summoned the commanders of royal troops in Paris, the duc d'Epernon and the maréchal de Schomberg, to remind them that he was the lieutenant general of the royal armies. He instructed them not to obey any orders not issued or countersigned by him—a direct challenge to the regent's ability to use the troops at her disposal to crush the opposition to Mazarin.[19]

It was a heady time for Mademoiselle as she divided her time between the Luxembourg, which served as the unofficial headquarters for the resurrected Fronde, the Palais de Justice, where judicial authority lent legitimacy to the rebellion, and the Palais-Royal, where a beleaguered regent and prime minister tried to stem the raging tide. The Luxembourg swarmed with Condé's supporters, with whom Mademoiselle made her formal peace. Under the circumstances, she concluded, her dislike of Condé was "unreasonable" and she resolved to go forward in partnership with her lifelong adversaries. Condé's representatives, glad of any support that might shore up Gaston's courage, responded to Mademoiselle's initiatives with effusive compliments and protestations of good will.[20]

Mademoiselle also attracted a good deal of attention from the Palais-Royal as Anne of Austria and Mazarin tried to use her to detach Gaston from his current alliance. Two emissaries of the court approached her with promises of huge, if unspecified, rewards for father and daughter if Gaston switched sides again. One of these envoys, Abel Servien, carried a direct appeal from the queen, which emphasized that Mademoiselle's own interests would be especially well served by a reconciliation between Gaston and the court.[21]

Mademoiselle relayed these overtures to Gaston and his advisers; with their consent she paid a visit to the queen to discuss matters further. At the Palais-Royal, Anne of Austria adopted a tone of sorrowful incomprehension: she did not understand why Gaston was so opposed to Mazarin and why he had waited so long to express himself. Mademoiselle's politic answer was that Gaston believed his duty to the young king and to the state compelled him to call for Mazarin's dismissal. Hitherto he had refrained from doing so out of respect for the regent and in the hopes that Mazarin would heed his advice. But Gaston had been treated with contempt (an allusion to the transfers of the princes), and this had led, inevitably, to Gaston's break with the court.[22]

On the evening of February 6, Mademoiselle was awakened by the noise of crowds gathering in the streets. Curious, she went to the terrace of the Tuileries. In the distance, near the Porte de la Conférence, at the western extremity of the gardens, she observed a small battle between some of her own guards and an unidentified troop, which was driven off. Several prisoners were taken; they turned out to be royal officers sent to secure the gate to protect Mazarin's flight from Paris. Mademoiselle immediately sent word to the Luxembourg, only to learn that Gaston was aware of Mazarin's intentions and had promised Anne not to pursue her fallen minister. Mademoiselle was instructed to release her prisoners.[23]

Mazarin, still hoping to salvage his position, withdrew to Saint-Germain to wait for the regent and the young king to slip surreptitiously out of Paris and join him there. The cardinal knew that as long as he controlled the king's person, his was the ultimate political authority. But the city was filled with rumors of the court's intended flight. To prevent it, Gondi, in Gaston's name, called out the city militia to take up positions at the gates and major crossroads in the city and at all the entrances to the Palais-Royal. These citizen troopers were often commanded by nobles attached to Condé and were reinforced by cavalry loyal to the Condés. Within the palace, there were fears that Gaston, urged on by Gondi and others, would seize the young king, confine Anne of Austria to a convent, and assume the regency.[24]

Gaston could not bring himself to take such extreme measures. On the morning after Mazarin's flight, Mademoiselle arrived at the Luxembourg just as Gaston was about to enter his carriage for an appointment with the regent. She persuaded him not to go, warning that the queen had heard the rumors of his "grand designs" and might strike first. Monsieur decided to wait until Condé was free.[25]

In the meantime, Gaston sent the captain of his guard to the Palais-Royal each evening to confirm that the king and his mother had not somehow slipped away. Sometimes this was not enough for the anxious Parisians: on one famous occasion, the regent was forced to admit a crowd of townsmen into the palace to file past the royal bed to view the young king, awake but feigning sleep under the blankets. Although the unwanted visitors were said to have blessed the king as they passed through his chamber, it was Louis XIV's most humiliating memory.[26]

On February 8, Anne agreed to exile Mazarin; the next day, the parlement banished the cardinal and his family, giving him two weeks to leave the country. At the same time, Anne promised to release the captive princes, subject to certain conditions. But Mazarin, moving with events, arrived at Le Havre on February 13 to free the prisoners himself, without any conditions. The cardinal then withdrew into imperial territory as a guest of the elector of Cologne.

On February 16, Condé entered Paris to a hero's welcome. The route along the road from Saint-Denis into the city was lined with the carriages of the high nobility and other dignitaries. Foremost among them was Gaston, accompanied by Gondi and Beaufort. The royal palace, Mademoiselle recollected, was deserted, with most of the court on the road. Eventually it refilled with courtiers, including Mademoiselle, curious to see how the queen would receive the liberated princes. In spite of herself, Mademoiselle admired the enormous self-control of the queen when the moment arrived. The three princes made their bows. There was an exchange of conventional compliments and a little banter. The conversation was strained; the princes did not linger but withdrew to dine with Gaston at the Luxembourg.[27]

At the Luxembourg, the atmosphere was triumphant. Condé regaled his audience with an account of Mazarin's fawning announcement to the princes of their liberation and his attempt to keep his composure through a dinner shared with the princes. Condé had all but mocked him at the table and had insulted him as they parted. Condé also made a point that day of seeking out Mademoiselle to confirm their reconciliation. In front of a laughing crowd of friends, the two admitted their years of mutual antipathy. Condé found some excuse for his silence during her bout of smallpox; Mademoiselle confessed that she had foolishly urged Gaston to support the princes' arrest. The laughter sealed the promises of future friendship.[28]

This new alliance soon led to another matrimonial fantasy on the part of Mademoiselle. In the spring of 1651, Condé's wife fell ill, and for a few days was in extremis. There were suggestions that Mademoiselle was the perfect candidate to fill the position of first princess of the blood. Mademoiselle spent a few hours speculating on the possibility with her secretary, Louis de Préfontaine. Condé, she maintained, was as distinguished by his talents as by his rank. Mademoiselle put aside for once her many battles over precedence with the Condés and remembered that they were of the "same blood" and the "same name." The obstacles to such a match were political: the concentration of power that such an alliance would create might not be acceptable to the regent, because Gaston, sustained by such a son-in-law, would control the state. This pleasant fantasy dissipated with the recovery of the princess de Condé, leaving Mademoiselle free to look elsewhere for an establishment.[29]

Mademoiselle also purged herself of the dream of an imperial match. During the siege of Bordeaux, the court had actually permitted her to send Saujon to Vienna in search of an imperial alliance. This public and unconventional attempt to secure a husband probably met with ridicule at the French court. Mademoiselle soon became disenchanted and professed to ignore Saujon's reports on his efforts. About the time of Condé's release, Saujon returned with the announcement that the emperor had become engaged to a daughter of the duke of Mantua. Mademoiselle would not admit her disappointment. God, she concluded, did not wish to bestow her hand on a man who did not deserve her.[30]

In the same season, her English suitor returned to the lists. Charles Stuart, after suffering a defeat at the hands of Cromwell's troops at Worcester, reappeared in Paris in October 1651 with stories of his narrow escape, a head of hair cropped close (to disguise him while in hiding), and a professed interest in renewing his courtship of Mademoiselle. This episode bore a close resemblance to earlier ones. Through intermediaries, Charles swore his affection for Mademoiselle, and Henrietta Maria swooped down with encouraging words. Mademoiselle vacillated. She was torn between her interest in a crown, even a titular one, and her fear that once she was married, Charles Stuart would squander her estates in vain attempts to regain his throne.

Gaston was of no help. His daughter, he told Henrietta Maria, was not his to give, but was at the disposal of the king and of the state. In the end, Gaston conceded that his daughter's fears of impoverishment were reasonable. His secretary, Léonard Goulas, painted Mademoiselle a dreary picture of a life shorn of wealth. Instead of an asset to Gaston, she would become yet another burden. This was enough for Mademoiselle, who had heard that Charles's advisers were already planning to scale back her household and sell her possessions. Her refusal caused consternation on the side of the English exiles, and inspired an act of royal boorishness. On her next visit to Henrietta Maria, Charles insisted on his right to a large armchair while she made do with a smaller chair: this was undoubtedly his right as a king, but not as a suitor. Mademoiselle ignored the insult.[31]

Mademoiselle's detached attitude toward the outcome of these various matrimonial proposals becomes more understandable in the light of yet another possibility that loomed large in the same period: the chance of a marriage with the boy king Louis XIV. As mentioned above, Mazarin and the regent had approached Mademoiselle in late 1650 to use her influence to persuade Gaston to rally to the court. In this portion of her *Mémoires*, Mademoiselle only alludes to the proposals made at that time: that Gaston would have carte blanche with respect to family matters, and that Mademoiselle's own "interests" would be well served by such a reconciliation. Mazarin and Anne of Austria, in their desperation, were prepared to offer Gaston the king's engagement to one of his daughters. Gaston was free to decide whether the bride would be Mademoiselle, who was eleven years older than Louis, or Mademoiselle's half sister, Marguerite-Louise, who was about five at the time.

Gaston was tempted, particularly by the possibility of the crown for Marguerite-Louise, the candidate whom the regent considered more suitable, on the grounds of age and temperament. Gaston finally decided that the terms offered by the Condés and the Old Fronde were too enticing, and he remained firm in his demands for Mazarin's departure. Mademoiselle was dismissive of the initiative, most likely because she realized that Gaston had committed himself to the Condés. She may also have been put off by the ambiguity of the situation: Gaston might have chosen the candidature of Marguerite-Louise over hers. According to Madame de Motteville, when a representative of the regent approached Mademoiselle about an alliance between the Luxembourg and the Palais-Royal, to be sealed with a marriage, she replied that she preferred to see her father remain on the side of the princes. The astounded emissary, the future duchess de Navailles, suggested that Mademoiselle make herself queen and then free the princes, but Mademoiselle was not persuaded, in spite of her desire to trade her coronet for a queen's "closed crown."[32]

This was only the opening episode in the comedy of *mon petit mari*. In the course of 1651, the regent and the exiled Mazarin saw this offer to Gaston as a powerful weapon in the complicated struggle for power that followed Condé's triumphant return. The efforts of the court were eased considerably by the inability of Condé to maintain the cohesion of the aristocratic and parlementary forces that had driven Mazarin away. By the late summer of 1651, the alliance of the Old and New Frondes was badly fractured. Some leading Frondeurs, including Gondi, the duchess de Chevreuse, and the Princess Palatine, had broken with Condé and were seeking a means of reconciliation with the court. Others, par-ticularly members of the parlementary opposition, were sobered by the approach of the king's legal majority, in September 1651. Thereafter, it would be impossible to justify their rebellion as a defense of the true interests of a minor king. These political shifts occurred against a back-ground of growing hostility between Condé, who suspected that the regent was seeking a pretext for his rearrest, and the regent, who feared that Condé intended to rekindle a civil war to carve a separate kingdom out of the provinces he and his allies controlled, if not to seize the crown of France for himself. By August 1651, the queen was openly accusing Condé of treasonable correspondence with Spain.[33]

Gaston was still a key figure in any calculation of power, and the court believed that his eldest daughter exercised considerable influence over him. In August 1651, Madame de Choisy told Mademoiselle that she wished to make her queen of France. Mademoiselle's first reaction was laughter. But she began to take the proposal more seriously when Choisy revealed several days later that she was acting on behalf of the Princess Palatine, Anne de Gonzague. The bargain was crass: the Palatine wanted a bribe of 300,000 écus (900,000 livres) and an appointment as superin-tendent of the new queen's household, an office that conferred consider-able rights of patronage on its holder. Madame de Choisy's husband was

to be the new queen's chancellor. The wedding would be held immediately after the proclamation of the king's majority, that is, in mid-
September. The hook came last: as part of the bargain, Gaston was to
support the return of Mazarin as the king's chief minister.

Mademoiselle was not sure what to make of all this. She was convinced that Gaston would never agree to Mazarin's return, certainly not
in exchange for her marriage to the king. Rather sadly, she reminded
Choisy that Gaston had been of little help in the past in her matrimonial
quests, and she did not believe he would be interested in this proposal.
Choisy was reassuring: Gaston would be a fool not to accept Mazarin's
recall as the price for his becoming the king's father-in-law. This conversation was followed by a visit from the Princess Palatine, who treated the
entire matter as settled.[34]

Having broken with Condé for the moment, Anne de Gonzague
was working with the regent to build support for Mazarin's return, in
exchange for her nomination as superintendent of the future queen's
household. Among other issues, there was the question of who would be
the king's bride. Although Anne of Austria was known to prefer a Spanish infanta for the king, the war with Spain precluded any immediate
marriage. Mademoiselle was sufficiently royal to serve in the same role,
was rich enough in her own right to reward her friends, and was Gaston's
daughter. Whatever the reservations on the side of the regent, the Palatine was authorized to approach Gaston and Mademoiselle.[35]

Caught up in the game, Mademoiselle gave free rein to her vivid
imagination, even concluding that the cynical proposal of the Palatine
was not the only way to obtain the closed crown. In the course of the
summer, she had been out riding a number of times with the young king,
who evidently enjoyed these excursions. The regent, suspecting that
the king was attracted to one of Mademoiselle's ladies, the comtesse de
Frontenac, forbade the king to join any more of these riding parties.
Mademoiselle believed that she, not Frontenac, was of interest to the
king. If so, Louis might prefer her as his bride over his mother's choice of
the Spanish infanta. Mademoiselle was sufficiently naïve to believe that a
union based on the king's supposed attraction was at least as likely as one
born of the bargain offered by Madame de Choisy and the Princess
Palatine.[36]

In September 1651, the king's majority was proclaimed at a solemn
ceremony at the parlement of Paris. In an extraordinary expression of
disrespect, Condé was not present. Shortly thereafter, hostilities broke

out between Condé and his partisans, based at Bordeaux, and the royal government, which moved to Poitiers to oversee the campaign. Gaston remained in Paris, torn between his duty to the king and his ties to Condé. In the hopes of keeping his allegiance, the court continued the negotiations for Mademoiselle's marriage. The Princess Palatine and Madame de Choisy arranged an "accidental" meeting with Mademoiselle in the gardens of the Tuileries to reopen the topic. To signal her interest, Mademoiselle wrote a number of times to a Guise uncle to express support for the royalists, knowing her correspondence would be opened by the government.[37]

In the late fall of 1651, the Palatine met again with Mademoiselle at the home of Madame de Choisy. She told Mademoiselle that the king was about to recall Mazarin to office and asked her to help secure Gaston's consent to this step. Gondi had already urged Gaston to do so, and she wanted Mademoiselle to second these efforts. Mademoiselle duly followed these instructions, meeting with Gaston and Gondi, with whom she had been on poor terms for years.[38]

With the passage of time, Mademoiselle came to doubt that the Palatine was able to deliver on her proposal, perhaps in part because of Gaston's public opposition to the recall of Mazarin. This did not prevent a request by Madame de Choisy for an immediate payment of 200,000 écus to the Princess Palatine. Mademoiselle, who had finally gained control of her finances in late 1650, promised to speak to her financial officials. But the Palatine saw no reason to involve Mademoiselle's staff; instead, she would arrange a loan from "friends," which Mademoiselle would guarantee to repay. Mademoiselle began to suspect that the Palatine's initiative had become little more than a scheme to coax money out of her.

Happily, events overtook this latest proposal. At the end of December 1651, Mazarin crossed into France near Sedan at the head of a small army of mercenary troops. The parlement of Paris responded by putting a price on Mazarin's head and petitioning Gaston to arrest him. Gaston, who had already mustered troops, declared his solidarity with Condé at the end of January. Mademoiselle asked Madame de Choisy to thank the Princess Palatine for her efforts and to tell her that she preferred to use her money to make war on Mazarin, which she saw as a quicker way to become queen of France.[39]

Mademoiselle encouraged Gaston to formalize the alliance with Condé, thereby contradicting the advice of Gondi, who preferred to see

Gaston remain the independent third force. She was rewarded with more flattery from Condé. His emissary, the comte de Fiesque, assured Mademoiselle that the prince wished to see her on the throne of France. It was a promise that Condé's supporters were to repeat frequently in an attempt to use Mademoiselle as a counterweight to Gondi. The alliance of Orléans and Condé was thus renewed, and the Luxembourg was once more a center of opposition to the royal government. Gaston's anterooms were filled with Condé's partisans, and Mademoiselle was the belle of the balls she hosted in their honor.[40]

By early March, however, the court seemed to have the upper hand. The royal armies had inflicted a number of defeats on Condé's forces in the southwest, and Mazarin felt sufficiently confident of the outcome to move the court back to Paris. By the middle of the month, the royal army and the court were at Blois, en route to Paris by way of Orléans. At the same time, Gaston's troops, under Beaufort, had linked up at Château-dun with a Condéan force under the command of Beaufort's brother-in-law, the duc de Nemours. The two dukes, who detested each other, could not agree on a course of action. Nemours, a fierce partisan of Condé's, wished to engage the royal army, whereas Beaufort preferred a defensive strategy, using the rebel troops to bar the royal progress toward Paris.

Matters were complicated further by the situation within Orléans. The court had expected the city to open its gates to the royal forces. The intendant in residence and the governor of the city were both inclined to obey, but the populace, terrified by reports of pillage and destruction by the royal army, rioted in protest. The town officials sent to Gaston, asking their feudal overlord for instructions and protection.[41]

Momentarily, the retention of Orléans had become important in the struggle against Mazarin. By denying the city to Mazarin, the princes could delay his return to the capital, and use it to guard a line of communication between Paris and Condé's forces operating below the Loire. In Paris, Condé's partisans, seconded by Mademoiselle, encouraged Gaston to go in person to secure Orléans, only to be told by Gaston that he believed that his abandonment of Paris would be a fatal error. Gaston added that the delegation from Orléans had also suggested Mademoiselle as an acceptable substitute. Mademoiselle jumped at the opportunity, as did Condé's partisans and Beaufort, who had put in an appearance at the Luxembourg. The only opposition seemed to come from Gondi (recently elevated to the College of Cardinals and now called the cardinal de Retz), who thought the idea ridiculous. Gaston, after a day or two of deliberation, overcame his hesitations and sent Henri de Rohan-Chabot to Mademoiselle with orders to leave for Orléans. Once there, she was to heed the advice of two of his agents, the comtes de Gramont and de Fiesque, and the bishop of Orléans, Alphonse d'Elbène, a veteran of Gaston's conspiracies against Richelieu. For good measure, Condé also sent along one of his agents, a *parlementaire* named Fouquet-Croissy.[42]

At the Luxembourg, Mademoiselle was the center of contrived adulation on the part of Condé's supporters. Late in the afternoon of March 25, to the cheers of bystanders and with a farewell wave from Gaston, Mademoiselle's carriages rolled out of the courtyard of the Luxembourg. Four of her ladies, Rohan-Chabot, and a small escort of Gaston's bodyguards accompanied Mademoiselle.[43]

At Chastres, where she spent the night, Mademoiselle was joined by the duc de Beaufort. The next day, near Etampes, Mademoiselle's party was joined by a large escort of horsemen drawn from Gaston's cavalry regiments. In the interests of speed, Mademoiselle abandoned her carriages and took to the saddle. The troops, she said, were delighted at this, as she "assumed command." At Toury she met with Nemours and the other senior officers of the two armies and presided over her first *conseil de guerre* as Beaufort, Nemours, and Rohan-Chabot wrangled over the deployment of troops. For Mademoiselle, the details were all secondary, except for Gaston's directive that under no circumstances were the princely armies to cross the Loire and move south to relieve Condé's partisans. Such a step, Gaston feared, would leave him marooned in Paris without any means of defense against Mazarin's troops. Mademoiselle repeated Gaston's orders in open council and warned against attempts to divide the princely forces by means of such disharmony.[44]

On the morning of March 27, Mademoiselle, with a small escort, was on the outskirts of Orléans. Her presence was an embarrassment to the municipal authorities. They had recently refused entrance to Mathieu Molé, a senior royal official who had been sent to secure the town for the king, and they dared not open the gates to a representative of their feudal lord while the king was still in the vicinity. But Mademoiselle was determined to gain entry. Escorted by her ladies and a handful of Gaston's bodyguards, she set up temporary headquarters at an inn just outside the city while deliberating on a means of entry.

By now, word of Mademoiselle's presence had spread. When Mademoiselle paraded along the moat, people on the walls cheered, but when she urged them to throw open the gates, there was no response. Similarly, an officer of the city guard called his troops to attention in honor of Mademoiselle but met her demand that he open a nearby gate with bows but no action. The governor of the city, the marquis de Sourdis, learning of her presence, sent a plate of confitures, but refused to admit her. The entire episode verged on the ridiculous. But Mademoiselle would not accept failure. Turning to Mesdames de Frontenac and Fiesque, she swore either to break down the gates or, failing that, to scale the walls.

A solution was at hand. Mademoiselle came across a group of boat-men who offered to help: Mademoiselle did not know that this encoun-ter had been arranged by Fouquet-Croissy. After a short harangue to encourage her newfound friends, Mademoiselle accepted a proposal from the boatmen that she force an entry through a gate known as the Porte Brulée, which they would batter down. To inspire her champions with her presence, she climbed up a knoll in the vicinity, climbing "like a cat" and tearing her clothes on brambles and hedges. Her ladies im-plored her to return; Mademoiselle ordered them to be silent. One of them, Madame de Bréauté, "the most cowardly creature in the world," became hysterical. This added to Mademoiselle's high spirits.[45]

To permit Mademoiselle to cross the moat, some of the boatmen improvised a footbridge by placing two boats end to end. A ladder was placed in the second and braced against the rampart to permit Made-moiselle to climb up to the quay. In the meantime, aided by a party of sympathetic citizens working on the other side of the wall, other boat-men had smashed in part of the gate. This second effort was not entirely spontaneous either, but had been organized by the comte de Gramont, an agent of Gaston's in the city. The guards posted at the gate did nothing to hinder the boatmen or Gramont's volunteers. By now the municipal authorities, already menaced by the agents of Gaston and Condé, had decided to make the best of the inevitable and were assembling in robes of office for a ceremonial welcome to the princess.

Mademoiselle had ordered her own bodyguards to return to the main gate of the city and wait to be admitted: she wished to show the citizens of Orléans that she had complete confidence in their loyalty. The mo-ment came: the opening was wide enough for Mademoiselle to pass through. Gramont gave her a sign to advance, and a footman rushed forward to assist her across a muddy ditch. As she entered, Mademoiselle gave her hand to a gallant captain; there was a drumroll and Mademoi-selle, placed in a sedan chair, was carried off in triumph, with cries of "*Vive le roi, et les princes! et point de Mazarin.*" After a few hundred yards,

Mademoiselle stopped and waited for her ladies to catch up with her. She then proceeded to her lodging, led by the drummers and a company of the town militia. On the way, she was met by the sheepish governor and the municipal officials. Mademoiselle was forgiving. Now that she was in the town, they had nothing to fear, since she would be responsible for matters in the future. The rest of the day passed with the usual formalities and a supper provided by the governor. Mademoiselle summoned the rest of her escort, sent word to Beaufort and Nemours of her successful entry, and dispatched a courier to Gaston to advise him that the capital city of his appanage had been taken by his eldest daughter.[46]

Gaston reacted to the news with words of praise that Mademoiselle cherished for the rest of her life; the securing of Orléans, he wrote, was an action "worthy of the granddaughter of Henri the Great." Condé, who arrived at Lorris a few days later to take command of the rebel forces, offered his own congratulations and promises of solidarity.[47]

Condé's arrival ended one of Mademoiselle's problems, maintaining peace between Nemours and Beaufort. These two could not agree on anything, and once even drew their swords in her presence during a quarrel about a military setback. It took all of Mademoiselle's powers of persuasion to bring about a superficial reconciliation between the two.[48]

With the excitement over, Mademoiselle settled into a routine. She appeared frequently in public, making a round of visits to the local churches and convents. She received the mayor and other local officials daily and restored some order in the city by putting an end to misbehavior by marauding soldiers. She issued safe-conduct passes and even read intercepted private mail, amusing herself with the details of other people's business affairs and family problems. Although she made an effort to tolerate the company of local worthies, her aristocratic instincts flared when the town fathers balked at receiving Condé within the walls. She summoned the municipal authorities, ordered them to admit the prince, and threatened suspected Mazarin partisans. When some claimed that the Condé name was disliked in Orléans because of the actions of Condé's grandfather there during the civil wars of the preceding century, Mademoiselle warned them that it was not for the "bourgeoisie of Orléans, or any in France, to speak thus of princes of the blood." To Mademoiselle, the intentions of princes were like "mysteries of the faith." Ordinary mortals were never to question their motives, but were to believe that their actions were intended for the general good and the safety of the state.[49]

Developments in the field made it possible for Mademoiselle to leave this increasingly tiresome outpost under honorable conditions. A sequence of military engagements at the end of the first week in April, known collectively as the battle of Bléneau, ended in a victory for Condé's troops over those commanded by the maréchal d'Hocquincourt. But the victory was blunted by Turenne, who commanded the royal rear guard and mounted a strong defense, saving the king's army from a complete rout and robbing the victory of much of its significance. Immediately thereafter, both armies fell back, by different routes, toward Paris. By the end of the month, the royal government was installed at Saint-Germain, and Condé had returned to the capital, leaving his army in the field. Control of Orléans was no longer of vital importance to either side.[50]

Mademoiselle, who had followed the campaign with some anxiety, was impatient to regain Paris. She wrote frequently to Gaston, asking permission to return, but received no answer. Mademoiselle decided not to wait any longer and set out on May 2. Since the weather was fair, Mademoiselle and her ladies abandoned their carriage for saddles. Near Angerville she was met by a large escort. Gaston had dubbed Mesdames de Fiesque and Frontenac the *maréchales-de-camp* of his daughter's army. The quip was well known, and to add to the merriment, the commander of a squadron of German mercenaries who formed part of the escort ordered his men to present arms in a proper military salute to the two maréchales. At Etampes, Mademoiselle entered the Frondeur camp to the beat of drums and the booming of cannon. The royal forces nearby were almost as courteous. At Chastres she came under the protection of a royalist escort sent by Turenne, who had gallantly agreed to issue her a safe-conduct.[51]

At Bourg-la-Reine, on the outskirts of Paris, Condé was waiting with Beaufort, Rohan-Chabot, and a number of other grandees to escort Mademoiselle into the city. Crowds cheered her passage, and aristocratic Parisians bowed from their carriages. The only vocal detractor of any importance was Gondi, who repeated a jest comparing the fall of Orléans to that of Jericho, with the substitution of Mademoiselle's violins for Joshua's trumpets. At the Luxembourg, Gaston was gracious, and Mademoiselle's triumph was enhanced by the sour greetings of her stepmother and a backhanded compliment from Henrietta Maria, who compared her with Joan of Arc, the original Maid of Orléans, who had saved Orléans and driven away the English—in this case, Charles Stuart.[52]

In the weeks that followed, Mademoiselle's apartments at the Tuileries were crowded with Frondeurs anxious to curry favor with the self-styled "queen of Paris." Gaston and Condé were frequent visitors, leading to the widespread impression that Mademoiselle had become the confidante of both. Mademoiselle corrected the record for posterity, noting that although Condé sought her opinion on all matters politic, Gaston rarely confided in her, a fact that Mademoiselle was sorry to disclose. "Those who read these *Mémoires* and will know me only through them, will easily decide that I deserved" Gaston's confidence.[53]

The politics of the final phase of the Fronde became even more confusing in the spring and summer of 1652. Many influential members of the parlement of Paris were opposed to Condé's presence in Paris. A number of aristocratic rebels had found their way back to the royalist camp, and within the entourages of Gaston and Condé there emerged advocates for an accommodation with the court. Even the duc de Nemours, a fierce partisan of Condé's, privately warned Mademoiselle shortly after her return to Paris that without a quick peace, all would be lost, including Mademoiselle's hopes for the crown of France, a caution that Mademoiselle dismissed out of hand.[54]

In her euphoria, Mademoiselle did not see that the military balance had shifted decisively against the princes. On May 4, the very day of her triumphant return to Paris, Turenne defeated the rebel forces in battle. The Frondeur casualties included officers who had recently entertained Mademoiselle at Etampes. The princely faction received a temporary reprieve with the arrival outside Paris of a mercenary army in Spanish pay under the command of the deposed duke of Lorraine, Charles IV, the brother of Gaston's wife. The duke was received warmly, and Mademoiselle put her house at Bois-le-Vicomte at his disposal. But the welcome soon gave way to dismay. Lorraine made the very quick calculation that he had more to gain from a bargain with the court than from an alliance with the Fronde. After a truce of several weeks' duration, an accord was reached through the mediation of Charles Stuart. The duke, well bribed, withdrew from the vicinity of Paris.[55]

Mademoiselle and the princes directed as much indignation and scorn at the English exiles as at Lorraine. Although negotiations had continued on all sides throughout the period, Mademoiselle saw an explanation for this event in personal terms. She attributed Lorraine's behavior to a plot by her stepmother to substitute one of Gaston's younger daughters as the king's bride in Mademoiselle's place. With her habitual lack of tact, Mademoiselle did nothing to hide her feelings, berating her stepmother "like a dog" and accusing her English relatives of betraying friendship, kinship, and their own best interests.[56]

At the end of June, Condé decided to concentrate his outnumbered troops, battered in a number of encounters with Turenne, at Charenton. While withdrawing through the Bois de Boulogne and the plain of Saint-Denis, Condé's vanguard was intercepted and defeated by Turenne's cavalry. Knowing it would be impossible to attain Charenton, Condé gave orders to fall back to the Faubourg Saint-Antoine. If all else failed, the princely army could take shelter behind the city's walls—that is, if the municipal officers would admit them. That they would do so was by no means certain. Parisians had fresh memories of the cruel behavior of troops under Condé's command in 1648–49; and Condé had been on poor terms with the parlement and the municipal government ever since his return to Paris in May. The military governor of Paris, the maréchal de l'Hôpital, was known to harbor royalist sympathies. He and the municipal authorities had declared their neutrality in the conflict between the two armies, refusing to help or admit either side. For this reason, Condé was forced to march his troops around the city walls rather than through the city. The one senior figure in Paris who might be able to prevail over municipal neutrality and the maréchal's malevolence was Gaston d'Orléans.

On the evening of July 1, Mademoiselle had a premonition that she might be called upon to do something "unexpected," as at Orléans. She stayed at her window until two in the morning, listening to the sound of drums and trumpets in the distance, as Condé's troops, refused entry at the nearby Porte de la Conférence, marched outside the walls. For the moment all she could do was speculate with Préfontaine on the outcome of Condé's maneuver.[57]

At six in the morning she was awakened by the comte de Fiesque, who told her that Condé was under attack and that his troops had been refused entry to the city at the Porte Saint-Denis. Condé had sent to Gaston to ask him to intervene, but Gaston, claiming to be ill, had refused. Fiesque had come to beg Mademoiselle not to abandon the prince in his hour of peril.

Mademoiselle dressed hastily and set out for the Luxembourg. There, to her astonishment, she found Gaston up and about, well enough to confer in his palace, but not well enough to see to Condé's relief. Mademoiselle reminded him that by failing to act he endangered not only

Condé and his partisans, but also many of their own supporters serving under Condé's orders. Mademoiselle's entreaties were joined by those of the duchess de Nemours, whose husband and brother were under fire with Condé, and by the pleas of Condé's emissaries, Rohan-Chabot and Chavigny. After more than an hour, during which he remained silent and apparently indifferent, Gaston finally authorized Mademoiselle to go to the Hôtel de Ville to request the city to admit Condé.[58]

At the Hôtel de Ville, Mademoiselle, armed with a letter from Gaston, met with the maréchal, the provost of the city, and the other municipal authorities. She asked that the city militia, already under arms, be sent to Condé's assistance. The city fathers refused. Mademoiselle deliberately saved her major request for last. But when she proposed that the city open its gates to Condé's troops, the reaction was consternation. Mademoiselle reminded them that she spoke for Gaston, and warned that if Condé was defeated and his army destroyed, the royal army would turn on Paris. To this, the maréchal countered that were it not for the proximity of Condé's troops, the royal army would not be approaching Paris. This sparked an exchange between the maréchal and the duchess de Nemours, which Mademoiselle cut short: the choice was to save Condé or to allow him to perish, to the shame of Paris. The council withdrew to another room to deliberate. They returned with reluctant permission for the rebel army to enter the city, a decision that was probably aided by the presence of a large and threatening mob gathered in front of the building. When Mademoiselle, escorted by L'Hôpital, stepped outside the building, a group of thugs hissed at the maréchal and called on Mademoiselle to give the order to drown him in the Seine. Mademoiselle refused to do so, told them of the council's decision, and remained there in her carriage until the maréchal had returned safely inside.[59]

As Mademoiselle made her way to the Rue Saint-Antoine, she encountered many wounded soldiers making their way to the rear. Among them were some of her good friends. She came upon the duc de la Rochefoucauld, blinded, his face covered in blood, being led away by his son and one of Condé's secretaries. Guitaut, another of Condé's lieutenants, crossed paths with Mademoiselle just as she reached the Rue Saint-Antoine. Mademoiselle remembered him "pale as death," his clothing unfastened, but still in the saddle, suffering from a massive body wound. The sight of the suffering and death around her was to give her at least one sleepless night, with "all these poor dead men on my mind."[60] Sending Rohan-Chabot forward to inform any municipal officials in the area of an order from the Hôtel de Ville to put themselves under her authority, Mademoiselle installed herself in a house close to the Bastille, with windows overlooking the street. There she received the first of several visits from Condé, who appeared in a cloud of dust, his hair tousled, his clothes bloody, his cuirass dented, and his sword in hand: he had lost the scabbard in battle. He offered his excuses, then burst into tears at the thought that many of his friends were dead or mortally wounded. Mademoiselle was touched. Condé had a reputation for coldness; this only proved that he was "solicitous for those he loved." She felt sure that at least some of those friends whom she had met on the way were likely to survive. The word that Mademoiselle had secured a line of retreat was welcome, but Condé was not willing to abandon the field to the "Mazarinists" in the middle of the day.[61]

With his troop outnumbered more than two to one by those of Turenne, the one general in the royal service who was his peer, Condé had given a matchless performance that day. The Porte Saint-Antoine opened onto a *place* formed at the intersection of three large avenues. Condé made good use of barricades prepared by the city militia for the defense of the gate. He also sent firing parties to occupy buildings that lined the avenues. Turenne sent formations rushing down the avenues, hoping to split Condé's forces into isolated groups that could be overwhelmed by the numerically superior royal forces. But Turenne's charges were met with ambushes, small arms fire from the houses and barricades, and furious counterattacks. In an episode that became legendary, the right wing of the royal army, commanded by the comte de Saint-Mesgrin, swept up the Rue de Charonne, smashing the troops commanded by one of Condé's lieutenants, and driving them almost to the Porte Saint-Antoine. At this point, Condé, at the head of a picked troop of noblemen, led a charge in person, fighting hand to hand and throwing Saint-Mesgrin back in confusion. The engagement ended in a reversal and the virtual destruction of Turenne's right wing. Among the royalist casualties was Paul Mancini, Mazarin's sixteen-year-old nephew, carried mortally wounded from the field.[62]

Throughout the day the stories of such encounters accumulated as Mademoiselle and other aristocratic ladies watched the procession of the wounded and the movements of troops through the streets. Mademoiselle was greatly distressed by the accusations of some around her that Gaston had been secretly negotiating with the court, and that he had abandoned Condé to his fate. "Monsieur's behavior toward M. le Prince, so contrary to his own interests, left me in despair." When word reached Mademoiselle that Gaston was on his way to confer with her and Condé, she sent for Condé and asked him, for her sake, not to reproach Gaston for his behavior. Condé was much too clever a general to take on another battle for no particularly good reason. He and Mademoiselle agreed that Gaston was with them in spirit, and blamed Gaston's occasional wavering on Retz's bad influence.[63]

Gaston, miraculously cured of his earlier illness, was all smiles and encouragement. He and Condé decided that the army should withdraw behind the city walls before nightfall, and Gaston then went off to the Hôtel de Ville, supposedly to thank the local officials for their assistance to Condé.[64]

It was time to retreat. The battle had raged for more than ten hours in suffocating July heat. As the day wore on, Condé's troops came under heavy artillery fire when the royal guns, under the command of the maréchal de la Ferté, reached the field. In anticipation of victory, the young king and Mazarin, surrounded by courtiers and officials, had gathered on the heights of Charonne to watch the destruction of Condé's army. A closed carriage stood by to carry Condé off to prison—assuming that he survived.

Mademoiselle was able to observe the king's party from the parapet of the Bastille, which she entered after Gaston had taken his leave. In the distance she could also see the royal troops massing for a final assault. The governor of the Bastille, Louvières, was a Frondeur; ironically, he was the son of Broussel, the magistrate whose arrest in August 1648, with Condé's connivance, had sparked the first Fronde. Louvières volunteered to follow any orders he received from Mademoiselle, provided he had a written authorization from Gaston. Luckily, Mademoiselle had already pried a note from Gaston, ordering Louvières to assist Condé and to fire on any of "the enemy" within the range of his guns.[65]

The cannon of the fortress were normally turned inward on the city. Mademoiselle instructed Louvières to rotate them outward, overlooking the Porte Saint-Antoine and aimed at the royal army.[66] Condé, whose observations of Turenne's movements were confirmed by a note from Mademoiselle, had ordered a general withdrawal into the city. But his rebel army was still in jeopardy if the royal troops acted quickly enough to overcome his rear guard and charge through the open gates.

Mademoiselle and the prince had correctly guessed Turenne's intentions. But the advancing royal forces were stopped by the cannon of the Bastille, firing at close range into the royal lines and mowing down the leading formations. For good measure, a few rounds were directed at the observers on the Charonne. Most contemporaries credited Mademoiselle with directing the fire. Mademoiselle, somewhat coyly, would admit only to giving the order to fire "while I was leaving" the Bastille.[67] Turenne was forced to recall his troops. Under cover of the guns of the fortress, Condé's army slipped through the gates to safety within the city walls.

Mademoiselle could not resist recording the account she heard later of the reaction within the royal party. When the first salvos were fired, there was rejoicing: the cardinal believed that the Bastille had turned its guns on Condé's troops. When more volleys followed, some speculated that they were only a salute in honor of Mademoiselle, whom the court knew to be in the vicinity of the Bastille. But the maréchal de Villeroy, the king's former governor, remarked that if Mademoiselle was there, she would have given the order to fire on the royal troops. Mademoiselle's informer did not provide her with Mazarin's reaction when the truth became obvious. It was left to Voltaire, writing a century later, to credit the cardinal with the remark found in every popular account: Mademoiselle "has just killed her husband."[68]

For her part, Mademoiselle went home and wrote a long letter narrating the events of the day, including a roll call of the dead and wounded and making note of the "twenty volleys" fired from the Bastille that had tipped the balance and saved the prince de Condé.

The memory of that episode was to remain vivid in the years ahead, as evidenced by the expanded account of it in her *Mémoires*. Mademoiselle's sense of having performed an extraordinary feat and rendered a great service to her party, overcame her feeling of sorrow at the loss of life on both sides: "When I thought about it that evening, and every time I've thought about it since, that I had saved that army, I admit that this was a great satisfaction to me and at the same time a great astonishment, to think that I had also let the cannon of the king of Spain into Paris, and let pass the red flags with the cross of St. Andrew."[69]

That night, at the Luxembourg, Mademoiselle was the toast of the Fronde; only Gaston seemed somewhat reserved in his congratulations. Mademoiselle, warmed by Condé's enthusiastic gratitude and praise, attributed Gaston's attitude to embarrassment that his daughter had taken his rightful place at Condé's side.[70]

Two days later, on July 4, Condé and Gaston appeared before an ad hoc assembly at the Hôtel de Ville that included representatives from the parlement, the municipal government, the most important guilds, the clergy, and the university. The princes intended to use this body to proclaim the king a prisoner of Mazarin's and to set up a government in opposition pending the king's "liberation." Gaston was to be declared lieutenant general of the kingdom, and Condé commander of the army.

But Gaston and Condé no longer commanded the undivided allegiance of these representatives of the elite strata of Paris. The assembly was not interested in such a scheme and confined itself to a declaration urging the king to dismiss Mazarin and return to his capital. The frustrated princes left hurriedly, taking care to display their dissatisfaction to a large and unruly crowd that had gathered in front of the Hôtel de Ville. The crowd, transformed into a mob and urged on by agents of Condé, turned violent. They broke down the doors of the Hôtel de Ville and massacred a few guards who tried to stop them. Once inside, they hunted down the notables, who had taken refuge in the building's rabbit warren of rooms and corridors. Some lucky ones escaped; some bought their way out; others were dragged from their hiding places and murdered. The crowd made no attempt to distinguish princely friend from Mazarinist foe: all within the building were fair game.[71]

Mademoiselle was at the Luxembourg, in Gaston's apartments, chatting with Condé and a few ladies, when a citizen, out of breath from fear and exertion, stumbled into the room with word of the carnage. Gaston had been changing in his bedroom; he now appeared in his shirt, all astonishment, forgetting for once the conventions of polite society. He asked Condé to go at once to the Hôtel de Ville to quiet the mob and rescue the victims. Condé refused. He was not, he said, the man for such a task. He suggested Beaufort instead, the favorite of the common people of Paris. To her credit, Mademoiselle volunteered to go and even suggested a political justification: to put the rescued notables in their debt while demonstrating the princes' hold on the Paris mob. She adds, probably an untruth, that Condé offered to go along, but she declined his services.[72]

She set out with a large escort provided by Gaston and Condé. On the way they identified a number of corpses flung onto carts or lying in the street. On a flimsy pretext, her escort forced her to return to the Luxembourg. But Gaston, alarmed by the reports of the massacre, sent her out again. It was now after midnight. Her entourage was actually smaller, a number of her protectors having crept away in the confusion. As she journeyed back to the Hôtel de Ville, she recruited impromptu reinforcements from militia patrols on the streets. Beaufort, who commanded her guards, rode ahead to clear the road. Even for Mademoiselle, well known and surrounded by servants and troops, the situation was dangerous. At one point, her carriage was stopped, and a street tough put his hand on the carriage door and asked if Condé was within. When Mademoiselle answered in the negative, he walked away. With the change of angle, Mademoiselle could see that he was carrying a pistol. It occurred to her that he might have been an assassin, and she "was sorry I hadn't thought of it at first; I would have had him arrested."

With Beaufort by her side, Mademoiselle passed through the main doors of the building, which were still smoldering, and took up her position in the great hall. While Beaufort and his men cleared the building, Mademoiselle rescued the provost, Antoine Le Fèvre, who had opposed Mademoiselle's request to open the city gates to Condé's army two days earlier. He offered his resignation on the spot, but Mademoiselle was magnanimous. Resignation would look like duress and could wait for another day. "I would be distressed to demand something from a man whose life I had just saved." Mademoiselle also attempted to find maréchal de l'Hôpital. But the maréchal had saved himself, leaving in disguise before Mademoiselle could rescue him. By four in the morning, all was quiet, and Mademoiselle went home to the Tuileries.[73]

Mademoiselle suspected that Condé and her father knew more about the massacre than they were willing to admit, but she refrained from asking. "I never spoke to them about it, and I was glad to be ignorant of the details, because if they had done wrong, I would have been very upset to know about it."[74]

Two days later, a rump assembly gave Gaston and Condé the declarations they required. Broussel replaced Le Fèvre as provost, and Beaufort assumed L'Hôpital's post as military governor of Paris. Mademoiselle was at the Luxembourg when Broussel arrived to take his oath of office before Gaston. Mademoiselle had the sense to see that this was only playacting: the ceremony, she said, was a "comedy."[75]

The violence and intimidation at the Hôtel de Ville put an end to any support the princes might have enjoyed within the circles of notables in Paris. In retrospect, Mademoiselle was to characterize it as a "knockout blow" (*coup de massue*) for the Fronde, which destroyed public confidence in the princes and their cause.[76] Henceforth, the princes' hold on the city rested on their feeble army and on paid street thugs. The Fronde disintegrated visibly. Troop desertions were endemic. Aristocrats as well as various other dignitaries began to treat privately with the court, and royal agents were active in the city, rallying support for the Crown.

The Frondeurs could not even refrain from turning on one another. At the end of July, the long feud between Beaufort and his brother-in-law, the duc de Nemours, ended in a duel behind the hôtel de Vendôme, a stone's throw from the Louvre and the Tuileries. Nemours was shot dead; two of Beaufort's three seconds were carried off the field mortally wounded; only the third, also wounded, survived.[77] Two days later, Condé, visiting Gaston at the Luxembourg, intervened in a dispute over precedence, taking the side of a La Trémouille against Charles de Lorraine, comte de Rieux, the heir of the duc d'Elbeuf. Words led to blows, and Condé and Rieux drew swords. The quarrel might have ended in more bloodshed except for the intervention of Condé's friend Rohan-Chabot, who managed to get Rieux out of the room and out of Condé's line of sight. Gaston reacted to the disturbance with royal logic, sending Rieux to the Bastille for showing disrespect to a prince of the blood.[78]

When not quarreling among themselves, the leaders of the Fronde were busy reorganizing their troops. The surviving companies and regiments were named for the nobles who sponsored them. At the cost of a heavy subsidy, Mademoiselle was allowed to sponsor a regiment of cavalry, "Mademoiselle's own." This gave Mademoiselle the opportunity to play at appointing the officers, usually nominees of her father or Condé, to attend reviews in her honor, and to meddle in military matters. At one point, a brief flare-up with Condé over the treatment of one of "her" officers led to another reconciliation and renewed protestations of friendship.[79]

From her unguarded remarks about Condé, it was clear that Mademoiselle was much taken with him. News from Bordeaux that Condé's wife was dying led to renewed speculation that Mademoiselle would be her successor. One evening, she remembered, "I went to take a walk while at Renard's: M. le Prince was also there; we walked the path twice without saying a word to one another; I think he believed everyone was watching, and I had the same thought. For my part, I had in mind all the things Madame de Frontenac had said to me; thus, we were both very embarrassed." Once more, however, the unwanted princess de Condé defeated death and her doctors, putting an end to Mademoiselle's pleasant fantasy.[80]

Mademoiselle soon had more serious things to worry about. No amount of posturing by its aristocratic proponents could stop or even slow the collapse of the Fronde in Paris. The court, now based in Pontoise, had moved rapidly to undermine any basis of support for the insurrectionary régime headed by Gaston and Condé. It had replied to the proclamation of the princes by convening the parlement at Pontoise, forcing members to choose between royal legality and princely insubordination. Enough judges chose to go to Pontoise to set up a functioning body there and to deprive the Fronde of any claims to judicial approval. In addition, Louis XIV, coached by Mazarin, accepted his chief minister's resignation and allowed him to withdraw again into temporary exile. Without the hated Mazarin in office, it was difficult to justify the continuance of hostilities. Mazarin's agents, however, remained in secret contact with the leading aristocratic Frondeurs. This became embarrassingly public when a dispatch from the abbé Basile Fouquet, one of the cardinal's chief agents, fell into Beaufort's hands. The report confirmed that Gaston had been in contact with the court and also suggested that a number of Condé's advisers were urging him to bargain for terms. Condé was upset; Mademoiselle was mortified; Gaston shrugged it off, telling his daughter that Condé, too, had been meeting with the abbé.[81]

The princely party obtained a temporary reprieve in early September, thanks to the return of the duke of Lorraine and his army. Turenne was reluctant to engage the duke, while Lorraine, as in the previous episode, was more interested in a bribe than in a battle. The opposing forces confined themselves to maneuvers and to pillaging the countryside around Paris. With this unexpected protection, the Fronde in Paris survived through September in the face of growing public opposition. Late in the month, several thousand people demonstrated outside the Palais-Royal to call for the return of the king. Mademoiselle's attempt to spark a counterdemonstration by appearing in front of the palace failed. Outraged at the "sedition," Mademoiselle wanted to hang the ringleaders. Gaston, who knew the game was up, forbade her to take any such action.[82] Others, too, knew that defeat was at hand. Broussel resigned as provost the day after the demonstration, while Beaufort, at the insistence of the municipal authorities, stepped down as governor of Paris. Delegations from the guilds and militia, armed with passes from Gaston, met with the court to discuss the king's return to his capital.[83]

Matters were brought to a head by the duke of Lorraine's decision to withdraw from Paris. Condé, uncertain of his fate at the king's hands, chose to leave with Lorraine. For Mademoiselle, it was a sad occasion.

Condé and Lorraine scheduled their departure for October 13. The previous afternoon they paid a farewell call on Mademoiselle. Condé appeared in a splendid costume, red and gold, and silver and black on gray, with a blue scarf under an unbuttoned coat. There were false promises that he and Lorraine would return after settling the troops into winter quarters. The three attended Mass together, where Mademoiselle suddenly felt alone and isolated: there were already rumors that the king would return and send them all into exile. "I confess that I wept while saying farewell to them."[84]

The end came quickly. On the day Condé left, a delegation of militia captains went to petition for the king's return to Paris. Although some Frondeurs, including Mademoiselle, urged Gaston to block the king's return, Gaston thought otherwise. He preferred to act as a last-minute mediator between the court and the rebels, and seek a general amnesty for the Frondeurs.[85]

Time had run out, and Louis XIV had no need for any more negotiations. On October 18, the king advised Gaston by letter of his intention to enter Paris the following Monday, October 21. There was no assurance of amnesty.[86] On that day, accompanied by his mother, Anne of Austria, by his younger brother, Philippe, by Mademoiselle's rejected suitor, Charles Stuart, and by Turenne, the king made a triumphal entry into Paris at the head of his troops. The previous Saturday, the king's maître d'hôtel had delivered a letter from the king to Mademoiselle. It was cold and to the point. Louis advised her that he had decided to lodge his brother at the Tuileries and that, accordingly, Mademoiselle was to vacate her apartments by noon the next day. Until she could find a suitable substitute, she would be permitted to stay at the hôtel de Ventadour.[87]

The blow was severe. Mademoiselle loved the Tuileries, "the most pleasant lodging in the world," her home since her eighth day on earth, with its royal associations so bound up with her own identity.[88] In a daze, she went to the Luxembourg to see Gaston, who told her to obey the king's orders. Other "friends" suggested that she barricade herself in the Arsenal and defy the court. Madame de Châtillon, one of Condé's partisans, had the sense to ridicule the idea. Mademoiselle took refuge temporarily at the home of the comtesse de Fiesque. In her confusion, it did not seem strange to her that Gaston had not offered her a place at the Luxembourg. Because gestures from Gaston were rare, she wrote bitterly, she did not realize at first that her father had made no attempt to help her.[89]

On October 21, Mademoiselle learned that Gaston had been ordered to leave Paris. She went to see him, and they fell into a quarrel. She accused her father of betraying Condé and the Fronde. Mademoiselle had heard the charge frequently from others that week, coupled with the suggestion that Gaston, as part of a bargain with the court, would abandon Mademoiselle to her fate. Gaston's reaction seemed to confirm her suspicions. He replied that he had nothing to answer for. When she asked about the rumors that she was to be exiled, he replied that he could not intervene on her behalf and that she had brought her disgrace upon herself.

Mademoiselle reminded him that her actions at Orléans and at the Porte Saint-Antoine were at his orders and was astounded at his sarcastic reply that whatever happened in the future, she could take consolation in remembering the praise heaped on her at the time. Mademoiselle asserted that all she had done had been in Gaston's service and that she would do it again, as this had been her duty as his daughter. She asked Gaston to permit her to stay at the Luxembourg. Gaston refused. There was no room, he asserted, nor would he consider evicting any of his officials to make room: they were all necessary for his service. Mademoiselle then suggested that she move into the nearby, vacant, hôtel de Condé. Gaston refused to permit this, which led his daughter to inquire:

"Where, then, Monsieur, do you wish me to go?"

"Wherever you want," replied Gaston, who then turned on his heels and left the room.[90]

The breach was a serious one. Gaston, whose relationship with the court remained ambiguous, had probably been warned not to permit Mademoiselle to remain with him. A letter from Mazarin documents the cardinal's fear that if Mademoiselle stayed with Gaston, she would lure him back into Condé's camp.[91] Several days later, Gaston, en route to Limours, summoned Préfontaine, Mademoiselle's secretary, to restate his position. His daughter, he said, had to accept that the Fronde was over, and should not waste time with fantasies of carrying on the struggle. She would be well advised to retire to Bois-le-Vicomte, or any other of her properties, and live quietly. Under no circumstances was she to try to join him; if she did, he would send her away.

Mademoiselle wrote: "I was abandoned in my disgrace by the one who had caused it. His refusal of a place to stay came back to me, and I have not forgotten it."[92]

Mademoiselle as an adolescent. The inscription celebrates her royal lineage, as further evidenced by the arms of Gaston d'Orléans (France with a silver label of three points). Courtesy, Bibliothèque Nationale de France.

Map of Paris in 1620, with an east-west orientation, from Zeiller's *Topographia Gallia* (1655). The palace and gardens of the Tuileries are clearly visible in the foreground. At the bottom of the garden is the Porte de la Conférence. At the top of the map the Bastille and the Porte Saint-Antoine are equally prominent. Courtesy, Yale University Library, Map Collection.

89

Opposite page: Saint-Fargeau from an aerial perspective, after Victor Petit. Despite some later construction, this nineteenth-century engraving shows the château largely as Mademoiselle would have known it, although the gardens were later re-landscaped in the English "romantic" style. Courtesy, Archives départementales de l'Yonne, Auxerre.

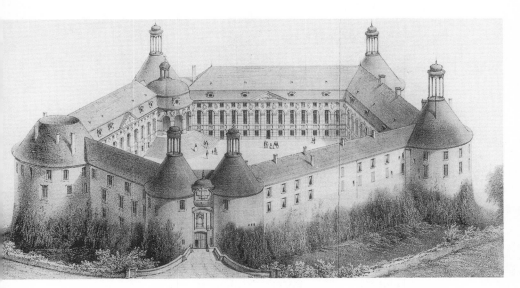

The Château de Saint-Fargeau. The forbidding medieval exterior masks the magnificent *cour d'honneur* designed for Mademoiselle by François LeVau. At the head of the staircase, the chapel; to the left were Mademoiselle's *grands appartements*, with a *salle des gardes* occupying the opposite section, to the right of the photo. Courtesy, Messrs. Jacques and Michel Guyot, current proprietors of the château. Photos: Collection of M. Daniel Allix.

ANNE MARIE LOVISE D'ORLÉANS *Souueraine de Dombes, Princesse de la Roche sur Yon, Dauphine d'Auuergne, Duchesse de Montpensier, de S.te Fargeau, et de Chastelleraud. Comtesse de Barsur Seine et de Mortain &c Seule Fille de Gaston Fils de France Duc d'Orléans.*

Mademoiselle on horseback, about 1652. This somewhat satirical view of Mademoiselle clearly is based on her exploits at the siege of Orléans. Courtesy, Bibliothèque Nationale de France.

Opposite page: The Château d'Eu, after Gagnières. This vast landed estate was to become Mademoiselle's principal country residence and the source of a significant portion of her revenues. This is a rare near-contemporary view of the château. The coat of arms to the right is that of the duc du Maine. Courtesy, Bibliothèque Nationale de France.

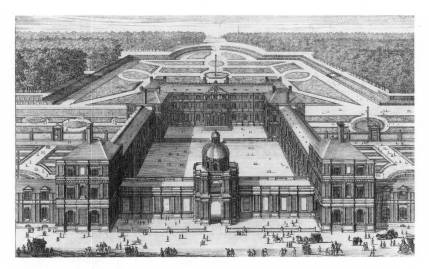

View of the Palais d'Orléans, also called the Luxembourg. This was Mademoiselle's Paris residence after her return from exile in 1657. She occupied the east
wing, shown here on the left. The west wing housed her stepmother and later,
her half sister the duchess de Guise. Courtesy, Bibliothèque Nationale de
France.

Veüe du Chasteau de
LA VILLE D'EV
en Normandie, dans le pais de Caux,
dessiné du costé de l'eglise N. Dame
en dedans de la Ville.

Contemporary portrait of Mademoiselle by an unknown artist, which still hangs at Saint-Fargeau. Mademoiselle is pointing to the architectural plans for the château's renovation. The building itself is in the background. Courtesy of Messrs. Jacques and Michel Guyot, current proprietors of the château. Photo: Jacques Leroy.

The Château de Choisy, after Jean Mariette. Mademoiselle's last building project, of which she was inordinately proud. In her will, she left the mansion to the dauphin Louis. Courtesy, Bibliothèque Nationale de France.

Louis II de Bourbon, prince de Condé, by David Téniers le Jeune (1653). Courtesy of the Musée de Chantilly. Photo: Lauros-Giraudon.

Antonin de Caumont, Duc de Lauzun and de Saint-Fargeau, as he is styled in this engraving. Lauzun is wearing the insignia of the Garter conferred on him by James II. Louis XIV would never make him a Knight of the Holy Spirit. Courtesy, Bibliothèque Nationale de France.

Mademoiselle in her middle years, probably about 1666, the date of the engraving. As Mademoiselle aged, her features took on the classic heavyset Bourbon look. Courtesy, Bibliothèque Nationale de France.

Portrait of Mademoiselle by Pierre Le Bourguignon (1671). Mademoiselle is dressed as Athena/Minerva and is pointing to a miniature of Gaston displayed on her shield. Tradition identifies the two figures on the relief as representations of Mesdames de Fiesque and de Frontenac. Courtesy, Musée de Versailles. Photo: RMN—Gérard Blot.

Allegorical portrait of the royal family by Jean Nocret (1670). Louis XIV and his kin are dressed as the gods of Olympus. To the right, Louis as Apollo, attended by his wife and children. Philippe d'Orléans as Poseidon is to the left, accompanied by Henrietta Stuart and their children. The seated figure in the center is Anne of Austria as Ceres. Mademoiselle as Diana, wearing a crescent decoration, stands to the side of Louis. Her half sisters are portrayed as the three Graces and stand between Anne and Louis. Courtesy, Musée de Versailles. Photo: RMN.

While I did my needlework, I had books read aloud; it was during this time that I began to love reading, as I have ever since.

MADEMOISELLE

As soon as these ladies joined the Princess Aurélie at the Château of the Six Towers, we thought only of amusing ourselves. The balls, the theater, the walks, the discussions and readings, together with the good living, provided something to please everybody, and we all found this life so sweet and pleasant that no one missed the distractions of Paris and court ballets.

JEAN REGNAULT DE SEGRAIS

4 The Pastimes of the Princess Aurélie

MADEMOISELLE'S EXIT FROM PARIS WAS SUITABLY THEATRICAL. Initially, she remained in hiding at the home of Madame de Montmort, the sister-in-law of Madame de Frontenac. She still hoped, against all probability, for a sudden victory by Condé and Lorraine that would bring about a peace on favorable terms. Mademoiselle imagined herself taking part in some popular uprising or other spectacular event that would force the court to bargain with its princely opponents.[1]

After several days, it became clear that no such occurrences were likely and that Gaston was firm in his refusal to let her join him. Mademoiselle had already decided against retiring to Bois-le-Vicomte. Préfontaine explained to Gaston that the château was being used as a convalescent home for wounded soldiers and that the surrounding countryside was still full of marauding troops. The unspoken reason was that Bois-le-Vicomte was too close to Paris for an escape if the king chose to arrest Mademoiselle.[2]

Without announcing her itinerary, Mademoiselle left the capital, accompanied by Madame de Frontenac, a handful of her servants, and Jules von Hohenlohe, called "Hollac" by Mademoiselle, an officer serving under Condé in Mademoiselle's regiment.[3] Her destination was a country house at Pont-sur-Seine that belonged to a friend, Madame Le Bouthillier, the mother of a prominent Frondeur, Léon Le Bouthillier de Chavigny.

Mademoiselle traveled incognito. At a roadside inn she introduced herself to a fellow guest, a Dominican friar from Paris, as "Madame Dupré," the widow of a nobleman, en route to Orléans to live with her brother and sister-in-law. The Dominican belonged to one of the fashionable monasteries in Paris. Among the court figures he claimed to know well were Gaston d'Orléans and his daughter Mademoiselle de Montpensier. The monk professed his admiration for the princess, adding that his interlocutor was of the same body type as the princess; because the widow refused to remove her traveling mask, he did not know if there was a facial resemblance. The "widow" found the episode diverting. She was even more amused by the discomfort of her staff, who had been instructed to sit with her at table as part of the masquerade. Her ladies and Hohenlohe were promoted to brother, sister, and cousin, and treated with familiarity.[4] The performance cannot have been very convincing, as even Mademoiselle suspected.[5]

While at Pont, Mademoiselle remained in contact with Gaston, as well as with Condé and the duke of Lorraine. These last two, who sympathized with her plight, were loud in their denunciations of Gaston's behavior and free with advice. Lorraine suggested that she withdraw to the château of Encerville, which belonged to her grandmother Guise and which was on the frontier, only a few miles from Stenay, where he and Condé intended to garrison their troops. In an emergency Mademoiselle could rely on them for help.[6]

An officer of Condé's, the comte de Saint-Mars, brought her a more daring proposal. Condé urged her to go to Harfleur, in Normandy, where she would be under the protection of the duc de Longueville, Condé's brother-in-law and the governor of Normandy. There she could secretly repair the fortifications and secure the place for some future use. If the court moved against her, Longueville would rise, and help would be available from Spanish-held Ostende. If all else failed, she could escape by sea: a repetition of Madame de Longueville's famous flight from Dieppe in 1650.

Mindful of Gaston's earlier warnings, Mademoiselle had the sense to dismiss Condé's proposal. She told Saint-Mars that she intended to comply with Gaston's orders to withdraw to one of her estates and refrain from "open warfare" with the court. She had chosen her property at Saint-Fargeau as her refuge. It was three days' journey from Paris, close enough for her to keep abreast of events, and roughly the same distance from Blois, where Gaston intended to take up residence. Stenay, Condé's base of operations, was only four days away, thus facilitating communication and, if necessary, flight in an emergency.[7]

Mademoiselle had already given Condé proof of her continuing allegiance to the Fronde. Before Saint-Mars's arrival, she sent Hohenlohe back to Condé with instructions that he and the comte d'Escars were to remain in Condé's service with the troops raised in her name and still paid by her. The two officers were to assume that any future orders to return had been forced from her and should be disregarded. If necessary, she would find a secret and undeniably authentic way to relay orders to them.[8]

Mademoiselle had reason to believe that her movements were watched. While still at Pont, she had received a letter from the king forwarded by the senior Madame de Fiesque, temporarily left behind in Paris. In it, Louis announced that he was pleased by her choice of Saint-Fargeau, and assured her that she could stay there undisturbed. In spite of her astonishment that the king knew her plans, Mademoiselle put up a good front, writing the king to thank him for his kind intentions and protesting her loyalty to his person.[9]

With this formal exchange, Mademoiselle began five long years of exile. Its duration was in part caused by Mademoiselle's unswerving support of Condé, as evidenced by the troops she continued to pay and by her frequent correspondence in cipher with the rebel prince. The normal channel for these exchanges was the comte de Fiesque, son of the senior comtesse and husband of the younger one, who had followed Condé into the service of Spain, a fact well known at court. Even as Mademoiselle had prepared to leave Paris in October 1652, Mazarin had identified her as one of Condé's warmest partisans, known to be in frequent contact with the prince, and a bad influence on Gaston.[10] Given the timing, it is likely that Gaston's refusal to receive Mademoiselle into his household was largely due to the court's determination to break any remaining links between Gaston and Condé. Because Mademoiselle was viewed as the intermediary between the two, her isolation was bound to last as long as there was any possibility of a renewed alliance between the junior branches of the royal family.

Saint-Fargeau, Mademoiselle's place of exile, lay in the valley of the Loing, in the district known as La Puisaye, part of the modern department of the Yonne, almost midway between Auxerre and Cosne-sur-Loire, in a remote, heavily wooded area, rarely visited. Mademoiselle had never seen the estate until her arrival in November 1652. Her first impression, at two in the morning, was entirely negative: the drawbridge was broken; the courtyard was overgrown with knee-high grass. The building itself was an imposing late medieval castle, but virtually empty. There were signs of neglect and disrepair everywhere: broken doors, shutterless windows, dirt, and decay. She was shown to a large empty room with a pillar in the center supporting the ceiling. The sight of this dungeon-like accommodation brought on a nervous fit: overcome with anger and fatigue, Mademoiselle wept uncontrollably. She refused to spend what little remained of the night under this roof. The short-term solution was to commandeer the nearby residence of an estate official, a comfortable house with a few books and a well-stocked larder, where Mademoiselle remained for several days to rest and regain control of her nerves.[11]

When she returned to her forlorn château for a second look, Mademoiselle discovered an apartment that had been constructed some years earlier for the duc de Bellegarde, who had stayed there from time to time as a guest of Gaston's. The suite was not to her taste, and she moved into the "attic" while it was remodeled. Until her furniture arrived from Bois-le-Vicomte, she made use of a bed belonging to the newly married steward of the estate.[12]

Within a few weeks, thanks largely to the efforts of Préfontaine, life assumed a certain normality. The household staff arrived from Paris, along with the comtesses de Fiesque. In the company of the Fiesques and the comtesse de Frontenac, Mademoiselle, who had always lived in the heart of Paris and at the center of the royal court, took to the role of a country aristocrat. To her surprise, she discovered that it was possible to keep up with events in the capital even at a distance. Couriers and letters brought word of the important developments: the banishment of prominent Frondeurs, the arrest of the cardinal de Retz in December 1652, the collapse of the Fronde in Bordeaux in the summer of 1653, and the progress of Condé's campaigns. The same sources and the occasional gazette brought her news of court ceremonials, aristocratic weddings, and the latest gossip and scandal.

As Mademoiselle had guessed correctly, Saint-Fargeau was well situated for the paying and receiving of calls. Except in winter, when road conditions and a harsh climate discouraged traffic, Saint-Fargeau offered hospitality to a stream of visitors. Many came from Paris, perhaps out of curiosity to see how the princess was adjusting to country life. Mesdames de Monglat and Lavardin, for example, came together in 1655, bringing with them the charming young marquise de Sévigné. This last lady remained on good terms with Mademoiselle and wrote one of her earliest surviving letters to the "*belle et charmante princesse*" of Saint-Fargeau.[13]

There were also guests from the Loire valley, including, very frequently, Madame de Sully and other members of the Béthune family. Still others came from nearby Burgundy, including Gabrielle de Mortemart, marquise de Thianges, of a family celebrated for wit and charm. Madame de Thianges was also notorious for her eccentric ways. She would often keep Mademoiselle and her entourage up until the early hours of the morning, filling their ears with tales told in the inimitable Mortemart style. Then, after retiring to her rooms, she would stay up until dawn, playing at various parlor games with the pages, valets, and ladies' maids, creating an uproar that interfered with other people's sleep. These antics shocked one of Mademoiselle's more prudish houseguests, Catherine de Vandy, a reaction that increased Mademoiselle's appreciation of her Mortemart friend.[14]

On a day-to-day basis, Mademoiselle was dependent on her two former comrades-at-arms, the younger Fiesque and Madame de Frontenac, for companionship—the senior Fiesque was simply tolerated. Though of very different backgrounds, both women were well known in the fashionable salons of Paris. Gilonne d'Harcourt, comtesse de Fiesque, belonged to a distinguished Norman aristocratic family and served as a Parisian "godmother" to Norman literati looking for introductions to high society and suitable employment. Among her protégés was one of Mademoiselle's private secretaries and literary tutor, Jean Regnault de Segrais, a native of Caen, whose importance in Mademoiselle's intellectual development is discussed below.[15]

Mademoiselle's other boon companion, Anne de la Grange-Trianon, came from a parlementary background. A relative of Madame Le Bouthillier's, she owed her position in society largely to her personal qualities. At the age of sixteen, she had eloped with Louis de Buade, comte de Frontenac, whose family had been attached to the royal household for several generations. The marriage produced one son, put out to board and largely ignored by both of his parents. The attraction between the two had long since faded, and the couple lived mostly apart, with alternating periods of estrangement and reconciliation.

The occasional attempt at rapprochement brought Mademoiselle into contact with Louis de Frontenac, later famous as the governor of French Canada. Mademoiselle's word for him was "extravagant." At first, her tolerance annoyed Madame de Frontenac, who was on very bad terms with her lawfully wedded husband at the time of Mademoiselle's arrival at Saint-Fargeau. He would sometimes appear uninvited, and Mademoiselle was treated to a number of violent and vulgar scenes between the spouses. For her part, Mademoiselle drew a lesson from their bad example: marriage had to be founded on reason and practical considerations, rather than upon passion. After all, she reasoned, "passion soon ceases . . . and one is unhappy for the rest of one's life." For Mademoiselle, this point of view came naturally, for "I had always had a great aversion for love . . . which seemed to me a passion unworthy of a cultivated spirit!"[16]

The Frontenacs eventually achieved a modus vivendi, and by the end of Mademoiselle's stay at Saint-Fargeau, the couple found common ground in criticisms of Mademoiselle's household arrangements. Madame de Frontenac complained about the quality of the food served at Mademoiselle's table, which, her husband insisted, was not as good as that served at his own residence of Ile Savary, near Blois. Madame de Frontenac blamed Mademoiselle's stinginess for her poor hospitality; her husband gallantly shifted the responsibility to Mademoiselle's staff. Mademoiselle dismissed both criticisms with royal disdain. The Frontenacs, said Mademoiselle, were the kind of people who enjoyed stews (*ragoûts*), something never served at Mademoiselle's table, in spite of the Frontenacs' repeated hints. "Normally, tables of people of my rank are not served like those of the bourgeoisie, and since she had such [bourgeois] tastes, she disliked anything which wasn't the same."[17]

Frontenac liked to design men's clothing, and to show off his creations. Once, on a visit to Chambord in Mademoiselle's entourage, he left a number of these items on a dressing table in Mademoiselle's bedroom. Shortly afterward, Gaston entered his daughter's apartment for an impromptu visit, and was astounded to find breeches and doublets in his daughter's room.[18]

To provide an appropriate setting for her activities, Mademoiselle undertook the transformation of Saint-Fargeau from a grim fortress into an attractive country seat worthy of a royal princess and comparable to the fine residences she had visited on the Loire. She reached this decision early in her exile, after declining the opportunity to buy Châteauneuf-sur-Loire and relocate there. She did not like the grounds at Châteauneuf, nor did she relish the proximity to Blois.[19]

Instead, she began a reconstruction of Saint-Fargeau. She spent much of her first winter overseeing the redesign of the grounds. Mademoiselle had brush removed and holes filled to create a long alley ending in a broad terrace overlooking the château, the woods, and the surrounding countryside. The effect was to open up the space around the building and set it off from the vast, dark woods nearby. She installed parterres and flower beds in the style of the century, and even a croquet lawn. All this was intended to provide a tranquil and elegant setting for the château.[20]

In 1654, Mademoiselle engaged a prominent architect, François LeVau, the brother of Louis LeVau, to oversee her building program. LeVau came well recommended. He had recently completed an extensive renovation of the Hôtel de Sully on the Rue Saint-Antoine in Paris and had also worked on the abbé de La Rivière's residence on the Place Royale. LeVau's work at Saint-Fargeau continued during the remainder of Mademoiselle's stay, so most of her pastimes there occurred against a backdrop of construction noises: stone splitting, wood cutting, sawing and hammering, and the shouts of workmen. She spent more than 200,000 livres on the project, with results that were little short of spectacular.[21]

The building constructed by Jacques Coeur two centuries earlier was an unusual pentagonal fortress built of brick, its five sides connected by large round towers, with the main entrance flanked by twin towers. As befitted its military origins, its walls were several stories high, and deep ditches, easily flooded and transformed into an impassable moat, surrounded the entire building. The interior would have been dank and gloomy even on a sunny day.

LeVau expanded the buildings by constructing a new set of inner walls with contemporary façades decorated with Mademoiselle's monogram. He enlarged the windows on the courtyard side to illuminate the interior of the building and those facing the exterior to provide perspectives on the park. LeVau took care to use brick and stone that harmonized with the materials in the old towers, five of which he decorated with elongated cupolas. In the court of honor, a grand semicircular stairway led to the principal entrance and to the magnificent domed chapel, where kneeling angels above the altar displayed Mademoiselle's arms. The chapel separated two wings of the building, with a suite of state apartments situated immediately to the left (when facing the chapel). To the right, occupying the adjacent wing, was a vast hall.[22]

Before hiring LeVau, Mademoiselle had begun remodeling the apartments formerly occupied by the duc de Bellegarde, in the wing of the château opposite the court of honor, between the entrance tower and the clock tower. By the fall of 1653, these were ready for Mademoiselle, and were the rooms she occupied for most of her stay at Saint-Fargeau. Her suite included an antechamber which Mademoiselle used for dining and for playing billiards, a long gallery which connected that room to her bedroom, a dressing room, a study (*cabinet*), and a second, smaller study as a place of retreat. At Selles, Mademoiselle had admired the Béthune family's collection of portraits of famous men of the time of Henri IV, modeled after the gallery at the Luxembourg adorned with Rubens's famous paintings of Henri IV and Marie de Medici.[23] She borrowed the idea for her own gallery, which was hung with portraits of Mademoiselle's close relatives, beginning with her royal grandparents and including all of her crowned aunts and uncles of England, Spain, and Savoy, as well as the Condés and the Guises. The place of honor, however, was reserved for her maternal grandfather, Henri de Bourbon, duc de Montpensier. He was not the greatest of these grandees, but he was the master of Saint-Fargeau. If he had not left it to her, she would not have had it to show off. The whole apartment was decorated with mirrors and paintings. After eight months in the attic she found herself in an "enchanted palace."[24]

Mademoiselle also decided in her first year that a theater would provide an additional diversion. A large hall that spanned the entrance towers of the château was converted into a well-lit and well-appointed theater. Mademoiselle engaged a troop of actors from Tours to spend several weeks each winter at Saint-Fargeau offering performances of the fashionable comedies of the day. There was also music. Mademoiselle arranged for a number of musical presentations at the château to amuse her guests. One of these, a full-blown *ballet de cour*, the *Ballet de l'Eloquence*, was performed in the winter of 1655 and made enough of a sensation to become the subject of a popular pamphlet. There was, however, one spectacular lost opportunity. Among Mademoiselle's junior staff was an Italian musician originally engaged by Mademoiselle to teach her Italian. At the time of her exile, the young man begged Mademoiselle for a dismissal to permit him to stay in Paris and pursue his musical career. Mademoiselle graciously agreed to let "Jean-Baptiste," that is, Jean-Baptiste Lully, remain behind.[25]

Outdoor sports also provided distractions for Mademoiselle and her circle. The woods around Saint-Fargeau provided ample opportunity for hunting. Hitherto, Mademoiselle had not liked dogs, nor did she have any special affinity for horses. In the country she changed her mind, importing hunting dogs from England and fine mounts from Germany, and taking great pride in showing them to visitors.[26] Many an hour was passed in the saddle following the chase.[27] If it was too icy to ride, a long walk on the grounds was substituted.[28] Weather permitting, the princess often played shuttlecock for several hours in the morning and then again in the afternoon. There was also croquet (*mail*). Mademoiselle's usual opponent was Madame de Frontenac, who was something of a bad sport, frequently disputing calls, even though she won her fair share of matches.[29]

The châteaux of the Loire were close enough for excursions in season. The Béthune family were happy to receive her at Selles; her fellow exile Beaufort entertained her at Chenonceaux; the abbess of Fontevrault was always pleased to see her niece, as were many other châtelaines. There was even a quick visit to Champigny to fortify Mademoiselle's resolve to regain the tombs of her Montpensier ancestors. In spite of her disgrace at court, local officials usually treated Mademoiselle as a royal visitor. At Amboise, for example, Mademoiselle was received with full honors. The governor of the town, the same marquis de Sourdis who had been so embarrassed by Mademoiselle's arrival at Orléans in 1652, ordered the cannons fired in her honor. The irony of this belated tribute was not lost on Mademoiselle.[30]

At Tours, Mademoiselle came upon an adolescent half brother, the product of Gaston's old liaison with Louison Roger. Gaston had refused to acknowledge the boy, but Mademoiselle could not bear the thought that a Bourbon, even a bastard one, was languishing among the bourgeoisie. She took him home and saw to his education and eventual career as a soldier. He also needed some kind of aristocratic surname. This gave Mademoiselle momentary pause. Most of her estates carried titles that had been borne by princes: this would not do for the son of Mademoiselle Roger. Then she remembered a modest property she owned nearby called Charny. Her half brother was transformed into Louis, chevalier de Charny, a member of Mademoiselle's household.[31]

Mademoiselle, now in her mid-twenties, continued to be of interest as a possible bride within international royal circles. Early in her years of exile, Mademoiselle rejected a proposal of marriage from the young elector of Bavaria,[32] and another pressing offer from a minor German prince, Philip William, duke of Neuburg, whose capital city was Düsseldorf. Mademoiselle considered an alliance with a mere duke of Neuburg totally unsuitable, and was not swayed by her stepmother's argument that Austrian archduchesses and princesses of Lorraine had set ample precedents for such unions. "I replied that others could marry as they pleased, but as for me, I was not persuaded to marry like that."[33]

At Gaston's insistence, Mademoiselle met with an emissary of Philip William's, a Jesuit priest. She listened politely to the cleric's description of the beauties of Düsseldorf and his paean to the prince's personal qualities before repeating her refusal. In desperation, the Jesuit noted that the prince's first wife, a Polish princess, had died of joy upon his return from a trip. This gave Mademoiselle a perfect opening: she dared not marry the prince for fear of falling too much in love and suffering a similar fate.[34]

The senior Madame de Fiesque, who had encouraged Mademoiselle to accept Neuburg's proposal, accused Mademoiselle of a secret understanding to marry Condé in the event of his wife's death, even if it meant breaking his son's engagement to Mademoiselle's half sister. This gave Mademoiselle an opportunity to repeat her grand theme of rationality in marriage. If Condé returned to court, and if his wife died, such a marriage would be possible, provided the king desired it for the good of the royal house and Gaston consented. For herself, she would gladly accept him as a husband, since she considered Condé "great, heroic, and worthy of the name he bears." That being said, however, she resented the idea that she could marry like the heroines in romances, as if Condé were Amadis, come to claim his Oriane and cleaving in twain anyone in his path. The image alone was offensive to the dignity of a princess of France.[35]

Despite Mademoiselle's insistence that Saint-Fargeau provided a "pleasant enough life," free from boredom, time must have passed slowly.[36] Mademoiselle would never admit this; indeed, she opens her

Mémoires by trumpeting her discovery that a person of her rank, born for the court, could find happiness in a country retreat.[37] But Mademoiselle's behavior, and that of her constant companions, the three countesses, suggest periodic bouts of cabin fever. There were endless small disputes, and the senior Madame de Fiesque even managed to pick quarrels with Préfontaine. Louis de Préfontaine, a relative of Gaston's chancellor Choisy and the brother of a prominent theologian, had served in the French delegation that negotiated the Peace of Westphalia. This diplomatic background and his own patient temperament were of great use to him in this turbulent household. The death of the elder Madame de Fiesque in October 1653 relieved Mademoiselle of a companion she no longer appreciated, but also left the younger countess and Madame de Frontenac free to compose their own differences. To Mademoiselle's dismay, the two found common cause in blaming Mademoiselle for their increasingly tedious exile.[38]

For Mademoiselle at least, the restoration of Saint-Fargeau had provided a major diversion. It had also stimulated her interest in the history of the property and the means by which it had passed into her hands. Documents preserved at the château indicated that Antoine de Chabannes, a famous warrior of the fifteenth century, had purchased the estate from the heirs of Jacques Coeur. Through intermarriages, the property descended through the families of Chabannes, Anjou, and Bourbon-Montpensier to Mademoiselle. She adds that her research stimulated an interest in genealogy, and she invited the genealogist Pierre d'Hozier to Saint-Fargeau to teach her more about the Chabannes lineage. She had a room in the château decorated with the Chabannes family tree and the blazons of families related to them. This presentation is probably a literary conceit to allow Mademoiselle to show off her knowledge and her pedigree without seeming boastful. Mademoiselle, as was typical of aristocrats of that time, knew a great deal about her ancestry: Saint-Simon was to say that she "counted cousins" (*cousinait*).[39] Mademoiselle adds that Hozier confirmed that the Bourbons were the "greatest and most illustrious house in the world," a characterization "pleasant enough" to a person of her temperament.[40]

The theater and genealogy were not her only intellectual exercises. It was during these years at Saint-Fargeau that Mademoiselle acquired a taste for reading. While doing her needlework or during meals, Mademoiselle had books read aloud. What precisely was read we can only surmise from occasional literary allusions in her writings, but the fare probably included the fashionable poets of the day, the windy romances produced by the *Précieuses*, and the works of other popular authors, such as Cervantes, Malherbe, Tasso, and Marguerite d'Angoulême.[41]

Mademoiselle's tutor in matters literary was Jean Regnault de Segrais (1624–1701), who, though forgotten today except by academic specialists, was a member in good standing of the Parisian literati, a minor poet and writer, and a classicist known later in life for his translations of Virgil.[42] A Norman by birth, Segrais had ingratiated himself with the younger Fiesques. Under their patronage, he had been introduced to the hôtel de Rambouillet and to the circle of writers around Condé. In 1648 the Fiesques secured Segrais an appointment as a private secretary to Mademoiselle. He earned his keep by composing poems and odes for special occasions, including one that celebrated Mademoiselle's securing of Orléans in 1652. She is, of course, compared to her glorious predecessor, the original Maid of Orléans (Joan of Arc), with a sly allusion to Mademoiselle's rejection of Charles Stuart as a suitor.[43]

Segrais remained with Mademoiselle at Saint-Fargeau throughout her years of exile. Although the references to him are rare in Mademoiselle's *Mémoires*,[44] it was under his guidance that Mademoiselle, in her own words, "began to love reading."[45] Among Segrais's works is a collection of six short stories in the genre of travelers' tales called *Les Nouvelles Françaises, ou, Les Divertissements de la Princesse Aurélie*, which was first published in 1656. In this work, Princess Aurélie and five of her ladies are living in voluntary exile in the "château of the Six Towers," having earned the displeasure of the "victorious prince" who governs France.[46] Their chosen retreat is tranquil: the nearby river is pure, the fields are always in flower, the trees provide welcome shade.[47] Princess Aurélie is a paragon of virtues: courageous, proud but not vainglorious, constant in adversity.[48] Her companions, under fanciful names, are easily identified: the beautiful Frontenie (Madame de Frontenac); the pleasant Gélonide (Gilonne d'Harcourt, comtesse de Fiesque); the warm and friendly Aplanice (Madame de Valençay); the sensitive Silerite (Madame de Mauny); and the formidable Uralie (Madame de Choisy).[49] All share in the distribution of graces and virtues, and each is ready to pass a day with a story for the edification of the company. The format of six stories, a "hexaméron," recalls the *Heptaméron*, a popular work in Mademoiselle's day, by Marguerite d'Angoulême, an ancestor of Mademoiselle's, a fact to which Segrais refers early in the text.[50]

Some of the stories contain allusions to the Fronde, particularly the fifth, *Aronde, ou, les Amants Deguisés*, with obvious references to Mademoiselle, Condé, and Charles II. The hero and heroine of the story, Charles, comte de Clermont, and Agnes de Bourgogne, who later became duc and duchess de Bourbon, were historical persons, ancestors of Mademoiselle, although the story is entirely fictitious. In it the brave and virtuous Agnes saves her father's city of Brussels from his enemies by rallying the citizens to his cause. Later, she falls into disgrace with her father, partly at the instigation of a servant in the pay of a suitor, the exiled English duke of Clarence. All ends well: Agnes and Charles wed and become progenitors of the greatest dynasty in the world.[51]

It is somewhat surprising to learn that Mademoiselle had attempted a literary exercise of her own before leaving Paris. In the middle of the Fronde, Mademoiselle somehow found time to write a satirical work called *Histoire de Jeanne Lambert d'Herbigny, Marquise de Fouquerolles*. The supposed subject of this exercise was the wife of a counselor of the parlement of Paris and a former friend of Mademoiselle's, with whom the princess had had a falling out. At the time of Mademoiselle's exile, the manuscript was forwarded to Saint-Fargeau with other papers, but it was seized by royal troops. Happily for Mademoiselle, the documents were returned to her after an appeal to Turenne.[52]

On a whim, Mademoiselle decided to have the piece published, together with a short sequel, the *Suite . . . à . . . Fouquerolles*, a *Manifesto*, possibly also by Mademoiselle, and several other short pieces written by Madame de Frontenac and the younger Fiesques. Mademoiselle's staff found a small printing press at Auxerre, which she had installed at the château. There the work was printed anonymously. The only ones in on the secret were Mademoiselle, Madame de Frontenac, Préfontaine, and Préfontaine's unnamed "clerk." One wonders if this last was Segrais.

Mademoiselle's *Histoire* and the *Suite* are of some interest here. The *Histoire* supposedly recounts the attempts of Madame de Fouquerolles, in alliance with Mademoiselle de Saujon, to gain control of Mademoiselle's household by securing the appointments of friends and allies to key positions and by blocking the appointments of others, such as Préfontaine, who are loyal to Mademoiselle. The plotters are thwarted by Mademoiselle, who sees through their villainy, and become the laughingstock of Mademoiselle's true friends. Underneath the fluff one finds not only some interesting characterizations by Mademoiselle of herself and her entourage but also narratives of some of the events that later appeared in Mademoiselle's *Mémoires*, such as Saujon's unsuccessful mission to Vienna. The *Suite* also provides an account of Mademoiselle's exploits at Orléans in 1652 and concludes with the collapse of the Fronde in Paris and Mademoiselle's flight. In an extraordinary rewriting of recent history, the princess insists that she and Gaston parted on the best of terms, but were kept apart by the court's fear that Mademoiselle would encourage Gaston to continue the struggle against Mazarin.[53]

This attempt by Mademoiselle to create some record of her part in contemporary events is not surprising. Mademoiselle had a lively interest in history, as evidenced by a comparison, in her *Mémoires*, of an episode in the Fronde to the famous Day of the Barricades of 1588. While at Orléans, she lectured Condé's critics on the roles of Henri IV and the prince's forefather during an earlier capture of Orléans.[54] During the Fronde, Mademoiselle began Italian lessons, and she resumed her efforts toward the end of her stay at Saint-Fargeau, intending to learn it well enough to read Tasso.[55] One of Mademoiselle's contemporaries, Pierre-Daniel Huet, bishop of Avranches, a friend of Segrais's, and another literary figure of the day, bore witness to Mademoiselle's tastes in reading. Huet met Mademoiselle at Forges in 1657. While her ladies dressed her hair, Mademoiselle had Huet read aloud in her presence, mostly history and romances (*romans*), that is, the traditional stories of heroes and heroines whose exploits, in remote times and places, were larger than life. In the discussions that followed, Mademoiselle's range of knowledge and her intellectual curiosity impressed the learned cleric.[56]

The history of Henri IV was of special interest to Mademoiselle. During her visit to Selles in 1653, as in the childhood visit recounted earlier in her *Mémoires*, Mademoiselle spent some time examining the mementos of her grandfather kept there. These included the portraits of his officials, as well as letters and documents written by him and his ministers.[57] As noted earlier, a partial edition of the duc de Sully's memoirs was published in 1638, and it seems likely that Mademoiselle was familiar with it.[58]

In 1649, at the beginning of the Fronde, Marguerite de Valois's *Mémoires*, first published in 1628, made a sensational reappearance in a new edition. Although covering only the years 1569–82, it dealt with many significant episodes in the civil wars of the preceding century from the perspective of a member of the royal family, sister of the last three Valois kings and first, if repudiated, wife of Henri IV.[59]

Once more, there was a tie to Mademoiselle's heroic grandfather. Marguerite de Valois, who survived until 1615, had remained on good terms with Henri after their divorce. Her vast Paris residence on the left bank of the Seine, on the site of the present Ecole des Beaux-Arts, faced the Louvre. She became a confidante of Marie de Medici, and was Gaston's godmother. It is entirely possible that Gaston shared his childhood memories of her with his daughter. In any event, Mademoiselle was more than a little impressed by Marguerite's memoirs. The example of Marguerite's work, and the urging of her circle of ladies, she says, inspired her to write an account of the events she had witnessed.[60]

The first part of Mademoiselle's *Mémoires*, covering all the events from her birth to the massacre at the Hôtel de Ville, was written rapidly, probably in the first year of her exile.[61] Mademoiselle devoted time after dinner every day to writing.[62] Préfontaine was delegated the task of cleaning up the text: Mademoiselle was only too aware of her limitations.[63]

The degree to which Segrais helped Mademoiselle with the composition of her *Mémoires*, and, conversely, Mademoiselle's influence on the *Nouvelles Françaises*, remain unresolved questions. One distinguished contemporary scholar who has flagged the stylistic similarities between the *Nouvelles Françaises* and the *Mémoires* of Mademoiselle suggests that Mademoiselle was Segrais's secret collaborator. Another has argued that a close comparison of the *Mémoires* with her later works, with which Segrais is certain to have assisted, proves the opposite, namely, that Segrais's influence on the *Mémoires* was minimal.[64]

It should be added that Segrais could have helped Mademoiselle only with the first part of her *Mémoires*, written before 1660. He left her service by the time she began the second part. Whatever Segrais's contribution, the *Mémoires* come down to us in a single, consistent, and recognizable voice, in spite of having been written in three parts at decades-long intervals. There can be no doubt that we encounter Mademoiselle in those pages and no one else.

The first part of Mademoiselle's *Mémoires* is divided into two sections: one covering the events through the massacre at the Hôtel de Ville (1652), and the second covering subsequent events through 1659. The first section (penned, as noted above, in such great haste) fills nearly five hundred pages in the Chéruel edition, and serves as Mademoiselle's apologia for the events that led to her exile. It is an indictment of the powerful ministers who, in Mademoiselle's eyes, had broken with the great traditions of the French monarchy as practiced by Henri IV.[65]

What is perhaps more intriguing is the provenance of the second section of the *Mémoires*, on the years spent largely in exile. In the Chéruel edition, this section takes up more than seven hundred pages. It seems to have been completed no later than 1660, and with notes and papers available to the writer for ready reference.[66] Admittedly, many pages are spent describing the little world Mademoiselle created for herself at Saint-Fargeau, while others provide self-contained episodes, such as her encounters with Queen Christina of Sweden. But underneath the flotsam and jetsam, we find a significant recurring theme: Mademoiselle's growing disillusionment with her father and her betrayal at his hands. It is, in fact, a new theme to explain a significant turning point in Mademoiselle's life and a shift in her sense of identity.

The trail picks up in a discussion of the most mundane of matters, one scarcely mentioned earlier: Mademoiselle's financial and business affairs. In December 1650, Mademoiselle had at last been given control of her inheritance. This gave her the opportunity to assemble a senior staff, including Préfontaine, to manage her fortune. Although this emancipation had long been a goal of Mademoiselle's, she had been too caught up in the events of the Fronde to devote any time to business matters. Peace and exile at Saint-Fargeau now provided the leisure to do so. Under Préfontaine's tutelage, Mademoiselle learned such useful skills as regulating her household accounts and ferreting out false expenses and exaggerated costs. She modeled herself on the revered infanta Isabella and the grand duchess Christina of Tuscany, who were well known for their aptitude in such matters.[67] Who would ever have thought, she marvels, that she would come to know the costs of brick and mortar, the price of plaster, and a journeyman's wages? By the time Préfontaine left her service in 1655, her accounts were in order, and her expenditures paid out of current revenues. She was even in a position to consider spending 800,000 écus to purchase the neighboring duchy of Nevers, because she knew where to find the money to fund it.[68]

In learning about her affairs, Mademoiselle was able to detect fraud and waste at much higher levels than those of her stewards and bailiffs. Thanks in part to Préfontaine's work and in part to her own curiosity, Mademoiselle became aware of the many irregularities committed by Gaston and his officers in the management of her fortune during her minority. This revelation and its consequences were to poison her relationship with her father and color her *Mémoires* in an unexpected way.

In her account of these years, Mademoiselle spends many pages recounting her long struggle to obtain some compensation for the misuse of her revenues. As early as 1647, she had asked Gaston to relinquish control of her financial affairs, but Gaston had temporized and delayed matters until late 1650.[69]

Shortly after her arrival at Saint-Fargeau, Mademoiselle took up the question of Gaston's stewardship. Her persistent requests for papers, documents, and accounts were met with foot-dragging by Gaston's officers and tantrums from Gaston, who saw Mademoiselle's inquiries as a threat. During the years that he had been the guardian of Mademoiselle's fortune, Gaston had helped himself to whatever he needed, as he once admitted to Madame de Motteville.[70] He had also made Mademoiselle a co-obligor for some of his borrowings. He now feared that any compensation for misuse of Mademoiselle's revenues would undermine his already precarious financial situation, and that of his younger daughters by Marguerite de Lorraine. Gaston's dilemma stemmed from the peculiar nature of his own fortune, which consisted of estates held from the Crown as an appanage and various pensions. In the absence of a male heir, most of this would revert to the Crown at his death, leaving Mademoiselle's half sisters virtually destitute. To provide for their future, Gaston needed whatever money he could cobble together for their dowries; any compensation to Mademoiselle for the earlier use of her money was out of the question. But Gaston also knew that if matters remained unsettled at his death, Mademoiselle could bring suit against her half sisters or their heirs for what little would be available. So some resolution, preferably at Mademoiselle's expense, had to be reached.

From Mademoiselle's point of view, some financial settlement was a matter of simple justice. It was easy for her to assert the claim because she believed that the fault lay not with Gaston but with his officials, who had managed her day-to-day affairs. In time, not even Mademoiselle could swallow this fiction, as Gaston's complicity became only too evident. To the accusation that she was indifferent to her sisters' plight, she retorted that "it would be better for them to rely on my generosity than to swindle from me."[71]

In reading Mademoiselle, it is clear that the financial issues were only a means to avenge herself for so many other wrongs and slights, some real, some imagined or exaggerated, at the hands of Gaston. Mademoiselle's furious quarrel with her stepmother in 1652 and her frequent expressions of disdain for her stepmother's penurious condition reflected Mademoiselle's anger that her sisters had become rivals: one sister, after all, had been considered as a bride for Louis XIV, while another had been betrothed to Condé's heir, the duc d'Enghien. It seemed evident to Mademoiselle that Gaston was more concerned about their future than about her lingering unmarried status.[72]

Gaston countered Mademoiselle's demands for reparations with accusations of gross disrespect for her stepmother and, indirectly, for him, because of her frequent and tactless comparisons of her mother's vast inheritance to her stepmother's lack of possessions.[73] The contempt, Gaston charged, extended to the children of his second marriage.[74] Mademoiselle, he asserted, looked forward to the day when her sisters would find themselves in the poorhouse so that she would have the satisfaction of refusing them help.[75] At one point in their prolonged dispute, he accused Mademoiselle of making a will that left her entire estate to Condé's son simply to spite her sisters. Mademoiselle retorted that she was too young to worry about wills and testaments, but that, in any event, neither Gaston nor her sisters had a right to expect anything better from her.[76]

In taking up arms against Gaston, Mademoiselle was at a considerable disadvantage. To begin with, there was the psychological advantage Gaston commanded as her father, whose approval she had always sought. In the course of their exchanges, Gaston played the offended parent to the hilt, alternating outbursts of temper with fair words and promises of reconciliation, provided that matters were settled on his terms. In addition, Gaston, as head of the family, could bring to bear his traditional and socially sanctioned authority over an unmarried daughter. Although Mademoiselle had attained her legal majority, the weight of custom in aristocratic circles was against her, all the more so because she was not, strictly speaking, a private person. She was a member of the royal house, and their quarrel touched on the honor of the dynasty. There was always the possibility that the Crown would intervene to avoid a public scandal, and not necessarily to Mademoiselle's advantage. Gaston was only in semidisgrace; since leaving Paris, he had worked to regain the good graces of the court in order to secure his pensions and the future of his younger daughters. Mademoiselle, still the rebel, remained in full disgrace and could not appeal to the king for help.

Mademoiselle's position was further weakened by an untimely episode in April 1653. A courier carrying letters from Condé to Gaston and to Mademoiselle was captured by royal troops. From the content of the letters, it was evident that Gaston had kept his word and had broken with the rebel prince. It was also clear that Mademoiselle had not done so. At

Gaston's behest, she had written some months earlier to Hohenlohe and d'Escars ordering them to return to France with her troops. Acting on Mademoiselle's secret instructions, they had refused to obey.[77] Mazarin sent Georges de la Feuillade, archbishop of Embrun, to Gaston with copies of these letters, and a proposal that the king sequester Mademoiselle's revenues to prevent any more of her money from reaching Condé. Gaston could nominate the trustees and thereby effectively regain control of her finances. Embrun went even further, speculating that if Condé advanced into France at the head of his troops, Mademoiselle might take to the field to meet him. In such circumstances, the king would look to Gaston for help.

All this made it clear to Gaston that he did not need to worry about royal interference in his quarrels with Mademoiselle. In reply, Gaston deflected the question of resuming control over Mademoiselle's property but implied that if circumstances so warranted, he would make Mademoiselle a prisoner in his household, an ironic stance given his earlier refusal to provide his eldest daughter with a bed under his roof. Much of this got back to Mademoiselle through a calculated indiscretion by the archbishop.[78] Fearing some kind of house arrest, she thereafter declined Gaston's repeated invitations to Blois for as long as possible. When she finally went, in May 1653, she feigned illness and took to bed. Gaston, unpredictable as always, was kindness personified. He visited frequently, assured her that he would never use violence against her, and was full of praise for Préfontaine. He refused, however, to discuss their financial disputes, although he raised no objection to her wish to sue Richelieu's heirs for the return of Champigny.[79]

Mademoiselle next saw Gaston at Orléans in early November 1653. Once more, the evasive if amiable Gaston refused to discuss the dispute between them.[80] Scarcely a month later, however, a sergeant appeared at Saint-Fargeau to serve a writ on Mademoiselle: Gaston had counterattacked by initiating a lawsuit claiming that Mademoiselle owed him money. His officials, directed by his chancellor Jean de Choisy, had done a few calculations of their own. Gaston's officers now refused to provide any accounting whatsoever for Mademoiselle's revenues from the Dombes or the Beaujolais and only a partial report for her Norman revenues, citing various legal theories that established Gaston's right to these revenues during her tutelage. After leaving these revenues unreported, they calculated that in the years 1627–50, Gaston had collected approximately 1,890,000 livres in revenues from the rest of her property but had spent a total of about 3,980,000 livres on her behalf. It was Gaston, therefore, who was owed money, more than 2,000,000 livres. Gaston's officials further argued that both the *droit écrit* that applied to most of Mademoiselle's property on or south of the Loire and the customary law that applied to her properties in the north of the kingdom supported Gaston's right to have borrowed money in her name during her minority. If this was not enough, Gaston's lawyers were prepared to argue that the same laws gave Gaston lifelong rights to at least part of Mademoiselle's revenues, notwithstanding the emancipation of 1650. Astonished, Mademoiselle wrote to Blois to protest, taking care to lay the blame on Gaston's subordinates rather than on Gaston himself.[81] Gaston replied with a threat to seize her properties and revenues if she would not come to terms.[82]

On the advice of Préfontaine, Mademoiselle asked the comte de Béthune, as a family friend, to intercede with Gaston. When Béthune's efforts brought no response, Mademoiselle suggested that the matter be put to arbitration: an earlier offer had been dismissed by Gaston as beneath his dignity.[83] This time, she proposed that her grandmother Guise act as arbitrator. Although Mademoiselle and Madame de Guise had never been close, the old lady was her grandmother and might be expected to be fair to her late daughter's only child. On the other hand, Madame de Guise and Gaston were former allies, and the Guises were a branch of the Lorraine family, to which Gaston's wife belonged. Madame de Guise might therefore be assumed to have a certain amount of goodwill toward both sides. Gaston agreed in principle, but found various pretexts to delay matters. Mademoiselle was relieved that they had found a mechanism for resolving their dispute without the embarrassment of a lawsuit.[84]

From Mademoiselle's vantage point, Madame de Guise turned out to be a less than satisfactory choice. The duchess showed little haste and even less direction in executing her mandate. From late 1653 until the spring of 1655, there was virtually no movement, just an occasional request for more information. The most critical aspect of the arbitration was the appointment of examiners and legal experts. Guise's proposal to appoint a tribunal of bishops and military officers (*maréchaux*), when the need was for experts in financial matters (*maîtres des comptes*), who would also be familiar with the laws governing properties in *pays de droit écrit* (Roman law), drove Mademoiselle to distraction.[85]

Mademoiselle's requests for haste were met by silence from Madame de Guise, whereas Gaston blamed Mademoiselle for the delays.[86] Once, on a visit to Blois at Easter 1655, Mademoiselle suggested to Gaston that they convene an ad hoc panel of jurists from Orléans to hear the case and offer their findings on an advisory basis. If nothing else, Mademoiselle asserted, they would be able to determine whether the self-interest of their respective servants rather than any real issues was the driving force in their dispute. Gaston replied by accusing Mademoiselle of trickery, fuming that it was all very well for her to suggest such a procedure, since she was familiar with the details. He, of course, would be helpless without his advisers. The outburst reduced Mademoiselle to tears.[87]

At long last, in the spring of 1655, Madame de Guise was ready to act. She had chosen as examiners three counselors from the parlement of Paris who were acceptable to both sides. After reviewing more documents, Madame de Guise summoned Gaston and Mademoiselle to Orléans in May 1655 to announce her findings. As part of her arbitration, she insisted that both sides agree to sign the documentation without reading it beforehand. Mademoiselle found this very strange, but she had confidence in the integrity of the experts chosen by Madame de Guise. Mademoiselle had learned that the examiners, while relieving Gaston of some obligations, had nevertheless determined that Gaston should be solely responsible for the debts contracted during her minority, because he alone had enjoyed the related proceeds; and that he would also be obliged to pay her significant sums in compensation for the use of her revenues.[88] A ceremonial signing brought together Gaston and Mademoiselle in the presence of the duc de Beaufort, the comte de Béthune, the bishop of Orléans, and a number of other witnesses. There was a formal rite of reconciliation between father and daughter.[89]

The next day Mademoiselle read the documents she had signed blindly. To her dismay, they bore little resemblance to what she had expected. She was held responsible for half of the debts for which Gaston had contracted jointly during her minority. On the other hand, after disqualifying many transactions, the document calculated Gaston's liability to her at 800,000 livres. But even the 800,000 livres was an illusion. Without the concurrence of the examiners, Madame de Guise had determined that Gaston was entitled to a lifetime annual pension of 40,000 livres from Mademoiselle's revenues; this claim of Gaston's on Mademoiselle's revenues was capitalized and set off against the 800,000 livres of liability. On a net basis, therefore, Gaston owed nothing, and Mademoiselle was liable for "her" share of Gaston's debts.[90]

The more Mademoiselle and Préfontaine examined the totals, the more numerical errors they uncovered in the calculation of the 800,000 livres liability. The three parlementary examiners were queried; they asserted that Madame de Guise had altered their findings without authorization, and volunteered to return to Orléans to testify to that effect.[91] Mademoiselle was conciliatory. Madame de Guise was asked to review her working papers. The reply was evasive: the old duchess was not sure she still had them. In front of Beaufort, Béthune, Mademoiselle de Guise, and others, Mademoiselle repeated her request that the transaction be reviewed for an "error in calculation." Madame de Guise refused; an incensed Mademoiselle de Guise accused her niece of insolence toward her grandmother. This sparked a loud dispute during which Mademoiselle accused her grandmother of allowing Monsieur to swindle her granddaughter for the benefit of his daughters by Marguerite de Lorraine.[92] She could see now that Gaston's fortune was "based on what they could steal from me."[93]

For his part, Gaston pressed Mademoiselle to sign a separate codicil confirming that his liability of 800,000 livres would be netted against his supposed pension rights. Mademoiselle replied that she would do so, but with a clause reserving her rights in the event of an error in calculation. This was completely unacceptable to Gaston. Mademoiselle tried in vain to persuade Gaston that if no provision was made for this contingency, her heirs and those of her sisters might well find themselves someday in litigation with one another. In front of Beaufort and other witnesses Mademoiselle did secure Gaston's formal consent to her efforts to regain Champigny from the Richelieu family, because this might be embarrassing for Gaston's officials, who had negotiated the original transaction. Gaston, a man easily bored with business matters, agreed to all this, and, if Mademoiselle is to be believed, parted with his daughter on civil terms.[94]

The lull did not last. Mademoiselle's staff were able to obtain copies of some of the working documents used by the examiners. These seemed to substantiate the assertion that there had been a serious error in calculation, and provoked yet another round of accusations between Mademoiselle, her father, and Madame de Guise.[95] In a show of force, and without any legal basis for his actions, Gaston forbade some of Mademoiselle's estate managers to forward revenues to Mademoiselle without express instructions from his own officers.[96] He also made scarcely veiled threats to imprison Mademoiselle at Amboise.[97]

While the conciliatory comte de Béthune worked to defuse the situation, Mademoiselle received word in July 1655 that she had won her case against the Richelieu family. The exchange of Champigny and Blois-le-Vicomte in 1635 was voided. Title to Champigny was to revert to Mademoiselle, along with damages for the destruction of the château and the depletion of the woodlands on the estate. At the same time, however, the parlement of Paris upheld the indemnification given to Richelieu by Gaston at the time of the transaction. This meant that the Richelieu family could have recourse to Gaston for the amount of damages that experts appointed by the court would determine.[98]

This new threat to Gaston's finances seemed more serious than the famous error in calculation, since it imposed a claim by a third party, Richelieu's heirs, who would not be as easily intimidated as Gaston's unmarried daughter. Gaston's wrath was fierce, and directed against Mademoiselle's confidential servants, Préfontaine and his assistant, Nau, whom Gaston held responsible for encouraging her to open up the entire question of his administration of her property.[99]

One day in early September, a nobleman of Gaston's entourage arrived at Saint-Fargeau with an order for Mademoiselle to dismiss Nau from her service. This was followed shortly afterward by a letter from Préfontaine's brother advising him that Gaston, out of consideration for past services, would permit Préfontaine to resign, provided that he acted immediately. Mademoiselle protested in vain that it was unheard of to force a woman of her age and station to dismiss her officials against her will. She considered an appeal to the king but concluded that it would be useless. With some difficulty Préfontaine persuaded her not to retire to a convent: an exit, he pointed out, might be more difficult than an entry.[100]

These events convinced Mademoiselle that the time had come to seek reconciliation with the court. There was simply no other power in France that could restrain Gaston. Part of the price of peace would have to be a repudiation of Condé. This was easier than it might have been at the beginning of Mademoiselle's exile. For some time, there had been signs of strain between Condé and the mistress of Saint-Fargeau. When Stenay fell to French troops in August 1654, the cipher used to encode letters between the two fell into French hands. Condé sent her a new one, with assurances that he had had all of her letters burned.[101] The new cipher was not used very much. Mademoiselle did not have any reason to write: some months later, Condé was complaining of her long silence and the apparent change in her feelings for him, a silence she broke only to complain about Condé's treatment of Hohenlohe.[102]

Late in 1655, Mademoiselle politely rebuffed an offer from Condé to intervene in her quarrel with Gaston, and advised the prince of her decision to make her peace with the court. To facilitate this, she asked Condé to cease all correspondence for the time being, while Béthune was dispatched to the court to sound out Mazarin on a possible reconciliation. The cardinal was sympathetic but insisted that Mademoiselle cease all relations with Condé as a sign of good faith. Béthune had been able to show Mazarin proof that the princess had already done so: probably a copy of Mademoiselle's letter to the prince.[103]

In the fall of 1656, Hohenlohe, who had been on bad terms with Condé for some time, announced his decision to return to France with what remained of his troops. Condé had him arrested and flung into prison.[104] Mademoiselle interpreted this as ingratitude and disrespect on Condé's part, because Hohenlohe was her "client."[105] Through the medium of Madame de Longueville, Mademoiselle made her feelings known.[106] Condé dismissed the protest as a pretext for Mademoiselle to abandon his cause. He had lived without her good graces in the past; he would manage in the future.[107] Mazarin was delighted at what seemed to be a real breach between the two.[108]

Knowing that she was no match for Gaston at the game of court politics, Mademoiselle journeyed to Auxerre to record a formal protest before a notary against any concessions she might be forced to offer Gaston.[109] She then appealed to her cousin Beaufort to intervene with her father. The answer was simple. Monsieur had initiated an appeal to overturn the judgment upholding his indemnification of Richelieu's heirs. The price of Gaston's peace with Mademoiselle was a counter-indemnification in the event that his suit failed. Practically speaking, this meant that Mademoiselle would not seek damages from the Richelieus. Mademoiselle, who was prepared by now to forsake her direct claims on Gaston, would not agree to waive her claims against the Richelieu family for the damage to Champigny. This provoked an exchange of very long letters. Gaston accused Mademoiselle of breaking her word to him to drop the suit against the Richelieus. Mademoiselle responded with her own version of events and insisted on her duty to right the wrongs done by cardinal de Richelieu to Gaston and to her Montpensier forebears.

Each blamed the other's confidential servants for providing bad advice and fostering the hostility between them.[110]

In the interim, the king intervened, removing to his own council a final decision on the settlement prepared by Madame de Guise, while leaving the question of Gaston's indemnification for Champigny before the parlement of Paris.[111] At the same time, Mazarin sent word through Béthune that the king still preferred to see these matters resolved amicably between the principals.[112] In late August, when returning from Forges, Mademoiselle stopped at Saint-Cloud for an interview with the chancellor of France, Pierre Séguier, to provide him with her version of the quarrel with Gaston about his misuse of her revenues, as well as her position on the issue of Champigny.[113]

Through all of this, Mademoiselle remained on poor terms with her father, having to endure frequent outbursts of temper, refusals to see her, and accusations that she was motivated by a desire to beggar her sisters. This endless psychological warfare took its toll on Mademoiselle's household as well. Gaston's refusal to agree to replacements for Nau and Préfontaine left Mademoiselle with the impossible task of managing her voluminous administrative and financial affairs without any professional assistance. The struggle had also disrupted Mademoiselle's inner circle. Faced with the prospect of endless exile in the provinces, Mesdames de Fiesque and Frontenac had begun a disengagement from the Montpensier household. Fiesque was openly contemptuous of Mademoiselle, blaming her for the deadlock with Gaston. After a violent quarrel with the princess, she quit the household to return to Paris. Madame de Frontenac behaved no better. By mid-1657, she and Mademoiselle were barely speaking.

By now, Mademoiselle had concluded that her own return to court and to a normal life, free from her father's interference, meant a capitulation to Gaston. To a large degree, this realization was driven by a new development. In late 1656, an *arrêt de conseil* by the king's council affirmed the terms of Madame de Guise's arbitration.[114] On this issue, therefore, there was no possibility of further resistance. Mademoiselle turned to Béthune and Beaufort to work out the details of her surrender. Mademoiselle's only satisfaction in the final documents lay in a waiver of any additional compensation that might arise from corrections of any errors in the original calculations. At best, this admission that errors might have occurred was a moral victory. While reading the document,

Mademoiselle added the caustic comment that the only clause missing was a stipulation that she forced her father to accept her money.[115]

In April 1657, the contentious issue of Champigny moved toward resolution. Here at least Mademoiselle obtained some satisfaction. The high court of Paris upheld the initial decision awarding Champigny to Mademoiselle but voided Gaston's indemnification of the Richelieus on the grounds that it had been extorted by the late cardinal de Richelieu. Any damages for Champigny, therefore, would be payable by the cardinal's heirs and not by Gaston. Gaston was delighted, and so was Mademoiselle. If nothing else, the verdict proved that she had been morally and legally correct to pursue the case, even at some risk to Gaston's interest: "It seemed to me that in avenging the insult to the shades of my [Montpensier] fathers, I somehow negated that done to me by the servants of His Royal Highness."[116]

By the end of this long and unequal struggle, Mademoiselle had come to see Gaston for what he was, as a man and as a prince. With respect to the man, she recounted a supposed conversation between Léonard Goulas and Gaston during which Goulas encouraged Gaston to act like an ancient Roman pater familias with rights of life and death over his children. Mademoiselle was shocked that Gaston had not reacted to the comment by having Goulas "thrown out the window," but had instead stood silent, as if in thought. Sadly, almost in terror, the overwrought princess remembered that the blood of the Medicis—"venom"—flowed in Gaston's veins, a thought that conjured up the image of murderous betrayal among close kin. She drew back, however, from the conclusion, and wondered if the thought itself showed her own taint from the same source. After further reflection, she decided that in her case, by contrast, the blood of the Bourbons, with its natural "goodness," predominated.[117]

With her sense of princely obligation in matters of state, Mademoiselle was just as disillusioned with Gaston as a *fils de France*. At the end of the day, Mademoiselle believed that her years of exile were due to the actions she had taken to support her father's politics during the Fronde. She was therefore thoroughly upset by an exchange with Gaston during a momentary truce in 1655. The two were seated in a carriage when Gaston told her he feared the monarchy could not last, citing examples of fallen monarchies that had begun their decline with events which resembled those in France in recent years. All of this was offered in a tone of resignation to the workings of Providence. Mademoiselle was scandalized. She rounded on her father: had these remarks come from the footman standing on the carriage step, she might accept them. But for Gaston, given who he was, it was inconceivable that he would stand by, and the thought that he might do so made her blood run cold.[118]

In spite of these reflections, which Mademoiselle intended for the eyes of her readers of a later generation, appearances had to be preserved. Once the final documents on the arbitration were signed, Mademoiselle wrote to Gaston and her stepmother. The responses were warm; Mademoiselle expected no less. Receiving them from Béthune, she asked for a preview, lest, she said sarcastically, she die of the joy and honor of such a reply.[119] This exchange was followed by a visit to Blois. Her sisters seemed genuinely pleased to see her. Her stepmother swore that she loved her as much as her own daughters. Gaston was awkward but followed his wife's lead. There was discussion of a possible match between Mademoiselle and the duke of Savoy, or even with the king's brother, Philippe. Gaston still hoped to marry his younger daughter Marguerite-Louise to the king. Mademoiselle doubted this would happen, and did not appreciate the thought that her younger sister would be exalted over her.[120]

Gaston did perform one useful service for Mademoiselle. Using the faithful Béthune once more as intermediary, he informed Mazarin and the king of his accommodation with his eldest daughter. As a result, he supported her request to pay her respects to the king and the queen mother in person: that meant, in effect, an end to her exile.[121] It was now the late spring of 1657; Gaston had paid his visit of reconciliation to the court in August 1656. Mademoiselle noted bitterly that since her offenses had been in her father's service, her rehabilitation should have been simultaneous with Gaston's. But Gaston, she believed, had refused to permit this while their own affairs remained in disarray, thus prolonging her exile by another year.[122] Now, however, all was in place for her reinstatement. Mazarin had been gracious to Béthune, and had made a point of praising Mademoiselle. As for her return to court, the cardinal reminded Béthune that the king was on campaign with the troops. Mademoiselle should wait until he returned so she could meet with him and the queen mother at the same time. Until then, she was free to go wherever she pleased, even Paris.[123]

During the last stages of Mademoiselle's quarrel with Gaston, there had been a few signs of a thaw in Mademoiselle's relationship with the court. This was probably the result of her breaking her ties with Condé. In February 1656, the widowed princess of Orange, elder daughter of Charles I and Henrietta Maria, began an extended visit to Paris. Gaston refused to permit Mademoiselle to accept an invitation to pay her respects to this cousin.[124] During the summer months, Henrietta Maria renewed her invitation, knowing that Mademoiselle would pass close to Paris on the way to Forges. This time neither Gaston nor the court objected. The meeting with Henrietta Maria and the princess of Orange took place at the magnificent château of Chilly, just outside Paris (Chilly-Mazarin, Essone). In addition to Dutch and English aristocrats, Henrietta's guests included most of the available French great ladies—duchesses and princesses—bidden to the reception. Although Mademoiselle does not say so explicitly, it is inconceivable that this very visible and ceremonial visit would have occurred without the tacit consent of Mazarin and Louis XIV.[125]

Some weeks later, on her return from Forges, Mademoiselle learned that Christina of Sweden was at Fontainebleau. Mademoiselle obtained the king's permission to call on the famous royal vagabond.[126] This was yet another step forward on Mademoiselle's road to rehabilitation as a member in good standing of the dynasty. To some degree, the visit with Henrietta Maria had been treated as a family affair, a useful pretext given the recent alliance between France and the Protectorate of Oliver Cromwell. The call on Christina was much more in the nature of an official visit, making it Mademoiselle's first appearance at an affair of state since the beginning of her exile. Mademoiselle hastened to make arrangements through her uncle Guise, who was acting as the king's personal representative to the Swedish queen during her stay in France. There were the usual questions about etiquette and precedence, but these were easily resolved. Christina was not particularly concerned about any of this and was perfectly happy to let Mademoiselle have her own way in such matters.[127]

The visit took place on September 6. In addition to Mesdames de Frontenac, Béthune, and Le Bouthillier, Mademoiselle was escorted by her uncle Guise, by the comte de Comminges on behalf of Anne of Austria, and by a bevy of royal officers. Mademoiselle gloried in the occasion, and her account of this encounter with the "queen of the Goths" is one of the great narrative pieces of her *Mémoires*. The visit went well. Mademoiselle had heard of Christina's peculiar habit of dressing, but she found the queen conventionally and elegantly arrayed in a gray silk dress trimmed with silver and gold, a flame-colored surcoat and a hat with black plumes. She had a fair complexion and blue eyes, but was short, her poor figure disguised with good tailoring. Overall, she reminded Mademoiselle of a "pretty little boy." Mademoiselle, to her immense satisfaction, had an armchair for the visit. For entertainment, there was a ballet followed by a comedy. Christina chatted amiably with the other guests and even queried the comte de Béthune about his famous collection of manuscripts. Mademoiselle presented Mesdames de Montglat and Fiesque, who had arrived late. So far, this was all standard fare for royalty. "She wanted to make it evident that she was acquainted with everyone and with the latest news."[128]

During the performance of the comedy, however, some of the unconventional aspects of Christina's personality emerged. She stretched herself out in her chair, moving her legs from one side to the other, eventually resting them on the arms of her chair. The queen would repeat, with unconcealed delight, lines from the stage that she found clever or amusing, peppering her own remarks with strong expletives that verged on the blasphemous. Her mood shifted without warning. Sometimes she would talk in an animated fashion, then grow quiet, sighing deeply and drifting into daydreams; then she would shake off the reverie like a person awaking suddenly. Mademoiselle found her "extraordinary."[129]

After the theater came a collation and fireworks. Some of the debris fell close by and startled Mademoiselle. The queen held her by the hand and teased her. How could the heroine of the Fronde be afraid of a few fireworks? There was much discussion of Condé, whom Christina claimed to admire, and a private talk afterward in the queen's bedroom. Christina expressed indignation at Gaston's treatment of Mademoiselle and offered to intervene. Mademoiselle, she asserted, was born to be a queen, indeed, queen of France. She would raise these matters with Mazarin. Mademoiselle asked her politely not to do so. The visit was a long one. It was daybreak before Mademoiselle saw her own bed.[130]

Several weeks later, on an impulse, Mademoiselle, who was visiting with Madame Le Bouthillier at Pont, sought out Christina, who was staying at Montargis. She arrived at ten in the evening, and was told that Christina had retired. Mademoiselle insisted that she be announced. She found the queen in bed and not very becoming in her nightclothes. They gossiped about the king's love affair with Marie Mancini, Mazarin's niece, and about the prince de Condé. The queen was tired, and Mademoiselle sensed afterward that the visit had lasted a little too long. She returned the next day to see Christina off on the first stage of a trip to Rome. With perfect inconsistency, the queen advised Mademoiselle never to marry and then offered to arrange a match between Mademoiselle and the duke of Savoy as she passed through Savoy. Mademoiselle declined: the dowager duchess was her aunt and things could be arranged en famille. Christina finally climbed into her carriage, accompanied only by male attendants. Mademoiselle found the absence of women "bizarre," even for a queen of the Goths.[131]

The two met twice more that year. In October 1657, Christina was at Orléans, and Mademoiselle, who was in the vicinity, hastened out to greet her. The visit was little more than a meeting of carriages on the road. Mademoiselle was startled by the queen's appearance. Christina was poorly dressed, and the prettiness she had admired earlier was not apparent. Christina, she added, was accompanied by her captain of the guard, Louis Sentinelli, and by her chief equerry, Francesco Monaldeschi.[132]

Mademoiselle saw the queen again the following December at Fontainebleau. The visit was not a success. Between the two encounters, in November 1657, Christina had had Monaldeschi put to death by Sentinelli, allegedly for reading her correspondence. The killing had taken place at Fontainebleau, reportedly in Christina's presence. In spite of repeated washing, the bloodstains in the flooring were still visible. As a sovereign Christina saw nothing wrong in the exercise of her powers of life and death. Her French hosts saw this judicial murder committed in a royal palace as a breach of hospitality and an insult.[133]

Mademoiselle recounts the story of Monaldeschi's last moments in some detail, and one suspects that she went to Fontainebleau to make up her own mind about Christina's behavior. She found the queen beautifully dressed, as at their first meeting. Unlike that first time, the atmosphere was strained, although, Mademoiselle insists, the queen was as civil to her as always. The conversation was deliberately casual. While they chatted, Mademoiselle could not put Monaldeschi's murder out of her mind, "I kept thinking about what she had done." By chance, she noticed Sentinelli's baton of command lying near Christina's bed, and "this made me think about the one who carried it, and what he had done." Sentinelli was known to be Christina's favorite; the baton recalled his part in the crime, and seems to have made Mademoiselle sick at heart. It was a "barbarous and cruel death . . . particularly [when ordered] by a woman."

Mademoiselle chose not to linger.[134]

It is marriage that has made men superior to us women, caused us to be called the fragile sex, subject to the male sex, often against our will and for family reasons that make us victims.

MADEMOISELLE

Mademoiselle gave me her horoscope and sent me to see a Minim priest at Perpignan who was known as a talented astrologer, to find out if she would ever get married. He said to me, "Monsieur, she will not marry; don't you see here that Jupiter and Mercury are in opposition? If it happens, the rules of our craft are wrong."

JEAN REGNAULT DE SEGRAIS

5   A Muse at the Court of Apollo

MADEMOISELLE REJOINED THE COURT IN THE SUMMER OF 1657. IN her version, the event was more a triumphal progress than the return of a prodigal. En route, she stopped at Saint-Cloud for a month, where she encountered a swarm of courtiers eager to welcome her. Some were old friends, like the princess de Carignan and Madame de Sévigné, who exchanged compliments with Mademoiselle and then hurried off to write Madame de La Fayette an account of the reunion.[1] Others were former adversaries, and Mademoiselle took pains to cultivate those identified with the cardinal, such as the elderly maréchal de Senneterre, whom Mademoiselle classified among the "birds of good omen" who flocked to her reception rooms.[2] It was a sign of the times that Carignan's daughter-in-law, to whom Mademoiselle was no less gracious, was Olympia Mancini, the cardinal's niece.

As for the cardinal himself, Mademoiselle was not subtle about the change in her attitude. The comte de Béthune brought word that Mazarin hoped Mademoiselle would consider addressing him as "Eminence." Béthune recommended against it: Gaston d'Orléans, he argued, had reserved this distinction for cardinals who were also papal nephews. "The cardinal," she replied, "is more useful and important to me" than any papal nephew. Not only would she accommodate the minister, but she even found a pretext to write Mazarin a day or two later in order to use the title.[3]

Mademoiselle's restoration also gave her the means to settle old scores, beginning with Madame de Frontenac, whom she refused to let accompany her to court. There were tears, but Mademoiselle was unmoved, remembering the times when Frontenac had "laughed while I wept."[4] When Frontenac's husband called at Saint-Cloud to protest, Mademoiselle remained adamant and accepted a pro forma offer of resignation.[5] Nor was Madame de Fiesque forgotten. The abbé Basile Fouquet, using his standing as one of Mazarin's trusted lieutenants, attempted to force a reconciliation on Mademoiselle. Mademoiselle would not budge. To her satisfaction, both the cardinal and the abbé's powerful brother, Nicolas Fouquet, the superintendent of finance, disavowed the abbé's actions, leaving Mademoiselle the victor. The abbé was left with no other recourse but complaints to his friends about Mademoiselle's "arrogance."[6]

Unexpectedly, Gaston d'Orléans approved of these dismissals. He also solved another problem for Mademoiselle, her lack of a residence in Paris, by offering her a suite of apartments at the Luxembourg. To other people, wrote Mademoiselle, nothing could be more ordinary than a father sheltering a daughter or permitting her a choice of servants. But between these two, such "favors" were so exceptional that they were the talk of their respective circles.[7]

A visit from Mademoiselle's childhood friend, Marie de Longueville, let the princess put another matter to rest. Longueville had recently become the duchess de Nemours, marrying Henri de Savoie, the younger brother and successor of the duke killed in the duel with Beaufort in 1652. Most of the family possessions had gone to the daughters of the late duke; Henri had inherited nothing but a small pension. To Mademoiselle, his courtship of the very rich Mademoiselle de Longueville was understandable; what was less so was Longueville's acceptance of, even passion for, a man "without property, position, or importance."[8] Longueville had turned down several more suitable matches. There was even a rumor that an engagement to Charles Stuart had fallen through at the last minute because of Mazarin's objections. Mademoiselle asked Henrietta Maria if there was any truth to the story and was pleased by her aunt's emphatic denials. It was obvious to Mademoiselle that a man who had courted her "would never lower himself to the level of Mademoiselle de Longueville."[9]

With her vanity thus assuaged, Mademoiselle set out on July 27 to meet the court at Sedan, having chosen a route that would take her through Rheims. Her swollen entourage included a royal secretary of state, Louis Phélypeaux de la Vrillière, and another of Mazarin's senior officials, Jean-Baptiste Colbert, who had charge of a shipment of bullion intended for the front. A troop of musketeers accompanied him to guard the treasure. This was a reminder that Mademoiselle was entering a war zone: Spanish troops were operating out of Rocroi, within striking distance of the convoy, and there were reports of enemy scouts in the vicinity. Given Mademoiselle's rescue of Condé and his Spanish allies at the Porte Saint-Antoine, there were jokes that she was in no danger, although the silver and the royal officials might be. Mademoiselle joined in the fun, promising Colbert her personal protection in the event of an ambush: to appease the enemy, they concluded, they would give La Vrillière up for ransom. In the meantime, the silver wagons were placed in front of Mademoiselle's carriage, with squads of cavalry surrounding the vehicles.

The danger never materialized, leaving Mademoiselle free to enjoy the ceremonial aspects of the trip: speeches by local officials, and local militiamen presenting arms in her honor. At Vandy the caravan was met by a regiment of German mercenaries sent to reinforce the escort, drawn up in parade formation to salute the princess. Once Mademoiselle's party reached the outskirts of Sedan, it was no longer in danger of attack. The Germans were dismissed with thanks and with money to drink to the princess's health.[10]

Anne of Austria was waiting for Mademoiselle in a nearby field. With trumpets sounding, Mademoiselle's party drove up at a gallop. At twenty paces from the queen, her carriage stopped abruptly. Mademoiselle gave the troops time to form a guard of honor, then descended and walked toward the queen. There was a required gesture of submission: Mademoiselle bowed low and kissed the hem of Anne's robe and then Anne's hands before the queen raised her up for an embrace. Anne was cordial but direct. Without much in the way of preface, she told Mademoiselle that she had never held the seizure of Orléans against her, but her rescue of Condé at the Porte Saint-Antoine was a different matter: for that episode, Mademoiselle said, the queen "would have strangled me." To this reproach, Mademoiselle offered a half apology: she regretted that her "duty [to Gaston] obliged me to behave the way I did."[11]

After this exchange, Anne remarked that Mademoiselle looked well in spite of some premature graying. Mademoiselle countered that gray hair came early on both sides of her family. There was a presentation of the queen's entourage, which included several of Mazarin's nieces. Mademoiselle then took her place in the queen's carriage for the drive into Sedan. On the way, Anne pointed out that the detachment of guards at the city gates had been increased in her niece's honor, a touch that delighted Mademoiselle.[12]

Although the strain of the encounter with the queen was over, Mademoiselle still had to make her peace with the young king. This would have to wait a while longer: Louis, his brother Philippe, and Mazarin were at the siege of Montmédy and were not expected at Sedan for a few more days. In the meantime, Mademoiselle resumed her place at the queen's side. To pass the time, there were pilgrimages to local churches and long talks with the queen and her ladies, which centered on Mademoiselle's recent disputes with Gaston. The queen was sympathetic, but not surprised: she had had her own experiences of Gaston's erratic behavior.[13]

On August 7, the king arrived at Sedan, fresh from the surrender of Montmédy. This is Louis XIV's first appearance in Mademoiselle's *Mémoires*, a warrior prince of nineteen, Mademoiselle's junior by eleven years. He came in time for dinner, booted and spurred, covered with the damp and dust of the road. Anne pretended to be scandalized. She would have preferred that Louis change his costume before she presented Mademoiselle. But Louis was too much the master to be ill at ease under his own roof. Anne introduced Mademoiselle as a young lady who regretted her bad behavior in the past and who would be "very good in the future." Louis, whom Mademoiselle thought quite handsome, laughed, as if Mademoiselle were guilty of some childish prank. He did not, however, embrace his cousin or address her directly, speaking instead either to his mother or to the courtiers around him. When Anne asked the king where Philippe was, Louis replied that his brother was coming by carriage: he was dressed up and did not wish to get dirty. This caused more laughter and sly glances at Mademoiselle: the princess had already picked up hints of a possible marriage between herself and the king's brother.[14]

Mademoiselle used the rest of this scene to illustrate the striking difference in temperament between the two brothers. The narrative continues with Louis's account of a recent skirmish. Several of his entourage pointed out that the king had been in the forefront of those seeking out the enemy. Philippe had "remained in his carriage" because he was not dressed for battle. At precisely this moment in the narrative, Philippe is announced. Unlike Louis, so careless of his appearance, the younger man was impeccably dressed in a gray court costume, with a feather in his hat and a fire-red ribbon across his shoulder. In contrast with Louis's coolness, Philippe was profuse in his welcome. He embraced Mademoiselle, drew her into a corner, and made small talk.[15]

To complete this ritual of reconciliation, Mademoiselle had to deal with the cardinal, who arrived immediately thereafter. Mademoiselle offered him the flattery of an embrace. They then chatted amiably and joked about Mademoiselle's good care of the royal silver wagons. There followed a dinner en famille with Mademoiselle at the royal table. They were serenaded by the king's violins during the meal, and there was dancing afterward. When the queen again expressed her joy at Mademoiselle's return, the king showed little enthusiasm. Although Mademoiselle spent much of the evening placed between the king and Philippe, Louis directed his attention to Marie Mancini, who stood to his other side. From time to time he would direct a word to Mademoiselle, but not very often. The frigidity intimidated Mademoiselle, and she rarely took the initiative to address the king, confessing that "I was afraid to question him."[16]

For the rest of her stay, Mademoiselle worked to ingratiate herself with this inner circle of queen, king, cardinal, and younger brother. She spent a great deal of time flattering Mazarin. In spite of the occasional jarring note, such as a hint by Mazarin that he had seen much of Mademoiselle's correspondence with Condé, the tone of the exchanges was conciliatory. Although the cardinal had worked hard to keep Gaston and Mademoiselle at loggerheads during her years of exile, he disavowed Gaston's actions and blamed the absent prince for many of Mademoiselle's problems, including the court's inability to find Mademoiselle a suitable royal alliance.[17] The queen seconded this explanation and also made a show of accepting at face value Mademoiselle's accounts of her quarrels with Mesdames de Fiesque and Frontenac. Fiesque, the queen commented, was "frivolous and a madwoman," and Frontenac had "neither birth nor merit" to recommend her.[18]

Mademoiselle was familiar with Anne and Mazarin, but finding common ground with her two royal cousins, whom she had last seen as silent children in Anne's entourage five years earlier, proved more difficult. Philippe, who did not have the burden of the crown, was the more approachable, and he continued to treat Mademoiselle with affection. To Mademoiselle's dismay, however, their conversations were always about trivial matters. Mademoiselle was surprised at his preoccupation with his wardrobe and his trifling pastimes. Because these were the things he cared about, she feigned an interest to flatter him.[19]

After several false starts, the king, too, seemed to warm to Mademoiselle. Here the bridge was Louis's interest in military matters. He liked to show off his household troops, and this provided an easy opening for Mademoiselle, who shared Louis's interest in fine uniforms and flashing swords. The discussion turned naturally to war and to battle. Playing up to the king's vanity, Mademoiselle compared his recent campaign to those of their grandfather, Henri IV. She even managed to turn a momentary embarrassment into a courtier's triumph. While showing off his troops, Louis asked if she had ever heard kettledrums play. She replied that she had, during the Fronde: they had belonged to the foreign allies of the Frondeurs. With an appropriate blush, she asked the king's pardon for the faux pas. Louis was gracious: they must not talk about the past.[20]

In spite of this public and apparently successful reconciliation with the court, Mademoiselle knew enough not to overstay her welcome. After all, Gaston's visit of reconciliation the previous year had lasted only three days. A suitable pretext for her departure was easily found: she was in need of a trip to the waters of Forges for her health, after which she wanted to visit Champigny before winter.[21]

Her departure on August 12 was almost as staged as her arrival. There were formal farewells and her coach was accompanied part of the way by a crowd of courtiers and royal officials. There was also an escort of household troops. To Mademoiselle's delight, these followed the same routine as when on duty with the king. They stood guard at every stop; at meals, they led the procession of dishes brought to her table; and at night, they slept in the antechamber to her bedroom.[22]

Mademoiselle's stay at Forges was uneventful. It was late in the season and most of the aristocratic clientele had already departed, with the exception of Condé's sister, the duchess de Longueville, with whom she had a joyful reunion. In the absence of good society, Mademoiselle was free to use the time to improve her mind. Segrais, who had accompanied the princess to his native Normandy, introduced her to his friend and fellow scholar Pierre-Daniel Huet, who, as mentioned earlier, found her knowledge of literature and history admirable. Mademoiselle also passed much of her time negotiating by courier with her father to put her household affairs in order. To the astonishment of many in her entourage, Gaston confirmed his offer of an apartment at the Luxembourg, but he was less accommodating about her household appointments.[23] It took weeks of exchanges, for example, before Gaston would ratify the nomination of a retired military officer named Brays, whom Mademoiselle had met at Forges in 1656, to a minor post.[24]

In October, on the way to Champigny, Mademoiselle stopped at Blois to present Brays and to plead for the reinstatement of Préfontaine and Nau. Gaston flatly refused to permit their return. Nor would he consent to the appointment of another former diplomat, Jacques Guilloire, as Préfontaine's replacement, on the grounds that Guilloire was known to be a good friend of Préfontaine's.[25] Mademoiselle took much of her frustration out on the Béthunes. The comte de Béthune and his wife had joined Mademoiselle's entourage at Sedan and had scarcely been out of her line of sight ever since. Too much of their company, and the comte's inability to soften Gaston, frayed Mademoiselle's nerves. When Madame de Béthune announced the couple's intention to remain with the princess until she married, Mademoiselle protested: "Fond as I am of these people, I don't want to live with them forever."[26] When she managed to leave for Amboise without them, she drew a sigh of relief.[27]

None of this detracted from Mademoiselle's joyful return to Champigny, this time as mistress of her recovered ancestral domains. Richelieu had demolished most of the château, but the wing that had housed her grandfather's pages had survived, as had the magnificent chapel housing the Montpensier tombs. Mademoiselle evidently decided not to rebuild the demolished portions, although she renovated apartments in the pages' wing for her own use, and arranged to restore the gardens and the chapel.[28]

Mademoiselle's visitors at Champigny included her good friends and cousins the duc and duchess de la Trémouille, whose ancestral estate of Thouars was in the vicinity. As a mark of her esteem, Mademoiselle paid them a return visit. Mademoiselle found everything at Thouars to her liking and could not resist drawing a contrast with the nearby château of Richelieu, where she had stayed so many years earlier. At Thouars she admired the courtyard, the terraces, and the extraordinary length of the façade. Everything about the exterior exuded dignity and bore witness that "its masters had owned the dwelling for a long time; this wasn't the case at Richelieu."[29] The interior was equally splendid; Mademoiselle liked the furnishings and the wall tableaux tracing the family's descent from the greatest houses in the kingdom, including the royal house. Mademoiselle was supportive of the La Trémouilles' claim to princely status, since "others with less right were daring to do so."[30]

Mademoiselle lingered at Champigny for a few weeks longer, working out the compensation due to her for the demolitions ordered by cardinal de Richelieu and tending to other business matters. She was back at Saint-Fargeau for Christmas. At Saint-Fargeau there was still work in progress to inspect, as well as a new hospital in the town that Mademoiselle had paid for and staffed with Sisters of Charity recruited from a Paris convent.[31]

Mademoiselle returned to the capital on the last day of 1657. For the first time in many years, Mademoiselle was able to enjoy the brilliance of a Paris season. The winter months were filled with balls and theater. Society revolved around the young king, whose taste for "gallantry" was already well established. A plethora of satellite royalty supplemented the splendor of the future Sun King, including Mademoiselle; the king's brother, Philippe; Henrietta Maria and her daughter, Henrietta Stuart; and Christina of Sweden, who had long since overstayed her welcome. Surrounded by crowds of young aristocrats, princes and princesses danced away the winter evenings. On February 6, the chancellor of France, Pierre Séguier, hosted a ball at his own sumptuous residence. With Mademoiselle as his partner, the king opened the dancing in the presence of the queen mother and the other royal guests. On the tenth of the same month, it was Mademoiselle's turn to hold a ball at the Luxembourg. On the fourteenth, Louis assembled the same cast at the Louvre to witness his debut in a new ballet called the *Ballet d'Alcidiane*. Mademoiselle and her few peers watched the spectacle from a temporary box, high above the crowd of ordinary spectators straining for a glimpse of the royal actor.[32]

Throughout this glittering period, Mademoiselle was not oblivious to the possibility of a marriage to her cousin Philippe. The season in Paris gave her the opportunity to study him closely, particularly since he often sought her out for conversation or an impromptu excursion. Although the affection was genuine, Mademoiselle's impressions of Philippe were mixed. She found him childish and easily led astray by the more ambitious members of his entourage. She was especially annoyed by his seeming lack of consideration for the feelings of others. For example, among those Mademoiselle encountered frequently was her cousin Henrietta Stuart. To avoid endless quarrels of precedence, the two princesses resorted to the expedient of walking hand in hand when they were together in public. When a rumor surfaced that Mademoiselle intended to claim precedence in the future, Henrietta's mother, the exiled Henrietta Maria, was offended, and Anne of Austria annoyed. To Mademoiselle's dismay, Philippe loudly and boorishly championed the seniority of a granddaughter of France over the daughter of an English king who was dependent on the court of France for her daily bread. Mademoiselle disavowed any such intention, and roundly scolded Philippe for bringing even more sorrow upon the head of their aunt Henrietta.[33]

If Mademoiselle disapproved of Philippe's insensitivity within the family circle, she was even more vexed by Philippe's civility to Mesdames de Fiesque and Frontenac. These two ladies were also much in evidence at the important social events of that winter, in spite of Mademoiselle's attempts to ostracize them. To Mademoiselle's dismay, Philippe spoke with them on several occasions, even in her presence, giving rise to harsh words from Mademoiselle and a quarrel that lasted a week before the queen mother mediated a peace.[34]

Mademoiselle was not sure whether the queen mother and Mazarin wanted to encourage a match with Philippe. She was also puzzled by Philippe's behavior, so much at variance with her idea of the princely vocation, and was confused about the role that the king intended for his brother. One day, while she was speaking with Mazarin, the subject turned to Philippe, and Mademoiselle characterized the prince as "childish." When Mazarin replied that he and the queen mother were in despair over Philippe's behavior, she countered that because they put up with it, the assumption at court was that they encouraged it. To the contrary, said the cardinal, they wished Philippe would ask for a posting to the army. This, said Mademoiselle, was her own advice to the prince. She then asked the cardinal if it was true that the queen disapproved of the tie between Philippe and herself. If so, it would be easy enough to break. Not so, replied the cardinal; they were pleased with the bond that had developed between the cousins, sure that Mademoiselle was a good influence.[35]

These were only words, however, and an episode in the spring of 1658 increased Mademoiselle's reservations about Philippe. In late April, the court departed for the northern frontier to open the campaign season against the Spanish foe. Mademoiselle, for reasons that are not clear, was left behind. The princess announced her plans to remain for a short time in Paris and then to depart for her annual visit at Forges.[36] Mademoiselle found that time passed slowly. She took drives along the Cours-la-Reine, visited convents and churches, and worked on a lawsuit against her Guise relatives to contest her grandmother Guise's will.[37] As the ranking member of the royal family in Paris, she felt obliged to entertain those aristocrats who had not accompanied the king. Her salon at the Luxembourg became the temporary refuge for those members of the fashionable world still in Paris.[38]

For the rest, there was little to do except wait for news from the front. In mid-June, Turenne, commanding a mixed French and English force, defeated a Spanish army under Condé on the outskirts of Dunkirk. Several days later, the Spanish garrison at Dunkirk surrendered, and on June 25 Louis entered the town in triumph. The news of the battle of the Dunes and the fall of Dunkirk caused widespread public rejoicing in Paris. As much as she disliked Turenne, Mademoiselle felt obliged to call on the victor's family to congratulate them. When Turenne's sister questioned her sincerity, Mademoiselle insisted, "I always celebrate the success of the king's arms."[39] She reserved for her *Mémoires* an assertion that the Spaniards had behaved poorly in battle and that Condé and his personal retainers had battled bravely against impossible odds.[40]

The rejoicing was soon silenced by a report that the king had fallen gravely ill of a fever at Mardyck. With each courier in succession, the medical bulletins worsened. For nearly two weeks, the king lay close to death. In Paris, prayers for his recovery were offered in all the churches. A private letter from a friend in the king's entourage warned Mademoiselle that the doctors had no hope. Fearing the worst, Mademoiselle postponed her trip to Forges until the crisis was resolved.[41] Mademoiselle did not hide her feelings: "I was much afflicted . . . the king was my first cousin; he treated me well; above all, it was terrifying to see a young king die and to think about the future and the queen's distress."[42]

Earlier, she had contrasted the king's military aptitude with Philippe's lack of enthusiasm for a prince's duties. While Louis was campaigning, Philippe had remained with the queen and her ladies, promenading on the beaches.[43] Now she was faced with the possibility that this immature and frivolous prince might soon be king. Much as she liked Philippe, he was "too childish to rule, or even to know what was good for him . . . not because Monsieur did not have a great deal of intelligence; but there was nothing solid there; without learning or experience, a state cannot be governed. His friends and cronies were more likely to ruin the state than not. . . . I have reason to believe that the dignity of office would not change Monsieur . . . and I have such love for my House and for its glory, that I would want those of it to be able to sustain its reputation as well as my grandfather did, or never to attain [the crown]."[44]

Louis's constitution proved to be strong enough to confound the ministrations of his doctors. On July 11, his fever began to subside; by the thirteenth it was gone; by the following week he was on the mend. Mademoiselle wrote that "everyone was overjoyed, myself especially."[45]

The contrast between the brothers preoccupied Mademoiselle in the months that followed. Mademoiselle had already begun to experiment with literary "portraits," that is, short physical and moral descriptions of people, a fashionable genre of the time. She turned to this device to express her views, recording her impressions of Philippe, Condé, and the king and creating, perhaps unconsciously, a meditation on power and the princely vocation.

In Philippe's portrait she dwells largely on his potential, rather than any accomplishments. Philippe carries himself like the son of kings and emperors; he is generous and pious; he dances well; and he loved to gamble and knew how to "lose money like a great prince." But his calling requires more than social graces and extravagant expenditures. The prince's ancestors provide the necessary models for his future conduct. His features recall those of Henri IV: his future actions in war and gallantry must sustain the comparison. Like his more remote ancestor, the emperor Charles V, he has shown his prudence and good judgment when surrounded by those less prudent than himself—Mademoiselle was surely using irony here. She could only hope that these ancestral qualities would eventually manifest themselves in some dramatic way, preferably in the traditional areas of war and statecraft suitable for a prince of such high birth. She wished him the conquest of his own kingdom, in fulfillment of a prophecy that a descendant of Henri IV would someday conquer the Ottoman Empire.[46]

If Philippe was the prince as trifler, the prince de Condé, still in exile, exemplifies par excellence the prince as warrior. Condé, too, has the proud look of a prince, and is also noted for his dancing and for his gallantry with the ladies. But such conventional aristocratic aptitudes pale before his military genius. The essential Condé is the man on horseback. Mademoiselle portrays Condé as she saw him on the day of the battle of the Porte Saint-Antoine: sword in hand, his cuirass battered and half dangling, filled with the joy of battle, the smoke and flame of cannon serving to frame the scene. To the physical endurance of a simple soldier he added the impatience of a great general who demanded the best from his subordinates. As for his personal courage, it was said that no one was cooler or more fearless in battle: "Nothing surprised him, danger reassured and calmed him, and he would give his orders with absolute calm. Compliments embarrassed him; he never wished to hear others speak of his great deeds, being convinced that he had never done enough, and he never found anything that exceeded his courage."[47]

Her portrait of Louis depicts the prince as ruler, whose role requires a range of talents. His personal qualities are well suited to the dignity of his office. The king is described as tall—a common misperception of Louis XIV—and well proportioned. He is handsome, proud, and majestic in bearing. He is athletic and enjoys his public appearances at ballets and other dances. With surprising insight, Mademoiselle notes the political significance of these performances and compares them to public spectacles arranged by Roman emperors in classical times. He has a passion for war and considerable personal courage, essential attributes in a seventeenth-century prince. He knows the military trade at all levels, from foot soldier to general. If by some misfortune he had to repeat Henri IV's feat of reconquering his own kingdom, he would be equal to the task. He has a good head for public business, and speaks well in the council chamber and in public. He knows a great deal of history, "the best knowledge kings can have," and draws lessons from the actions of his predecessors. He is gallant and pious and shows his good judgment in placing his confidence in Mazarin as his chief minister. In short, the king has earned "the love of his people, the respect of his court, and the terror of his enemies."[48]

These portraits formed part of a literary exercise that Mademoiselle had begun in the fall of 1657, when the genre had already been popularized by Mademoiselle de Scudéry's *Le Grand Cyrus* and *Clélie*. The composition and circulation of such portraits soon became a fashionable pastime. Mademoiselle had been drawn to this genre during her visit to Champigny in the fall of 1657, when the La Trémouilles had shown her a number of portraits they had composed, including a set of self-portraits. Mademoiselle was sufficiently intrigued to try her hand, beginning with a self-portrait, which she finished in November 1657 while still at Champigny.[49]

Mademoiselle begins with her physical attributes. She describes herself as tall, of medium build, with straight limbs, ash-blonde hair, poor teeth, and a prominent nose. Her proud look did not prevent her from behaving with civility and familiarity toward others. Though clean in her person, she was not particularly interested in clothes. She enjoyed reading "good solid books" and took a special pleasure in conversing with well-bred persons (*honnêtes gens*). She was constant in her friendships but made a bad enemy. She enjoyed the company of soldiers and talk of warfare. She was melancholy by nature, with a good deal of self-control acquired through her experiences in life. She had an aptitude for the management of her affairs. As for matters of the heart, "I have no inclination to gallantry . . . and the poetry I like the least is that of love."[50]

By late 1658, Mademoiselle had composed sixteen individual portraits and a collective sketch of the *Précieuses*. She wrote some of these while traveling; others were composed at home at the Luxembourg. The portraits include members of her entourage, such as Brays, Guilloire, and Mademoiselle de Vandy; close friends, such as the duchess d'Epernon and Madame de Thianges; and even one of her self-styled enemy, Madame de Fiesque.

These portraits and a number of others written by Mademoiselle's friends were widely circulated at court and among her callers at the Luxembourg. At some point, Mademoiselle decided to publish a selection of these exercises, fifty-nine in all, including the seventeen by her own hand and one of Madame de Sévigné by the comtesse de La Fayette. She entrusted the task of publication to Segrais and his friend Huet. The collection was published at Caen in January 1659 under the title *Divers Portraits Imprimés en MDCLIX*. If Segrais is to be believed, only about thirty copies were printed of this edition. The beautifully bound volumes, decorated with Mademoiselle's arms and dedicated by the "anonymous" editor to the princess, were distributed to her friends. The unsigned preface recounts the origins of the book and notes that Mademoiselle had ordered that it include the names of each author, and the date and place of composition, both to satisfy her own curiosity and to inform those who "in a hundred years will find this book in the bookshelves at Saint-Fargeau."[51]

These portraits form a kind of *tour d'horizon* of the court of France in the first decades of Louis XIV's reign and are a companion piece to the portion of Mademoiselle's *Mémoires* that covers the same years. This later section of Mademoiselle's *Mémoires* lacks a strong narrative theme. Instead, it offers innumerable sketches of various personalities of the time, punctuated by anecdotes of court life. Not surprisingly, many of the characters who feature prominently in the *Mémoires* are found in the *Divers Portraits*. To cite one example, Mademoiselle's discussion of Madame d'Epernon's dramatic life in the *Mémoires* is almost a draft of her portrait.[52]

The printed *Divers Portraits* was probably intended as a keepsake for Mademoiselle and her circle of friends. The survival of numerous manuscript copies in many archival collections suggests a wide circulation for these pieces. Almost simultaneously with Mademoiselle's publication, two commercial publishers, Charles de Sercy and Claude de Barbin, brought out a two-volume edition of 105 portraits called *Recueil des Portraits et Eloges en Vers et en Prose Dédié à S.A.R. Mademoiselle*. This included twenty-one of the portraits from the original *Divers Portraits* and was an attempt to capitalize on Mademoiselle's name: there was an elaborate dedication to Mademoiselle and stylized engravings of the subjects and of Mademoiselle's arms. This publication, reprinted with some variations in its content and title, went through a number of successful editions in the 1660s. Mademoiselle may have been amused by all this publicity: a copy of the Sercy-Barbin edition found its way to her library.

Mademoiselle's patronage of a seemingly insignificant aristocratic pastime was to have some interesting consequences. This kind of portrait or sketch was used by many generations of writers, from Saint-Simon, a master of the art, through Proust and beyond, and literary critics freely acknowledge Mademoiselle's influence in the introduction of the technique. Nor can Mademoiselle's influence in encouraging aristocratic women to publish be overlooked: at least forty-four, and possibly forty-seven, of the original *Divers Portraits* were written by women, including, as noted, La Fayette's first published work.[53]

Mademoiselle's attention to the publication of the *Divers Portraits* in the waning months of 1658 is all the more remarkable given her other activities during that period. In the late fall of that year, the court of France journeyed to Lyons for a meeting with the court of Savoy. The unspoken but well understood purpose of the meeting was a possible marriage between Louis XIV and the princess Marguerite of Savoy. But the entire episode was a cruel hoax; Anne of Austria had long set her hopes on a marriage of the king with her own niece, the infanta Maria Theresa of Spain, as part of the terms of peace between France and Spain. The meeting with the Savoy family was intended to force the hand of the Spanish king, and succeeded. By the end of the visit between the courts of France and Savoy, the king of Spain had formally offered his daughter's hand as a gage of peace.[54]

Mademoiselle's account of the trip to Lyons and her portrayal of her Savoyard cousins is lively, if condescending. Mademoiselle thought Charles Emmanuel was pretentious,[55] and agreed with the queen's characterization of her aunt Christine as "the greatest comedienne in the world."[56] In spite of herself, Mademoiselle was drawn to the princess Marguerite, the victim of this royal scam. Even after the game was apparent, Marguerite behaved with remarkable dignity, and won Mademoiselle's grudging admiration.[57] She and Mademoiselle had a private talk about marriage, using as a starting point the marital woes of Marguerite's absent sister, the electress of Bavaria.[58] When the two courts parted, Christine wept, while Marguerite finally let her guard down and shed a few tears, "more in anger than affection."[59]

Lyons was not far from one of Mademoiselle's important possessions, the principality of Dombes, which faced the Beaujolais from the opposite bank of the Saône. Dombes was in theory a part of the Holy Roman Empire, and this made Mademoiselle a sovereign princess. While the court was at Lyons, the parlement of Dombes received permission to come to the city to greet the king. As a symbol of their independence, however, the judges did not kneel before the king during the speech of welcome made by their presiding officer, the *premier président*. To Mademoiselle's satisfaction, the speeches of this worthy stressed the independence of the principality and Mademoiselle's sovereign status.[60]

Mademoiselle visited the principality shortly thereafter, in the week after Christmas 1658. It was her first visit, and a rare treat for the inhabitants: her Montpensier predecessors had never even owned a residence there. In preparation, Mademoiselle arranged to buy a house at Trévoux, the capital, with a terrace overlooking the river.[61] At Trévoux, her parlement appeared in robes of office to welcome her, and this time they knelt before her in recognition of her authority. In her role as sovereign, she reviewed the cases of a number of criminals, pardoning a few and commuting sentences for others. She was also pleased to discover that prayers were routinely offered for her health at Mass, another symbol of her sovereign status. In a diplomatic gesture, she ordered that the king be included as well. Before departing, Mademoiselle created a number of new offices connected with the parlement of Dombes and the administration of justice. These were for sale, thus providing Mademoiselle with the means of financing the trip to Lyons.[62]

The excursion also gave Mademoiselle an opportunity for yet another literary work. While still at Lyons, Mademoiselle had been visited by a certain Boussillet de Messimieux, who held the title of *chevalier d'honneur* to the parlement, a sinecure created by Gaston's administrators to raise money.[63] Messimieux had called on Mademoiselle to brief her on his endless quarrels with his parlementary colleagues. Scarcely able to contain her laughter at his Lilliputian seriousness, Mademoiselle promised to reward his efforts by appointing him governor of a newly purchased island domain, adding that she would send him its name and a description as soon as possible. Messimieux was waiting for Mademoiselle at Trévoux and supplemented the judges' greetings with his own soaring oratory. The amused princess hastened away to finish her account of this imaginary island. The next evening, Mademoiselle had this piece, entitled the *Relation de l'Isle Imaginaire*, read aloud in the presence of its "governor" and her assembled guests.[64]

The work begins with a laudatory dedication to "Monseigneur" de Messimieux, offering him a title reserved for princes, dukes, and ministers of state and repeats it several times for comic effect. The text proper takes the form of a tale by a shipwrecked adventurer who discovers an island paradise where a republic of animals has evolved into an aristocratic society dominated by greyhounds. The air is perfumed with the scent of fruit and pine trees; there is an abundance of grains. What is lacking is a human population. To remedy this, the author recommends the importation of all manner of folk, including Jesuits for learning and Jansenists for industry. One could not dispense with a parlement to administer justice, nor, above all, with a *chevalier d'honneur* to render his special services. We can only speculate as to when "Monseigneur" felt the nettle penetrate; Mademoiselle does not tell us, although she notes that thereafter Messimieux was referred to as "Monsieur le Gouverneur."[65]

Some months later, in the fall of 1659, Mademoiselle was at Bordeaux, accompanying the king on a long trip through the south of France in anticipation of peace with Spain and his marriage to the Spanish infanta.

While there, Mademoiselle was visited by an old friend, Julie de Mon-tausier, the daughter of the marquise de Rambouillet, who came on the pretext of mediating a dispute between Mademoiselle's companion, Ma-demoiselle de Vandy, and Mesdames de Fiesque and Frontenac. In real-ity, the reconciliation Montausier hoped for was between Mademoiselle and her former fellow exiles. Mademoiselle did not seem interested. At one point, borrowing a title from a work of Mademoiselle de Scudéry, Montausier rounded on poor Vandy, the surrogate for the princess, and exclaimed, "You are certainly proud, Princess of Paphlagonie," to which Mademoiselle responded, "The Princess of Paphlagonie is in a state of war with Queen Gilette," meaning Gilonne de Fiesque.[66] After an eve-ning of such banter, Mademoiselle decided to write a "history" of the princess for Madame de Montausier.[67]

The result was a roman à clef set in Paris during the Fronde, which imitates Scudéry's use of mythological settings and fanciful names. Se-grais has preserved for us the key to these pseudonyms: Mademoiselle de Vandy was Princess of Paphlagonie; Condé, Cyrus; Madame de Fiesque, Queen Gelatille; Madame de Frontenac, the Merchant Woman; and Ma-demoiselle, Queen of the Amazons.[68]

In a striking reversal of the usual gender hierarchy, all of the leading characters are women, the various queens and princesses in the story. Even the strongest males, Cyrus (Condé), the Italian prince (Fiesque), and the minister of Thrace (Basile Fouquet) are relegated to subordinate roles. There is a great deal of gentle satire in the work. Mademoiselle de Vandy's prudishness, for example, was a source of merriment to her friends. The Princess of Paphlagonie (Vandy) is similarly afflicted. In deference to her modesty, the word "love" cannot be pronounced in her presence; one simply speaks of "the other."[69] Not everyone was speared: Princess Aminte (Julie de Montausier) is described as "lovable and loved by everyone,"[70] and the daughter of the Goddess of Athens (Madame de Rambouillet) as a lady so "cultivated, wise, and knowledgeable" that she was worshipped as the true daughter of Jupiter.[71]

There follows a famous description of Madame de Rambouillet's re-ception rooms: "I see her in a recess where the sunlight does not pene-trate, but where light is not entirely banished. This lair is decorated on all sides with crystal vases filled with the most beautiful spring flowers, which bloom eternally in the gardens next to her temple . . . she is surrounded with pictures of those she likes; her contemplation of these portraits brings down blessings on the originals. There are many books

on the tables in the grotto; one can see that there is nothing commonplace about them. Only two or three people at a time can enter this
place, because the goddess dislikes noise and confusion."[72]

In the end, the Princess of Paphlagonie remains constant in her virtue
and is rewarded with a place among the company of virgins who attend
the goddess Diana through eternity. As a star in the heavens, she can still
be seen, in her translucent beauty, on certain days of the year.[73]

Madame de Montausier was delighted with the result, as was Mademoiselle's hostess in Bordeaux, Madame de Pontac, wife of the *premier
president* of the parlement of Bordeaux. At Pontac's urging, Mademoiselle published the work, together with the *Isle Imaginaire*, in a single
volume that appeared "anonymously" in a limited edition arranged by
Segrais some weeks afterward. In some circles, *Princesse de Paphlagonie*
was read as a satire on *Le Grand Cyrus*. This did not stop Mademoiselle
de Scudéry from expressing her admiration for the work, which she
professed to read "with great pleasure,"as did the comtesse de Maure,
another of Mademoiselle's *Précieuse* friends.[74]

The publication of this small volume brought to a close the period
of literary experimentation that marks Mademoiselle's return to court.
Shortly thereafter, sometime in 1660, Mademoiselle also put aside her
Mémoires, after recording the 1658–59 trip to Lyons, her visit to Dombes,
and the court season that followed. Seventeen years later, in 1677, she
picked up the thread of her narrative, beginning precisely where she had
left off. She provides her own explanation for this long hiatus: the pace of
court life, her many long trips, a second exile, and certain other issues, as
yet unresolved in 1677, had drawn her away from her *Mémoires*.[75] When
she took up her pen again, she resumed her work with strong narrative
themes, beginning with the events surrounding the marriage of the king
and the various projects to find her a spouse in the period 1659–61.

The long trip through the south of France that culminated in the
marriage of Louis XIV to the Spanish infanta began at the end of July
1659, when the court left Fontainebleau for Bordeaux. The peregrination
took the court to Toulouse and Montpellier, followed by several months
of wandering along the coasts of Provence and the Languedoc. By late
April, the royal party was back in Toulouse, preparing to meet with the
Spanish court at Saint-Jean-de-Luz.

For Mademoiselle, this was a journey of discovery to the remotest
parts of the realm, and her account is a vivid travelogue. With some of
these places, Mademoiselle was able to make a personal connection.

Nérac, on the road between Bordeaux and Toulouse, evoked memories of Marguerite de Valois and Henri IV. Mademoiselle admired the gardens and examined various artifacts dating from the period.[76] At Toulouse, the king and his mother stayed at the episcopal residence, an imposing structure that had been rebuilt in the prior century by one of Mademoiselle's Joyeuse relatives. This gave Mademoiselle an excuse to lecture her readers on the history of that family, concluding: "Thus I was pleased to see the respect and veneration for the family in the province, and the many indications of greatness which they have left behind."[77]

At Nîmes, which the court reached in January 1660, Mademoiselle toured the amphitheater and the other Roman relics, and then left to explore the papal enclave of Avignon. She stopped to climb the Pont du Gard and entered Avignon by the famous bridge, which she saw "by moonlight." This was more frightening than romantic: the Rhone was wide and flowed rapidly, while the bridge was "narrow, high, and in need of repair."[78] She was not impressed by the papal palace, which she thought "shabby" and badly furnished. She toured the town, admiring its fine walls, and stopped at a church famous as the site of many miracles, and at the local Carmelite convent. She even visited a synagogue, where she listened to the chanting of a service, but left with a very negative impression.[79]

At Salon, she visited the tomb of Nostradamus. Like many of her contemporaries, she was fascinated by his book of prophecies, which she mentions at the end of her *Isle Imaginaire*.[80] At Vaucluse the local fountain evoked the memory of Petrarch and his Laura. Mademoiselle knew the story, but her Italian had never been strong enough to tackle poetry.[81] At Narbonne, Mademoiselle came upon more relics of her Joyeuse ancestors, while at Perpignan she was struck by the Spanish-style housing and customs.[82]

Some sights left more disturbing memories. At Marseilles, the court toured a fleet of galleys. The gilded and painted ships made a brave show, but the sight of the galley rowers, convicted criminals or prisoners of war, shook Mademoiselle. Their heads were shaven, and they were nearly naked; sunburned and chained to their oars, they offered Mademoiselle a "glimpse of hell."[83] An excursion to the nearby château d'If just outside the harbor was also unnerving. Although the view was spectacular, it reminded her of a prison, and she had a lifelong dislike of prisons.[84]

At the end of January, Mademoiselle had a joyful reunion at Aix with the prince de Condé, returned at last from his long Spanish exile. His

reinstatement had been one of the last issues resolved in the long negotiations between France and Spain. At Condé's request, there were no
spectators present at his first meeting with the king and queen mother.
Mademoiselle heard that the king had received him graciously, chatting
about the Fronde and Condé's years in Flanders as if the prince's victories had been in his service. At a ball several days later, Mademoiselle and
Condé spent much of the evening laughing at the "foolish things" they
had done during the Fronde. The king, who was present for much of
this, took it in good humor, often joining in the banter.[85] Although
Condé seemed at home, his visit, like Mademoiselle's return to court in
1657, was only a first step toward rehabilitation. He declined a polite
invitation to stay with the court for the royal wedding and hastened off to
Paris and his estate at Chantilly.[86]

A few days earlier, at the grand *Te Deum* celebrating the peace between France and Spain, Mademoiselle had been seized with a presentiment of disaster. Condé's return provided a temporary distraction, but
the arrival of a messenger from Blois reawakened this sense of forebod-
ing.[87] The courier brought word that Gaston had fallen ill, but that his
physicians believed him out of danger. After reading the dispatch, Mademoiselle's own physician refused to confirm this optimistic prognosis.[88]

Mademoiselle had been on bad terms with her father for some
months. In late July 1659, during the first stage of the trip south, the court
had stopped at Chambord, for the classic comedy of unwilling host and
reluctant guests. The courtiers found fault with Gaston's hospitality; the
king and queen scarcely touched their food. Everyone mocked the old-
fashioned ways of the Orléans household and the awkward behavior of
Mademoiselle's half sisters. Louis and his mother made no secret of their
haste to be gone, whereas Gaston, annoyed at the bad manners of the
royal horde of locusts, made no attempt to detain them.[89]

On the morning of the court's departure, Gaston woke Mademoiselle
for a private farewell. Sitting on her bed, he predicted that the trip south
would probably last longer than expected. For himself, he sensed the
approach of death and was not sure that they would meet again. He
asked Mademoiselle to set aside her hard feelings toward her stepmother
and to look out for her half sisters, since their mother would be of little
use to them. There were tears, embraces, and promises before Gaston left
the room. The scene was so out of character for Gaston that Mademoiselle had trouble believing it had actually happened: "If I did not remem-

ber it so well, I would have thought it a dream, given all that had happened in the past."[90]

In a novel, this gentle scene of reconciliation would have been Mademoiselle's last encounter with her father. But in real life, yet another quarrel intervened. In the fall, while the court was at Bordeaux, Gaston wrote to complain that Mademoiselle had attempted to disrupt his negotiations to marry his second daughter, Marguerite-Louise, to the duke of Savoy. He accused Mademoiselle of writing secretly to Charles Emmanuel to warn him that her half sister was physically deformed. The supposed source of this revelation was the dowager duchess, Gaston's sister Christine, who had intercepted a letter to the duke in Mademoiselle's handwriting. Mademoiselle vehemently protested her innocence. On the advice of Mazarin, she wrote to Christine, demanding that either the letter be produced or that the story be retracted. She sent Brays to Turin with instructions to wait for an answer.[91]

By the time Brays reached Turin it was Christmas; after a diplomatic delay, Christine furnished him with a letter denying any knowledge of the alleged correspondence between Mademoiselle and the duke. It was late January before Brays caught up with the court at Aix. On the day that Mademoiselle had planned to work with Mazarin on a note to Gaston advising him of Brays' return and the reply from Savoy, a messenger arrived from Blois with news that Gaston was seriously ill.[92]

In an instant change of mood and in a state of near panic, Mademoiselle wished to leave immediately for Blois. Forewarned by Mademoiselle's doctor, a number of her friends, including the princess de Conti (Mazarin's niece Anna-Maria Martinozzi), were convinced that she would arrive too late. With Mazarin's help they persuaded her to wait a few days and to send a messenger to Blois for an update on Gaston's condition. Mademoiselle dispatched one of her valets, with instructions to turn back if he learned of Gaston's death while en route. A day or two later, Mademoiselle returned from Mass to find her staff assembled in her rooms: the valet was there, with word that Gaston had died on February 4. Mademoiselle went to bed with the knowledge that he had died still angry with her about the Savoy marriage.[93] To add to her sorrow, she learned several days later that he had blessed her half sisters while on his death bed, but no one had thought to ask about his absent daughter.[94]

Mademoiselle found some consolation in the rituals of death. She draped her rooms in black and put her entire household in mourning, down to the caparisons of her horses and mules.[95] As the sole representative of the Orléans family at court, Mademoiselle received formal visits of condolence from other members of the royal family, courtiers, delegations from the regional parlements, and other local officials. She also received the conventional assurances from the senior members of the family. Mazarin promised to find husbands for herself and her sisters,[96] while the king promised to be a "second father" to her.[97]

At the same time, Louis showed that curious indifference to the deaths of his close relatives that Saint-Simon, among others, was to remark upon. On his visit to Mademoiselle, the king could not resist a joke about his own brother. Gaston's death had provided Philippe with an opportunity to wear a grand mourning costume. The only other suitable occasion would have been the king's death, so Louis was relieved that Philippe could amuse himself at Gaston's expense, rather than his. He continued that Philippe "thinks he's going to inherit his appanage. He doesn't talk about anything else, but he doesn't have it yet."[98]

Although Mademoiselle continued to receive condolences from the various officials she encountered during the rest of her visit in Provence and Languedoc, the court soon forgot all but the formalities attached to the death of the king's uncle. By mid-May, the royal entourage had reached Saint-Jean-de-Luz. The Spanish king was just across the border, at Saint-Sebastian, preparing, like Louis, for the formal meetings and the wedding that would mark the end of a generation of warfare.

Mademoiselle devotes more than thirty pages in the Chéruel edition of her *Mémoires* to an account of the conferences on the nearby Isle of Pheasants and of the two wedding ceremonies, a Spanish service at Fontarabia on June 3 in the presence of Philip IV and then a French one at Saint-Jean-de-Luz on June 9. Her narrative is overflowing with descriptions of the actors and the settings and has always served as a major source for secondary accounts. Among other insights, she captures the intense curiosity that the French displayed about their longtime foe, and the seeming absence of any reciprocal interest by the Spaniards.[99]

Mademoiselle and her cousin Philippe were among the many French courtiers who wanted to attend the Spanish nuptial service. But Mazarin refused to allow Philippe, the heir presumptive to the crown, to cross onto foreign soil. Mademoiselle was also forbidden to attend, but the cardinal relented in the face of her argument that since women could not inherit the crown, daughters were "good for nothing in France" and at least "should be allowed to see what they want."[100] To avoid problems of protocol, Mademoiselle was to go incognito, in the train of Pierre Lenet, Condé's representative in Spain during the prince's years in exile. Mazarin did alert his Spanish counterpart, Don Luis de Haro, to the identity of the unknown lady dressed in mourning who would accompany Lenet.[101]

Mademoiselle's entourage set out at five in the morning on the day of the ceremony. By her standards, she traveled simply, accompanied only by Mademoiselle de Vandy, Mesdames de Navailles and Pontac, Guilloire, and a few servants. At Andaye, Mademoiselle's party was joined by Lenet and the bishop of Fréjus. A handsome ship decorated with blue hangings ferried them to Spain. There followed a two-hour trip to Fontarabia. At the church, Don Antonio Pimentel, a minister of state, had been detailed to escort the "relative of M. Lenet."[102] Mademoiselle was placed to one side of the high altar, not far from the place reserved for Philip IV.

Shortly thereafter, the king made his entry, wearing two of the most famous of the Spanish crown jewels, a fabulous diamond called the Mirror of Portugal, and a great pearl known as the Pilgrim. The infanta followed, walking alone up the aisle. Mademoiselle thought the king looked tired and worn out; Maria Theresa, soon to be queen of France, looked like a younger version of Anne of Austria. Don Luis de Haro, the proxy for the bridegroom, neither touched the infanta's hand nor offered her a ring during the exchange of wedding vows. At the end of the ceremony, the new queen knelt before her father and kissed his hand; the king embraced his daughter without returning the kiss and removed his hat. They marched out together, with Philip IV to the right.[103]

After the service, Mademoiselle followed the crowd to a nearby castle to watch the king dine on plates of gold. She managed to exchange glances with the king, who knew her identity, and to essay a few words in halting Spanish with Spanish courtiers who had recognized her. Mademoiselle then found her way to the new queen, who was dining in another room. There, Mademoiselle caught up with her friend Madame de Motteville, who served as interpreter. At the end of the meal, the new queen embraced the "unknown lady" and retired to her private apartments. One of her ladies was sent back to fetch Mademoiselle. In the relative privacy of the queen's chamber, all pretense was dropped. Maria Theresa asked a number of questions about various personalities at the French court and expressed her impatience to see her aunt Anne of Austria. Mademoiselle refused several invitations to stay for dinner; she was too anxious to return to France and give an account of the day to the cardinal and to the queen mother. A carriage was waiting, on the orders of the young queen, to take her back to the river and a waiting barge. The day closed for Mademoiselle with a ball on the French side. In honor of the event, Mademoiselle and two of her younger sisters, who had come from Blois for the celebrations, put off mourning for the evening and wore court costumes and jewels.[104]

Mademoiselle was also present at the conferences between the two kings held on the Isle of Pheasants. The pavilion where they met straddled the border between the two countries. Each side of the building was furnished separately by the two courts, and the chairs were arranged so that neither king ever left his own kingdom. In one of the more moving ceremonies, copies of the peace treaty were placed before the kings in the presence of the two courts. Each monarch swore on the Bible to observe the agreements. They embraced and swore "friendship as well as peace."[105]

There remained the handing over of the queen bride and the second, French wedding at Saint-Jean-de-Luz. Mademoiselle did not devote as many pages to describing this as she did the Spanish ceremony, perhaps because she was familiar with the ceremonial of the French court and felt no need to elaborate. Her sisters and the dowager princess de Carignan carried the queen's train, while Mademoiselle presented the queen's offering for the Mass and marched behind the bride. Mademoiselle was flattered that Spanish guests remarked on her resemblance to their late queen, her aunt Elisabeth of France, the mother of the new French queen.[106]

For herself, Mademoiselle seems to have given up on the idea of marriage. At the time of the king's illness in June 1658, she had had the sense to admit that she had no hopes of marrying the young king, and, as was evident, she had no inclination to marry Philippe.[107] One possible alternative had been the duke of Savoy, whom Gaston had seen as a match for his second daughter, Marguerite-Louise. Although Mademoiselle skirts the issue, Madame de Motteville recorded that at a meeting of the courts of Savoy and France in 1658, Mademoiselle had attempted to push her own candidacy for the duke's hand. But the duke feared that Mademoiselle, then thirty-one, might not be able to provide him with an heir. Mademoiselle's disappointment may have fueled her rage at her father's accusation of interference in the later negotiations on behalf of Marguerite-Louise.[108]

Shortly before Gaston's death, Mazarin approached Mademoiselle to reopen the subject of a marriage with Charles Stuart, whose restoration to the English throne was believed imminent. The princess stood on her dignity: having refused Charles once, she could not accept him now. In fact, she was "indifferent" to the whole subject of matrimony. She used the same expression when Gaston accused her of interfering in negotiations on Marguerite-Louise's behalf: "This subject was of no interest to me."[109]

Similarly, after Gaston's death, when Mazarin discussed various possible husbands for her sisters, coupled with a promise to find a suitable establishment for Mademoiselle, she commented that, "as for myself, who had no strong desire to marry, I listened to all that he said about the others with pleasure and without any regret."[110]

This professed lack of interest had been Mademoiselle's stock response since her return from exile. While at Saint-Jean-de-Luz, her feelings hardened into an outright hostility to the idea of the married state. When walking on the shore one day, she fantasized about a life far from the court, a life of contemplation unspoiled by marriage or romance. She returned to her quarters and penned a letter describing this idealized world, which she sent anonymously to Madame de Motteville.[111] Motteville guessed the author and replied to the princess, thus beginning a stylized correspondence that lasted for more than a year. Part of this survived and was printed anonymously, to Mademoiselle's supposed regret, in 1667.[112]

In her first letter, Mademoiselle proposes a rural retreat, a self-contained world of well-bred persons who delight in high-minded conversation and the cultivation of the mind. The setting is suitably utopian: a large and comfortable house not far from a riverbank but also close to the woods, with gardens and a croquet lawn. The furniture would be plain, but with plenty of bookcases, for "we would read a good deal."[113] Contacts with the outside would be restricted to essential business and family obligations. There would be exchanges of new books and verses, and people would be encouraged to write. There would also be music, with violins to serenade the company and singing. The food would be good—"nothing is more human than eating"—and Mademoiselle would encourage the consumption of cheeses and cakes. There would be fruit trees and picnics on the grass, and sheep to tend. This would not be some pagan utopia but a Christian community. Mademoiselle's plan called for a Carmelite convent to set an example of austerity, a church with learned doctors to provide sound sermons, and a hospital for the sick and for foundlings, where the company could help with the afflicted.

To all of this, Mademoiselle adds one important condition: the company would exclude married couples, and restrict membership to widows and widowers, and to those who had resolved not to marry. Moreover, within the community, love would not be permitted in any form, although worthwhile friendships were to be encouraged. To Mademoiselle, the program offered a "perfectly Christian and moral life, where innocent pleasures would not be banned. On the contrary, one can say that one can truly enjoy them there."[114]

Madame de Motteville penned an equally eloquent response, congratulating the "illustrious princess" on her wonderful proposal. It was, however, the plan of a princess: the residence was that of a princess, not of a shepherdess, as were various proposed conveniences, such as carriages; the sheep were only really there for amusement. Still, a life that joined Christian piety, the wisdom of ancient philosophers, and the fine manners found in the novels of the *Précieuses* would indeed be a paradise on earth, and Mademoiselle's little realm would be the envy of the kings of this earth. But Mademoiselle's high virtues, which made her the natural ruler of this fine domain, might be a little too lofty for her putative subjects. Madame de Motteville suggested somewhat simpler arrangements, such as small cabins rather than a great house, and fewer servants, just enough to take care of the sheep in bad weather. But Motteville hesitated at the banishment of love, fearing that "this wise and necessary law will be poorly obeyed."[115] Mademoiselle, after all, expected her subjects to have *l'esprit galant* and to write verses. If these exercises were permitted, one should expect the shepherdesses to listen, with the inevitable consequences. The only remedy was to permit "that common mistake legitimized by ancient custom and called marriage."[116] The shepherds and shepherdesses could be expected to choose their mates wisely.[117]

Mademoiselle's reply went beyond the conventional Catholic defense of celibacy as a preferred way of life. Friendship and harmless "gallantry," she wrote, were to be permitted in her utopia, but neither love nor marriage. It was better to permit those who felt the impulse to marry to leave rather than to endanger the harmony of the community. Whereas friendship was a necessity of the human condition, love was a dishonest passion, a "child without reason and unaware of it."[118] And marriage "has made men superior to us women, caused us to be called the fragile sex, subject to the male sex, often against our will and for family reasons that make us victims. At last, let us free ourselves from slavery, and let there be a corner of the world where we can say that women are their own masters and do not have the faults attributed to them, and let us solemnize this in the centuries to come with a way of life that will immortalize us."[119]

These comments challenged the routine assumption that in both the public and private spheres, women were limited to a subordinate role. The prominence of women in the Fronde, including the regent Anne of Austria and rebels such as Mademoiselle, had given new impetus to the study of "illustrious" women rulers in history. This raised questions about traditional assumptions of the "natural" exclusion of women from public life and their subordination to husbands in private life. Motteville took the bait, and willingly. She replied that she shared many of Mademoiselle's views on the irrationality of passion and the tyranny of the male sex, whose "usurpation" of the direction of the world had no rational basis: "The history books are full of women who have ruled empires with a singular prudence, found glory in commanding armies, and were admired for their talents. In the last century, there were no secrets in politics that were not known and practiced by Isabella of Castile, Elizabeth of England, the duchess of Parma, and Catherine de Medici."[120]

Even so, she reminded the princess that many of her subjects in this imaginary kingdom would not be able to emulate their virtuous ruler, and to enforce the ban on marriage would create unhappiness. Since Mademoiselle had "to rule over men, and not angels," marriage was a necessity.[121] Motteville repeated the traditional Christian arguments that marriage, ordained by God in the time of Adam, was the means for the perpetuation of nations and the social order.[122]

Mademoiselle paid tribute to her friend's scholarship and to the brilliance with which Motteville marshaled her authorities. By comparison, she admitted, her own remarks were mere "bagatelles."[123] She did not, however, concede the argument.

In a word, he has pleased me and I love him passionately.
MADEMOISELLE

We should get married too, dear friend. Given the mood of ladies today, at the very least we should marry foreign princesses!
ROGER DE BUSSY-RABUTIN

You have disgraced yourself and are the laughingstock of Europe!
GUILLOIRE

6 The Triumph of Venus

MADEMOISELLE RETURNED TO PARIS IN JULY 1660, A FEW WEEKS ahead of the court, to await the formal entry of the king and his bride. In the meantime, she arranged her own triumph, taking possession of the apartments in the Luxembourg formerly occupied by her stepmother. This was not done without considerable resistance from the old duchess, who had proposed that Mademoiselle move into less desirable space. There was the inevitable confrontation, for which Mademoiselle came well prepared, with Condé on call "in case of attack," and Mazarin on notice that the princess was prepared to take extreme measures. Faced with this formidable coalition, the duchess exchanged a few volleys for form's sake before leaving the field to Mademoiselle, who later came to regret her sharpness: "It would have been better if the two of us had treated one another differently."[1]

Mademoiselle's insistence on occupying those particular apartments is perhaps more revealing than she realized. The quarrel between the two women was largely over the titular status of head of the family, as surrogate for the late Gaston. The struggle manifested itself in many forms. Gaston's estate consisted mostly of debts, and the bulk of the Orléans properties and revenues had reverted to the Crown at Gaston's death. The duchess had to make do with a small widow's portion (*douaire*) for herself and her daughters. Mademoiselle used her residual claims against the estate, which could be asserted against the dower revenues, as a weapon in her battles with her stepmother. The arguments about the division of the Luxembourg continued intermittently for years. In 1665 the king intervened, awarding Mademoiselle the east wing of the building and leaving the widowed duchess the west wing, while certain areas, such as the main courtyard, the great staircase, and the chapel, were to be shared on an equal footing. This arrangement gave Mademoiselle use of the apartments that had belonged to her grandmother Marie de Medici and provided her with another restoration project.[2]

The customary memorial service for Gaston, which had been postponed until the king's return, provided another battlefield for the two women. The ceremonies were scheduled to take place at Notre Dame in November 1660. In a break with tradition, the duchess invited an obscure monk of her acquaintance to preach the sermon. Normally, a bishop or distinguished orator would have assumed this role. Despite Mademoiselle's objections, the court would not intervene, and Madame would not budge. Fearing a serious public embarrassment, Mademoiselle sent Segrais to coach the monk on court usage, but to no avail. The cleric was polite but not particularly interested in Segrais's counsel. The result, in Mademoiselle's eyes, was an unmitigated disaster: "He preached, and said none of the things he should have said; there were the most wonderful things in the world in Monsieur's life, which he could have highlighted admirably. He had him born without a father, not saying a word about Henri IV; made me a bastard by not mentioning his marriage to my mother, and spoke only of Madame and how she had 'converted' Monsieur, as if he had been a Turk. He spoke ill of the king of Spain and of M. le Prince [Condé], who was there, as was the Spanish ambassador. He heaped blame on the queen mother and the cardinal."[3]

The sequel was predictable: the Spanish ambassador sent a full report to his master, and the prince de Condé protested the monk's insolence. When the queen mother and Mazarin spoke to Mademoiselle, she had the satisfaction of blaming them for not intervening beforehand. There was the inevitable exchange between Madame and Mademoiselle, but without a clear victor. Mademoiselle worked herself into a rage, but Madame was not disturbed, telling her stepdaughter, "you get angry too quickly."[4]

At the time of Gaston's death, Mazarin had encouraged Mademoiselle to take an active part in matters that concerned her younger sisters, since the old duchess "was a woman who spoiled everything she got involved in."[5] This was an echo of Gaston's plea to Mademoiselle during their final meeting at Chambord to look after her sisters. Now for the first time she and her sisters were living under the same roof, in daily contact with one another, and Mademoiselle took these admonitions to heart.

Here again, a battlefront opened up. Mademoiselle had blamed her stepmother for her sisters' lack of savoir faire at the time of the court's visit to Chambord. Now that her sisters were candidates for great marriages, this supposed failing in their upbringing was all the more critical. The appointment of a new governess, Madame de Langeron, was not, she maintained, an improvement, because Langeron had "never seen the world and did not know how to live at court."[6]

Mademoiselle let it be known that her three sisters were welcome in her part of the Luxembourg. At first they were somewhat reserved, but this melted away after "three days." For young women raised far from the glitter of the court and domiciled with a hypochondriac mother who passed much of her time in prayer and meditation, the appeal of Mademoiselle's invitation was understandable. Her apartments were filled with the cream of society, including many of the survivors of Madame de Rambouillet's salon, such as Madame de Sévigné, the duc de la Rochefoucauld, Madeleine de Scudéry, and Roger de Bussy-Rabutin. The young gallants of the king's circle dropped in from time to time, as did such intriguing visitors as the duke of Lorraine and his young nephew and heir, Charles de Lorraine. When no balls or receptions were scheduled at the Louvre, Mademoiselle would summon her violins for an evening of dancing at the Luxembourg.[7]

Mademoiselle took a special interest in the eldest of her half sisters, Marguerite-Louise, her goddaughter, who at age fifteen was "as beautiful as the day."[8] In spite of their earlier rivalry, when Marguerite-Louise had displaced Mademoiselle as Gaston's candidate for Louis XIV's hand during the Fronde and, later, as a possible bride for the duke of Savoy, Marguerite-Louise soon captured Mademoiselle's affection. She took the first step by asking Mademoiselle to permit her to keep company with her.[9] Before long, this younger sister had become a fixture in Mademoiselle's apartments. She would spend whole days there, far from her mother and her priests, often taking possession of Mademoiselle's study, where she and her young friends would do needlework and gossip. With mock exasperation, Mademoiselle would chase them away.[10]

Mademoiselle often brought Marguerite-Louise and her companions out with her to see a comedy or a royal ballet, or to dance at a ball. There were drives in the country and even a weeklong visit to Pont to stay with Madame Le Bouthillier. The old duchess d'Orléans disapproved of such activities; to Mademoiselle, this was one more proof of her stepmother's inadequacies as a parent. Speaking of the duchess's objection to the visit to Pont, Mademoiselle observed: "Madame did not want to let my sister go with me. . . . My stepmother had foolish ideas like that, which drove her [Marguerite-Louise] to despair, while in other matters she let her do whatever she wanted."[11]

Early in this relationship, Marguerite-Louise let slip her need for Mademoiselle's guidance. Her mother, she said, was a good woman, but one without any knowledge of court life, and she was badly advised by people like Madame de Choisy. The younger woman blamed Madame de Choisy for giving Gaston false hopes of a marriage between herself and Louis XIV and for mishandling the negotiations with the duke of Savoy, both subjects dear to Mademoiselle's heart. Marguerite-Louise now feared that the latest proposal, a match with Cosimo de Medici, the eldest son and heir of the grand duke of Tuscany, would also fail. She asked her older sister to help convey her interest in this marriage to Mazarin.[12] Mademoiselle was willing to oblige. The proposal to marry Marguerite-Louise to the Tuscan prince had first surfaced in 1658. At the time of Gaston's death, when Mazarin had discussed the future of her younger sisters with Mademoiselle, he had alluded to conversations about it with the Florentine resident, the abbé Pierre Bonzi.[13]

For once, the Orléans family seemed to agree on something. The duchess favored the match—all the more, according to Mademoiselle, because an earlier grand duchess had come from the family of Lorraine.[14] The cardinal was thus pleased with Mademoiselle's initiative and with an offer from Marguerite-Louise to meet with him privately to discuss the marriage further.[15]

While awaiting a formal offer, the time passed quickly. The winter of 1660–61 was a brilliant season of "merrymaking and pleasures," even if marred by a fire at the Louvre and the death of Mazarin in March, which Mademoiselle passed over with the casual remark that he was "not mourned very much even by those who owed him the most: such is the lot of *favoris*."[16] The focus instead was on the weddings of a younger generation, including two of Mazarin's nieces, followed on April 1, 1661, by the infinitely more important marriage of the king's brother Philippe, now duc d'Orléans, to Henrietta Stuart.[17]

Marguerite-Louise and the *affaire de Toscane* had not been forgotten. In early April, Bonzi, now bishop of Béziers, received his commission as "ambassador extraordinary" of Florence and made a formal request for the hand of the princess. To Mademoiselle's astonishment, her sister, hitherto so enthusiastic, now seemed to have changed her mind and was "in despair." The unhappiness became public during a visit to a Carmelite convent in the company of the queen and queen mother. When Maria Theresa playfully asked the princess to send her some perfumes from Florence, Marguerite-Louise burst into tears and left the room. An attendant returned shortly to report that Marguerite-Louise had given way to a tantrum. Mademoiselle went looking for her sister, and found her with Madame d'Aiguillon. There her sister raged away, denouncing the Tuscan marriage and calling the king a "tyrant" for forcing her hand. Afterward, the queen, who had been briefed earlier by Béziers, told Mademoiselle to take her sister away, warning that if Marguerite-Louise "played the madwoman" in front of Louis, he might send her to a convent on the spot. She reminded Mademoiselle that her sister had wanted the match and that Louis had committed himself: now was not the time to change one's mind. Mademoiselle, equally dismayed, took her sister home to the Luxembourg. Once there, Marguerite-Louise again reversed herself, declared herself ready to marry the Tuscan prince, and begged Mademoiselle to intercede with the king and queen to forgive her for her outburst. Mademoiselle sent a note to the Louvre and brought her sister there the following day to apologize in person.[18]

But Marguerite-Louise's behavior continued to be erratic. She snubbed Béziers publicly when he put in appearances at the Luxembourg, and his visits soon ceased. Marguerite-Louise spent much of her time away from the palace, out riding or hunting, and often returned late in the evening. To make matters worse, she was not usually accompanied by an older woman of suitable rank, but only by young servants and an undergoverness. Polite society was scandalized by the identity of her other habitual companions: prince Charles de Lorraine and his male friends. An unmarried princess, all but affianced, did not behave in such a fashion. "One was astonished at these excursions and that Madame permitted them."[19]

Charles de Lorraine was a frequent guest at the Luxembourg. He was, after all, the nephew of the old duchess, hence within the close family circle, and the heir to his uncle the duke, Charles IV, who had regained part of his duchy as a result of the peace between France and Spain. The two Lorraines were at home at the Luxembourg, often staying all evening.[20] At one point, the duke suggested a marriage between Mademoiselle and his heir; as part of the arrangement, he would abdicate in favor of his nephew. Although Mademoiselle thought the younger man was "awkward," "badly dressed," and the butt of courtiers' jokes, she was flattered by the duke's proposal.[21] Marguerite-Louise teased her out of the idea without Mademoiselle suspecting any ulterior motive:

> "Sister, do you really want this pauper? Those Lorraines are the stupidest people in the world! You'd be just as stupid to want anything to do with them!"
>
> "How nice, little girl! Show a little more respect for your mother's relatives. M. de Lorraine does me much honor. When there has been a daughter of France in the family, a granddaughter can certainly join it."
>
> She let fly at her cousin, really working herself up. I didn't understand why.[22]

But it now became only too apparent why Marguerite-Louise had objected to a marriage between her elder sister and a prince she favored for herself. There was no time, however, to give way to private rancor. Family honor, dynastic pride, and the interests of the king all required a rapid conclusion of the Florentine alliance. On April 19, Béziers performed the wedding ceremony in the chapel of the Louvre. Mademoiselle's uncle, the duc de Guise, served as proxy for the absent groom. There was a dinner at the Luxembourg and formal visits to the Louvre to call on the king and queen and to Saint-Cloud to call on Philippe and Henrietta.[23]

This new status did nothing to change Marguerite-Louise's behavior.

On the day appointed for the reception of the diplomatic corps, she announced she would go hunting. Mademoiselle thought her sister was joking, until summoned to the stables by the servants. Marguerite-Louise was already in the saddle when Mademoiselle arrived. Mademoiselle made her get down and led her by the hand back into the palace. "One can well imagine what the papal nuncio and the Venetian ambassador would have said if they had not found her home. Béziers was very grateful to me."[24]

These visits by dignitaries and members of the nobility consumed a good two weeks and were held in Mademoiselle's apartments, so that Mademoiselle could keep matters on track. She would stand by her sister and help her return the flowery compliments of well-wishers. "Without this help, I don't think she would have said a word."[25]

Béziers arranged for a quick exit from Paris. Marguerite-Louise was to travel south to Marseilles, where she would embark for Italy by sea. Mademoiselle agreed to accompany her as far as Saint-Fargeau. To the despair of Béziers and the king's ministers, the new princess of Tuscany continued to misbehave, making no effort to hide her feelings. At Saint-Fargeau, she slipped away one afternoon at three o'clock and had not returned by evening. Béziers feared that she had run away, but Mademoiselle was not as worried: the bride was on foot and could not get far. Marguerite-Louise reappeared at two in the morning. She announced that she had been touring the countryside and admiring the beautiful scenery. Mademoiselle was sarcastic, and Béziers incredulous.[26]

Marguerite-Louise was supposed to leave a day or two later, but she persuaded Béziers to extend her stay for another week, pleading that it was probably the last time she would see Mademoiselle. Shortly afterward, to the astonishment of Mademoiselle and the indignation of Béziers, Charles de Lorraine rode into the courtyard of the château. At this point in the story, Mademoiselle claims, letters from friends in Paris and some plain speaking on the part of Béziers made her fully aware of the relationship between Marguerite-Louise and Charles de Lorraine. Mademoiselle apologized to Béziers for her blindness; the bishop was kind enough to throw the blame on the old duchess for not supervising her daughter more carefully.[27]

Mademoiselle demanded to know why her sister had not confided in her. Had she known of Marguerite-Louise's feelings, she would have tried to arrange a marriage with the Lorraine prince. Marguerite-Louise's answer was out of a storybook: Charles loved her but could not marry her because of her relative poverty. So she had urged him to transfer his affections and seek her older sister's hand. Mademoiselle was touched but insisted that although she had been flattered by the proposal, she did not care for the prince, and would never marry him.[28]

The prince's visit soon came to an end, and he took the road to Paris. It was time for the sisters to part. They said their tearful farewells on the church steps at Cosne, on the banks of the Loire.[29] As in the case of Gaston and Mademoiselle, this was a false happy ending, soon followed by disillusionment. With Marguerite-Louise's carriage scarcely out of sight, another visitor arrived at Saint-Fargeau, the comte de Fürstenberg, a member of the duke of Lorraine's entourage and a friend of Mademoiselle's. He told Mademoiselle that Marguerite-Louise had only expressed an aversion to her Tuscan future after it became known that duke Charles was seeking Mademoiselle's hand for his nephew. Motivated by thwarted passion, Marguerite-Louise had urged the Lorraines to drop the idea. Mademoiselle suspected that she and the duke of Lorraine had been deceived by her sister and his nephew, and made to look foolish at court. Fearing public ridicule if she showed her face too soon in Paris, Mademoiselle lingered a month at Saint-Fargeau to allow matters to quiet down. She also made it clear that she had no further interest in the subject of a marriage between herself and Charles de Lorraine. She covered her feelings with a witticism. When questioned about the proposal, she would simply say that she had a fear of wolves, and Nancy, an open city, was often infested with them.[30]

This unhappy experience marked the end of any rapprochement between Mademoiselle and her sisters. Mademoiselle had no part in the marriage of her youngest sister, Françoise-Madeleine, born in 1648, to the duke of Savoy in March 1663. This was entirely the handiwork of her stepmother and her aunt Christine, the dowager duchess, and Mademoiselle took refuge at Saint-Fargeau at the time of the wedding. Her younger sister was said to resemble her and, as a child, had called her *ma petite maman*. In more recent years, her stepmother and Madame de Langeron had kept them apart, and they were no longer close. While traveling south, the new duchess of Savoy passed close to Saint-Fargeau, and sent a retainer with greetings for Mademoiselle, who was pleased by the gesture.[31]

In January 1664, the young duchess died suddenly, scarcely a month after her mother-in-law, the dowager duchess Christine. Mademoiselle was already in mourning when she received word of her sister's death.

Mademoiselle had long disliked Christine and felt very little grief on the loss of her aunt. She did, however, express real sorrow for Françoise-Madeleine.[32]

Elisabeth d'Orléans, the second of Mademoiselle's half sisters, born in 1646, had long been considered a possible match for Henri-Jules de Bourbon, duc d'Enghien, Condé's only son and heir. But Condé chose otherwise, marrying his son in December 1663 to the princess Anne of the Palatinate, daughter of the famous Frondeuse Anne de Gonzague, Princess Palatine. Anne's sister, the queen of Poland, endowed the bride with a dowry that impressed even the Condés. Mademoiselle did not attend the wedding but heard much about the show the Condés put on for the occasion. The king and the rest of the royal family graced the ceremony, and the bride's jewelry, a gift of the Polish queen, dazzled the spectators. The only dissenters, apparently, were Mademoiselle, her stepmother, and Condé's wife. Mademoiselle would not concede that Condé had done well by his son. She insisted that "people were astonished that M. le Prince preferred the money and jewels of Poland to the rank of a granddaughter of France," and conveyed her disapproval to Condé when next they met.[33] To Mademoiselle, it was a question not just of rank but also of propriety: in a rare compliment to her detested stepmother, Mademoiselle insisted that from the point of view of character and reputation, the old duchess d'Orléans was a more suitable connection for the Condés than the Palatine.[34] Mademoiselle's comments were of little interest to the Condés. The marriage was bound up with the ambitions of the Condés to gain the crown of Poland, hopes which Louis XIV encouraged if for no other reason than to block rival candidates who might be clients of the Habsburgs.[35]

Elisabeth d'Orléans remained single until May 1667, when she was wed suddenly and without much fanfare to her cousin Louis-Joseph, duc de Guise. Mademoiselle learned of the match while at Forges. When Mademoiselle next saw the king, he was offhand. The old duchess, he said, had appeared one day to ask his permission, adding that she wished to see her daughter married before she died. Louis consented, the engagement was announced, and the ceremony followed a few days later. The king continued, "They asked me for nothing; I gave her nothing. I wash my hands of it."[36]

These matrimonial shuffles suggested that Mademoiselle had fallen into the second rank of candidates. Some of this neglect was no doubt due to her advancing age; the rest may be attributed to her attitude. In a further exchange of letters with Madame de Motteville in the summer of 1661, Mademoiselle remained true to her resolution not to marry, in spite of Motteville's arguments that the princess should put the "public good" ahead of her private reservations. In her *Mémoires*, however, Mademoiselle's feelings are somewhat more ambiguous. After a brief discussion with Mazarin in early 1661 about the duke of Savoy, Mademoiselle confessed: "There were moments when I really wished to marry, and others when I didn't care at all; but I was happy that they talked about it and people knew I was not forgotten, and that there was concern about an establishment for me; in fact, if things had been brought to the point of closure, I'm not sure I would have wanted to."[37]

In addition to the halfhearted initiative with Savoy and the complicated proposal from the duke of Lorraine, there was a final offer from the restored Charles II, or, rather, from his mother, Henrietta Maria, conveyed through Madame de Motteville. Mademoiselle's response was classic, so much so that one can assume she was playing to her audience. Having refused Charles Stuart when he was a refugee, she said, she could hardly accept him in his hour of triumph. If she did, her earlier refusals would cloud the relationship, and they would never be happy together. As for marriage in general, it was in the hands of God, and she would await his will "with no impatience."[38] This recital makes wonderful theater, and the account may be more fiction than not. There is some contemporary English evidence to suggest that whatever Henrietta Maria thought, Charles II had taken a violent dislike to the cousin who had spurned his earlier advances, and he refused even to consider the possibility of such a marriage.[39]

Mademoiselle's subsequent actions are consistent with her determination to decide for herself when and if she would marry, notwithstanding lip service to the dream of an establishment and periodic restatements of her duty to marry in the king's service if so required. This last was the working assumption of the dynasty. When the duke of Lorraine had suggested a marriage between his nephew and Mademoiselle, her reply was that "the king was the master and one had to deal with him."[40]

Mademoiselle's adherence to this principle was soon tested in an unexpected way. In the late winter of 1662, Mademoiselle was surprised to learn that the maréchal de Turenne had called several times at the Luxembourg while she had not been home. Intrigued, Mademoiselle arranged to see him a day or two later. As a grandson of William the Silent and Charlotte de Bourbon-Montpensier, a great-aunt of Mademoiselle's,

Turenne had his place on Mademoiselle's family tree, but the two had never been close, even though his sister Madame de la Trémouille was one of her best friends. In fact, Mademoiselle used to mock Turenne's Montpensier ancestor, a Protestant heroine of the previous century who had fled the convent to embrace the Protestant faith and marry William of Orange. From time to time, as heiress of the Montpensiers, Mademoiselle would even threaten to reinstate old inheritance lawsuits against Turenne's family. Nevertheless, when Turenne sat down by the fireside with Mademoiselle, he put on an avuncular pose (he was her senior by sixteen years) and announced that he had come to marry her off. The intended groom was the young king of Portugal, Alfonso VI, whose domineering mother, Luisa de Guzman, held the reins of power. Portugal had risen in 1640 to regain its independence under a Braganza prince, John IV, the father of the present king. Spain had not yet conceded the loss of its sovereignty, and the war between Portugal and Spain survived the Peace of the Pyrenees (1659). After the death of John IV, his widow had carried on the struggle on behalf of the present king, Alfonso VI. France supported the Portuguese insurgency, and it was Luisa de Guzman who supposedly saw in Mademoiselle a worthy successor as the power behind the throne: Alfonso, it would seem, had certain mental and physical handicaps and required a consort who would guide his hand.

However great a soldier, Turenne was not much of a diplomat, and the two soon clashed. To Mademoiselle's flat refusal, Turenne retorted that women of her rank had no will except that of the king. But when Mademoiselle asked if Turenne's proposal was actually the king's, he denied it: this was purely a "family matter." The more Turenne talked about the details, the more implausible this seemed. When Turenne noted that the Portuguese had a large army and Mademoiselle could choose new senior commanders for them from available French officers, Mademoiselle was incredulous. How could the maréchal propose the seconding of French officers without Louis being aware of his scheme? Before Turenne could reply, she offered two reasons for her refusal. Her marriage would become the cause of "an eternal war" between France and Spain for the benefit of a rebel. Alternatively, she could well imagine the failure of the revolt and her return to France after squandering her personal fortune in her husband's cause. Saddled with a "stupid and paralytic husband," she would be reduced to living on royal charity while "playing the queen" in some provincial town. For this scenario, Mademoiselle could conjure up fresh recollections of the miserable experiences of her English royal relatives, as well as her earlier misgivings about marrying the exiled Charles Stuart. It was better, she concluded, to be Mademoiselle in France, with her huge income, free to come and go as she pleased, happy to be her own mistress.

Turenne responded sarcastically. The king was still the king, and Mademoiselle, for all her wealth and rank, was his subject. When he was not freely obeyed, he could punish with exile, house arrest, or confinement to a convent. In the end, after useless suffering, one obeyed. Mademoiselle was not intimidated, warning that "people like you don't threaten people like me." Having come to the edge, the two now retreated behind insincere compliments, while Mademoiselle made a final plea that Turenne drop the idea.[41] For all her bravado, Mademoiselle realized that Turenne was unlikely to have approached her in the first place, to say nothing of threatening her with royal displeasure, without some involvement by the king. Rather than embarrass Louis with a direct inquiry, Mademoiselle tried to determine through her friends the Navailles whether the proposal originated with the king. Mademoiselle's instincts were right. Louis wanted to help the Portuguese while avoiding an open breach with his Spanish father-in-law, and Turenne had been assigned a key role in the implementation of this policy. The Navailles brought Mademoiselle the reply that Turenne was not acting on his own initiative, but that the king was not yet ready to speak to Mademoiselle about the matter.[42]

Mademoiselle wrote to the king, reminding him that she was still hopeful of an establishment and assuring the king of her wish to be of service to him through a suitable match. She entrusted the letter to the king's first gentleman of the bedchamber, the duc de Saint-Aignan, after telling him the story of Turenne's approach. Saint-Aignan delivered the letter and reported back to Mademoiselle that the king had read it but had decided not to reply; Saint-Aignan advised her not to pursue the subject.[43]

Although neither Turenne nor the Navailles raised the matter again, Mademoiselle soon noticed a coolness in the king's manner. Fearing that she had offended him, she approached Anne of Austria, hoping for a sympathetic hearing, since the Spanish-born Anne might be assumed to be hostile to the Portuguese alliance. But Anne was evasive, saying only that if the king wanted the Portuguese marriage, it was a pity, but the king was the master, and she could not interfere.[44] Mademoiselle had already committed one false step in not taking the strong hint from the Navailles that Turenne was not acting without authorization. Now she committed two other faults in Louis's eyes. The first was to propose an alternative match. Learning that Béziers was about to accept an appointment by Louis as ambassador to Venice, Mademoiselle approached the king with a suggestion. Since Béziers would pass near Turin on the way to Venice, he could stop there to negotiate her marriage with the duke of Savoy. Louis asked her pointedly how she knew about Béziers's appointment and travel plans. To the reply that everyone at court was talking about it, Louis simply answered, "You are mistaken." He continued, in a cold, dry voice: "I will think about you when it is convenient for me, and I will marry you off where it will be of use to me."[45]

Mademoiselle's second mistake in judgment only became evident some weeks later, when she was at Forges to take her seasonal cure. She received a note from Saint-Aignan, returning to her a letter which she had written to her half brother, the comte de Charny, which had fallen into French hands. Charny had taken service in the Spanish army at the time of the Peace of the Pyrenees and was now serving against the Portuguese. In the letter, Mademoiselle expressed the wish that Charny would win a great battle against the Portuguese and see the rebel king hanged, even though, she added, Alfonso's sister, Catherine de Braganza, had recently entered Mademoiselle's cousinage as the wife of Charles II.[46]

Although Mademoiselle makes light of the episode in her *Mémoires*, treating the letter as an extended joke, she had certainly committed a singular indiscretion, particularly since the letter was written after Turenne's initial approach.[47] The text of Mademoiselle's letter does not survive, but it is probable that Mademoiselle made some allusion in it to Turenne's proposal that she marry the Portuguese king. Louis cannot have been expected to appreciate the humor. Hoping to stave off embarrassing questions from the Spanish court, he instructed his envoy in Spain to treat the whole episode as an idle fantasy on the part of the princess. Moreover, partly as a result of Mademoiselle's soundings, many people were aware of Turenne's initiative and its true origin. In Louis's eyes, Mademoiselle had now gone beyond a refusal to defiance and mockery and had managed to create a diplomatic incident in the process.[48]

The royal response was not slow to arrive. From Forges, Mademoiselle had gone to visit the château and county of Eu, which she had recently purchased from the Guises. In October, just before her return to Paris, the marquis de Gesvres, captain of the king's guards, was announced. He told Mademoiselle that the king wished her to go to Saint-Fargeau and stay there until further notice. Mademoiselle protested that she had done nothing to deserve banishment, and blamed the order on Turenne, who had threatened her with exile the previous wint⎵ ⎵⎵vres declined to convey such a message to the king and took his leave.[49]

Mademoiselle prepared to counterattack. When another nobleman arrived with a letter from Turenne, she wrote back, scornfully calling him a "man of his word" and telling him how proud she was of his behavior. Nor was she silent thereafter, notifying her friends that she had been exiled at Turenne's initiative for refusing the Portuguese marriage. She also wrote to the king, Anne of Austria, and Philippe d'Orléans protesting her treatment. None deigned to reply, although Anne let it be known that the king was furious with his cousin. Mademoiselle insisted that she was not troubled by the silence and had a "clean conscience."[50]

Mademoiselle arrived at Saint-Fargeau in November 1662. During the winter months of 1662–63, Turenne used several intermediaries to pursue the matter with Mademoiselle, hoping that exile might soften her attitude. But Mademoiselle would not be moved. Instead, she took advantage of Louis's refusal to speak directly to her about the Portuguese marriage, keeping up the pretense that Turenne's proposals were "private" rather than official and heaping scorn on the maréchal for his bullying tactics. She insisted that she did not know the reason for her banishment and repeatedly demanded an explanation from the king. She also warned that this inexplicable punishment would never work: her removal from the court only made her give some thought to a voluntary, permanent retirement from public life.[51]

To justify her refusal to her readers, Mademoiselle recounts conversations at Saint-Fargeau with an emissary of Turenne, an acquaintance named La Richardière, recently returned from Portugal, and, in an obvious literary fiction, with an unnamed "wandering monk" staying temporarily in the vicinity who, by a happy coincidence, had also just returned from Portugal. The picture was hardly encouraging: Alfonso was partially paralyzed, mentally defective, and given to bouts of rage and to impulsive violence. Turenne's own envoy depicted Alfonso as "malicious, ignorant . . . debauched; cruel and taking pleasure in killing."[52] La Richardière added that the rumor of a marriage between Mademoiselle and Alfonso had caused great rejoicing among the French troops in Portugal. The Portuguese, he told her, disliked the French almost as much as they did their Spanish enemies and resident Frenchmen lived in constant fear of assassination at the hands of their allies. Mademoiselle's marriage would bring them a protector.[53]

Mademoiselle wrote Turenne that his envoy had been no more persuasive than his master. She was firm in her resolution not to marry the Portuguese king and concluded with regrets that she could assure Turenne only of her continued esteem, not her friendship. Through another acquaintance she sent an even stronger message, telling Turenne that his tenacious pursuit of the proposal had "mortally" offended her.[54]

Roger de Bussy-Rabutin, a good friend and regular correspondent of the princess, has left an account that confirms Mademoiselle's anger and revulsion. Bussy-Rabutin stopped at Saint-Fargeau for a short visit in the spring of 1663. Mademoiselle complained bitterly of Turenne's behavior and voiced her fear that she would be compelled to sell her estates to finance the Portuguese struggle. She could well imagine herself returning in defeat as a "poor princess without a kingdom or fortune." She also discussed Alfonso's personal defects and asked Bussy-Rabutin laughingly if "it was decent [honnête] to refuse a husband because he was disabled." Bussy thought so, as, no doubt, did many of her other friends.[55]

In the winter of 1662–63, Mademoiselle was stricken with a severe respiratory illness. Although she had survived her first exile at Saint-Fargeau without any health problems, she blamed this lingering malady on the climate at Saint-Fargeau. The snow and rain of winter had replenished the ponds and streams that bordered the château and left the grounds damp and swampy. She wrote to the king to describe her physical deterioration and to ask for permission to move to Eu. Otherwise, she feared she would never recover, and protested that she "had done nothing to deserve such a death."[56] Louis sent word through Turenne that she could move to Eu but that his clemency was intended to remind her of her duty in the matter of Portugal. To drive the point home, Turenne sent her a portrait of Alfonso as an adolescent, which Mademoiselle dismissed as bearing little resemblance to the original.[57]

Mademoiselle took advantage of this permission to relocate immediately to her vast domain of Eu. Eu had been one of the major possessions of the Guise family, but the Guises, laboring under the debts of several generations, were badly in need of money. In 1657, shortly after her return from her first exile, Mademoiselle had contracted with the guardians of her future brother-in-law to purchase the property, although the sale was not consummated until 1660, when the princess paid her Guise relatives 2.5 million livres for the estate.

Eu was a property very much to Mademoiselle's taste. The county of Eu was one of the most senior lay peerages in the kingdom; its possession gave Mademoiselle one more grand title to add to her long list, and also made her one of the great landladies of Normandy. Its acquisition was also a financial coup, increasing her revenues by more than 100,000 livres per annum. While rents, feudal dues, and purchased regalian rights provided substantial income, more than half of the revenues derived from extensive commercial woodlands, about 14,000 acres in all, divided into a number of separate parcels. The district from Le Tréport to Aumale, which followed the bank of the Bresle, was home to a flourishing commercial glassware industry that made good use of Mademoiselle's wood, and the princess took care to obtain royal confirmation of her right to authorize the establishment of additional glassworks.

The château also had many historical associations that intrigued Mademoiselle. Some of the buildings dated back to the medieval counts, who had belonged to a branch of the royal family; the rest had been constructed by the greatest of the Guises, Henri-le-Balafré, the rival of Mademoiselle's grandfather Henri IV. The modern part of the château, however, had never been finished, and the grounds were not to Mademoiselle's satisfaction. As at Saint-Fargeau, Mademoiselle used her time in exile to embark on a program of restoration and construction, which seems to have been substantially completed by about 1670. The interior of the château was modernized, with a suite for Mademoiselle's use, a number of apartments to accommodate visitors, and a portrait gallery dedicated to members of the Guise family. The buildings were repaired and enlarged, with Mademoiselle's monogram carved in the stone and woodwork. Mademoiselle also had two buildings constructed: a small house for her pages, and a pavilion overlooking the bay at Le Tréport called the *Pavillon de Mademoiselle*.[58]

Unlike Saint-Fargeau, Eu was not far off the beaten track. In the late spring and summer months, many of Mademoiselle's friends from court were nearby at Forges. There were also a number of noble families with estates in the area, as well as dignitaries such as the duc de Longueville, governor of the province, and the duc de Navailles, governor of Le Havre, within visiting distance.[59] Although Mademoiselle wrote to Bussy-Rabutin in November 1663 that Eu was a "desert" in the winter, thanks to the poor roads and the wind and rain, she later recalled that the winter of 1663–64 was exceptionally mild.[60] Mademoiselle also discovered a number of interesting local gentry whom she welcomed, so that her "court was large." When not presiding over her assemblies, the princess passed the time reading, overseeing an army of workmen, and writing, presumably, personal and business letters that do not survive. There were also church services and visits to the local convents, and time "passed unnoticed."[61]

Mademoiselle did not lack news of the court or of the Parisian social whirl. Thanks to faithful correspondents and the availability of gazettes, she knew all the details of the Condé match with the daughter of the Princess Palatine, of the scandals surrounding the duke of Lorraine's infatuation with a servant girl, and of the deaths in close succession of her aunt the dower duchess of Savoy and of her sister the young duchess.[62]

In spite of local diversions, by the spring of 1664 Mademoiselle had grown weary of her routine. She sensed that the Portuguese proposal was no longer quite so important to the king and that the time had come to attempt an accommodation with the court. She had had no communication with Louis since the beginning of her exile, except for the permission to move from Saint-Fargeau to Eu. Mademoiselle accepted that she would have to take the first step.[63] When she learned that the queen was pregnant, she recognized the necessary pretext. She wrote to Colbert in late March to express her joy at the news and her desire to offer her congratulations in person. In late May, Louis responded, writing that the past was forgotten, and granting her permission to return to court if she wished.[64]

Mademoiselle set out immediately for Paris. The recent death of her uncle the duc de Guise gave her friends a reason to call at the Luxembourg and set the stage for a surprising reconciliation with Madame de Fiesque.[65] The princess continued on to Fontainebleau to join the court. Her welcome was civil if not effusive. Turenne attempted a rapprochement, but Mademoiselle rejected his overtures and snubbed him publicly.[66] She also took the time to tell Condé exactly what she thought of his son's marriage to the daughter of Anne de Gonzague.[67] Having thus defied France's most distinguished soldiers, Mademoiselle moved directly against the centers of power. After a few days, she felt bold enough to ask Anne of Austria and then the king for an explanation of her disgrace, wanting to know if Turenne had misrepresented her position on the Portuguese marriage. She received the same answer from mother and son: it was better to forget the past and not speak any more about it.[68] The first time she dined with the king, however, she refused to admit to any boredom during her exile.[69] To prove her point, she left after a few days to return to Eu and the Norman countryside.[70]

Louis's unexplained change of heart may have had a great deal to do with the sudden death of Mademoiselle's sister, the duchess of Savoy, in January 1664. The duke would need a new consort, and there were already rumors that Mademoiselle would be the next duchess.[71] While at Fontainebleau, Mademoiselle expressed a strong interest in succeeding her sister, and Louis promised Mademoiselle that he would do what he could. Mademoiselle could not bring herself to acknowledge the sequel: in spite of intense diplomatic activity on her behalf, Charles-Emmanuel was no longer interested in the richest woman in France. Instead, in May 1665, he married a distant cousin, Marie-Jeanne-Baptiste de Savoie, daughter of that duc de Nemours killed by Beaufort in 1652 and of Beaufort's sister Elisabeth de Vendôme.[72] Through her mother, the bride was the great-granddaughter of Henri IV, though not of equivalent rank to Mademoiselle. Louis's need to find another bride for Charles-Emmanuel with ties to the French royal house was thereby satisfied without Mademoiselle's help. Ironically, the bride's younger sister, Marie-Françoise-Elisabeth, was to solve Louis's Portuguese problem by agreeing to marry Alfonso in 1666.

Mademoiselle did not rejoice in the good fortune of her cousins of Savoie-Nemours. To begin with, she did not see any charm or beauty in either sister.[73] The Savoy marriage was beneath Charles-Emmanuel, because his predecessors for generations had married daughters of kings.[74] As for the younger sister, who, "carried away with joy at being a queen," had taken Mademoiselle's place as Alfonso's consort, Mademoiselle could not resist recording the sequel. A year or two later, the new queen was calling her husband "a drunk, and a brute who killed in cold blood." She conspired with her husband's brother to overthrow Alfonso, annul her marriage, and marry his brother, who assumed the crown as Peter II. The second husband turned out to be not much better, but because "there wasn't a third brother and she has had children, she will probably stay with this one."[75]

For the moment, Mademoiselle settled back into a routine of attendance at court broken by trips to Eu and Forges, where, as at the Luxembourg, she could preside over her own assemblies. For Mademoiselle, these middle years of the decade were defined by the failing health of the queen mother. In May 1664, Anne of Austria, who had been ill most of the previous year, began complaining of breast pains. The diagnosis of the royal physicians was breast cancer. The treatments were more than useless. Anne survived for another eighteen months, enduring the attentions of her doctors and bearing her suffering with courage.

Mademoiselle heard of Anne's illness in the summer of 1664, while she was staying at Eu, and directly from Anne some months later.[76] In November, during a brief stay in Paris, Mademoiselle called on Anne. One topic of discussion was the appearance of a comet over the skies of Paris, a traditional herald of disaster. The old queen, who was visibly failing, remarked sadly that the comet's message was intended for her, reducing Mademoiselle to tears.[77] In August 1665, the queen mother appeared to be near death, and Mademoiselle cut short her stay at Forges to rush back to Paris. But Anne of Austria rallied for the last time: the crisis passed, and Mademoiselle resumed her Norman holiday.[78] In September, when the princess saw her aunt again, it was evident that the disease had gained the upper hand.[79]

The final episode of Anne of Austria's life unfolded in January 1666. There are two detailed accounts of the queen's death that have long been used by historians, the first by Madame de Motteville and the second by Mademoiselle. Motteville's account, an exercise in hagiography, focuses on the queen's piety and Christian resignation. Mademoiselle offers a far more human account of the event, with attention to the actions and reactions of the king and other members of the family.

It was customary to expose the relics of Saint Geneviève, the patron of Paris, when a member of the royal family was in extremis. Louis approved of this action, although he agreed with Mademoiselle's warning that "miracles didn't happen every day" and "we no longer lived in a time when they did happen."[80] Mademoiselle was present at the procession of the relics before going to the Louvre to attend the dying woman. Once there, she had a word with one of Condé's surgeons, whom she trusted. His diagnosis was blunt: "She's a dead woman."[81]

Mademoiselle's skepticism about miracles should not be interpreted to mean doubts about her faith. On the contrary, it meant that it was time to tell Anne to prepare for death. This was Mademoiselle's advice to Louis, but the doctors warned that saying this to the queen mother directly might hasten the end. This drove Louis, barely in control of his emotions, into a fury. "What!" he said, "They would flatter her and let her die without the sacraments, after six months of sickness. I will not have this on my conscience. We have no more time for flattery."[82] Mademoiselle observed that Anne took the news like a good Christian, but fearfully, as evidenced by a change in her voice as she gave the command to summon her confessor.[83]

Before the queen mother received the last sacraments, she called members of the family to her bedside for private farewells. To Mademoiselle's surprise, neither she nor Condé was summoned. At the end, the old queen had no time for those who had troubled her regency with princely rebellion. For the ritual of extreme unction, the crystal cross and candlesticks from the chapel of the palace were brought into the queen's bedroom. Mademoiselle, who admired these pieces, was struck by the contrast between the brilliance of the crystal and the approaching darkness of death.[84]

It was now late in the day on Tuesday, January 19: the death vigil had commenced. Philippe d'Orléans stayed by the bed; the king stood back a few feet. At one moment, thinking his mother had expired, Louis fell back, "half fainting," on Mademoiselle and Mademoiselle d'Elbeuf. With Condé's help, they dragged him off to a small room nearby, and loosened his buttons to allow him to breathe. Louis remained in this cabinet, while other members of the family moved back and forth from this room to the bedroom of the dying queen. A crowd of courtiers moved in and out of the queen's room at will. Even for Mademoiselle, who had lived all of her life in public view, this lack of privacy was distasteful.[85]

At midnight, the priests began celebrating Mass in an oratory adjacent to the queen's bedroom. At five in the morning, Anne was served bouillon, which she drank "like a person in great need of nourishment."[86] At six o'clock, the bells of Notre Dame could be heard in the distance. Mademoiselle was with the king in the nearby cabinet when Philippe d'Orléans suddenly cried out. Anne was gone. As was customary, the queen's will was opened and read aloud before the company departed. Louis wept as the formalities were completed. Mademoiselle went home to sleep.[87]

For Mademoiselle, as for Louis XIV, the death of the former regent marked the end of an era. Anne of Austria had lived her life at the center of the struggles recounted earlier in Mademoiselle's *Mémoires*. With her death, the age of Richelieu and Mazarin was but a memory. The future was now entirely in the hands of a younger generation. For Louis, the last constraints on his private behavior were buried with his grief. For Mademoiselle, the old court was irretrievably gone, and a new period was opening in her life.

After recording the old queen's final trip to Saint-Denis, this second segment of Mademoiselle's *Mémoires* moves quickly toward its principal subject, her attraction to one of the king's companions, the comte de Lauzun, and the scandal caused by her failed attempt to marry him. Mademoiselle, who had insisted all her life that she abhorred "gallantry" and was not "tender-hearted," who had denounced marriage as "slavery" in her correspondence with Madame de Motteville, found herself drawn irresistibly into the great emotional event of her life.

The object of Mademoiselle's passion was a favorite courtier of Louis XIV, Antonin Nompar de Caumont, comte de Lauzun. Mademoiselle's junior by six years, Lauzun was born in 1633 at the château of the same name, which still stands, not far from the confluence of the Lot and the Garonne. The Caumonts were an old noble family of the Agenais district. Antonin's father, Gabriel de Caumont, headed the junior branch of the family; his mother, Charlotte, belonged to the senior branch, and was a granddaughter of Jacques Nompar de Caumont, duc de la Force and maréchal of France, who had escaped the Saint Bartholomew's Day Massacre (August 1572) and fought alongside Henri IV in the civil wars of the late sixteenth century.

Although well connected, the Lauzun branch was poor. Antonin, one of eight children, was a second son, destined to make his own way in the world. At the age of fourteen, he was sent to Paris to be raised in the household of his father's cousin, the maréchal duc de Gramont. Since his father was still living, Antonin made his appearance in Paris society as the marquis de Puyguilhem, a junior title in the family. During the winter months, he attended one of the fashionable academies in the city where young noblemen learned skills useful in warfare, such as applied mathematics, fencing, a smattering of languages, as well as the poise and manners expected of a nobleman. In the summer months he served in the Gramont regiment under the eyes of his patron.[88]

By the mid-1650s, Antonin had attained the rank of captain, and in 1658 became colonel of a regiment of dragoons. He had a reputation for courage under fire, and was commended by Turenne for his performance in the campaign of 1658, notably at the Battle of the Dunes (June 1658) and at the fall of Oudenarde, where, ironically, he faced the regiments of Condé and Hollac, so dear to Mademoiselle.[89] Although he had earned his reputation for bravery, it cannot have hurt that Turenne, who brought Lauzun's record to Mazarin's attention, was another family connection, married to Charlotte de Caumont (d. 1660), the first cousin of Antonin's mother.

By the time Mademoiselle returned from her first exile in 1657, Antonin had begun to make his mark on the far more treacherous battlefields of the court. Here too, his family connections served him well. His Gramont cousins were members of the king's entourage, and Lauzun's cultivation of Mazarin's nieces, the Mancini sisters, brought him into proximity with the king at play. Mademoiselle and Antonin crossed paths briefly during the carnival season of 1659. One evening, Mademoiselle, two ladies of the court, and the king's brother, Philippe, attended a masquerade dressed as peasant girls from the Bresse. The "shepherds" who escorted them included the comte de Guiche, son of the maréchal de Gramont and a favorite of Philippe's, and Guiche's cousin Puyguilhem.[90]

Throughout the 1660s, Antonin belonged to the small group of courtiers who surrounded Louis XIV in his pursuit of private pleasures. He also acquired a reputation of his own as a ladies' man, his name linked with some of the same women found on Louis XIV's long list of conquests. The attraction cannot have been physical. Judging by his portraits, his features were plain and his nose was often reddish or inflamed, possibly from some medical problem not diagnosed in the seventeenth century. His blond hair, often unkempt, was beginning to gray prematurely; not unlike Condé, he was notorious for his slovenly appearance.[91]

Antonin's attraction lay not in his person but in his personality: until the end of his very long life—he died at ninety in 1723—he was famous for his flashing wit and devastating bons mots. He would lead his prey on, demolish him or her with an unexpected sally, and withdraw from a circle of laughing spectators before the victim could recover his (or her) balance. He was the master of the practical joke and turned many a solemn ceremony into comedy by persuading a participant to commit some faux pas. Saint-Simon, who later became Lauzun's brother-in-law, recorded a number of these episodes, and bore witness to the effectiveness of Lauzun's wit and charm. Lauzun combined these qualities with others that made him less appealing: a short temper, a domineering personality, which extended to physical assaults on women, and an egotism that interfered with his extraordinary effort to be the most visible and obsequious of Louis XIV's courtiers. This was particularly evident in the pursuit of women, where he had the effrontery to undertake a rivalry with the king.

In 1664 one of Lauzun's old flames, his cousin Catherine-Charlotte de Gramont, now princess of Monaco, returned to the French court on a mission for her husband. Lauzun wished to renew his ties with his

cousin, but the princess preferred the king to the colonel. Louis suggested that Antonin inspect his regiment of dragoons, which was gar-
risoned in faraway Béarn. Lauzun refused, offered to resign his commission, and threatened never again to draw his sword in Louis's service.
The king sent him to the Bastille for six months, where, in spite of his
complaints to the contrary, he was treated well and, ironically, was a
fellow prisoner with Roger de Bussy-Rabutin, who had been sent there
for publishing his *Histoire Amoureuse des Gaules*. When Antonin reappeared at court in December 1665 with a six months' beard on his chin,
Louis laughed and readmitted him to his inner circle.[92]

Lauzun's revenge fell on Madame de Monaco: he managed to place
himself close to the princess one evening in May 1666, when she was
seated with a group of ladies on the parquet floor at Versailles. Antonin
joined this group, launched a barb at one of the company, and, while
they were distracted with laughter, turned on his heel and "accidentally"
stepped on the hand of the princess, breaking several bones and inflict-
ing severe pain. An embarrassed Louis felt obliged to treat the matter as
an accident and to accept at face value Lauzun's hypocritical expressions
of contrition.[93]

This episode did nothing to diminish his favor with Louis XIV, who
continued to be amused by his favorite's antics. Antonin may have owed
some of this tolerance to his friendship with the marquise de Montespan,
who had become the king's mistress sometime in 1667. In 1668, he was
appointed colonel-general of dragoons, a new post created especially for
him by the king. He was also promised the much more lucrative and
prestigious post of grand master of the artillery. But the announcement
did not come on the expected day. Louvois, the minister of war, had
objected, perhaps because Lauzun was aligned with Turenne and a number of other soldiers who opposed Louvois's proposed reforms of the
army. Faced with the minister's reservations, Louis postponed a decision.
Antonin turned to Montespan for support. But rather than promote his
candidature, she told the king privately that the appointment would lead
to confrontations between Louvois and the headstrong Antonin.

When he learned of this, Antonin sought Montespan out at the next
ball, listened to her falsified version of her entreaties to Louis on his
behalf, and then repeated to her the actual conversation she had had with
the king. When the king reprimanded his wayward colonel-general, Antonin defied his sovereign to his face, breaking his sword over his knee
and vowing never again to draw it in the service of a king who broke his

word. For once, he did not carry the scene. Louis replied by opening the nearest window and throwing his cane out "for fear of striking a gentleman." He then sent his rebellious officer off for a second visit to the Bastille.[94]

The sequel, as with so much in Antonin's life, reads like an episode out of a Dumas novel. The miscreant was released within a few days on the intercession, astonishingly, of Montespan herself. Instead of the post of grand master of the artillery, he was offered a commission as captain of the king's bodyguard, one of the most senior appointments in the royal household. The four captains of the guard, who served in three-month rotations, were often chosen from the *maréchaux* of France, and took their orders directly from the king. The minister of war, the detested Louvois, had no authority over them. Puyguilhem accepted, but only after an initial refusal, to drive home the importance he put on his independence.[95]

In spite of his shortcomings, Lauzun continued to enjoy the confidence of both Louis and his mistress. Shortly after assuming his new duties, Lauzun was entrusted with an extraordinary mission. On the night of March 31, 1670, Madame de Montespan gave birth in secret to a son who would later become the duc du Maine. Lauzun had the honor of smuggling the child out of the palace of Saint-Germain in the dead of night and depositing the infant at the Paris home of a confidante of Montespan's, the Widow Scarron, later Madame de Maintenon, who would serve as the governess to the royal, if yet unacknowledged, child.[96]

About the same time as he accepted his commission as captain of the guards, Antonin assumed the title "comte de Lauzun." His father had died, and his older brother, who remained at home, was willing to permit his younger brother to use the name under which he became known to history. Puyguilhem, the cadet of Gascony, had become the Lauzun of Mademoiselle's story.

When Mademoiselle sat down in 1677 to write her account of her passion for Lauzun, she overlooked her earlier mention of their encounter at the carnival in 1659. Instead, she set her initial glimpse of him at the wedding of Louis XIV at Saint-Jean-de-Luz in 1660. She remembered her surprise at seeing the king escorted by two companies of halbardiers she had never seen before, called the "crowsbeaks" (*becs à corbin*) after the shape of their weapons. These companies were activated only for the occasional ceremonial event. One was commanded by the marquis d'Humières, and the other by Puyguilhem, "a younger son of the house of

Lauzun, who have always held this post." The two commanders fell into an argument, which Puyguilhem won, carrying himself with an assurance that promised he was "not destined, evidently, for small matters."[97]

Mademoiselle committed a number of chronological errors in her hasty account of Lauzun's deeds in these early years. For example, she puts his first imprisonment in the Bastille in 1662, three years too soon, but uses the event as a springboard to discuss his standing with the women of the court. "He was the handsomest and best-made man at court, with the grandest bearing. All of the women wanted him, and he was not cruel to them." She added that he had a reputation as a man of "merit," a point supposedly conceded even by his enemies.[98]

In June 1662, Mademoiselle joined thousands of her fellow Parisians to witness a stylized equestrian parade, or carousel, held in front of the Tuileries in honor of the birth of a dauphin to Louis XIV and Maria Theresa. The participants were organized into five squads, each representing a different mythical group. The king, dressed as "emperor of the Romans," led the first; his brother, Philippe, was "king of the Persians," and Condé, "emperor of the Turks." Among the Turks of the day was Puyguilhem. Mademoiselle remembered him bearing a shield decorated with a rocket rising toward the clouds with a motto in Spanish or Italian meaning "Everything to the highest degree." Mademoiselle added that she had the meaning of the device and motto explained more than once. In fact, she was mistaken. His shield bore a sunflower turned toward the sun (and the Sun King) with the motto "Do not despise the one who loves you."[99]

Mademoiselle's second exile (1662–64) precluded any further development in this relationship, and the following years were equally barren. In June 1666, Louis held a grand review of his household troops at Moret. Lauzun, always ready to put his best foot forward, showed off his dragoons to good effect and had the honor of receiving the king in his own regimental tents, which were magnificently appointed for the occasion. Mademoiselle, away at Forges, read about this in the *Gazette*, with more details provided by friends at court.[100] But the relationship was still casual: "I held M. de Puyguilhem in high esteem; he pleased me. I found him good company, but I had no ordinary ties with him."[101]

The campaign of 1667 in Flanders gave Mademoiselle the opportunity to see her Gascon colonel perform heroically under fire. For her readers, she offers an image of Lauzun as a valiant and brilliant soldier, the envy of lesser men, but protected from harm by the king's esteem and gratitude for his services.[102] Given Lauzun's prominence in the king's entourage, Mademoiselle and Lauzun must have crossed paths frequently, if casually, with many opportunities for banter, but Mademoiselle's *Mémoires* sets her first exchange of words with Lauzun in 1669. After a long account of Lauzun's quarrel with Louvois and his failure to obtain the grand mastership of the artillery, Mademoiselle notes that Lauzun took up his duties as captain of the king's guard with great aplomb. When Mademoiselle congratulated him on his new distinction, Lauzun thanked her and added that since she had begun speaking with him, he had had good luck. This was Mademoiselle's cue: from that time, they spoke frequently. Mademoiselle found his conversation "extraordinary" and very much to her liking.[103]

The two began to be more aware of one another, and Mademoiselle was pleased that Lauzun distinguished himself at a grand function at Versailles in honor of Cosimo de Medici, Mademoiselle's brother-in-law.[104] After the Medici prince left Paris, as Mademoiselle was preparing to depart for Eu, Lauzun called on her to offer his services for any dealings she might have with the court. He said that he sensed she had confidence in him and this pleased him. Apparently, Mademoiselle was also pleased. When she returned to Paris in December, she sought Lauzun out frequently for more of the conversation that she found so intriguing.[105]

Although Mademoiselle's sentiments are evident, we do not know Lauzun's first reactions to these overtures by the king's aging spinster cousin. Mademoiselle cannot have been physically attractive to him. Her portraits suggest that she had grown heavier in her features as the years advanced. Her nose had taken on the characteristic Bourbon prominence, and her complexion had never recovered from the bout of smallpox she had suffered many years earlier. Mademoiselle's dislike of gallantry was well known at court, as evidenced by the absence of the slightest rumor of any love affair. Her old friend the duchess de Nemours is supposed to have remarked that Mademoiselle did not believe that she should have a "joyful heart" outside of marriage.[106] Apart from Mademoiselle's own temperament, which made a simple seduction unthinkable, there were other considerations for a shrewd courtier such as Lauzun. Any liaison with an unmarried princess of the blood, and the resulting scandal, would have ended his career, if not more. Given his

ambitions and evident vanity, his initial impulse was probably oppor-
tunistic: to use the infatuation of the princess as a way of furthering his
career, even if he could not be sure how to employ her good offices.

Mademoiselle dated her determination to marry Lauzun to the winter of 1670. She was, she wrote, tired of her solitary state and wanted
to marry. Upon reflection, she concluded that someone had to be the
source of this inspiration: "I looked around, I thought about it, and
I could not determine who it was. Finally, after several troubled days, I
realized it was Lauzun who had slipped into my heart and whom I
loved . . . all I needed for my happiness was to have a husband like him,
whom I would love dearly and who would love me; once in a lifetime, it
was essential to know the joy of being loved by someone worth loving."[107]

She realized how important her casual encounters with Lauzun had
become and how bored she was on the days when their paths did not
cross. From his behavior toward her, she was convinced that his feelings
were the same, even if he did not dare to show it.[108]

As evidenced by her attempt to chronicle her interaction with Lauzun
over the preceding decade, Mademoiselle refused to concede the suddenness of her passion. Instead, she preferred the image of a predestination
made manifest over time and ultimately irresistible. Calling Corneille to
her aid, she quoted from his *Suite du Menteur* (IV, i):

> Quand les ordres du ciel nous ont fait l'un pour l'autre,
> Lise, c'est un accord bientôt fait que le nôtre.
> Sa main entre les coeurs, par un secret pouvoir
> Sème l'intelligence avant que de se voir.[109]

Loosely:

> When Heaven has decreed us made for one another,
> Lisa, it doesn't take us long to agree.
> Its mysterious power plants the seeds of communion
> In our hearts even before we meet.

The poetry expressed her conviction that God sometimes preor-
dained marriages. A novena in late winter gave Mademoiselle an occasion for fervent prayer. When she rose from her knees, she was sure that
God had "inspired me to act."[110]

Mademoiselle had need of both poetry and religion. In her fantasies,
she constructed a plan for Lauzun's "elevation." She imagined his grati-

tude and enduring affection, as well as the fury of her heirs, cheated out of an inheritance they did not deserve.[111]

Mademoiselle's plans were in defiance of two social conventions of major significance in the seventeenth century: those of rank and gender. As a close relative of the king, such a marriage to a nobleman who was neither the head of a great family nor otherwise of exceptional distinction was virtually unimaginable and only too evidently a misalliance. As a single woman, it was unseemly to take the initiative in the selection of a husband, all the more so within a dynastic context.

In seventeenth-century France, as elsewhere in Western Europe, public authority and the social hierarchy were often viewed as analogous to, and stemming from, the patriarchal family structures of private life. Paternal authority and royal authority were mirror images: the king was father of his people, and the father was a monarch in his own household. Marriage was an important element in this model of society, since its purpose was to maintain or advance the family fortunes and validate the family position in the social hierarchy by an alliance with another family of comparable standing. The choice of mate was largely the prerogative of parents, made with little regard for the wishes of the principals. Marriages of affinity did exist, but if contracted without parental consent, they were viewed as a threat to the order of society and a defiance of legitimate authority. This was particularly so if the marriage in question was viewed as a misalliance.

In the case of Mademoiselle, the public and private spheres met in a very visible way. As a member of the royal family, the pater familias was the king himself, so any defiance of the conventions challenged both monarchical and patriarchal images of authority.[112] Mademoiselle did not dare to confide her intentions to anyone, although she was sorely tempted to speak with Philippe d'Orléans's wife, Henrietta of England, who had become a good friend and who, Mademoiselle believed, would approve. Instead, she realized, she had to proceed slowly.[113]

The nine months that followed constituted her courtship of Lauzun, recounted by Mademoiselle in loving detail. Apart from issues of propriety and rank, there was a practical problem. Privacy in the modern sense was little understood or desired in the seventeenth century. Persons of even modest station in life lived surrounded by servants. A great princess like Mademoiselle lived amid ladies in waiting, courtiers, and servants. Finding an inconspicuous way to exchange confidences with

Lauzun would be difficult, to say nothing of finding a way to convey her interest without opening herself to gossip.

An ephemeral rumor that she might marry Charles de Lorraine gave Mademoiselle a pretext to treat Lauzun as her confidant in matters matrimonial. When she expressed her reservations, Lauzun agreed. He understood her dismay at the thought of greedy heirs waiting to dismember her estate; but at her age, and given her exalted rank, a foreign marriage offered her little. It would be better to find a worthy candidate in France whom she could elevate, for she had enough wealth to "make a man equal in power and grandeur to sovereigns," and who would always be in her debt.[114] The problem, Lauzun added slyly, was finding someone worthy of the honor.[115]

Lauzun, who must have suspected Mademoiselle's intentions quite early on, never slipped out of the role of disinterested friend and counselor in the days and weeks that followed. Once, he played devil's advocate, marshaling all the arguments against a marriage; the next time he saw her, he reversed himself and provided reasons why she should marry. Somewhat cruelly, he criticized Mademoiselle for dressing as if she were still fifteen, and for passing her time at balls and banquets. This was unseemly in a single woman of forty. Given her rank, he conceded, an occasional appearance at a court function was permissible out of respect for the king. Otherwise, the only proper pastimes for the aging princess—Mademoiselle was forty-four—were prayer and good works. Unless, of course, she married: a married woman of any age could go anywhere without comment and dress up "to please her husband." So perhaps this was the solution, and he would give some thought to possible candidates. After this exchange, Mademoiselle believed that Lauzun had all but said "take me." But he dared not say it, so it was for her to carry the matter forward.[116]

In the spring of 1670, Louis XIV announced his plans for a royal progress through the Flemish lands acquired in 1668 at the Peace of Aix-la-Chapelle, an exercise that would blend the splendor of the court with a display of military might. Mademoiselle was to travel in the queen's entourage, as would the king's two mistresses, Mademoiselle de la Vallière and Madame de Montespan. Lauzun, who made the perfect parade ground soldier, was appointed to command the military escort. The preparations for this assignment kept Lauzun away from Mademoiselle for weeks on end. When they crossed paths occasionally, the presence of others kept the conversation innocuous. At Noyon, they managed to have a private moment. But when she asked him teasingly if she had to wait until the end of the expedition for his recommendation, he replied, "We must think only about the trip."[117]

Once on the road, Mademoiselle had to content herself with glimpses of her hero riding at the king's side, or issuing orders to his subordinates with an air of authority "which became him well."[118] The nearness to her intended gave wings to Mademoiselle's spirit. In spite of rainy, miserable weather, impassable roads, poor food, and squalid living conditions, even for members of the royal party, Mademoiselle was in raptures: "Everything pleased me: this trip seemed to be made for me; I thought everyone wanted only to please me, and I considered Lauzun as everyone and all the rest, with the exception of the king, nothing."[119]

From her vantage point in the king's carriage, Mademoiselle paid close attention to the interaction between the king and Lauzun. Whenever possible, Mademoiselle would call Louis's attention to Lauzun's many "achievements," and took a secret delight in Louis's compliments to Lauzun on his performance.[120] Mademoiselle believed that she did all of this without betraying her feelings about Lauzun to others. On one occasion, Lauzun stood bareheaded in a pouring rain alongside the king's carriage to receive the king's orders. Frantic that he might catch a cold, Mademoiselle interrupted several times to urge the king to command Lauzun to cover himself. "I said it so often I was afraid someone would notice."[121]

Not too long afterward, Mademoiselle and her paladin spent a wet evening together. There had been a rumor that Louis intended to offer him the hand of his fading mistress, Louise de la Vallière. This led to a monologue by Lauzun on the ideal woman. The lucky lady would have to be virtuous beyond reproach; nothing else was acceptable, even, he said slyly, "if it were you, who are above everyone else." But, replied Mademoiselle, she could pass the test. To this, Lauzun replied, "No fairy tales from the *Peau d'Ane* when we are speaking seriously."[122]

In addition to Lauzun's reticence, Mademoiselle had to contend with three alternative candidates for her hand, including one of her own making. Shortly before setting out on the Flemish expedition, Mademoiselle had hinted that she might consider a proposal from the young duc de Longueville, Condé's nephew. Mademoiselle floated the suggestion in the hope of "getting people used to" the idea of her marrying someday.[123] Although Charles-Paris de Longueville, born during the Fronde, was more than twenty years Mademoiselle's junior, the Condé clan saw Mademoiselle's millions as suitable compensation for the disparity in ages. The Longueville candidacy surfaced from time to time in those months without ever reaching the stage of a formal proposal.[124]

The second candidate was none other than her old suitor Charles II of England. In early June 1670, Charles Colbert de Croissy returned from a diplomatic mission to England. He brought with him gossip from London that Charles II had decided to repudiate his childless queen, Catherine of Braganza, and that he might replace her with Mademoiselle. Louis and Philippe d'Orléans teased her about the possibility while out for a drive in the royal carriage. To Mademoiselle's dismay, Louis asked Mademoiselle in a more serious tone if she would consider the possibility. Luckily for Mademoiselle, Maria Theresa had already expressed her outrage at the idea of repudiating Catherine, and Mademoiselle was able to pick up on this. It would violate her conscience to marry a man with a living wife shut up in a convent. Louis seemed to take this response well, although Philippe and Madame de Montespan raved on maliciously about the joys of such a match, reducing Mademoiselle to tears. She had enough presence of mind to attribute this reaction to sorrow at the thought of leaving Louis. The subject died a natural death; Charles II chose not to repudiate his wife, who was well liked in her adopted country.[125]

In the meantime, the Longueville candidacy built momentum and rumors flew at court. Mademoiselle's old friend Madame de Thianges, the sister of Madame de Montespan, actually raised the subject with the king, who seemed taken aback. Madame de Thianges reminded Louis that he had consented to the marriage of Mademoiselle's sister Elisabeth to the duc de Guise; Longueville, son of a princess of the blood, was at least as suitable a match for a granddaughter of Henri IV.[126]

Lauzun remained discreetly aloof. When Mademoiselle finally ran him to earth, he was sarcastic. Madame de Thianges, he pointed out, had good reason to champion Longueville's cause: she was his mistress. Later that evening they spoke again, and the discussion was tense. He maintained that she had lost confidence in him and that she intended to marry Longueville without asking his opinion. She replied that she intended to marry, but Longueville was not her choice. She wanted to speak with Lauzun about it the next day and would then approach the king. Lauzun thought this a good plan, saying, "I'm beginning to want all of this finished as much as you do." Mademoiselle was convinced that Lauzun refrained from declaring himself openly out of respect for her rank and a desire to leave her free to change her mind without embarrassment.[127]

The next day, Mademoiselle encountered Lauzun's sister, Madame de Nogent. She told Nogent that she intended to solicit the king's permission to marry. She confided in Nogent that her choice would not be Longueville but a worthy gentleman who, she believed, shared her feelings but dared not express them. Nogent tried to guess, but did not succeed. Mademoiselle told her that the candidate would call that evening.[128] Before Mademoiselle could take this any further, a captain of the guard appeared with the astonishing news that Henrietta Stuart was dying. Mademoiselle set off immediately for Saint-Cloud with the king and queen. While climbing into the carriage, the queen told Mademoiselle of the widespread belief that Henrietta had been poisoned. There were those who whispered that her husband, Philippe d'Orléans, and his entourage were guilty of the crime. Mademoiselle found this unbelievable: "We are good people in our family."[129]

Mademoiselle's description of Henrietta's deathbed agonies is chilling. Although the queen and her companions wept, the rest of the spectators seemed completely indifferent. Mademoiselle was astounded that Henrietta was dying without the last sacraments and without a confessor present. When she insisted that Philippe see to this, his first concern was to pick a fashionable clergyman whose assistance would make good copy for the *Gazette*. Happily for Philippe's sense of occasion, the choice fell on Bossuet, whose funeral oration would later immortalize the event. Unlike Anne of Austria, Henrietta Stuart did not part from Mademoiselle without a few private words. "You are losing a good friend. I was beginning to know you and to love you."[130] Mademoiselle could not find the strength to reply. When she took her leave, she was too overcome to approach the dying woman and said farewell from the foot of the bed.[131] Mingled with the tears for Henrietta were tears for herself. Mademoiselle realized immediately that she might very well be Henrietta's replacement. She was determined to continue down the path she had chosen, although how to do so if the king desired otherwise gave her a sleepless night.[132]

The unwanted offer came the very next day, which Mademoiselle spent at Versailles with Louis and Maria Theresa. The king, upset by Henrietta's death, had shut himself up in his room with the two ladies. After dinner, he took Mademoiselle aside and said bluntly, "There is a place vacant here. Do you want to fill it?" Mademoiselle replied that

Louis was the master. Surprised at this formal response, Louis asked if she was averse to the idea. Mademoiselle's silence was taken for consent, and Louis promised to speak to his brother.[133]

As luck would have it, Philippe's first reply was equally polite but evasive. Although he was willing to announce the engagement, he felt the wedding should be put off until the winter months for the sake of propriety. Mademoiselle suggested instead that the entire matter be deferred until the fall, after her annual excursion to Forges, and Louis agreed to this.[134]

When Mademoiselle returned to Paris some months later, she detected a change in enthusiasm on the part of both brothers. Philippe treated her with a noticeable coolness. Louis was equally offhand, joking that in spite of her protests to the contrary, she did not seem worried too much by the delay.[135] A few days later, Louis brought her Philippe's thoughts on such a marriage. Philippe was mostly interested in the material questions. In the event that the couple had no children, Monsieur insisted that Mademoiselle's entire fortune be left to his eldest daughter by Henrietta, who was to be betrothed to the dauphin. Louis had trouble keeping a straight face when Mademoiselle expressed her surprise at the idea of marrying without the intention of having children. Philippe, the king conceded, had said a number of such foolish things, which Louis had warned him would injure his reputation. The queen, who was in earshot, added a few choice remarks. As for the disposition of her fortune, Mademoiselle remarked rather pointedly that the dauphin was not a lad who would have to marry for money. Louis found this sally hilarious. Adopting a more serious tone, Louis warned Mademoiselle that he was prepared to lavish money and possessions on Philippe, but he would never offer him the governorship of any province, or, by implication, any position of real authority, even at Mademoiselle's request.

Louis then brought up the rumor that she was about to ask his permission to marry just before Henrietta's death, and wanted to know if Longueville was her choice. Mademoiselle equivocated. When the queen asserted that it could be no other, because it had to be a prince, Mademoiselle tested the waters. Alluding to her sister's marriage to the duc de Guise, she replied that she was rich enough to transform any husband of hers into a greater nobleman than Guise was, and she hoped the king, having permitted the Guise marriage, would allow her to make her own choice. The king, startled, replied that he would not force anyone into an unwanted match.[136]

As the exchange suggested, a number of considerations had caused Louis to have second thoughts about the proposed marriage to Philippe. The last year of Henrietta's life had been marred by a series of violent confrontations between Philippe and his wife. At issue was the domination of the Orléans household by a coterie of Philippe's male favorites, of whom the most prominent was Philippe de Lorraine, a junior member of that prolific family. To pacify Henrietta, who was secretly negotiating a treaty with her brother Charles II on Louis's behalf, Louis had ordered Lorraine arrested. The arrest had taken place in Philippe's presence in his own apartments at Saint-Germain. Monsieur had responded by withdrawing to the remote château of Villers-Cotterets. From there, he bombarded Louis and his ministers with violent protests over the insult to his dignity and the ill-treatment of Lorraine, who had been confined under harsh conditions at the château d'If, in the harbor of Marseilles. The uproar was enormous and was resolved with an unannounced compromise. Philippe returned to court without any public concessions by the king, while Louis freed Lorraine and allowed him to go into comfortable exile in Italy.[137]

With hindsight, we know that Philippe d'Orléans spent his life as the palest of satellites in the orbit of the Sun King. But to Louis, Philippe's actions may have conjured up memories of the clashes between Gaston and Louis XIII. Louis's assertion to Mademoiselle that he would never give Philippe the governorship of a province, which might serve as a base for launching rebellion, was thus no idle thought. It may have occurred to Louis that Mademoiselle's millions might also provide Philippe with a dangerous amount of independence.[138] So Louis's remarks to Mademoiselle may have been intended to signal his own reservations and to provide Mademoiselle with a pretext to decline an offer for which she clearly had little enthusiasm.

Apart from her determination to marry Lauzun, the arrest of Philippe de Lorraine brought into focus another good reason for Mademoiselle to dislike the idea of a union with Philippe: the problem of Philippe's entourage. Mademoiselle was well aware of her cousin's attraction to men, and Philippe's orientation in itself was not an issue. The issue was the same one that had troubled Henrietta of England: the prominence of a coterie of favorites who had used Monsieur's inclinations to gain control of his household and dominate his affairs. She had witnessed the violent quarrels between Henrietta and Philippe after Lorraine's arrest and had tried to warn Philippe of the damage to his reputation that these scenes had caused.[139] Shortly after the rambling discussion with Louis and Maria Theresa recounted above, Mademoiselle was approached by one of Monsieur's entourage, the chevalier de Beuvron, who told her that he and the exiled chevalier de Lorraine approved of her proposed marriage to Philippe, and assumed she would be suitably—and tangibly—grateful for their endorsement. Mademoiselle reported these remarks to the king, who pronounced the man a "fool" and regretted that Philippe surrounded himself with such people.[140]

It was now mid-October, and Mademoiselle was convinced that the king had serious reservations about the marriage. Shortly after the exchange with Beuvron, she told Louis that she had decided against the marriage. "I would not be happy for a thousand reasons that Your Majesty knows; so I beg you not to talk about it any more." She added that she and Philippe would always get along well as cousins, but it was best to leave matters where they were. When the king, feigning surprise, asked if he should tell Philippe that she had decided never to marry, she corrected him: "No, Sire, but I do not want to marry him." Louis, she noted, did not seem upset, although Philippe, who may have wanted the marriage for all the reasons that did not appeal to the king or to Mademoiselle, was angry at the snub.[141]

Mademoiselle's household officials, in particular Guilloire and Segrais, were relieved at this outcome. Guilloire had feared that the integration of Mademoiselle's staff with Philippe's would diminish his authority, and Segrais was a strong partisan of a marriage between Mademoiselle and Longueville. Segrais, with the help of well-placed seconds, had alternated warnings about the horrors of the Orléans household with praise for the young Longueville. Mademoiselle was diverted by the effort. "I listened to them and said nothing. I laughed to myself as I watched them take so much trouble for nothing."[142]

Mademoiselle might have used her time more profitably if she had reflected on Lauzun's behavior after the death of Madame. Like the rest of the court, he was caught off guard by the suddenness of Henrietta's death. In speaking to Mademoiselle, he was able to hide behind his role of disinterested adviser. This gave his remarks an ambiguity that Mademoiselle chose to interpret in the way most appealing to her. Thus, their first exchange after the death of Henrietta was a brief remark by Lauzun, "I'm afraid this will ruin all our plans," and Mademoiselle's reply, "No, no matter what happens," a promise that Mademoiselle repeated at the next opportunity.[143] Lauzun heard of the proposal for a match between the princess and Philippe within hours of Louis's first words to Mademoiselle on the subject. Seeking her out, he congratulated her and asked to remain her friend. "I would be very pleased, since I prefer your greatness to my joy and good fortune; I owe you too much to have any other feelings." Mademoiselle was touched: "He had never said so much to me."[144]

To Mademoiselle, this exchange had revealed Lauzun's true feelings. When he encouraged her later the same day to marry Monsieur, she believed he was unselfishly putting her interests ahead of his inclinations. Mademoiselle insisted that she knew where her happiness lay, and it was not with Monsieur. Lauzun persisted, urging her to take her place as the new second lady of the realm. Every time she passed in state, he would rejoice, remembering their many talks about finding her a proper establishment. Mademoiselle thought she detected a forced cheerfulness in these remarks, and went back to her rooms for a good cry.[145]

In their next conversation, Mademoiselle ridiculed the "advantages" she would gain by exchanging her role of Mademoiselle for that of Madame: it came down to a better seat in the king's carriage. On the personal side, she refused to submit to the rule of the chevalier de Lorraine or any other of Monsieur's favorites. "I want to be happy, and I am convinced I won't be with Monsieur." Lauzun then asked Mademoiselle not to speak with him any more. He feared that if the marriage with Philippe fell through, the prince would blame him for the failure. Mademoiselle, reduced again to weeping, saw Lauzun's request as another proof of Lauzun's affection, a lover's noble sacrifice of his own happiness for the benefit of his beloved.[146] To a third party, the exchange reveals Lauzun's good instincts at avoiding even the suggestion of a rivalry with the king's brother. If Mademoiselle married Philippe, no one would suspect his game. If Mademoiselle managed to avoid the match, his involvement would not be evident.

All of these discussions took place within a few days of Henrietta's death. Mademoiselle, as indicated earlier, retreated to Forges to gain time, and then came back to court in the fall to put an end to the proposal. Upon her return, Lauzun kept his distance while she attempted to verify a change of heart by Louis XIV. There were a few hurried and ambiguous words on the way to church, otherwise silence.[147] One day at Chambord, the two crossed paths while Mademoiselle was chatting with Mesdames de Montespan and de la Vallière. Mademoiselle asked Lauzun to adjust a ribbon on her sleeve, but he refused, claiming to be too clumsy with his hands.[148] Even after the match with Philippe d'Orléans was dropped, Lauzun continued to avoid her. Monsieur, in a pique at his rejection, was blaming it on unnamed "friends of Mademoiselle" who were not friends of his. Lauzun wanted to be sure that this did not mean him.[149]

In late November, Mademoiselle caught up with Lauzun at Versailles. She wished to return to her earlier idea of selecting a match by herself, and she was ready to announce her decision. He stopped her, saying that if she named someone he did not find suitable, their friendship would be at an end. After a few more teasing conversations of this sort, the princess gave Lauzun a sealed paper with the name of her choice written on it. Lauzun was to open it privately and return it to her with his comments. On it, the princess had written, "It's you."[150] The next time the two spoke, Lauzun accused her of making fun of him. "I'm not stupid enough to take it seriously." He followed this with a letter accusing her of abusing his friendship. But then he suggested that if she was sincere he just might be amenable to the proposal.[151]

Mademoiselle made use of Lauzun's sister Madame de Nogent to re-peat her intention. One evening shortly after her exchange with Lauzun, she and Nogent passed an evening together in Mademoiselle's rooms. The princess handed Nogent a paper with three names on it—Philippe d'Orléans, Longueville, and Lauzun—and asked her to guess which of the three she intended to marry. Nogent replied by flinging herself at Mademoiselle's knees.[152]

This melodramatic episode may have convinced Lauzun beyond any shadow of a doubt, and he probably discussed Mademoiselle's proposi-tion with a few close friends. When Mademoiselle took a stroll in the gardens at Versailles a day or so later, the duc de Luxembourg joked with her that she was well enough heeled "to make the fortune of a younger son of good family." He added that as a member of the Montmorency family, which ranked as the most senior of the nobility of France, he could only welcome a match between a princess of the blood and a French nobleman. Even more directly, the marquis de Dangeau teased her about her evident pleasure in Lauzun's company.[153]

Finally, at Mademoiselle's insistence, she and Lauzun reviewed all the reasons why she had chosen him. Most importantly, she held him in high esteem, and it was easy, she argued, to move from esteem to love. Lauzun played devil's advocate, refusing to take her offer seriously but willing to humor her. He raised the obvious objections, starting with rank. She would be marrying a "servant" (*domestique*) of her cousin the king, and his status would not change, because he would not give up his post as captain of the guard. The princess found this admirable: Louis was her master as well, and she saw Lauzun's service as an honor. Arguably this was the case, but there was another more intractable question about rank. Lauzun was a nobleman of good family, but not a prince: the disparity of their positions in society was too great. To this, Mademoiselle replied that she was rich enough to make him the greatest nobleman of the kingdom. Lauzun passed to other matters, in no particular order. He expected to spend much of his time waiting on the king, so a wife would not see much of him. He was satisfied with his current position and had no ambition for high office. He doubted, for example, that he would accept a governorship if offered one by the king. He was also temperamental and often retreated to his room for long hours of solitude. Mademoiselle found none of this objectionable. They passed to physical attributes. Mademoiselle considered his person perfectly acceptable. For herself, she knew her teeth were bad; this was a "defect of the breed" (*un défaut de race*), but a breed "better than most." Lauzun was suitably diplomatic on this subject. He kept insisting that her proposal was all a fantasy: "The more you talk about it the less I believe." This conversation took place while they strolled along a gallery at Versailles, out of range of Mademoiselle's ladies—and of any fireplaces—and they broke off the discussion when it grew too cold to continue.

Lauzun returned a few hours later to say that there were times when he believed her and gave way to joy, but he kept telling himself it was all an illusion. Discussions of this type continued for the next few days. Among the fantasies Lauzun now found appealing was the stray thought that he might accept a governorship, or even ask for it, if it would please her. She began to tell him about her many estates, especially Eu, where she hoped to welcome him. He thought he could manage this: a troop under his command was stationed at Gisors, not too far away from Eu, and he owed it a visit. He could thus blend the king's service with Mademoiselle's invitation. These ambiguous remarks were the closest to a positive reply that Mademoiselle could get from Lauzun.[154]

The court returned to Paris for the Christmas season. From this point on, Lauzun and Mademoiselle spent many hours debating the best way to secure the king's consent to their union. Lauzun finally yielded to Mademoiselle's wishes in early December.[155] He approved the text of a letter that Mademoiselle entrusted to Bontemps, the king's very discreet valet. In it, Mademoiselle told the king of her desire to marry and of her choice of Lauzun, whose devotion to the king's service was especially appealing to her. She then apologized for her earlier objections to her sister Elisabeth's marriage to Guise as a misalliance, assured the king that she had thought about her proposal for a long time, and asked the king, "as the greatest favor he could ever grant her," to allow her to marry Lauzun.[156]

Louis's reply was brief, and noncommittal. He expressed his surprise at Mademoiselle's request, asked her not to be hasty, and to think well on the matter. He added that he would not stop her and assured her of his affections.[157] Mademoiselle was upset that Louis had not given his outright consent, but Lauzun took another tack. She was doing something she shouldn't, and the king was asking her to think hard about it. Lauzun thought this was "admirable" and for good measure asked Mademoiselle not to be seen too often with him.[158]

Except for Lauzun's sister, Madame de Nogent, no one else was supposed to be in on the secret. In the meantime, the two continued their normal routines at court. Lauzun was with the king on many occasions, but neither ever mentioned the letter. For her part, Mademoiselle continued to welcome Longueville to her receptions as a means of concealing her intentions. Much of this deception may have been intended for her own staff, whom she no longer trusted. She also made endless appearances at the queen's apartments, where Lauzun was often to be found and where they could exchange a few inconspicuous words.[159]

Matters came to a head on December 8. Lauzun heard that Guilloire had somehow learned of their plans and had gone to Louvois to ask if the king had consented to the engagement. Mademoiselle wanted to dismiss Guilloire on the spot, but Lauzun had no time to waste on a squabble with servants. It was essential to see the king immediately and get his permission before Louvois could act. Always hedging his bets, he told Mademoiselle to see the king and withdraw her proposal. Mademoiselle was willing to see Louis, but rejected the rest of this insincere suggestion. Lauzun's parting advice was to "speak what is in your heart."[160]

Mademoiselle went to the Tuileries to wait in the queen's apartments for the king to return from a night at the gaming table. The astonished Louis found her there at two in the morning. In spite of his fatigue, he drew her aside so they could speak privately. Mademoiselle spoke rapidly, blurting out that she had come to secure the king's consent to her marriage with Lauzun. Turning the usual arguments upside down,

Mademoiselle insisted that she saw more honor in marrying the king's subject than in marrying a foreign prince, particularly when her choice was a man such as Lauzun. She insisted that Louis would be praised for elevating Lauzun and for giving her "joy and peace in my life." She renounced her earlier ideas on misalliances: "I would never have believed in such a thing earlier, but everything changes." The only harm done in the whole business was to her false pride.[161]

Louis could not resist reminding Mademoiselle that at the time of her sister Elisabeth's marriage to the duc de Guise she had objected to the match as beneath the dignity of the royal family. But he then drew the logical political conclusion that, having permitted the marriage with Guise, who, as a member of the Lorraine family, was considered a "foreign prince," he could not forbid Mademoiselle to marry one of his own noblemen without offending the high aristocracy of France. Still, Louis was uneasy about Mademoiselle's choice. Lauzun was almost too much a favorite at court, and people might see the king's hand in the match. But, he conceded, "you are old enough to know what is good for you." He concluded, rather grandly: "I do not advise you to do this; I do not forbid you to do it; but I ask you to think hard about it. No one knows about this, but many people suspect something. The ministers have spoken to me of it. There are many people who don't like Lauzun. So take your precautions."[162]

No one overheard this conversation, but several days later, Louise de la Vallière congratulated Madame de Nogent on her brother's good fortune. Both Lauzun and Mademoiselle interpreted these remarks as evidence of the king's consent.[163] The proposal and the king's apparent consent were still secret, known only to a handful of people. There were now two possible ways to proceed: either to marry immediately and announce it afterward, or to announce the betrothal and hold a grand wedding. Lauzun chose this second course of action, persuaded at last that the king and Madame de Montespan were in favor of the match.[164]

Apparently he interpreted the king's comments to Mademoiselle as an indication that Louis saw the marriage as a way to flatter the high nobility of the kingdom. With this in mind, Lauzun asked four of his close friends, the ducs de Montausier and Créqui, the maréchal d'Albret, and the marquis de Guitry, to seek an audience with the king and solicit the king's consent. This delegation was drawn from the cream of the French aristocracy, and the symbolism would be evident to the denizens of the court.[165]

The date chosen was Monday, December 15. The king received Lauzun's emissaries in his council room, with his brother, Philippe, also present. Wanting to be nearby, Mademoiselle paid a visit to the queen and accompanied her to Mass at a nearby convent. While she sat uncomfortably through the sermon, an attendant advised her that Montausier was waiting outside. The duke gave her a quick account of what had transpired. In spite of the protests of Philippe d'Orléans and the silence of his ministers, the king had consented to the match as an indication of the esteem in which he held the high aristocracy of the realm. Montausier and his fellow delegates thanked the king "in the name of all the nobility of the kingdom."[166]

Within the royal family, Louis had to deal with the objections of Philippe and Maria Theresa, but neither Lauzun nor Mademoiselle took this seriously. Lauzun remarked that "Monsieur and the queen do not tell the king what to do."[167] Mademoiselle took this a step further. Angered by Philippe's accusation that Louis had masterminded the proposal to benefit a favorite, she forced her way into the king's council chamber. Philippe had left, but the ministers were still there. Denouncing the reports that Louis had instigated the marriage, she demanded to know what "liars" had put this idea into Philippe's head. She emphasized that the proposal was of her own making and that Louis had counseled her to think carefully before going forward. After alluding to the relative standing of foreign princes and French noblemen once more, Mademoiselle launched into a eulogy of Lauzun, whose talents and zeal in Louis's service made him so worthy of an alliance with the royal family. Even Mademoiselle admitted that her harangue was too long. Louis cut her off by saying that he was "persuaded."[168]

Word soon spread of this outcome. The Luxembourg filled up with courtiers, some "astonished," some "happy," and some "upset."[169] Among those truly amazed was Mademoiselle's good friend the marquise de Sévigné, who immortalized the moment in a letter known to every generation of students of French literature:

> I am going to tell you the most astonishing thing, the most surprising, the most wonderful, the most miraculous, the most triumphant, the most astounding, the most unheard of . . . something people cannot believe in Paris (so how could you believe it in Lyons?) . . . I can't make up my mind to tell you what it is . . . guess who Lauzun is going to marry on Sunday at the Louvre? . . . I'll have to tell you after all: on Sunday at

the Louvre he is marrying, with the king's permission, Mademoiselle, Mademoiselle de . . . Mademoiselle . . . guess the name: he is marrying Mademoiselle . . . la Grande Mademoiselle; Mademoiselle, daughter of the late Monsieur; Mademoiselle, granddaughter of Henri IV . . . Mademoiselle, the king's first cousin; Mademoiselle, destined for the throne, Mademoiselle, the only match in France worthy of Monsieur. . . . There is a fine subject for discussion. If you scream, if you are beside yourself, if you say we are lying, and that we are making fun of you . . . we'll say you're right, since we have done the same.[170]

He is like God; one must await his will with submission, and hope for everything from his justice and goodness, with no impatience, in order to draw more merit from it. This is a real sermon; but I assure you, I have need of it, and I practice what I preach.

MADEMOISELLE

So this is the gratitude for all I have done for the king's children.

MADEMOISELLE

I don't think the king cares much about Mademoiselle's anger, but I think it even less likely that she will go back to Lauzun; she has had the leisure to face reality, and I think she is certainly ashamed now of her attachment to such a nonentity.

ROGER DE BUSSY-RABUTIN

7   The Mask of Apollo and the End of Illusions

MADEMOISELLE CALLED THE THREE DAYS THAT FOLLOWED THE announcement of her engagement the "happiest moments of my life."[1] She and Lauzun spent the hours receiving the congratulations of courtiers, decorating an apartment for him at the Luxembourg, discussing the arrangements for the wedding ceremony, and waiting for the lawyers to draw up the marriage contract. There was a good deal of banter about Lauzun's earlier amorous exploits—Mademoiselle played the forgiving if vigilant bride—and the archbishop of Rheims, Louvois's brother, vied with the archbishop of Paris for the honor of presiding over the ceremony.[2]

Mademoiselle threw herself into these activities with passionate enthusiasm. For her, the marriage was the opportunity to graft a new line of Orléans-Montpensier onto the old. She had already insisted that Lauzun adopt her blue and red livery, which had been Gaston's, and add the royal fleur-de-lis to the insignia of his cavalry command.[3] By Wednesday evening, December 17, 1670, the lawyers had drawn up deeds of gift bestowing on Lauzun joint and several ownership of the duchy of Montpensier and the principality of Dombes. Mademoiselle presented him to the assembled company as the "duc de Montpensier" and asked them henceforth not to refer to him by any other name."[4] Madame de Sévigné, who inaccurately added a few more properties to the list, marveled at his good fortune "while waiting for more."[5]

All of this gaiety did not entirely eradicate a certain unease, at least on Mademoiselle's part. With the exception of Mademoiselle herself, almost no contemporary commentator believed that Lauzun was in love with Mademoiselle. He was viewed as a wily courtier who had taken advantage of the inexplicable infatuation of the princess: an achievement condemned by some, admired by others. The real question was whether Mademoiselle had originated the proposal or whether, as Philippe d'Orléans asserted publicly, the king had engineered the match to benefit a favorite courtier,[6] an accusation that troubled Louis in the wake of his original consent.[7]

The royal family had many reasons to dislike the match. Mademoiselle, hitherto so sensitive to minute questions of rank and precedence, cannot have had any illusions as to the reaction of her royal relatives. The attempt to link her engagement to the larger question of the relative standing of the highest French nobility and the cadre of foreign princes at court initially offered Louis some room for maneuver. This, however, was not enough for the royal family. Maria Theresa spent an entire evening arguing with the king, while Philippe d'Orléans bellowed that Mademoiselle should be confined to a madhouse and Lauzun thrown out a window. Philippe had personal as well as dynastic reasons to dislike Lauzun. As a friend of his late wife Henrietta, Lauzun was automatically suspect; more importantly, he had taken part in the notorious arrest of the chevalier de Lorraine. How could Philippe welcome into the family a witness to his humiliation?[8]

Mademoiselle's stepmother bestirred herself to write a long letter of protest to the king and was joined in her efforts by her daughter, the duchess de Guise, and by the rest of the Guise-Lorraine clan, gathered, said Mademoiselle, "in a body to do battle with me."[9] The collateral relatives were just as indignant. The prince de Condé threatened to blow out Lauzun's brains on the steps of the church. The elderly princess de Carignan, last of the Bourbon-Soissons line, warned Madame de Montespan that if she continued to support the match she would earn the enmity of the entire royal family.[10]

Material considerations also figured in the opposition of Mademoiselle's relatives. Mademoiselle was well aware that her kinfolk had begun to consider the division of her property after her death, provoking a resentment that Lauzun had shrewdly played upon.[11] At the time of the proposal that Mademoiselle marry Philippe d'Orléans, Philippe's designs on Mademoiselle's property became only too evident.[12] The Longueville candidacy was the chosen vehicle for the cupidity of the Condés, and even without such a marriage the Condés were close enough in blood and influential enough at court to expect to share in the windfall that would follow Mademoiselle's death, provided she died unmarried.[13] Even the queen had some thoughts on the matter. Her reaction to Mademoiselle's announcement was a cold remark that it would be better that she never marry and that she leave her fortune to the queen's second son, the little duc d'Anjou (1668–1671), a proposal that Mademoiselle denounced as "shameful."[14]

While a few noblemen took Louis's words at face value and thanked both the king and his cousin for the honor bestowed on their caste by such a marriage, most of the high aristocracy were also indignant. The king's former governor, the maréchal de Villeroy, spoke for them when he added his voice to the chorus of those who objected to the marriage. Within the circle of powerful parlementary families, who were often the source as well of the king's administrative officers, there was evidently consternation at the damage to the royal image. When Madame de Sévigné warned Mademoiselle that the "entire kingdom" was talking about the announcement, it was these groups—her own social circles—that she had in mind.[15]

Mademoiselle was enough of a dynast to understand these objections. What was involved here were the conventions of a society that believed deeply that differences in rank were almost divine in origin and not to be breached lightly. The manuscript of her *Mémoires* contains a number of extraneous documents that bear on these points: a genealogical study of the Caumonts to prove their long and illustrious pedigree; another study questioning the princely status of the Lorraine family prior to the fifteenth century; and a list of earlier marriages between princesses of the royal house and members of the high nobility.[16] These arguments about the suitability of a marriage between a princess of Mademoiselle's rank and a nobleman described by an Italian diplomat as a "gentleman of good family, favorite of a great king, but that's all," may seem strange to modern eyes, but they were taken seriously by Mademoiselle's contemporaries, and cannot be dismissed as inspired by simple greed or envy.[17]

Olivier d'Ormesson, a well-placed member of the parlement of Paris, suggested in his *Journal* yet another undercurrent to this controversy, the ill will between Lauzun and Louvois. Louvois's chief rival was Colbert, who had always been on good terms with both Mademoiselle and Lauzun. Colbert was charged with reviewing the terms of the marriage contract and obtaining the king's signature on it. Given Colbert's prominent role, there were those who interpreted this marriage as another episode in the rivalry between Colbert and Louvois and an indication that the balance between the two was tipping in Colbert's favor. The fact that such a rumor was circulating in official circles makes it likely that it had reached Louis's ears as well.[18]

If all of this were not enough, Mademoiselle had to contend with opposition within her own household. Segrais, who still championed an alliance with the duc de Longueville, made no secret of his feelings. Guilloire went still further, behaving, said Mademoiselle, "like a madman."[19] She could not bring herself to record Guilloire's reprimand, but according to Segrais, who was present, Guilloire told her that she had disgraced herself and was "the laughingstock of Europe."[20]

Although much of this opposition crystallized in the three days following Louis's public consent, there had been warning signals from the beginning. Montausier, who served as governor to the dauphin, was a practiced courtier and understood the nuances of Louis's grudging approval. When he first brought Mademoiselle word of the king's consent, he urged the couple to marry the same evening. Mademoiselle, whose instincts were reinforced by her recent exchange with the queen, agreed. But Lauzun refused to hurry, convinced that the king would not be swayed by the objections of the queen or his brother and afraid that undue haste would ruin the impression of "moderation" in the face of good fortune that he wished to convey.[21]

Lauzun's idea of "moderation" was curious. His first plan was a wedding at Versailles, with Madame de Montespan as the unofficial hostess; but the royal mistress found an excuse to beg off. He then proposed a wedding in the queen's chapel at the Tuileries, with the court in attendance and with the king and queen escorting the newlyweds back to the Luxembourg.[22]

In the meantime, a chorus seconded Montausier's early warning. On Tuesday, Rochefort, one of Lauzun's fellow captains of the guard, urged them to marry without delay, as did Guitry, who warned the couple of the growing opposition within the royal family. Guitry also told them that the chapel at the Tuileries would not be available—hardly a surprise given the queen's opposition—leaving the couple without a place for the ceremony.

On Wednesday morning, a frantic Montausier appeared at the Luxembourg with Lauzun in tow. He had just upbraided Lauzun for not taking his advice to marry immediately, and Lauzun had put the blame for the delay on Mademoiselle. It was her turn to be astounded. She had deferred to Lauzun, who did not wish them to seem too much like a man "whose good fortune had gone to his head" and a young lady "in great haste to marry." Montausier asked Lauzun sarcastically if he wanted a wedding fit for "crowned heads," and insisted that they focus on a time and place. They concluded that Saint-Fargeau and Eu were too far away, since Lauzun wished to return to attendance on the king the day after the ceremony. Lauzun then volunteered the house of the duc de Richelieu at Conflans, with the ceremony set for Thursday.[23] Later that day Madame Colbert came to warn that Lauzun was the object of much envy and spite, and the following morning Madame de Sévigné cautioned Mademoiselle that the delay was a temptation for "God and the king." But Mademoiselle seemed "full of confidence" and Sévigné went away thinking that her counsels had fallen on deaf ears.[24]

Late on Wednesday, the Richelieus declined the honor of hosting the wedding. Madame de Richelieu held a high post in the queen's household and dared not risk the queen's wrath. The Créqui family came to the rescue, offering the use of their estate at Charenton. By now, it was Thursday morning, and another piece of bad news awaited the couple. The lawyers had not been able to finish the marriage contract in time to obtain the king's signature and hold the wedding that day.[25]

Mademoiselle shared the Catholic dislike for Friday weddings, so the ceremony would therefore have to be postponed another day. She asked Colbert to obtain the king's signature on Friday morning; she and Lauzun would leave that afternoon for Charenton. The ceremony would be held at midnight between Friday and Saturday, and the two would return to the Luxembourg the next day. The local curate would officiate; the archbishops, it seems, were no longer available.[26]

By early Thursday evening, December 18, the arrangements were in place. The crowds had drifted away, and Mademoiselle and Lauzun were free to sit by the fire and make small talk, until Lauzun excused himself to take care of last-minute business. By eight o'clock, Mademoiselle was alone with Lauzun's sister, Madame de Nogent, and was surprised by a sudden, unexplained urge to weep.[27]

A messenger from the king appeared unexpectedly at Mademoiselle's door and told her that the king wished to see her. Mademoiselle understood instantly. Turning to Madame de Nogent, the princess exclaimed, "My engagement is broken." In a fog, with only Nogent to accompany her, she ordered her carriage and drove to the Tuileries. Rochefort, who was on duty, stopped her briefly in the king's antechamber; the princess knew that this was to permit some other person to enter the king's rooms without being seen by her. When she entered, she found the king "all alone, agitated, and sad."[28]

Louis came right to the point. His reputation abroad was being damaged by the accusation that he was sacrificing her to make Lauzun's fortune. Under the circumstances, he could not permit them to marry. He added rather melodramatically, "Hit me if you want. There is nothing you could do that I wouldn't deserve and wouldn't endure." This threw Mademoiselle into a flood of grief and tears. Had the king forbidden them at the beginning, it would be different, but now, what of appearances? And what, she asked anxiously, would happen to Lauzun? Nothing, the king assured her. As Mademoiselle tells it, the two sank to the floor holding one another, and the king "cried as much as I did." The king asked her why she had not acted quickly, rather than allow time for "reflections." The princess answered that Louis had given his word and that had been enough for her and Lauzun, who could never have imagined that he would break it. Mademoiselle continued, "You gave him to me. You are taking him away. You are breaking my heart."

A cough broke the mood. Someone was hidden in the room listening, perhaps to make sure that Louis did not reverse himself again. Mademoiselle recognized the cough. She asked the king rhetorically to whom he was sacrificing her, then answered the question. It was not, she hoped, to Condé, whose life she had once saved and who now made common cause with the family of Lorraine out of hatred for a man (Lauzun) devoted to the king. She continued to plead until Louis cut her short. All of this was pointless. If she obeyed him now, there was nothing he would ever refuse her. But he would not yield to her tears. "Kings must satisfy the public." With a few more polite words, he embraced her once more and showed her to the door.[29]

Mademoiselle returned home in a fury, smashing the windows of her carriage on the way. François de Choisy, who was at Mademoiselle's apartments at the time of her arrival, remembered the scene. Two footmen appeared and ordered the crowd to leave immediately. Choisy lingered long enough to see the princess at the end of the *salle des gardes* "like a fury, disheveled, her arms raised in threats to heaven and earth."[30]

Shortly thereafter, Lauzun arrived with Montausier, Guitry, and Créqui. Lauzun had been instructed by the king to thank Mademoiselle for the honor she had intended for him and to assure her that Louis would reward both of them for their sacrifice. Lauzun then suggested that Mademoiselle see the king the next day and thank him for preventing her from taking a step she would soon have regretted. The princess could not believe her ears. She drew Lauzun aside for a private word in her *ruelle* (the space near her bed). She wept and got the reaction she had hoped for: he wept along with her, but then took his leave.[31]

Once more, Lauzun had found the balance between disappointed suitor and obedient courtier. Earlier the same evening, immediately after speaking with Mademoiselle, Louis had summoned Lauzun's emissaries to tell them of his decision, and had then spoken directly with Lauzun. Louis was the first to say that Lauzun received the news with "fidelity and submission."[32] In the days that followed, Lauzun did not waver from his posture of sorrowful and dignified obedience, playing his part with "firmness, courage, and sorrow mixed with deep respect," in what Madame de Sévigné called a "perfect piece of theater."[33]

Louis's official explanation of the rupture was contained in a letter to his ambassadors written shortly thereafter and widely reprinted all over Europe. In this version, Louis had been surprised at his cousin's request and had gently tried to change her mind. She persisted, however, and "found a way to involve the high nobility of the kingdom" by evoking his consent to the marriage of her sister with a "foreign prince," the duc de Guise. She and Lauzun's delegates maintained that a refusal to consent to her request to wed Lauzun would therefore offend his own nobility. The king gave his "tacit consent to the marriage, shrugging my shoulders at my cousin's behavior, and saying only that she was forty-five years old and could do what she pleased." Shortly afterward, Louis heard a rumor that Mademoiselle had told people that he, the king, had fostered the match. Although she reaffirmed in front of Montausier and his ministers that the marriage was of her own volition, the rumors persisted and grew louder. It was even said that his resistance to the match was "a feint and a comedy, and that in fact I was very pleased to procure such great wealth for the comte de Lauzun, whom, as everyone knows, I am fond of and hold in high esteem." With his reputation at stake, Louis decided to forbid the marriage. He told his cousin that she could choose anyone else from the nobility of France and "I would take her to the church myself." He added that Mademoiselle had been distraught and Lauzun had behaved well.[34]

As chronicled by Madame de Sévigné and others, the behavior reported by Louis continued. Lauzun went about his normal routine as if nothing unusual had happened, while Mademoiselle was prostrate with grief. For nearly a week, she remained shut up in her apartments, admitting only a select few. The king came for a second bout of tears; the queen called, and also Philippe d'Orléans, to whom Mademoiselle had little to say. She refused to see either her stepmother or her sister the duchess de Guise, but she did receive a few close friends. Madame de Sévigné, who visited three times in those first few days, was surprised at her own compassion for a person of such elevated rank.[35] Even Sévigné's cynical cousin Roger de Bussy-Rabutin, who had originally laughed at the announcement of Mademoiselle's marriage, was moved to pity by the reports of her emotional collapse, the result of what his correspondent Madame de Scudéry called a "grand passion in the heart of an honorable person like her."[36]

In spite of their sympathy, it was almost impossible for Mademoiselle's friends to say or do the right thing. Mademoiselle took umbrage at an exchange between Mesdames de Sévigné, de la Fayette, and de Longueville on the motives for her engagement to Lauzun and found Louise de la Vallière's attempts to console her "stupid." Even her dear friends the Epernons came in for their share of disapproval. In her grief and rage, Mademoiselle believed that many failed her in her hour of need. She was to remark to the king that as a result of the Lauzun episode, she had lost all of her friends.[37]

On Christmas Eve Mademoiselle returned to court and her normal routine. This was largely at the insistence of Lauzun, who feared the consequences if the princess continued her withdrawal from public life.[38] One of Mademoiselle's worries was put to rest when Louis agreed that she could still see Lauzun in the role of adviser. This gave Mademoiselle some hope that the king might someday permit them to wed.[39]

Mademoiselle found it difficult to control her feelings. At various functions, the sight or even the thought of Lauzun brought her to tears. Embarrassed by these outbursts, Lauzun threatened to avoid her if she persisted in this behavior.[40] He even felt obliged to warn her that she was neglecting her appearance.[41] But these admonitions had little effect. Once, at a ball at Vincennes, Mademoiselle was dancing with the duc de Villeroy when she suddenly broke down and began weeping in full view of the assembled court. In one of the inimitable gestures for which he was famous, Louis came to her rescue. He walked over to Mademoiselle, removed his hat and positioned it in front of her to hide her contorted features from the spectators. He led her gently off the floor, announcing, "My cousin is not well."[42]

Mademoiselle's tears were mingled with a rage that she directed at those of her household who, she felt, had betrayed her. She could not forgive Guilloire for his reprimand, nor for his evident satisfaction at the collapse of the engagement. Nor could she tolerate Segrais, who had continued to advocate a marriage with Longueville and, Mademoiselle charged, worked actively behind the scenes with Longueville's friends to resurrect his candidacy.[43] At Lauzun's insistence, however, she initially took no action against them. Finally, she found an appropriate pretext. Sometime in mid-March she was visited by the new archbishop of Paris, François de Harlay de Champvallon. The archbishop told Mademoiselle that shortly after he took office in January, Guilloire and Segrais had called on him. They told him that Mademoiselle was still seeing Lauzun and they asked the archbishop to intervene. The archbishop should forbid Mademoiselle, as a matter of conscience, to see Lauzun any more. Alternatively, the archbishop might suggest to the king that Lauzun be posted abroad as an ambassador, or be given a field command, to remove him from the court and Mademoiselle's line of sight. Seeing no moral issue and doubting his right to suggest political appointments to the king, the archbishop had refused to take any such actions. The two men then approached the king's confessor, Father Ferrier, with the same propositions. Ferrier also declined to involve himself, but reported this approach to the king and to Lauzun.[44]

After confirming the archbishop's account, Mademoiselle dismissed both Guilloire and Segrais from her service. A number of friends attempted to intercede, but Mademoiselle was adamant. In the case of Segrais, the duc de Montausier and Madame de Sévigné, among others, asked Mademoiselle to reconsider, but to no avail. The princess, said Sévigné, was "unyielding."[45] Mademoiselle believed that Segrais had egged Guilloire on.[46] She negotiated a settlement with Guilloire of 50,000 livres for his prior services, but she refused to give a penny to Segrais.[47] With the king's consent, she replaced Guilloire with a nominee of Lauzun, Marc-Antoine Rollinde.[48]

Even more surprising was the dismissal of her confessor, the abbé de Saint-Léger. A stray remark by the abbé led her to suspect that he might have betrayed the seal of the confessional and told Guilloire of her plans at the time Guilloire had first approached Louvois about Mademoiselle's marriage. The abbé had also opposed the marriage after the initial public announcement. Thereafter, Mademoiselle had refused his services, going instead to an Augustinian monk who lived near Saint-Germain. Once Guilloire and Segrais departed, Mademoiselle forced his resignation. Mademoiselle rounded out the dismissals by ridding herself of her personal maid, Madelon.[49]

Philippe d'Orléans found these abrupt dismissals very curious and raised the subject one day when they were at the king's table. To Mademoiselle's pleasure, the king weighed in on her side, denouncing in particular monks who meddled in worldly affairs. The king's remarks, said Mademoiselle, "ended the discussion and pleased me; it showed that he was happy that I had rid myself of all those servants who were not friends of M. de Lauzun."[50]

By the time this incident took place, it was early April 1671, and the court had accompanied the king on another Flemish campaign. This gave Mademoiselle a chance to see Lauzun frequently, and the change in the tone of the *Mémoires* is startling. Although Mademoiselle occasionally records more weeping whenever they parted, she had clearly regained her equilibrium. The interactions with Lauzun were usually lighthearted, and the two of them spent much time conniving to keep Lauzun in the king's line of sight.[51]

This change of tone is difficult to explain; as recently as early March, a correspondent of Bussy-Rabutin's characterized the princess as weepy and despondent, although constantly in Lauzun's company.[52] Yet by early

April, Mademoiselle was sufficiently recovered to take on Philippe d'Orléans at table. The change is paralleled by a series of events in late winter
that indicate that Lauzun continued to be in high favor. After the breach
of the engagement, Lauzun had returned Mademoiselle's deeds of gift.
She had them reissued over the objections of her lawyers.[53] There is no
indication that the king tried to intervene. In January, Louis granted
Lauzun the *grandes entrées*, meaning the right to enter the royal apartments at will, a distinction reserved for royal princes and a select number
of courtiers, and a large sum of money to settle his debts.[54] At the end of
February, Louis offered Lauzun the baton of a maréchal of France, which
Lauzun refused on the grounds that he had done nothing to earn it.[55] He
did, however, accept the governorship of Berry at the end of March, just
before embarking on the campaign.[56] Shortly thereafter, there were rumors that Lauzun was negotiating an exchange of this governorship for
that of Languedoc, which had once been held by Gaston. In the king's
presence, Philippe d'Orléans asked pointedly about Mademoiselle's role
in the proposed exchange. To Mademoiselle's relief, Louis cut off the
discussion.[57]

One may well wonder if the change in Mademoiselle's mood and the
indications of high favor to Lauzun are indications of a secret marriage
between Mademoiselle and Lauzun during the spring of 1671, perhaps
with the king's consent. Many of Mademoiselle's contemporaries believed that she and Lauzun married in secret, as have most modern
biographers of the two. Bussy-Rabutin speculated on the possibility of a
secret alliance as early as March 1671, while Saint-Simon was convinced
of it.[58]

The issue is timing, and here there is no consensus. Most modern
writers have followed the lead of the duc de la Force, who argued in a 1913
work that the union did not come about until the 1680s. The notable
exception to this is Arvède Barine, who maintained in a study published
about the same time as La Force's book that there was a great deal of
"evidence" that the marriage had taken place sometime in the spring of
1671.[59] The third possibility, that they never married, also has a few
adherents.[60] The question cannot be answered with any certainty, although a close reading of the text of Mademoiselle's *Mémoires* can be
used to support Barine's conclusion. The abrupt change in tone noted
above is obvious to the reader. There are also some passages in this
portion of the text that are quite intriguing, such as the following dialogue between Lauzun (first speaker) and Mademoiselle:

"You have not changed."

"No, and I will never change."

Mademoiselle continues: "The rumor was rampant that we had married before leaving Paris, and the *Gazette de Hollande* [reported] it. Someone had brought it to me. He laughed, and I didn't say anything. I sent it to him."[61]

Mademoiselle follows this several pages later with an account of an earlier conversation with Lauzun, dating from their engagement, when he expressed a wish to distinguish himself in the Flemish campaign. If he fell in combat, people would say, "His conduct in all things makes him stand out from all the others and justifies the choice Mademoiselle has made."[62] In the fall months, at the end of the campaign, the two were back in Paris. Mademoiselle remarks: "I was often in and out of Paris, where people continued to say that we had been married. Neither he nor I said anything, and only our closest friends dared to speak to us about it, and we laughed in their faces, without saying anything more than 'the king knows what there is to know.' "[63]

It should be noted that there are other passages in the same section of the *Mémoires* where Mademoiselle expresses her wish that the king would permit them to marry and asserts that Charles II had offered to help if he could.[64] Taken alone, these would suggest that the two had not yet married. But taken together, the various passages, against the background of Mademoiselle's dramatic shift in mood, might be interpreted as a veiled disclosure that the two had been secretly married and the issue was obtaining the king's public consent.

These few months were the last in which Mademoiselle was to enjoy any vestige of happiness. In the fall of 1671, after the court's return to Saint-Germain, Mademoiselle and Lauzun continued to see one another on terms of easy familiarity. One day in late November, Mademoiselle was dining in public at the Luxembourg. Madame de Nogent was called from the table. Mademoiselle thought nothing of it and continued her meal. When she returned to her bedroom, Madame de Fiesque approached her and began speaking, "Monsieur de Lauzun . . ." The princess cut her off, thinking that Fiesque was announcing his arrival, and that, as usual, he had entered through her dressing room and was waiting in an adjacent private room. "What manners he has. I thought he was at Saint-Germain," the princess said laughing. But Fiesque stopped her: Lauzun had just been arrested at Saint-Germain by his colleague Rochefort. Mademoiselle and Madame de Nogent were in a state of near shock for several hours, until Mademoiselle recovered sufficiently to hear the details from Rollinde.[65]

A few days earlier, there had been a false report that Lauzun had been arrested.[66] In Mademoiselle's account, this rumor and a strange presentiment when she parted from Lauzun at Saint-Germain were the only hints that anything was amiss.[67] Mademoiselle hurried off to Saint-Germain, where she attended the king's supper; the two did not speak. Mademoiselle felt it would have been "imprudent," since the king "was prepared for anything I might have said to him." Instead, she spent her time staring at him through tears, while the king looked "sad and embarrassed." He remarked afterward that he was pleased with Mademoiselle's delicacy in not confronting him.[68]

Lauzun's arrest made almost as much of a sensation as the announcement of his engagement to the princess a year earlier, all the more so because no reason for the arrest was given. A month later, Madame de Sévigné wrote that "no one knows any more than I do."[69] In another letter, the inquisitive marquise drew a conclusion probably held by many: "The king has said nothing, and this silence is declaration enough of the seriousness of his crime."[70]

Louis never did say anything publicly, leaving his contemporaries and later generations to their speculations. A contemporary observer, the marquis de la Fare, and later Voltaire, believed that Lauzun's crime was a secret marriage to Mademoiselle against the king's wishes,[71] and, as noted above, passages of Mademoiselle's *Mémoires* can be cited as evidence that they had married.[72] But the weight of contemporary explanations points elsewhere. The consensus of most commentators is that the arrest stemmed from a sequence of bitter confrontations between Lauzun and Madame de Montespan in the course of 1671. Lauzun, in these versions, blamed Montespan for the failed engagement and showed his contempt with harsh words and insults in public on a number of occasions. Given Lauzun's history of violent behavior, the reports of such outbursts are certainly plausible. If Saint-Simon is to be believed, Montespan and Louvois called Louis's attention to these confrontations and accused Lauzun of arrogance and ingratitude.[73]

Saint-Simon's explanation is consistent with a few contemporary remarks by the protagonists. Madame Scarron, later Madame de Maintenon, governess of Louis's illegitimate children by Montespan, alluded to Lauzun's rages in a guarded conversation about a year later,[74] while the marquis de Saint-Maurice reported that after Lauzun's arrest armed guards were posted in Montespan's apartments and accompanied her whenever she left the palace.[75] Lauzun always claimed that he owed his fall to the malice of "powerful enemies,"[76] while Louis, in a rare public comment shortly after the arrest, dwelled on Lauzun's ingratitude, remarking that Lauzun had never even "deigned" to thank him for the governorship of Berry.[77]

A surviving dispatch from Francesco Nerli, the papal nuncio in Paris, provides a plausible account of the immediate events surrounding Lauzun's arrest. According to Nerli, Lauzun's influential relative, the maréchal de Gramont, was told privately that Lauzun had had a violent exchange with Montespan in late November. The king ordered Lauzun to apologize and gave him five days to comply. Lauzun refused and his arrest followed.[78] This account is compatible with Saint-Maurice's reports of the posting of guards around Montespan. Such defiance of the king would have been completely in character for Lauzun, who had a long history of insolence in his relations with Louis and Montespan. This explanation might be even more plausible if he had indeed secretly married Mademoiselle with the acquiescence of those two, because the revelation of such a secret would have given the lie to Louis's published account of his dissolution of the engagement. But if Lauzun did behave in the manner described by the nuncio, his almost infallible courtier's instinct had deserted him, and he did not realize that his conduct had gone well beyond what Louis was prepared to tolerate.

Lauzun's fate was intended to be exemplary. At the moment of his arrest, he asked Rochefort to be taken to the king or to Montespan. This was refused, on the king's explicit orders, as was a request to write to either.[79] In spite of his repeated demands, no explanation was offered for his arrest, nor was he allowed to communicate with anyone. After a brief stay in the Bastille, Lauzun was transported south to an undisclosed destination in the care of the incorruptible Charles d'Artagnan, captain of the musketeers. The cortege eventually arrived at the remote fortress of Pignerol (Pinerolo), a French outpost not far from Turin. Those distant walls already held another famous prisoner, Nicolas Fouquet, the fallen royal minister, serving a life sentence. Only now did Lauzun realize that he was indeed "lost."[80]

With Louis's approval, and under the supervision of Louvois, Lauzun was wrapped in a blanket of silence. He was shut up in a small ground-floor apartment, with bars and shutters on his windows that blocked out much of the daylight. His only companion was a manservant, and his only link to the outside world was the prison governor, Bénigne de Saint-Mars, a protégé of Louvois's. Louvois instructed Saint-Mars not to permit his prisoner to write to the king under any pretext whatsoever. There would be no visitors, nor any correspondence with family or friends, nor any contact between Lauzun and Fouquet. His reading material, which only became available in the second year of his captivity, was restricted to religious books and devotional tracts. On several occasions, Louvois repeated that Lauzun was to have no news of or communication with the outside world. Initially, Lauzun was also denied any exercise. Saint-Mars followed these instructions with a pedantic severity, promising the minister that Lauzun would spend his time *in pace*—that is, he would experience a living death—and Louvois repeatedly encouraged this approach. All of these details, together with reports of Lauzun's behavior in prison, are preserved in an extensive correspondence between Saint-Mars and Louvois. To the modern eye, it is only too evident that Louvois had set up a régime of psychological torture intended to break the will of the prisoner.[81]

At the beginning of his captivity, Lauzun was told that the king had given his governorship of Berry to the prince de Marcillac, and about a year later he was ordered to resign his commission as captain of the guard. Lauzun attempted to use his letter of resignation, addressed to the king, as a means of protesting his treatment, but it was returned as unacceptable. After interminable negotiations the duc de Luxembourg was appointed to replace him, with some financial compensation to Lauzun for his lost captaincy. The captive's defiance during this episode only increased Louis's irritation, and the outcome can only have convinced Lauzun of the hopelessness of his situation. Upon his arrival at Pignerol, he is supposed to have muttered *"in saecula saeculorum,"* a religious expression meaning "forever and ever." When the story reached Paris, there were those, said Madame de Sévigné, whose reply was "amen," that is, "let it be so," and others whose response was "not so."[82]

Mademoiselle was in the front ranks of this latter group. At the moment of Lauzun's arrest, her inclination was to withdraw from court in protest, just as Philippe d'Orléans had done at the time of the chevalier de Lorraine's arrest. On second thought, Mademoiselle concluded that Lauzun was better served by her remaining at court, in the hope of moving the king to pity. There was no question of direct defiance. In a letter to Bussy-Rabutin several years later, she was to compare the king's position to that of God, and to counsel "submission" to his will while relying on his "justice and goodness." For the rest, as she stated in her *Mémoires*, there was nothing she could do except "weep endlessly, speak with his friends, and . . . ask God for the patience to bear . . . our cross."[83]

Ironically, her first opportunity to display her constancy in the face of adversity was at the wedding of her cousin Philippe d'Orléans to Elisabeth-Charlotte of the Palatinate, who was taking the place Mademoiselle had refused to fill. The balls and ballets brought back memories of happier times and of festivals Lauzun had graced.[84] She had no doubt that Lauzun's feelings were reciprocal. She sought out d'Artagnan and his nephew of the same name for their accounts of Lauzun's journey into captivity. She recorded with some pleasure Lauzun's supposed remarks about her goodness and affection for him and his fears that these might change in his absence.[85] She rejected with scorn the reports that royal officials discovered letters and portraits during their search of Lauzun's rooms that compromised many of the leading ladies of the court. She resolved to ignore stories of such conquests for fear of harming Lauzun still further by appearing to be resentful.[86]

In addition to this kind of scandalous gossip, Mademoiselle had to put up with the many fictionalized and sensational versions of her relationship with Lauzun that circulated in the European press. One of these, for example, a pamphlet called *Les Amours de Mademoiselle et de Monsieur de Lauzun*, appeared in 1672 and was frequently reprinted in succeeding years in Holland and Germany. In it, Lauzun is portrayed as an ambitious schemer urged on by friends, and Mademoiselle as a foolish, infatuated woman manipulated by a cunning and ambitious fortune hunter. Similarly, a fable in verse called *The Eagle, the Sparrow, and the Parrot* tells the story of a proud female eagle, member of the family that reigns over the bird kingdom. The eagle is seduced by a villainous and cunning sparrow, to the dismay of the other birds. But order is restored when the senior eagle, head of the family, steps in, puts an end to the liaison in spite of the "shameful" attitude of the female eagle, and reprimands the sparrow for forgetting his duty and the respect due to royalty. The other birds of the kingdom rejoice in this exercise of royal authority to defend the social equilibrium. Works of this type, reflecting the widespread disapproval of the liaison by contemporaries, are completely at variance with Mademoiselle's story of a princess who chose for herself and an honorable soldier who was reluctant to accept her affection.[87]

The second part of Mademoiselle's *Mémoires*, which is basically an attempt to answer her critics, breaks off in April 1676, shortly after an abortive attempt by Lauzun to escape from Pignerol. Her account of the years between his arrest in November 1671 and his foiled escape in 1676 is largely a chronicle of Mademoiselle's many failed efforts to obtain clemency from the king. The king apparently refused to discuss the subject directly, and Mademoiselle was left to make allusions to Lauzun or to hope that others would do so. In 1672, for example, the duke of Buckingham, while on a diplomatic mission to the French court, dared to ask the king about his friend Lauzun. A vague reply from Louis implied that someday Lauzun might be released and gave Mademoiselle unjustified hopes.[88] Mademoiselle continued to follow the court on its various excursions into the provinces and on campaign, because she believed that her presence in these settings would remind Louis of Lauzun and his past services. Louis, however, remained evasive, even as he expressed his regrets for her troubled state of mind.[89] On one occasion in 1673, while the court was in the vicinity of Strasbourg, a naïve local official with some past ties to the court asked the king about a number of his old aristocratic acquaintances. An amused Louis was happy to bring him up to date, until the unwary man asked about Lauzun. When the king did not reply, he repeated the question several times, even asking the reason for the silence. The only answer was a royal stare and jeers from the courtiers who accompanied the king.[90]

For Mademoiselle, almost all other events were filtered through the prism of Lauzun. Her constant companion in those years was Madame de Nogent. Although Mademoiselle occasionally found her honorary sister-in-law trying, Nogent and Lauzun's former subaltern and comrade, Henri de Barrail, were the only other people on earth who shared her constant preoccupation with Lauzun's fate.[91] In June 1672, Madame de Nogent lost her husband at the famous engagement known as the "Crossing of the Rhine." Lauzun's friend Guitry was also killed, along with a number of other prominent courtiers, including the duc de Longueville. Madame de Nogent took the news badly, and Mademoiselle did what she could to console her. She could not help seeing the hand of Providence, however, in Lauzun's imprisonment. Otherwise, she was convinced, he would have perished alongside his brother-in-law and Guitry.[92]

Within her own family, Mademoiselle took a hard line. In April 1672, she refused to see her dying stepmother, who, Mademoiselle noted, did not ask to see her. She also refused to act as chief mourner at the funeral, staying away with the king's permission and allowing the place of honor to fall to a young princess of equivalent rank, Philippe d'Orléans's daughter Marie-Louise (1662–1689), also known as "Mademoiselle" in court circles.[93]

After her stepmother's death, Mademoiselle rejected an olive branch offered by her sister Elisabeth, the duchess de Guise, and made a show of her complete indifference to the death of Elisabeth's young son, the duc de Guise, in 1675.[94] Shortly after her son's death, the duchess de Guise wished to sell her half of the Luxembourg to the Condés. Although Mademoiselle had long ago reconciled with Madame de Longueville, she had no use for the rest of the Condé clan.[95] Mademoiselle took her protests to the king, refusing to live under the same roof with the Condés and accusing them of acting against her in 1671 out of cupidity. The king assured her that he would not permit the transaction without her consent. Madame de Longueville smoothed matters over, blaming the whole idea on Condé's son, Henri-Jules, duc d'Enghien, and on Madame de Guise. Since Mademoiselle was prepared to believe the worst of her sister and of Henri-Jules, she accepted this explanation and apologies from the Condés.[96]

The marital misfortunes of her other sister, Marguerite-Louise, grand duchess of Tuscany, offered Mademoiselle a modest amount of diversion. Mademoiselle liked her brother-in-law, the grand duke Cosimo. At the time of her engagement, he alone of her entire extended family had written her a congratulatory note, in which he expressed his high regard for Lauzun.[97] His own marriage to Marguerite-Louise, however, had been a failure, in spite of the birth of three children. At the end of 1673, the grand duchess withdrew to a convent outside Florence, and the couple exchanged formal letters to record that the marriage had broken down beyond repair.[98] With Louis's reluctant permission, Marguerite-Louise returned to Paris in 1675, where she took up residence in a specially built house on the grounds of a convent at Montmartre. The king's welcome was decidedly cool, but Mademoiselle made an effort to help her sister settle in at court.[99]

None of these episodes, nor the routine of court life and gossip, kept Mademoiselle from her efforts on Lauzun's behalf. Among her greatest frustrations was her inability to secure any amelioration of Lauzun's captivity. From the beginning, Mademoiselle put the blame for the brutal treatment of Lauzun on Louvois's shoulders, saying that she refused to believe that Louis was responsible for these "harsh measures."[100] In

1674, Lauzun fell ill, and there were concerns about his survival. Mademoiselle wrote a long letter imploring the king to ease Lauzun's plight. Louis accepted the note from her hands, but took no action.[101]

In February 1676, Lauzun attempted a daring escape from Pignerol. He tunneled out of his cell and managed to reach the courtyard of the building. He approached a servant girl and offered her a bribe to guide him out of the fortress. But an officer recognized the prisoner, intervened, and took him back to his cell. Lauzun had left two letters in his cell, addressed to Louis and to Louvois. In them, he announced his intention of seeking service with one of Louis's allies, as the only way he could put his sword to use for the king. Mademoiselle was at Fontainebleau when word arrived of this latest adventure. The text of the letters made the gossip circuit of the palace corridors, and Mademoiselle found herself once more at the center of unwanted attention from curious courtiers. One wonders how many of the onlookers shared Madame de Sévigné's reaction: Lauzun would have been better off had he perished in the attempt.[102] Mademoiselle wrote Louis once more, asking him to consider the plight of Lauzun. Once more, there was no response.[103]

If anything, the restrictions became still harsher at Pignerol. Louvois reminded an embarrassed Saint-Mars that Lauzun was to have no news whatsoever of Mademoiselle, and that Saint-Mars would answer for any clandestine communications between the two.[104] Mademoiselle, who had had no direct contact with Lauzun since his arrest, may have decided that matters were truly hopeless. In August 1677, she reopened her *Mémoires* to write the account of the years from the marriage of the king in 1660 to her own doomed bid for happiness. The narrative ends abruptly in April 1676, just after Lauzun's attempted escape.[105]

We cannot tell exactly when Mademoiselle finished this part of her *Mémoires*, but it was probably prior to 1680.[106] Ironically, the first small improvements in Lauzun's living conditions occurred just after Mademoiselle began writing. In September 1677, Lauzun was allowed to have visitors: his sister Nogent, a younger brother, and a family lawyer, in order to deal with pressing family matters. Madame de Nogent and her younger brother brought back to Paris shocking reports of a broken man, ailing and semilucid. The ensuing uproar instigated a series of gradual improvements. Over the next two years, Lauzun was allowed access to Fouquet and also permitted to dine at Saint-Mars's table, even when the governor had outside guests, and to go riding under escort. His reading list was expanded to include gazettes with current news of the world of court and politics, and he was allowed to write to his relatives, although not to Mademoiselle.[107]

Throughout these years, Mademoiselle remained constant in her affection for Lauzun, in spite of occasional doubts. There were many who asserted that Lauzun had merely taken advantage of her infatuation and that after the rupture of the engagement, he had gone back to his courtier's routine unperturbed. Mademoiselle refused to believe these slanders, although she found herself struggling "against myself," with only Barrail to speak for Lauzun.[108] At one point, she even considered semi-retirement to a Carmelite convent, but Barrail convinced her that this would not be in Lauzun's best interests, since it might lead eventually to a complete withdrawal from court, leaving Lauzun with no advocate at all.[109]

Mademoiselle's hopes revived in March 1680, when Barrail was allowed to spend a week at Pignerol. Upon his return, he spoke at length with Madame de Montespan, without disclosing the substance of his conversation to Mademoiselle. Montespan, who had always been on good terms with Mademoiselle, had promised to help Lauzun if an opportunity arose. Although she was no longer the reigning favorite of the king, she continued to have a good deal of influence over him, and Mademoiselle saw Montespan as the best means she had to move the king to clemency.[110]

Barrail's visit to Pignerol coincided with the celebrations that marked the wedding of the dauphin to Marie-Anne of Bavaria.[111] The occasion was no doubt a reminder to Montespan that her children by the king were also growing up. The eldest, Louis, duc du Maine, was now ten years old and needed to be provided for. Both Montespan and the children's governess, Madame de Maintenon, formerly the widow Scarron, saw Mademoiselle's millions as part of the solution. Mademoiselle knew the children well, and Maine was supposed to have a special affection for her. So when Montespan urged Mademoiselle to think of something she could do that would please the king enough to agree to "her heart's desire," it did not take very long for Mademoiselle, with the help of Lauzun's friends, to come up with the answer. She sent Barrail with a proposal: she would make Maine her heir if the king would release Lauzun and let her marry him.[112]

In retrospect, Mademoiselle saw that she had been overmatched by Montespan, a far abler and more practiced player who knew how to move the game along. Montespan agreed to sound out the king. She returned with word that Louis could never consent to Mademoiselle marrying Lauzun, given the public position he had taken in his letter of 1671 to his ambassadors. Still, Montespan assured Mademoiselle, "in time, circumstances change."[113] She advised Mademoiselle to offer to make Maine her heir without mentioning Lauzun, thus allowing the king to reciprocate with a gracious gesture, without the appearance of a bargain.[114] Mademoiselle authorized Montespan to convey this revised proposal. The king came up to her a day later and thanked her for her generosity. He realized that his cousin was doing this out of affection for him, and Louis hoped the boy would someday be "worthy" of the honor she did him.[115]

Thereafter, Montespan was all smiles, and Louis uncommonly gracious. Maine, who had been away with Madame de Maintenon, called to thank Mademoiselle for her good intentions, which had not yet been publicly announced. Still, Louis had not yet said anything about Lauzun. To Mademoiselle's anxious inquiries, Montespan simply replied, "Patience."[116]

Now it was time for specifics. Montespan demanded that Mademoiselle deed over the principality of Dombes and the county of Eu, two of her richest domains, which she had already bestowed on Lauzun.[117] Mademoiselle demurred; she intended to make Maine her heir upon her death, but not to dismember her estates during her lifetime. This was not what Montespan and the king had in mind. Colbert was brought into the discussions. To Mademoiselle, Montespan was all gentleness, but with Barrail she was direct: "The king is not mocked. When you promise something, you do it." Barrail, who acted as Lauzun's representative, was key, because both of these properties had already been deeded to Lauzun, and his consent would be necessary for the proposed donation to be valid. Through Barrail, Lauzun's verbal consent was obtained. All of this took some time, and Mademoiselle assented only when Barrail was threatened with the Bastille if negotiations failed.[118] In early February 1681, in the presence of Colbert, Montespan, and Barrail, Mademoiselle signed over these properties to the duc du Maine, but reserved their use and income for the remainder of her lifetime. Montespan assured the reluctant donor that the king looked upon her more as a "sister" than as a cousin, and would soon show her his gratitude.[119]

Mademoiselle began almost immediately to press for Lauzun's release, but there were still some difficulties to overcome. Louis could not bring himself to do openly what Montespan had implied privately. Montespan finally told Mademoiselle that Louis would never permit her to marry Lauzun publicly, nor would he allow Lauzun to call himself the duc de Montpensier. He would make Lauzun a duke, and Mademoiselle could marry him in secret. Officially, the king would take no notice. Mademoiselle was outraged. How, she asked, could Lauzun live with her if they were not publicly wed? What would people say? Montespan, who had lived for years in double adultery with Louis XIV, could not understand these scruples. Since they *would* be married, she emphasized, Mademoiselle's conscience should be clear. Other people would be silent out of respect for the king. In the end, the princess would be "a thousand times happier," because Lauzun "will love you all the more; secrets add to the taste of things."[120]

Shortly thereafter, Montespan told Mademoiselle that Louis would release Lauzun, but he would not permit him to return directly to Paris. Instead, Lauzun was to be sent to the spa of Bourbon-l'Archambault, under a kind of house arrest, with an escort of guards. There was worse to come. Montespan reiterated Louis's refusal to countenance a public marriage between the princess and Lauzun. Mademoiselle's protests were brushed aside. Half truthfully, Montespan insisted, "I never promised you anything." The former mistress, said Mademoiselle, had what she wanted, and listened to Mademoiselle's barbed comments in silence. Barrail, who witnessed this exchange, did his best to calm the princess. He had just come from Pignerol, with confirmation that Lauzun would sign a written waiver of his claims to Dombes and Eu, and Barrail was more interested in freeing Lauzun than in confronting Montespan about false promises.[121]

Under the circumstances, Mademoiselle decided to make the best of the situation. She thanked the king for his clemency and got him to agree that Lauzun would be escorted to Bourbon-l'Archambault by a contingent of musketeers, rather than by Saint-Mars, whom Lauzun detested. Barrail was received by the king and entrusted with the order of release. On April 22, 1681, Lauzun took his leave of the grim prison in which he had spent ten years of his life: he was now forty-eight years old; Mademoiselle was weeks away from her fifty-fourth birthday.[122]

Mademoiselle was not to see Lauzun for nearly a year. He spent most of the summer and fall at Bourbon-l'Archambault, stayed briefly in Chalon-sur-Saône, and then passed the winter months at Amboise. During this time, he was technically under house arrest, although free to do what he pleased. Barrail continued to be his emissary to Mademoiselle and to the court. Lauzun's partial release, at least in his own eyes and Barrail's, was only a first step. There remained any number of issues to resolve.

At the time of Barrail's visit to Pignerol in 1681, Barrail and Lauzun had begun a secret correspondence, which continued throughout this period, and which Saint-Simon, allowed to read it many years later, was to pronounce "very interesting." From the surviving portions, it is clear that Lauzun was an active party to the negotiations with the court for his full freedom, the restitution of his forfeited commissions and offices, and suitable compensation for the properties formerly deeded to him by Mademoiselle and now bestowed upon the duc du Maine. Without a written renunciation by Lauzun of Mademoiselle's earlier donations to him, Montespan and the king feared that Lauzun might someday challenge the gifts to Maine, which had not yet been publicly announced or registered with parlement. But Lauzun wanted compensation for his sacrifice, and there was a common consensus among the participants that this, too, would have to be at Mademoiselle's expense.[123]

Since Lauzun was still under house arrest far from the court, it fell to Barrail to represent his friend. In the months of discussion that followed, Barrail would present written proposals to Montespan. The king remained offstage, using Montespan and Colbert as his spokespersons. Lauzun and Barrail were welcome to wrest as much as they could from Mademoiselle, provided that any new donations by Mademoiselle were accompanied by Lauzun's renunciation of the former gifts that would now benefit Maine. At the same time, Louis would not compromise his dignity by permitting any action or declaration that might suggest, however remotely, that Lauzun's imprisonment had been an injustice. This made it virtually impossible to permit Lauzun to return to court on his old footing, to resume his place as a captain of the guard, or to hold any equivalent distinction. Nor, as already indicated to Mademoiselle, could Louis permit a public marriage between Lauzun and Mademoiselle.

This last consideration seems to have been the least important item on the agenda in Lauzun's eyes. The critical issues for him were his rehabilitation at court and compensation from the king for his lost offices, and from Mademoiselle for the properties he was now obliged to renounce. Neither Lauzun's ordering of priorities nor Louis's was well received by Mademoiselle. She was willing to champion Lauzun's interests at court but unwilling to deed over any more of her properties to Lauzun without a public marriage. Mademoiselle's feelings and her sense of dignity, however, mattered little to anyone else involved in the negotiations. The battle raged for months, with Montespan and Colbert willing to compensate Lauzun with Mademoiselle's property, but taking a more reserved position on the issues of royal compensation for Lauzun's lost offices and his return to court. Beneath the wrangling, there lurked the unspoken threat that Lauzun could be returned to Pignerol or sent into exile abroad. By the late summer of 1681, after a number of alternatives had been reviewed and discarded, Mademoiselle's quasi-opponents agreed on a proposal that provided Lauzun with the duchy of Châtellerault, several other properties, and a pension derived from her *rentes* on the salt tax from the Languedoc. In spite of the urgings of Colbert and Montespan, Mademoiselle still hesitated, angry that she was expected to lead a *"vie libertine"* with Lauzun and increasingly troubled by Lauzun's demands; at one point, she actually referred to him as a "swindler."

By September, worn down by the combined efforts of Barrail, Montespan, and Colbert, she agreed to deed over the properties in question to Lauzun and to accept that, for the moment at least, she could not wed Lauzun publicly. Leaving Mademoiselle no time for second thoughts, Montespan left immediately for Bourbon-l'Archambault. There she secured Lauzun's written renunciation of his claims to Dombes, Eu, and Montpensier (which was not part of the gift to Maine). In addition to the gifts wrung from Mademoiselle, Montespan promised Lauzun to seek compensation from the king for his forfeited offices.[124]

Montespan returned to Fontainebleau at the end of September 1681; there she continued the discussions on Lauzun's behalf. At the last minute, the possibility that collateral heirs might challenge the alienation of Châtellerault caused a scramble. With Colbert's help, Mademoiselle was prevailed upon to substitute Saint-Fargeau, although she had refused months earlier even to consider it. By now, the king was very anxious, writing directly to Colbert with instructions to expedite matters and ordering him to tell Mademoiselle that the bargaining was over: for the moment, Louis would do no more for Lauzun. A cornered Mademoiselle signed the deeds of gift at Choisy on October 29, with Barrail signing on Lauzun's behalf. Mademoiselle ceded Saint-Fargeau to Lauzun, hoping the king would confer the ducal title on him, as well as the barony of Thiers in Auvergne, and a pension of 10,000 livres. By her calculations, these gifts would provide Lauzun an income of 40,000 livres. Lauzun, who considered this inadequate compensation for the sacrifice of such princely possessions as Eu and Dombes, had pressed for properties and pensions at the level of 100,000 livres. Even Barrail was embarrassed by this naked rapacity. In the end Lauzun accepted gracelessly, letting all and sundry know that her gift was "so little that he could hardly accept it."[125]

When the news of the donations to Maine and to Lauzun were published, the reaction was mixed. Some thought Mademoiselle had been foolish, while others, friends of Lauzun or Montespan, called to wish her well. The only compliment the princess considered disinterested was that of Philippe d'Orléans, who had been told of the donations before the public announcement. Since the king was pleased, said Philippe, and it made her happy, Philippe was also happy.[126]

During all these months, Lauzun did little to show his gratitude to Mademoiselle, or even to communicate with her except through Barrail, restricting his comments to the various points under negotiation. After a decade of solitude at Pignerol, it is not surprising that Lauzun wished to make some use of his limited freedom. But the reports reaching Mademoiselle suggested a bit too much freedom. Lauzun's name was linked with a number of women: Madame d'Humières at Bourbon; Madame de Chamilly at Chalon; Madame d'Alluye at Amboise. These adventures caused Mademoiselle a great deal of public humiliation. Humières returned to Paris to tell people about her pleasant stay at Bourbon. If this were not enough, a letter from Lauzun to Humières fell into Mademoiselle's hands. Mademoiselle read it and burned it.[127] Madame de Chamilly spoke to the princess of her frequent correspondence with Lauzun. Mademoiselle, still working to secure his freedom, was pained by this revelation.[128] From Amboise came news that Lauzun was constantly at the Alluye residence, where he was engaged in "flirtations with the ladies."[129] All of these reports redoubled Mademoiselle's fears that in freeing Lauzun she might have lost him. Barrail often bore the brunt of Mademoiselle's anger, even while negotiating the compensation arrangements for Lauzun. For Mademoiselle, the solution was to be found in Lauzun's return to court and to her company, but her repeated entreaties for Lauzun's recall to Paris brought counsels of patience.[130]

In early March 1682, Mademoiselle was told that Lauzun could return and that the king would see him, but only once. He would be free thereafter to go wherever he wanted, except the court. For want of better, Mademoiselle was forced to accept this, and with it, the congratulations of courtiers who flocked to her doors when the news became public.[131]

Lauzun arrived at Saint-Germain to pay his respects to the king while an anxious Mademoiselle waited in Montespan's rooms. Lauzun had been famous before his disgrace for his pranks. Hoping to amuse the king, he appeared in an old-fashioned coat that was in tatters and too short for him: Louis did not laugh. While speaking, Lauzun repeatedly threw himself on his knees before the king: Louis was not moved. Lauzun was then led away to Mademoiselle, who thought his behavior on such an occasion astonishing. Montespan withdrew to permit them a few private words, but Mademoiselle, overcome with emotion, followed Montespan out of the room. Lauzun left for formal visits to the rest of the royal family. He did return eventually to thank Mademoiselle profusely for all she had done to secure his freedom. Mademoiselle, still not sure of herself, "didn't say a word. I was astonished."[132]

Lauzun hurried off to call on Louvois and Colbert while Mademoiselle tried to gauge the family's impressions of Lauzun. At dinner, the young dauphine, Marie-Anne of Bavaria, and Philippe d'Orléans's wife, Elisabeth-Charlotte, pronounced Lauzun handsome and distinguished. Philippe made a few kind remarks. The king did not say a word. From Montespan, Mademoiselle learned that Louis had mocked Lauzun's obsequious manners, observing that Lauzun had not changed in this regard. But clearly, the king had found the whole performance distasteful. A day or two later, Montespan suggested that the princess return to Paris, where she could be with Lauzun.[133]

It was soon apparent that Lauzun had little interest in being with Mademoiselle: he did not see her again for five days, and when he did so he began their first truly private discussion with criticism of her manner of dressing as inappropriate for her age. Mademoiselle found this so painful to recall that she crossed out her original account and rewrote the story as a commentary by Lauzun on the queen's wardrobe.[134] Lauzun excused himself with a promise to return that evening. He did not come, but spent the evening with another woman.[135]

It was a poor beginning to what were to be two of the most trying and disappointing years of Mademoiselle's life. If anything militates against the idea of a secret marriage between the two in those years, it is Mademoiselle's account of the unremitting unhappiness she experienced at Lauzun's hands. Every encounter with Lauzun was tense, with scarcely a pleasant moment. Lauzun was always known for his eccentric personality, even before his imprisonment. There can be little doubt, however, that ten years of captivity under harsh conditions had exacerbated the more extreme traits of his personality. Bitter at his long imprisonment and frustrated by his inability to regain the king's good graces, Lauzun blamed Mademoiselle for his plight. He was prone to sudden mood swings and temper tantrums. Conversations would shift from civility to acrimony without warning, and the tone would quickly become accusatory. Mademoiselle remarked on the inconsistency of his manner toward her: on one day a tone of "respect and gratitude," and on the next that of a "furious ingrate."[136] The longer they were together, the more rapid the shift; on one occasion she complained that he was never the same from one quarter of an hour to the next.[137] Mademoiselle and others, like Montespan, ascribed the change in Lauzun's personality to his confinement, and hoped that in time he would regain some equilibrium.[138]

Lauzun betrayed his true feelings very soon after his return to Paris. One afternoon he was out walking with Mademoiselle and Madame de Montespan in a convent garden at Chaillot. The conversation had been casual and lighthearted. Suddenly, Lauzun turned on Mademoiselle and told her that "he was the unhappiest man in the world because I had gotten mixed up in his affairs." He insisted that in 1680 he had been in the last stages of negotiating his rehabilitation when Mademoiselle's efforts had superseded his, and he complained bitterly that he had left prison a pauper. Losing her temper, Montespan told Lauzun that without Mademoiselle, he would never have gotten out of prison, and reminded him that the king, thanks to Mademoiselle's intervention, had agreed to pay him a huge sum, 948,000 livres, in compensation for his various forfeited offices. Mademoiselle joined the fray, which Montespan somehow brought to a gracious end. Montespan began laughing, blamed Lauzun's strange notions on too long a time in prison, and asked Mademoiselle to overlook his outburst.[139]

Some months later, Mademoiselle made plans to spend time with Lauzun at Eu, but Lauzun claimed that the king had forbidden him to go. Mademoiselle sent a note to Montespan, who quickly wrote back that, on the contrary, the king expected Lauzun to go. With this settled, Lauzun had no further excuse. He arranged, however, to travel separately. To Mademoiselle's annoyance, he arrived three weeks after her. He liked the château, where, added Mademoiselle, "I had provided him very good accommodations."[140]

Mademoiselle put him up in a suite of rooms just above her own, connected by a secret staircase. The ceiling was decorated with a suggestive, if stylized, motif of angels, graces, and the Montpensier arms.[141] But Lauzun was a reluctant bridegroom. He would disappear in the morning to go riding by himself, and reappear in the evening without any explanation of his whereabouts. Somehow there was still time for quarreling. Saint-Simon, who heard Lauzun's version of events, speaks of physical violence on both sides.[142] After two weeks, Lauzun rode away on the pretext that his mother, who lived at the château of Lauzun, was very ill, and he wished to see her convert from her Huguenot faith to Catholicism before she died. But in Paris, he got the good news that she had recovered, so went no further on his mission of conversion, but remained in the capital to socialize with his friends.[143]

Lauzun did little to hide his infidelities. Somewhat belatedly, Mademoiselle discovered that he was infatuated with Marie-Madeleine Fouquet, the daughter of his former fellow prisoner, whom he had met at Pignerol during family visits by the Fouquets. Upon his return to Paris, he called frequently on the Fouquets and was often seen in public as Mademoiselle Fouquet's escort. Mademoiselle's steward, Rollinde, who lived in the same neighborhood as the Fouquets, knew of Lauzun's behavior but was too embarrassed to tell her.[144]

If this were not enough, Madame d'Alluye turned up one day at court, played cards at Mademoiselle's table, and filled her ears with tales of Lauzun's exploits during his stay at Amboise. By the time Lauzun appeared on the scene, the damage had been done. The princess suggested that he share these stories with Mademoiselle Fouquet, who might find them interesting.[145]

Lauzun constantly criticized Mademoiselle's spending habits and complained about his own poverty. In 1680, about the time negotiations began for Lauzun's freedom, Mademoiselle had bought a large tract of land just outside Paris at a village called Choisy-le-Roi. She had always wanted a country house close to Paris, but had never found one she liked. She engaged the architect Jacques Gabriel to design a small but elegant residence on the site, with windows overlooking the Seine. Le Nôtre was engaged to design the gardens, terraces, and orangery. As at Saint-Fargeau and Eu, Mademoiselle filled the rooms with family and ancestral portraits, as well as with works by the most fashionable artists of the day. The king's likeness was everywhere, and in a special place of honor hung a painting of Mademoiselle holding a miniature portrait of Gaston. Her pride in the house was boundless. Her earlier projects had been largely works of restoration, but Choisy was entirely of her own making. "It's my handiwork; I've done it all."[146] Madame de Montespan promised that the king would surprise her with little presents—statues, fountains, and treasures to embellish her rooms—in token of gratitude for her kindness to the duc de Maine.[147]

The work was not finished until 1686, but the château was already habitable by the time of Lauzun's release. Mademoiselle chose Choisy for her first meeting with Lauzun after his presentation at court. He was politic enough to pronounce himself "enchanted" by the place, but soon changed his tone. He reprimanded Rollinde for allowing Mademoiselle to spend so much money on such a project. He was just as blunt with the princess. On a subsequent visit, he dismissed her efforts as an immense folly: in his opinion, all she needed was a little place for picnics, without even overnight accommodations. He used the same line on her that he had on Rollinde: it would have been better to have given the money wasted on the project to him. Mademoiselle replied with a reminder of how much she had already done for him.[148]

Shortly thereafter, Mademoiselle made Lauzun a gift of diamonds to set as ornaments for his coat sleeves. After complaining about their poor quality, Lauzun sold them, telling friends he had done so because he "didn't have a cent to live on." She adds the needless detail that such behavior was unheard of and gave rise to much laughter.[149] Mademoiselle knew that Lauzun was a heavy gambler, and his losses often resulted in fresh complaints about her extravagance.[150]

In spite of his criticism of Mademoiselle's expenditures, Lauzun did not hesitate to propose another one on his behalf. He suggested that she evict her pages from their quarters at the Luxembourg and refurbish the space as a residence for him. He would keep his own table there, at Mademoiselle's expense, so he could host his friends to dinner and entertainment. Mademoiselle had to remind him that the king would not stand for such a public display of their relationship. Lauzun the penniless consoled himself for this refusal by buying the elegant town house on the Ile Saint-Louis still known as the Hôtel de Lauzun.[151]

Even more disturbing to Mademoiselle was Lauzun's suggestion that he should control her financial affairs. On a number of occasions, he offered to preside over the weekly meetings of her business advisers. Mademoiselle laughed this off.[152] In time, this became a more specific proposal that he should control her household and financial affairs; he assured the princess that he would get better results than her treasurer and other estate managers did. But he made the mistake of using the analogy of the chevalier de Lorraine's control over the affairs of Philippe d'Orléans. This put Mademoiselle on guard. Lauzun had always ridiculed the chevalier's control of the Orléans household. How could he propose a like arrangement for her? "It would be a fine thing if I had to ask you for money when I needed it."[153]

Lauzun repeated this proposal, complete with the comparison to the Orléans household, to Colbert. The minister, equally astounded, told Lauzun that the king would never permit it, and reported this conversation to Mademoiselle. He also told her sadly that she had done a great deal for a man who showed her no gratitude. He predicted that she might well ask the king to send him away again and that the king would grant that request more quickly than he had responded to her earlier pleas for Lauzun's recall.[154]

Colbert had good reason to be exasperated. He and Montespan had been Mademoiselle's principal conduits for her endless stream of requests on Lauzun's behalf, and he had not been any more successful than Montespan in obtaining additional concessions from the king. The problem, Colbert insisted, was Lauzun himself. At the beginning, the minister had promised Mademoiselle that he would try to help Lauzun, provided he conducted himself properly.[155] But reports of Lauzun's bizarre behavior and his abusive treatment of Mademoiselle had displeased the king, and Colbert could do little to advance Lauzun's interests under the circumstances. This warning, conveyed by Mademoiselle to Lauzun, sparked yet another violent argument between the two.[156]

Lauzun's erratic outbursts continued, and by the end of her first year with Lauzun, Mademoiselle had come to a sad conclusion: the real Lauzun, as opposed to her idealized fantasy during his years of imprisonment, was very much as she saw him in these moments of outburst, and she despaired of any change. "I began to know him really well, and to be tired of him. But I wanted to keep up my end of the game. After having done so much for him, I wished to finish the job, that is, to get him made a duke and readmitted to court."[157]

If quarrels over money and Lauzun's flirtations caused periodic uproars, Lauzun's thwarted ambitions provided a perpetual source of tension between the two. Unable to accept that a grudging semirehabilitation was the best he could expect, he pressed Mademoiselle to obtain the return of his forfeited posts, and berated her endlessly for her lack of success. He began with a demand that he be allowed to return to court. Mademoiselle dutifully relayed this to Montespan and Colbert, only to be told that this would depend on his behavior.[158] He then began to agitate for the return of his commission as captain of the king's guard. Given Louis's feelings, this was completely out of the question; as Montespan reminded him, he was lucky to receive a financial settlement for his forced resignation. But Lauzun insisted that he would have recovered his commission through his own efforts had Mademoiselle not intervened in 1681. His failure to do so was therefore her fault. This assertion provoked yet another argument between the couple.[159] Mademoiselle tried at the end of the shouting to persuade him that fits of rage would not advance his interests and that his own behavior impeded his rehabilitation.[160]

In addition to the return of his commission as a captain of the guard, Lauzun also dreamed of a high military command. Within hours of his return to Paris in 1682, he began to agitate for command of the king's troops in Savoy. He hoped to obtain this post through the intercession of his old friend Marie-Jeanne de Savoie-Nemours. When this tactic failed, he turned to Mademoiselle, who resented his ties to the duchess. Mademoiselle refused to help, saying sarcastically that Lauzun had no need of "a little lady like me" when he had the help of a great lady like "Your Madame Royale." The appointment never materialized, and the incident added to the growing estrangement between the two.[161]

Lauzun put in an appearance as a volunteer without a command at the siege of Courtrai in November 1683, in the suite of the comte de Vermandois, one of the king's illegitimate sons. Lauzun took the royal tolerance of his presence as a sign of rehabilitation. The following spring, he asked Mademoiselle to obtain a place for him in the upcoming campaign. He wanted to serve as an aide-de-camp to the king, with the rank of lieutenant general and full seniority from his earlier appointment in the 1660s. He also intimated that his failure to achieve a restoration of his rank was somehow due to Mademoiselle's refusal to help him. Mademoiselle brought the letter to Montespan and Madame de Maintenon. There was exasperation all around, ending in a quarrel between the princess and Montespan, during which Mademoiselle accused Montespan and Colbert of breaking their promises to help her with Lauzun's rehabilitation. All of this got back to Louis, who told Mademoiselle that he had his reasons for not wanting to see Lauzun and that he was not ready yet to agree to Lauzun's reinstatement.[162]

The king left for the front in late April 1684, without Lauzun. When the latter appeared at the Luxembourg some days later, Mademoiselle suggested that he leave Paris and spend some time on his estates to avoid any unpleasant comments on his absence from the army. He replied that he intended to leave, had come to say farewell, and hoped never to see her again. This comment galvanized Mademoiselle, resolving any lingering doubts. She shot back, "It would have been better if I had never seen you, but better late than never." Lauzun continued to rant, accusing her of ruining his life and holding her responsible for the king's refusal to take him on the campaign. Mademoiselle suggested that the king could tell him the real reasons for his decision. This enraged Lauzun all the more. When he finished his tirade, Mademoiselle said, "Farewell then," and retired to her bedroom. When she emerged some time later, he was still in her antechamber, making small talk with her ladies. The princess crossed the room, walked up to him, and ordered him out. In a huff, he went to Philippe d'Orléans to complain that she had turned him out like a dishonest servant—as indeed she had.[163]

Mademoiselle never saw Lauzun again, nor would she accept any communication from him, in spite of a number of efforts by Lauzun.[164] This final break occurred in May 1684. Mademoiselle lived on, a sad and disillusioned woman. She had, wrote Bussy-Rabutin to Madame de Sévigné, "the leisure to face reality, and I think she is certainly ashamed now of her attachment to such a nonentity."[165]

To occupy her time, Mademoiselle took part in the various festivities that marked the coming of age of yet another generation of the royal family, a clan that had expanded dramatically with many young Contis, Condés, and Orléans, as well as Louis XIV's legitimate and illegitimate offspring. In July 1686, for example, she gave a reception at Choisy in honor of the dauphin, with virtually all of the royal family—except the king—present. She also crossed swords with her two surviving sisters from time to time. As an additional pastime, there was another great lawsuit over the Guise inheritance following the death of her aunt Marie de Guise in 1688, in which Mademoiselle made common cause with the Condés. Mademoiselle was eventually awarded the principality of Joinville and a pension of 35,000 livres drawn from the Guise patrimony. Still, however, one senses from the tone of her *Mémoires* that she forced herself to take an interest in such matters.[166]

She also returned to writing. The last part of Mademoiselle's *Mémoires*, in which she chronicles the negotiations for Lauzun's release and the disillusionment that followed, date from 1689–90. This final segment is framed, so to speak, by two religious tracts, commentaries on the *Eight Beatitudes* and on the *Imitation of Jesus Christ*, written, respectively, in

1685 and 1693. While the last part of Mademoiselle's *Mémoires* reflects the deepening piety evidenced by these other writings, it also contains Mademoiselle's admission of self-inflicted injuries caused by her misplaced affection for Lauzun and records her pitiless manipulation by Montespan, with Louis XIV in the background, to force Lauzun's ransom at Mademoiselle's expense. For all her disillusionment with Lauzun, her accounts of her many disputes with Montespan and Colbert, surrogates for the king, indicate that Mademoiselle put some of the blame for Lauzun's behavior on Louis's refusal to rehabilitate Lauzun fully and to permit her to marry him publicly.

The last paragraph of Mademoiselle's *Mémoires*, written sometime in the second half of 1690, begins with a mention of Lauzun, and then breaks off abruptly: "M. de Lauzun lived as he always did, mysteriously, but making people talk about him, often by [doing] things that annoyed me. When I returned from Eu in 1688, all my servants were dressed in new liveries. One day, as I was walking in the park of . . ."[167]

Mademoiselle could not bring herself to write the rest of the story. Lauzun had gone to England to serve under James II, the ally of Louis XIV. At the time of the Glorious Revolution, Lauzun had smuggled James's infant son and his queen, Mary of Modena, out of England. He brought them safely to France at the end of December 1688. Since he was still forbidden to appear at court, he coolly sent to Louis for instructions. The result was inevitable. Louis wrote his congratulations in his own hand and received Lauzun in public. Within a few months, Louis had reinstated his privilege of the *grandes entrées*, and James II, a refugee at Saint-Germain, borrowed Notre Dame to bestow the Order of the Garter on the savior of his wife and son. There remained only a ducal title, which Louis conferred in 1692. "Lauzun," marveled Sévigné, "has found his way to Versailles by way of London."[168] La Bruyère was to write of Lauzun that "people do not dream the way he has lived."[169]

Louis never entirely forgave Lauzun, but his rehabilitation, for reasons of political expediency, was a final blow to Mademoiselle. Louis sent Colbert's son Seignelay to explain matters to her, and James II called in person at the Luxembourg to smooth things over, but in vain. Mademoiselle could only say that she deserved better after all she had done for the king's children.[170]

Mademoiselle found some solace in pious meditations. In spite of her conventional devotions and the endless rounds of convent visits in the days of Anne of Austria, Mademoiselle's faith had always been largely a matter of external conformity. At one point in the late 1650s, perhaps under the influence of Préfontaine, she had expressed a passing admiration for Jansenists, if not for Jansenism. In her later years, however, she was drawn to the austerity of the Carmelite movement and to the writings of the sixteenth-century Carmelite mystic Teresa of Avila.[171] In April 1685, only a few months after she broke with Lauzun, she published an anonymous study of the *Eight Beatitudes*. She deposited several copies in a Carmelite convent on the Rue de Grenelle, and forwarded another to her brother-in-law, Cosimo III de Medici.[172] In an attempt to draw some meaning from her sufferings, she concluded that "misfortunes and infidelities, the ingratitude of our friends, opposition in our families" were intended to detach a Christian from worldly concerns and to teach that true consolation lay in submission to the will of God.[173]

Mademoiselle's last work, a commentary on the *Imitation of Jesus Christ*, was probably completed in the final months of her life. It was published posthumously in 1694, in an edition of the *Imitation* prepared by Nicolas Fontaine.[174] Borrowing from the introduction to her *Mémoires* written forty years earlier, Mademoiselle confirms the conclusions she had reached in her study of the Beatitudes: "Greatness of birth and the advantages bestowed by wealth and by nature should provide all the elements of a happy life. But experience should have taught us that there are many people who have had all of these things and are not happy; that there are moments when one believes oneself happy, but it does not last . . . the events of my own past would give me enough proof of this without looking for examples elsewhere."[175]

And even more sadly: "But alas! Since the veil has fallen from my eyes, I have known that all the grandeur, all the vanity, and all the pomps and pleasures of the world, have been illusions and that, however much effort we make to possess and enjoy them, they are destroyed in a moment. And I have certainly seen that we are only actors who play a role in the theater, and that the persons portrayed are not our true selves."[176]

Outwardly, she carried on with what dignity she could manage, staying away from Versailles to avoid encounters with Lauzun and holding her own court at the Luxembourg. At least since 1670, she had routinely been called "La Grande Mademoiselle" to distinguish her from Philippe d'Orléans's daughters. In her last years, this designation had become routine. The original sense of the word may thus have been nothing more complicated than "senior," but in historical memory, the term has come to identify her as the female counterpart to the Grand Condé in the entourage of "Louis le Grand."[177]

In the pages of Dangeau's *Journal*, we can follow her infrequent appearances at court on festive occasions, when younger members of the family curried favor in the hopes of an inheritance. In February 1693 the princess attended a parade of the household troops at Versailles in honor of a visiting Danish prince. While the king presided, Mademoiselle, who still enjoyed the sight of flashing swords and smart salutes, sat in a place of honor with James II's queen, Mary of Modena.[178]

Scarcely a month later, in mid-March, she fell ill with a painful disease of the urinary tract. She died on the morning of April 5, 1693. Madame de Fiesque, long since restored to her position as *dame d'honneur*, was at her side. The princess was sixty-six years old. On her deathbed, the granddaughter of Henri IV, Segrais's Princess Aurélie of the Château of the Six Towers, refused to see Lauzun.[179]

Her will, dated 1685, revoked an earlier one that had made Lauzun her universal heir. There were a few modest bequests to hospitals and convents in her domains and small sums for faithful servants. She left Choisy to the dauphin and her remaining estates to Philippe d'Orléans, the cousin who had stood up for her as a little boy on the day she had braved Anne of Austria over the *affaire Saujon* and who had kept vigil at the Luxembourg during her last illness.[180] With her pride of race and sense of history, it would please her to know that many of her titles, including that of duchess de Montpensier, continue to this day to be borne by Philippe's descendants.

To the annoyance of the royal family, Lauzun appeared in full mourning after Mademoiselle's death and adopted a variation of her livery as his own.[181] In 1695 he married a fifteen-year-old girl, Geneviève de Lorges, the younger sister of the duchess de Saint-Simon. He lived until 1723, dying in his ninetieth year. Some years earlier, he had sold Saint-Fargeau to a banker.

I often digress from the subjects I start with; but there are certain diversions that are somewhat necessary to clarify matters for those who were not there in those days, or who were not informed about these things, and [other diversions] on matters that only I would care about.

MADEMOISELLE (1677)

Greatness of birth and the advantages bestowed by wealth and by nature should provide all the elements of a happy life. But experience should have taught us that there are many people who have had all of these things and are not happy; that there are moments when one believes oneself happy, but it does not last . . . the events of my own past would give me enough proof of this without looking for examples elsewhere.

MADEMOISELLE (1694)

8 The Muse's Lament

THE MANY PRINTINGS OF MADEMOISELLE'S WRITINGS THROUGH-
out the eighteenth century, the inclusion of her *Mémoires* in the great
nineteenth-century anthologies of Petitot and of Poujoulat, the success
of Chéruel's critical edition of 1858, its recent reprinting by Fayard (1985),
and the many biographies of the princess since the turn of the twentieth
century, based largely on the *Mémoires*, attest to the enduring public
interest in Mademoiselle's eventful life.

The best modern studies place Mademoiselle squarely in the history
of her own time.[1] Mademoiselle's life and her writings span much of the
seventeenth century and offer a running commentary on events as seen
at the highest levels of the aristocracy. The opposition to Richelieu, the
confusion and tragedy of the Fronde, the shift in the relationship be-

tween the Crown and the great nobility that is evident by the beginning of Louis XIV's personal rule, are all faithfully mirrored in the *Mémoires* of Mademoiselle. One can also find much evidence of the parallel shift in the taste, manners, and style of the Parisian elites, a shift that was to have profound effects on patterns of behavior for generations to come.[2]

This study ends, as it began, with the assertion that Mademoiselle's *Mémoires* are central to our understanding of her personality and of her contribution to the history and literature of her time. In spite of Mademoiselle's disclaimers that the *Mémoires* were not intended for publication, but were written as a source of consolation as she reflected on the "misfortune of my house," the princess clearly expected that they would someday reach a wide audience.[3] She resolved to provide the world with her own version of her life, and she took steps to ensure that more than one copy of her manuscript would survive.[4] There can be little doubt that the Mademoiselle we encounter in the *Mémoires* is Mademoiselle as she intended us to know her.

Not all of Mademoiselle's readers have reacted to her efforts with unqualified admiration. Voltaire, who owned a copy of the 1728 edition of the *Mémoires* and made good use of it in his *Age of Louis XIV*, thought her style unworthy of a princess, commenting that her accounts seemed to be "written by a chambermaid," more preoccupied with herself than with the great events she had witnessed.[5] Saint-Simon, Voltaire's rival chronicler of Louis XIV, owned both a manuscript copy of the *Mémoires* and a copy of the 1735 edition. While giving Mademoiselle high marks for the accuracy of her narratives and the quality of her portrayal of Lauzun and her other tormentors, he nevertheless found her recitals naïve.[6]

A century later, Sainte-Beuve, echoing his predecessors, called Mademoiselle a "*princesse romanesque*" whose life lacked the "taste, the grace, and the balance" that characterized the belle époque of Louis XIV. The author of the *Causeries du Lundi* found these faults reflected in the *Mémoires*, where she expressed herself "naïvely, proudly, and exactly as things came to her."[7] Adolphe Chéruel, in his edition of Mademoiselle's *Mémoires* (1858), felt obliged to defend his decision to strip away the "corrections" of his predecessors in order to present the "authentic" Mademoiselle, with her seventeenth-century syntax and her idiosyncratic style. There are still a few modern critics who find Mademoiselle's writing pedestrian, and inferior to that of many of her contemporaries. Gabrielle Verdier, for example, has characterized the *Mémoires* as "stuffed with repetitions and set phrases . . . weighed down with innu-

THE MUSE'S LAMENT ✤

merable incidents always introduced by the same conjunctions . . . full of grammatical errors and broken constructions." Another distinguished critic, Derek A. Watts, regrets the "relative banality of the literary expression" found in Mademoiselle's great work.[8]

Whatever the merits of Mademoiselle's style when compared to those of contemporaries like Retz, a number of characteristics of Mademoiselle's *Mémoires* are of interest to both the historian and the literary critic. To begin with, their very existence sets them apart. Although the memoir literature of the seventeenth century is immense, most of it is by men. Comparatively few memoirs were written by women of Mademoiselle's generation, and these vary greatly in quality and in scope: one might contrast, for example, the very distinguished effort of Madame de Motteville with the utterly unimpressive product of Marie de Longueville, duchess de Nemours. Virtually all the memoirs dealing with the Fronde, by men and women alike, are outer-directed, dealing with specific events and the narrator's part in them, sometimes presented as an apologia or simply as a record of the author's observations of important episodes. In the case of Motteville we are confronted with a lengthy work that, as indicated by its subtitle, is a biography of Anne of Austria. Motteville's own sentiments, although not her observations of Anne's, are carefully concealed. By contrast, Mademoiselle's rich narrative is always accompanied by a running commentary on her emotional responses to the events recounted. This is sometimes supplemented with an "insider's insight," secret knowledge that an outsider could not know.[9]

As a member of the royal family and an enormously wealthy woman in her own right, Mademoiselle was caught up in the issues of her class and gender in the seventeenth century, many of which were debated in learned circles and explored in the literature of the period. In the public sphere, the seventeenth century in France saw the resurgence of royal authority after the disruptions occasioned by the wars of religion in the preceding century. In private life, there was a new stress on paternal authority and, from available evidence, a corresponding decrease in the spheres of activity permitted to women. The two phenomena were symbiotic: the authority of the state and that of the pater familias were thought to complement one another, forming part of the natural order of things and sharing, ultimately, a divine origin.

Seventeenth-century women struggled against these broad trends to restrict the roles of women not only in the public domain, but in the realm of private and family matters as well.[10] A few women, drawn from the highest circles of the aristocracy, continued to play a visible and independent role in the public life of France throughout the first half of the century: one might cite Madame de Chevreuse, Madame de Longueville, Anne de Gonzague, and Mademoiselle herself. Mademoiselle's writings, with meditations on the ability of women to govern, accounts of the prominent role taken in the Fronde by women, and a narrative of her struggles to maintain her independence of choice in matters matrimonial, touch on many of these issues. The relationship between state and society, the shift in aristocratic attitudes and behavior in the course of the century, and the preoccupation of articulate society with the right ordering of family relationships can all be traced in the pages of Mademoiselle's *Mémoires*.

If Mademoiselle does not concern herself with political history as such after the Fronde, she maintained an interest throughout her life in the conflicts she observed at the intersections of public and private life. Certain themes are constant in Mademoiselle's *Mémoires*: authority and autonomy, with challenges to both royal and paternal authority, the clash between social convention and private inclination, the relationship of power and status, the complications of wealth and status in a society obsessed with questions of relative rank and standing. From her vantage point as a dynast, matters of public import often had private consequences, so that an *affaire d'état* was often an *affaire de famille* with consequences for the natural ordering of family relationships. At the same time, her rank and visibility gave a public import to what would otherwise have been private matters: her father's management of her property, her attempts to chart her own course in marriage, and her defiance of social convention—and dynastic principle—in selecting Lauzun as her mate. This dynamic drives a constant shifting of the boundary between the public and the private in Mademoiselle's narrative, often joining issues within a framework of conflicting values: for example, Mademoiselle's justification of her role in the Fronde sets her filial duty as Gaston's daughter in opposition to her duty of obedience to the king.

One of the most vexing problems in evaluating Mademoiselle's great work is to classify it. To some scholars, it is a typical mid-seventeenth-century aristocratic memoir. To others, it is a proto-autobiography or even a kind of journal. One critic has even insisted that it is a "deliberately unclassifiable" document, thus ascribing to Mademoiselle our twentieth-century deconstructionist confusion. Still others argue that the key to Mademoiselle's *Mémoires* is that it is a hybrid. Those parts of the work written after the event, when the outcome is known, conform to the more traditional notion of a historical memoir: with hindsight, the author comments on her role in certain famous events, or provides an insightful narrative on episodes of interest to a wider public. But other parts of Mademoiselle's *Mémoires* are closer to a journal, or even a diary, since she was recording events whose outcomes were not yet known.[11]

Where are the distinctions to be made? A review of the composition of the *Mémoires* is helpful here. The traditional chronology of the *Mémoires*, following Chéruel, divides them into three parts: the first, encompassing all the material written by 1659–60, thus including Mademoiselle's childhood recollections, the events of the Fronde, and her years at Saint-Fargeau; the second, covering the events from 1659 to 1676 and written by the princess in 1677; and a final part written in 1689–90 and chronicling Lauzun's release and the final break with him. But Mademoiselle herself states that the very first section of the *Mémoires*, beginning with recollections of her childhood and ending with the massacre at the Hôtel de Ville in 1652, was written as a single exercise early in her years of exile at Saint-Fargeau; the obvious conclusion is that the balance of the first part, dealing with her exile and her quarrels with Gaston, was written at some subsequent period.[12]

Had Mademoiselle ended her work with the events of the Fronde, it would have survived as a conventional memoir of the period, distinguished only by its unusual openness, vivid narrative, and the rank of the writer. It would have been comparable to the work of her distinguished predecessor and model, Marguerite de Valois.

Given the narrative content, this portion of the *Mémoires* is the most overtly political. To some extent, Mademoiselle's interpretation of the struggles against Richelieu and Mazarin is conventionally "high aristocratic," asserting her firm belief in the right, if not the duty, of revolt against "ministerial tyranny." This has a princely gloss: as evidenced by her remarks at Orléans and her carriage conversation with Gaston, Mademoiselle believed in a special role for members of the royal house, dynastic guardians of the state, whose actions, she insisted, were intended for the public weal.

Mademoiselle's assertion of such a role allowed her to critique ministerial actions from a different perspective than that available to lower-ranking aristocrats. If the good of the state is equated with the stability and sanctity of the royal house, then the princess could portray the damage inflicted by the ministerial régimes on members of the royal family as an assault on the stability and safety of the state itself. Echoing Gaston, who accused his royal brother of unfilial behavior at the behest of Richelieu, Mademoiselle chronicles the cardinal's assaults on the royal family as the actions of a dishonest steward: the seizure of Champigny is a theft of royal property; the exile of Marie de Medici is a theft of royal affection; the misalliance with the Condés is a theft of royal rank. Mademoiselle is scarcely less scathing in her treatment of Mazarin, criticizing the regent for repeating Louis XIII's error by surrendering royal authority to a *favori,* and justifying Gaston's break with the minister by the cardinal's refusal to recognize Gaston's special place as the guardian of his nephew's state. In both cases, Richelieu's and Mazarin's, the servant had helped himself to the master's portion and the master's place, with the inevitable consequences: confusion and rebellion.

Mademoiselle's view on the role of women in the public sphere is also evident in the first part of her *Mémoires,* in part because of her unspoken assumption that the role of women—at least aristocratic women—was indistinguishable from that of men. For at least three generations, since the religious wars of the previous century, women of the top social strata had played prominent roles in public affairs; in more recent times, France had been governed by women regents, Marie de Medici and Anne of Austria. Women had figured prominently in the opposition to Richelieu and, later, to Mazarin. The Fronde marked the high point of this phenomenon, pitting the regent Anne against a cast of aristocratic women rebels that included, among others, Mademoiselle herself, the Condé women, and the Princess Palatine, all of whom functioned on a level of political equality with their male counterparts. At Orléans, Mademoiselle "took command," with at least nominal authority over Beaufort and Nemours; her lecture to the Orléanais on the role of "princes" clearly encompassed royalty of both sexes.

Contemporaries were acutely aware of the prominence assumed by women in politics in this period, with predictably mixed commentary.[13] Mademoiselle came in for her share of the sarcasm, as evidenced by the satirical tone of many Mazarinades and cartoons, Retz's sour comments, and Henrietta Maria's biting references to Joan of Arc. But the activities of these great ladies led to considerable reflection on the natural fitness of women to play a part in public affairs and even to govern the state. Other writings of Mademoiselle, notably her correspondence with Motteville, emphasize the importance of this debate; in fact, Mademoiselle takes pains in her *Mémoires* to trace the origins of this exchange to conversations within the entourage of Anne of Austria. The idyllic retreat envisioned by Mademoiselle would be ruled by a woman (herself) with the inhabitants on a level of equality irrespective of gender. While it is Motteville who sings the praises of women rulers in the correspondence, Mademoiselle endorses this view and authenticates it in the *Mémoires*. The *Princesse de Paphlagonie*, written in the same period as the Motteville correspondence, reinforces this impression with its fictionalized account of the Fronde that deliberately inverts the "normal" gender roles, with women at the center of the narrative and in the critical roles, and men playing supporting parts.

Mademoiselle's endorsement of a natural and important role for women in the public sphere dovetails with her reflections on the autonomy of women in the sphere of family and private matters. Mademoiselle's personal experiences give rise to reflections and observations on the paradox of her time: women who had played a leading role in public life were subjected in private life to abuse without any effective restraint, as evidenced by her treatment at the hands of Gaston during her first exile (1652–57), or that of the princess de Condé somewhat later at the hands of the victor of Rocroi.

The shift in emphasis is evident as Mademoiselle continues her *Mémoires*, devoting many hundreds of pages to a justification of her confrontation with her father, recording her sense of betrayal at his hands and her emotional break with him. To justify her defiance of Gaston, Mademoiselle had to appeal once more to the natural order. If Gaston had forfeited his role as protector and had acted instead as a despoiler of his daughter's interests, then she could argue a natural right of resistance. For this reason, Mademoiselle chose to resume the narrative thread of events after the massacre at the Hôtel de Ville before proceeding to the long and confusing battle over Gaston's stewardship of her property. Gaston's abandonment of his daughter at the moment of the king's return to Paris, his refusal to offer her a refuge on his estates, and his apparent contempt for his daughter are the justifications for Mademoiselle's later actions. Having abandoned the "natural role" of the father as protector, Gaston is not convincing when he accuses his daughter of unnatural behavior in raising questions about his management of her property. Mademoiselle lost this battle largely because of the reconciliation between Gaston and the court. The poles of paternal and royal authority, so critical to the seventeenth-century mentality, were once more properly aligned. Mademoiselle, unable to appeal from one to the other, had lost her room to maneuver. These matters had scarcely been put to rest, and not to Mademoiselle's satisfaction, at the time of her return to court in 1657. From the internal evidence of the narrative, this segment of the *Mémoires* has the feel of a journal or diary, providing a chronicle or nearly simultaneous narrative of her struggle with Gaston.

The final portion of this part of the *Mémoires* is fairly dense, full of the amusements at the court of the young king, gossip about courtiers, and many interesting character sketches of her contemporaries. The writing corresponds to the time in which Mademoiselle was composing her *Divers Portraits* and reflects her experimentation with other forms of expression, namely the literary portrait, the letter, and the *nouvelle*, as alternatives and supplements to the narrative mode. But this was short-lived, and by the time Mademoiselle returned with the court to Paris in July 1660, her interest in these literary forms had waned.

This first part of Mademoiselle's *Mémoires* ends abruptly with the visit of Gaston to Paris in 1659 and with the rumors in the capital that peace between France and Spain was imminent. After she put down her pen, the princess did not resume the composition of her *Mémoires* until 1677. Mademoiselle later explained that the long hiatus was due to the press of events and the distractions of the court. The real reasons may lie else-where. Having finished her accounts of the battle with Gaston and her reconciliation with the court, Mademoiselle could not find a narrative theme to sustain her chronicle, nor could she satisfactorily resolve the questions she had raised about the contradictory roles of women in public and private life. These structural problems may have been com-pounded by some form of long-term depression following the death of Gaston in February 1660.

By the time Mademoiselle resumed writing her *Mémoires* in August 1677, the lack of a leitmotif was no longer a problem. Her involvement with Lauzun, her public humiliation at the hands of Louis XIV, and her continuing fears for the still-imprisoned Lauzun provided a framework for her narrative. Mademoiselle wished to reply to two widespread con-temporary interpretations of the *affaire Lauzun* that she found deeply offensive. The first was that the king had somehow engineered the entire episode to reward a favorite courtier. Ironically, Louis had used this "explanation" to good purpose, breaking the engagement to demon-strate the untruth of the accusation. The second interpretation, even more insulting to the princess, painted her as the victim of a scheming and insincere courtier. This is the underlying premise of the popular pamphlet *Les Amours de Mademoiselle et . . . Lauzun,* which first appeared in 1672 and soon became a seventeenth-century best-seller.[14]

Both explanations of her behavior struck hard at her self-image by portraying her either as a king's pawn or a courtier's dupe. To a large extent, the part of the *Mémoires* written to cover the years 1659–76 is an attempt to impeach these interpretations. Mademoiselle takes pains to demonstrate that she remained in control of her destiny, and that she had taken the initiative in her relationship with Lauzun. She reminds her readers that she refused kings and princes in those years, including Charles of England, Alfonso of Portugal, and Philippe d'Orléans, and endured a second bout of exile (1662–64) rather than submit to the king's wishes. She manages to condense the period 1659–66 into a mere 255 pages (in the Chéruel edition), inclusive of her accounts of the king's marriage, her second exile, and the death of Anne of Austria, to arrive at 1666, when Lauzun comes into focus at the moment of his appointment as captain-general of the royal dragoons. The way had already been prepared by a number of earlier comments. At the time of the king's marriage, Mademoiselle takes note of the old Spanish custom of marrying royal princesses to great noblemen; shortly thereafter, Lauzun, as commander of the *becs-à-corbin,* catches Mademoiselle's eye in a successful battle over precedence. Thereafter, the pair had no need of a king to urge them on. As suggested by her quotation from Corneille's *Suite du Menteur,* Mademoiselle believed that a higher power had sown the seed that she had nourished.[15]

In *Les Amours de Mademoiselle . . . et Lauzun,* Lauzun is portrayed as a devious and clever courtier, encouraged by his friends to woo Mademoiselle. The prize is her vast wealth and the prestige of a royal alliance. While there is never a suggestion that Lauzun harbors any real affection for the princess, there is more than a hint of physical seduction, and Lauzun is referred to as her lover.[16] By contrast, the Lauzun of Mademoiselle's *Mémoires* is initially a respectful and solicitous friend of the princess. It is the princess who concludes that she has fallen in love with Lauzun and that Lauzun's personal qualities make him a fit candidate for her hand: "Finally, after several troubled days I realized that it was Lauzun who had slipped into my heart, and whom I loved . . . once in a lifetime, it was essential to know the joy of being loved by someone worth loving."[17]

Thereafter, the text of the *Mémoires* is largely an account of the "courtship of Lauzun" by Mademoiselle and of their betrayal by jealous rivals and false friends. While Mademoiselle's treatment of Louvois, Orléans, and Condé is scathing, she is still respectful of the king. Louis is portrayed as caught between his public duty and his personal inclinations, and he alone within the royal family is shown as sympathetic to her plight.

The reasons for so forgiving a portrayal of the king are not hard to find. When Mademoiselle was writing this part of her *Mémoires*, Lauzun was still in prison. In spite of her constant battles with authority, Mademoiselle was to a large degree a believer in the religion of royalty: the king could not knowingly commit an injustice. Others, such as Louvois or jealous rivals, were responsible for Lauzun's disgrace, and Mademoiselle hoped to move the king to mercy. There was also the simple matter of prudence. Mademoiselle did not wish to write anything that would compromise her or put Lauzun further in jeopardy, if her writings somehow found their way to the king's study. Her inability to secure Lauzun's release or even a mitigation of his living conditions caused Mademoiselle to break off her writing once more after the failure of his attempted escape from Pignerol in 1676 and Louis's refusal to act on any of her pleas and entreaties.

By the time Mademoiselle began to write the final part of her *Mémoires*, around 1689, another decade had elapsed, a period that saw the collapse of all her hopes and the greatest betrayals she chronicled. Once again, Mademoiselle felt compelled to offer her own version of events. She makes little attempt to explain away Lauzun's behavior, leaving that to others, such as Madame de Montespan. Betrayal at the hands of ingrates was always the ultimate offense for Mademoiselle: Gaston had been ungrateful for her support during the Fronde; Condé had been ungrateful for her efforts to save his army at the battle of the Porte Saint-Antoine; Lauzun had been ungrateful for the financial sacrifices she had incurred to secure his release; Louis had been ungrateful for the benefits showered on his bastard son.

With little left to lose, Mademoiselle is ready to accuse even the king of betrayal. Her false friend, Montespan, acts as the king's surrogate in securing Lauzun's release in return for Mademoiselle's gifts of property to the young duc du Maine. And then the bargain is only half kept: Lauzun is denied the court, and his offices are not restored. Mademoiselle is not permitted the dignity of a public wedding. Her astonishment at the suggestion that she and Lauzun could live openly together without a publicly acknowledged marriage is surely not feigned, and there is more than a suggestion in the *Mémoires* that Lauzun might have behaved differently had he been restored to his former position at court. The end of Mademoiselle's *Mémoires* thus brings her back to one of its fundamental themes, her lifelong conflict with authority, often at the intersection of the public and private spheres.

Any sensitive reader of her *Mémoires* can readily observe that Mademoiselle's tie to Gaston was the deepest one of her life. Her preoccupation with her half sisters and her quarrels with her stepmother after her father's death underscore her need to be, in some emotional sense, the heir to Gaston. If Gaston the man was a predator, Gaston the prince was the source of his daughter's royal status and social position, and Mademoiselle never let her contemporaries forget this. It is striking that the surviving portraits of Mademoiselle that show her holding or pointing to a likeness of Gaston, including the one by Pierre Bourguignon (1671) that can still be seen at Versailles, were done many years after Gaston's death. After the loss of Gaston, Mademoiselle had no trouble in accepting Louis's invitation to regard him as her "second father." This would have been natural enough for any seventeenth-century aristocrat, and was all the more so for a member of the royal house dealing with the dynastic chief.

This commingling of roles, however, brought Mademoiselle to even more grief, as evidenced in her account of the *affaire Lauzun* and its aftermath. In the end, Mademoiselle came to see her "second father" very much as she saw the first: as a natural protector turned predator. However carefully constructed and superficially respectful, the characterization of Louis's behavior in the final part of the *Mémoires* is not flattering.

Gabrielle Verdier has argued that each portion of the *Mémoires* was instigated by a separate *trahison masculine* by, in order, Gaston, Louis, and Lauzun. This useful insight requires a caution: the theme of betrayal is not gender-specific in the *Mémoires*. Mademoiselle was sensitive to female betrayals as well: Anne of Austria betrayed their old alliance in the *affaire Saujon*; her friend Mademoiselle d'Epernon betrayed their friendship by entering a convent without telling her; the countesses betrayed Mademoiselle after she sheltered them at Saint-Fargeau; and Montespan betrayed her trust by deceiving her about the king's willingness to rehabilitate Lauzun and permit a public marriage in exchange for Mademoiselle's lavish gifts to the duc du Maine.[18]

The last betrayal, then, is the king's. Having broken with Lauzun, Mademoiselle found his rehabilitation by the king incomprehensible.

The political necessity that compelled Louis to make much of the rescuer of James II's wife and infant son found no justification in Mademoiselle's eyes. Her anger at the royal "ingratitude" was well known to contemporaries. Mademoiselle was able to write of her shattered hopes of a life with Lauzun; she could not bring herself to record her final humiliation at the hands of a king who denied her justice. The conclusion that runs through the last part of her *Mémoires* is that justice is found only in heaven. The rage here is mixed with indications of a new level of religious piety and resignation to the divine (as opposed to the royal) will. The conflict between these two positions, a Christian resignation to the injustice of the world and a rage at its consequences, is never resolved in the *Mémoires*.[19]

Mademoiselle's seeming preoccupation with marriage, another constant throughout her long work, cannot be separated from the other central themes of her *Mémoires*—power and authority, duty versus inclination—since marriage in the seventeenth century, at least in elite circles, was bound up with questions of social standing and family alliance. The word that Mademoiselle commonly uses for her marital projects is her "establishment." The writing of the *Mémoires* in parts widely separated in time permits us to trace the evolution of Mademoiselle's thinking on the subject. From childhood through the end of her first exile, Mademoiselle thought in the most conventional terms of her future "establishment," that is, of a match that would confirm her royal status. Her preference was for a crown matrimonial: either the French or the imperial diadem. Failing these, at the very least any proposed spouse had to come from the narrow circle of nonreigning Bourbons, Habsburgs, or Stuarts. Minor German or Italian princes were beneath her, and the specter of misalliance horrified her: the Condé match with Richelieu's niece, the marriage of the Rohan heiress with Henri de Chabot, even the marriage of inclination between her old friend Marie de Longueville and the penniless duc de Nemours, struck Mademoiselle as scandalous.

If there is anything unconventional about Mademoiselle's views, it is her attempt to portray herself as an active participant in the search for a suitable "establishment," even to the extent of flirting with treason in the *affaire Saujon*. If her preferences for a royal groom were as might be expected, her role was not, and throughout her *Mémoires* there is an insistence on her right of *choice*, which she will not concede to father, minister, or king. The rejection of eminently suitable matches—Charles

Stuart, Alfonso of Portugal, even Philippe d'Orléans—suggests a new sensibility at work as well as the influence of the literary circles around her.[20]

Her exchange of letters with Madame de Motteville at the time of the king's marriage indicates that as she entered her thirties, Mademoiselle adopted the views of some *Précieuses* that marriage, with its permanent subjugation of wife to husband, was not a desirable state. This assertion went hand in hand with Mademoiselle's frequently expressed belief that if women were capable of exercising authority in the public sphere, then they were entitled to autonomy in private matters as well. It was in this spirit that she told Turenne that she preferred to be Mademoiselle in France managing her vast estates rather than queen of almost anywhere else. The furious reaction of the king to Mademoiselle's vocal defiance speaks not only to the needs of Louis's foreign policy, but also to his exasperation with a declaration of feminine autonomy that flew in the face of the social conventions of the day.

Thereafter, much as Mademoiselle tries to conceal it by noting the occasional marriage proposal, Louis preferred to marginalize Mademoiselle, rather than call further attention to her defiance of royal authority. There were, after all, other princesses who could serve as instruments of French policy, including Mademoiselle's half sisters, and later, Philippe d'Orléans's daughters. The somewhat surprising proposal in 1670 that Mademoiselle should take the place of Henrietta Stuart as Philippe's second wife was due entirely to the unexpected vacancy caused by Henrietta's premature death. Mademoiselle used this event to underscore yet another theme in her *Mémoires*: the cupidity of her family and the envy her wealth inspired, even among royal princes. Philippe, it will be recalled, had proposed that Mademoiselle's money be left to one of his daughters by Henrietta, who would be betrothed to the dauphin. The Condés were not far behind, and both Maria Theresa and Louis XIV offered their own alternative candidates for Mademoiselle's wealth, if not her hand.

The second part of the *Mémoires*, covering her infatuation with Lauzun, thus suggests a shift in Mademoiselle's ideas on matrimony. The issue of the subjugation of the wife is muted in favor of the assertion of the right to choose: once more, Mademoiselle is in charge of her own destiny. Moreover, unlike the usual arrangement, whereby the wife's status is a function of her husband's, Mademoiselle bestows the status and wealth. By her act, Lauzun will become duc de Montpensier, one of the wealthiest noblemen in France, able to use Gaston's livery and display Mademoiselle's coat of arms—the royal arms differenced for Orléans. Only the king could ennoble, but Mademoiselle, as she boasted, could make a nobleman a near prince, greater than her sister's husband Guise. A cadet of Gascony would thereafter rank as the king's first cousin by marriage.[21]

Mademoiselle chronicles the fierce reaction of the extended royal family to her engagement. She ascribed much of this hostility to the cupidity of the queen, Philippe d'Orléans, and the Condés. As events indicated, there was obviously much truth in this. Nevertheless, in stressing the selfish interests of those who opposed the match, Mademoiselle ignores the widespread indignation in elite circles at this violation of hierarchical conventions and the lingering incomprehension and astonishment in polite society at her behavior. To substantiate this, one need only recall the comments of her friends Sévigné and Bussy-Rabutin, the furious arguments with her own confidential servants, and the satirical verses and pamphlets at her expense.

In the end, Mademoiselle was true to her view of herself as a rational actor who chose independently, first to have Lauzun, then to ransom him, and finally to dismiss him not simply for his evident ingratitude, his violent behavior, and his unconcealed infidelity but also because of his attempts to gain control of her affairs. Again, Mademoiselle's objections to those attempts would have seemed unconventional to contemporaries. Husbands normally assumed control of their wives' properties and business affairs, and Lauzun was widely assumed to be Mademoiselle's husband. Mademoiselle was able to win this battle because Lauzun could not summon the authority of state and society to enforce his authority as head of household. This was due partly to the nature of an unacknowledged secret marriage and partly to his own disgrace in the king's eyes. Once again, a misalignment of the normal alliance of public and private authority gave Mademoiselle room to maneuver.

Still, after yet another political shift, Mademoiselle was doomed to disappointment. When Louis, in a gesture to the dethroned James II, permitted Lauzun to return to court, Mademoiselle was powerless to interfere. The last pages of her *Mémoires* stop just short of this final defeat. Mademoiselle could not bear to chronicle her near despair at the king's "betrayal" of her honor.

Mademoiselle's detailed first-person narrative of certain contemporary events over the central decades of the seventeenth century has long been of use to traditional historians; in recent decades, her attitudes and approaches to many of the social issues of interest to her class and gender have attracted the attention of younger historians. Many of these questions are of interest to literary scholars as well, and Mademoiselle has found a second audience among them, not only for her *Mémoires* but also for her correspondence with Motteville, her *Divers Portraits*, and her small works of fiction.

Mademoiselle's reputation has benefited from the twentieth-century movement by some French literary critics away from formalistic studies of classical prose and toward the content of many of these writings, seeing in them an exploration of the inner self, the development of a psychology of self-awareness, and a medium for exploring the tension between the ideal and the real in the daily lives of the principals. Many of these developments in French literature date from the seventeenth century, and Mademoiselle's works can be set in this context. Her literary portraits, an early attempt at psychological profiling, enjoy a special status; her *Mémoires* are applauded for their straightforward narrative, their concentration on key episodes and events, and the running commentary by a narrator who separates the "self as actor" from the "self as retrospective commentator." Even her exchange of letters with Madame de Motteville, while making use of common literary props of the period—romantic shepherds, idealized settings, and so on—goes beyond the clichés to assertions about the roles and abilities of women at a time when society overall was decreasing the sphere of independence for women.[22]

Literary critics in the last generation have expended a great deal of ink tracing the development of the modern genre of autobiography out of its predecessor forms, the journal and the memoir literature of the sixteenth, seventeenth, and eighteenth centuries. In the process, they have set aside the comments of many illustrious predecessors and have identified Mademoiselle's *Mémoires* as an important contribution in the development of this genre. In a famous phrase, Marc Fumaroli calls memoirs a form of writing "at the crossroads of genres in prose," noting the relationship of memoirs not simply to history or autobiography but to the development of the modern forms of the novel. He cites Mademoiselle's writings as the best of the subgenre of the "worldly memoir" with its stress on the distinction between life "as she would have wanted to live it and life as she did live it."[23]

The little-read *Vie de Madame de Fouquerolles* should not be overlooked in tracing Mademoiselle's literary odyssey. In it one meets a number of characters who feature in the *Mémoires*, notably Saujon, and sees an attempt to narrate some of the early events of the Fronde. It also contains a number of character sketches and prototypes of the literary portrait, including a self-portrait. In her first self-description, Mademoiselle boasts about her powers of perception, which give her an ability to see through the false protestations of devotion by Fouquerolles and to discern her true intentions. This need to unmask others recurs throughout the *Mémoires* and is often used to great effect. Beneath the glitter of court life and high position, we glimpse the unhappiness of the great (Queen Maria Theresa, Henrietta Stuart) and the hypocrisy and greed of others (Philippe d'Orléans, Madame de Montespan, Lauzun). This becomes a justification for seeking one's true destiny elsewhere.[24]

Of Mademoiselle's other writings, until recently only the *Divers Portraits* has attracted significant critical attention, as an important contribution to a literary technique, the "portrait," which was to be perfected by Saint-Simon and has enjoyed a very long shelf life. Mademoiselle's collection may also be seen as a historical document, providing us with examples of the self-image and group values of the high aristocracy of France in the middle of the seventeenth century. Among the portraits executed by Mademoiselle for her collection, those of Philippe d'Orléans, Condé, and Louis XIV are among the most striking. Taken together, they form a kind of commentary on the princely vocation, as they portray "the prince" in three incarnations: the prince at play, the prince as warrior, and the prince as ruler.

Mademoiselle's use of the "portrait" is not confined to those found in the *Divers Portraits*. Emmanuèle Lesne (-Jaffro) has pointed out that Mademoiselle made good use of this technique in her *Mémoires*.[25] Within the *Mémoires*, portraits are sometimes split, with portions in various places in the text. With Lauzun, for example, Mademoiselle starts with her overall impression, from a distance as it were: "He was not destined, as it appeared, for small things" (3: 478).

Further in the text, his moral portrait is given in the first person, as part of an exchange between herself and Lauzun. Lauzun describes himself thus:

> I am of all men in the world the one who likes the least to talk, and it seems to me that you [Mademoiselle] very much enjoy conversation. I sometimes stay three or four hours all alone in my room, and if my valet

entered, I think I'd kill him. . . . I am very much the king's servant and I would hardly have any time left for a wife. So I would be a husband you would rarely see, and when you did, I wouldn't be very amusing. . . . You might think that I want a more important post than I have now, and that this elevation [from the marriage] would make me ambitious . . . not so; I want no other post than the one I have [captain of the guards]. . . . I have a special liking for what others dislike, constant attendance on the king . . . if they offered me a governorship I would refuse. (4: 178)

There is finally a physical portrait, which Mademoiselle puts in the third person:

He is a small man, but everyone says he has the most handsome and pleasing figure. He has good legs and a distinguished manner. His hair is blond but very mixed with gray, often unkempt and too thick. His eyes are blue but almost always reddened; a handsome face and a look of distinction. He has a pleasant smile. His nose is pointed and red; there is something superior about his whole appearance. His dress is often in disarray, but when he cares to take the trouble, he is very presentable. Here is the man. As for his disposition and his manners I defy anyone to understand, describe, or copy them. (4: 249)[26]

Mademoiselle's direct involvement with literary figures must be teased out. Her *Mémoires* are strangely reticent about her interest in the salon society that flourished in the first half of the seventeenth century. This is probably because of her later break with many in this circle, including Sévigné and Segrais, due to their sometimes vocal disapproval of her relationship with Lauzun.[27] Her earlier familiarity with the world of the salons is not surprising. Gaston, whose protégés included Vincent Voiture, was a noted patron of the arts and letters. Mademoiselle is known to have frequented Madame de Rambouillet's salon before the Fronde, and Julie de Montausier was a lifelong friend: it was at her urging that Mademoiselle produced the *Princesse de Paphlagonie*, with its striking description of Rambouillet's famous *chambre bleue*. Segrais was a member of Mademoiselle's household for many years, and influenced her modes of expression. Segrais was also linked to Madame de la Fayette, and it is striking that two of La Fayette's early works have some association with Mademoiselle: her portrait of Sévigné, which appeared in the *Divers Portraits*, and her first novel, *Princesse de Montpensier*, published in 1662, which is set at Champigny and which treats of an imaginary love affair a century earlier between an earlier Montpensier lady and a duc de Guise. Madame de Sévigné's letters provide ample evidence of her ties to the princess, despite the infrequent references to the marquise in the *Mémoires*.[28]

After Mademoiselle's return to court in 1657, she hosted her own salon at the Luxembourg, and her weekly *après-midis* have been portrayed as the aristocratic answer to the more pedantic and bourgeois crowd that gathered at the Scudéry residence. This is to shortchange both Mademoiselle and the Scudérys. Mademoiselle learned the technique of the literary portrait in the famous *romans* of Mademoiselle de Scudéry, *Clélie* and *Le Grand Cyrus*. She was also on good personal terms with the three Scudérys, as evidenced by her role as godmother to Georges de Scudéry's son in 1662. If her views on marriage, as expressed in the correspondence with Madame de Motteville, seem extreme, they can be traced to an exaggerated disdain for the married state found in certain *Précieuse* tracts.

On a different level, Mademoiselle was an admirer of Corneille, although she cites him only twice in her *Mémoires*, most notably to portray her attraction to Lauzun. Ironically, her choice of this particular passage from Corneille's *Suite du Menteur* lends itself to contradictory interpretation, for the image of an overpowering predestination is contrary to her general insistence on free choice and control over her destiny. Even modern critics are hesitant here. Jean Garapon cites the Corneillian tradition to argue that Mademoiselle believed in an *amour d'élection*, while Patricia Cholakian predicates a Corneillian determinism, or "will of heaven," in Mademoiselle's use of the quotation to explain her infatuation with Lauzun.[29]

On the other side of the house, both Molière's *Précieuses Ridicules* (1659) and his *Femmes Savantes* (1672) can be tied to the world of the salons, including Mademoiselle's at the Luxembourg. A famous scene in the *Femmes Savantes*, the furious argument between Trissotin and Vadius (III, iii) has been linked to a brawl in Mademoiselle's apartments one afternoon between the abbé Charles Cotin and the poet Gilles Ménage, when the latter, to the merriment of the company, unknowingly ridiculed a sonnet that had been written by the former. Mademoiselle was courageous enough to offer a performance of the complete version of *Tartuffe* to her guests in 1669 in spite of the frowns of the authorities.[30]

Writing from a feminist perspective, Faith Beasley argues that the entirety of the *Mémoires* can be read as an act of political and cultural subversion and that Mademoiselle set out to construct an interpretation of events that stressed the contributions of *women* to both the political developments of the day and to the cultural phenomenon of the time, the rise of salon society and the consequent transformation of aristocratic mores. This, Beasley insists, was due to Mademoiselle's perception that "official" history and conventional memoirs would minimize the contributions of women as a matter of course. Mademoiselle thus offers an alternative interpretation to the accepted, male-dominated version of events. Beasley's views are shared by others, including Gabrielle Verdier, and have been extended to cover Mademoiselle's other works as well.[31]

It is certainly true that Mademoiselle was acutely conscious of the growing limitations on a woman's freedom of action, even in the most rarefied circles of society. The paradoxical events of her own life can only have made this all the more evident: the woman who had saved Condé's army from annihilation and had secured Orléans for the princes could be forced by a father's command to dismiss her confidential servants. There is much evidence in her writings of her sensitivity on the matter: her musing on great rulers such as the infanta Isabella, her exchange with Madame de Motteville on the abilities of women to govern, even her fascination with the abbey of Fontevrault, where the abbess had jurisdiction over the monks residing on the premises.

But Mademoiselle's *Mémoires* cannot be treated simply as a chronicle, or as a detached narrative, or even as an alternative version of the history of her times. She was not interested in recording great events with a historian's precision, nor was she by nature a dispassionate observer. At no time does she suggest any grand theory of history to explain the public events she has witnessed. On any number of occasions, she indicates that she will leave such matters to others. Her themes are primarily subjective, and in the fashioning of her narrative, she freely shapes her account to suit her preconceptions. To cite several examples: she refuses to acknowledge that the restored Charles Stuart and the widowed duke of Savoy declined her hand, rather than the reverse, because this would contradict her constant assertion of self-determination in matters matrimonial. Nor can she accept the reality of Lauzun's fierce and eccentric behavior after his release. Mademoiselle expected a return, namely, love and gratitude, for her investment of a decade of her life and much treasure in the pursuit of Lauzun's freedom. The collapse of this investment and the resulting emotional crisis are the background to her final appeals to heaven and to posterity for the justice denied her in her lifetime.

Her sculpted narrative, built around certain subjective themes and intended to explain her failed search for happiness, creates a dilemma for scholars trying to classify Mademoiselle's great work. In the end, most critics have concluded, often with a mix of fascination and exasperation, that in fashioning a *personnage* for herself, Mademoiselle created a work that hybridizes the techniques of the historical novel and the preoccupations of autobiography, thereby skirting the boundaries between fiction and reality at Fumaroli's famous "crossroads of genres in prose."[32]

The very characteristics of Mademoiselle's writings that have dismayed critics from Voltaire to Sainte-Beuve attract the modern reader: her frankness, her display of emotion, her willingness to explore her own motivations. Mademoiselle's ability to control her narrative by distinguishing between herself as the omniscient narrator and herself as the protagonist at any given point in the *Mémoires* gives her writings a freshness and a modern appeal.[33] At the same time, the narrative quality of some of her set pieces stands comparison with the best of her contemporaries. Her version of the battle at the Porte Saint-Antoine in 1652 blends a tribute to Condé's heroism with her own horror at the sight of the wounded and dying and her wonder that she was responsible for Spanish troops marching through the streets of Paris. Her account of the death of Anne of Austria is a worthy precursor of Saint-Simon's famous accounts of the deaths of the Grand Dauphin and of the duc de Bourgogne a half-century later. Her own fear of death is not far away in her account of Anne of Austria's last hours, nor has Louis XIV ever been depicted in a more human way than in her account of his grief and torment as his mother lay dying.

One critic has noted that the *Mémoires* offer a vivid picture of the author "in her humanity and sensitivity," and another, Margaret McGowan, with wonderful insight, has noted that Mademoiselle is "her own witness, so to speak," and her *Mémoires* are intended to project her self-image, building "a monument for the future."[34] Jonathan Dewald has pointed out that the survival of the diaries of Louis XIII's physician Héroard allows the "possibility of real knowledge of a seventeenth-century man."[35] Arguably, the survival of Mademoiselle's *Mémoires*, written in parts separated by decades, permits the historian and the literary scholar to trace the evolution over time of a seventeenth-century woman. One may well debate whether it is the same person at the end as the one with whom the story begins, although, as Jean Garapon argues so eloquently, "the voice remains the same, just as noble."[36]

Mademoiselle opened her *Mémoires* with a lament about the "misfortune" of her house. She could have closed them on a similar note, but they break off in mid-sentence, and the reader is left without a final summation. As a placeholder for this unwritten conclusion, one might offer the following passage from her self-portrait, written in 1657:

> I have a good memory, and I am not lacking in judgment. I only hope that if people are to judge me, it would not be on the basis of the events Fate has decreed for me to date. If so, their opinion of me will not be favorable. To do me justice, admit that I have been less wanting in my behavior than Fate has been in its decrees. Had Fate been fairer, she would have treated me better.[37]

Mademoiselle's Writings

MADEMOISELLE'S *MÉMOIRES* WAS PUBLISHED FOR THE FIRST TIME in Paris in 1718, but the entire edition was suppressed by order of the regent, Philippe II d'Orléans, and his *lieutenant général de police*, Marc-René d'Argenson. Ten years later, in 1728, a new edition was successfully published in Paris by Le Breton, followed by a Dutch version in 1729 by J. F. Bernard (Amsterdam), which included some of Mademoiselle's other writings. Thereafter, the *Mémoires* was republished frequently: Amsterdam, 1730; Anvers, 1730; Amsterdam, 1735; Amsterdam, 1736; The Hague, 1741; Paris and London, 1746; Amsterdam, 1766; Maestricht, 1776; and Paris, 1806 and 1823.

The source of the earliest editions is not clear. The edition of 1735 published by J. Wetstein and G. Smith (Amsterdam) was derived from the manuscript copy entrusted by Mademoiselle to a prominent member of the parlement of Paris, Achille III de Harlay, who had been the executor of her will, and that manuscript is preserved at the Bibliothèque Nationale de France, Ms. Fr. 19588–92. The Wetstein edition, long considered the most accurate version, was the source of most editions published in the second half of the eighteenth century and the first decades of the nineteenth century. In addition to the *Mémoires*, the Wetstein edition included most of the other works of Mademoiselle and, inevitably, the *Amours de Mademoiselle . . . et Lauzun.*

Over time, various editors "corrected" the style and grammar of earlier editions, often truncating or rewriting sentences and paragraphs to conform to later stylistic norms. In 1824, Claude B. Petitot and Louis J. N. Monmerqué, using the Harlay manuscript as a guide, republished the 1735 edition, after removing what they considered the errors of their editorial predecessors, in their *Collection des Mémoires Relatifs à l'Histoire de France* (second series). Yet another edition based on the same 1735 text was published by Joseph-François Michaud and Jean-Joseph François Poujoulat in their *Nouvelle Collection des Mémoires pour Servir à l'Histoire de France* (third series) in 1838.

Surprisingly, both Petitot and Michaud chose to ignore the autograph version of Mademoiselle's *Mémoires*, which was known to both, and which was readily available at the Bibliothèque Royale (now, Bibliothèque Nationale de France). This may have been because the manuscript in Mademoiselle's hand was incomplete and was, according to Petitot, "practically illegible."

In 1858–59, Adolphe Chéruel brought out a new edition of the *Mémoires*, based on the autograph manuscript, Ms. Fr. 6698–99. This Herculean task involved correcting the phonetic spellings used by Mademoiselle but otherwise leaving her syntax more or less intact, dividing the work into chapters, identifying persons mentioned in the text, and adding a critical apparatus of notes and appendices consisting of excerpts from other contemporary sources.

The autograph copy of the manuscript lacks the first eighty-two folio pages and begins with the events of 1649. To reconstruct the missing text, Chéruel had to rely on the Harlay manuscript for the first 207 pages of his edition, which runs to more than 2,000 pages. In otherwise disregarding the Harlay version, Chéruel evidently dismissed the possibility that the Harlay manuscript may represent a rewriting sanctioned by Mademoiselle herself. Chéruel's version, reprinted several times, has superseded all others for scholarly purposes. Jean Garapon has pronounced the Chéruel version to be sound, although subject to certain minor corrections. In 1985, the French publishing firm Fayard reprinted Chéruel's text, but without his notes and critical apparatus, with a new introduction by Christian Bouyer.[1]

There are two other manuscript copies of the *Mémoires* at the Bibliothèque Nationale de France. One of these, Ms. Fr. 4154–56, belonged to Gros de Boze, the secretary of the Académie des Inscriptions, and has been at the Bibliothèque Nationale since 1728; the other, known as the Lancelot manuscript, Ms. Fr. 4157–60, is a 1721 copy of a manuscript belonging to the duc du Maine. An inscription in the Lancelot copy suggests that Maine may also have owned the mutilated autograph manuscript at the Bibliothèque Nationale.

There are two other manuscript copies of the *Mémoires* in major public collections. One of these belonged to the duc de Saint-Simon, and appears in an inventory of the duke's papers made after his death in 1755. Together with the original of the duke's memoirs and other papers, this version of Mademoiselle's work is still preserved at the Archives du Ministère des Affaires Etrangères, series Mémoires et Documents: France, vols. 70–74. How Saint-Simon acquired this copy is not certain. Given his dislike of the Harlays and also of Louis-Germain de Chauvelin, who inherited the Harlay collection of manuscripts, it seems unlikely that the duke solicited it directly from any of these. No attempt has ever been made to compare the Saint-Simon version, in a very clear handwriting, with the other extant manuscripts.

Yet another copy survives at the British Library, Egerton Ms. 1679, about which little is known but which would appear to be a reproduction of the Harlay manuscript, acquired at auction from the estate of a private party in 1856. It too has never been compared with the autograph manuscript.[2]

As Garapon has observed, we know very little about the actual composition of the *Mémoires*, and we can only surmise that Mademoiselle made use of letters, notes, or possibly journal entries that are now lost. There is some evidence that supports this view. For example, a letter written by Mademoiselle in July 1652 describing the battle at the Porte Saint-Antoine includes some of the same details as the account in the *Mémoires*: in both, Mademoiselle lists various aristocratic casualties, notes the perils Condé experienced, and rejoices at the salutary effects of a few "volleys from the Bastille." A number of her letters from the 1650s dealing with the *comptes de tutelle* survive and are consistent with her presentation in the *Mémoires*, and one may assume that she had access to copies of these letters at the time she wrote the relevant sections of her *Mémoires*. To cite another example, her vivid narrative of the marriage of Louis XIV in 1660, in particular, of the ceremonies on the Spanish side of the border, was written in the late 1670s. The exceptional richness of detail suggests some source dating from the actual event. Two letters by Mademoiselle de Vandy, who accompanied Mademoiselle to the Spanish service, have survived, and are strikingly similar to Mademoiselle's account. Since Vandy remained in Mademoiselle's circle until her death in 1685, it is quite possible that Mademoiselle had access to these pieces.[3]

Unfortunately, Mademoiselle still lacks her Pléiade. In spite of Garapon's reassurances, a modern edition of the *Mémoires* is needed that takes into account all of the known manuscript versions of the text. Until a contemporary scholar braves Mademoiselle's nearly illegible handwriting and her phonetic spelling to produce a modern critical edition of the *Mémoires*, there will be any number of issues and uncertainties about the texts.[4]

As far as I can determine, there have only been two English translations of the *Mémoires*, a three-volume translation published by H. Colburn (London, 1848) and a very abridged one-volume translation by Grace Hart Seely published in London (1928) and New York (1929).

Mademoiselle's original collection of fifty-nine literary portraits, seventeen of which were written by her, and including the famous portrait of Madame de Sévigné by Madame de La Fayette, was originally published at Caen at the end of 1658 or the very beginning of 1659 under the title *Divers Portraits Imprimés en l'Année 1659* in an edition limited to no more than sixty copies. This edition, which did not have a royal "privilege," or license for publishing, was followed almost immediately, in January 1659, by a second version published by Charles de Sercy and Claude de Barbin and called *Recueil des Portraits et Eloges en Vers et en Prose Dédié à Son Altesse Royale Mademoiselle*. This edition, in two volumes, each more than three hundred pages long, included twenty-one of the portraits published in the *Divers Portraits*, of which only three were by Mademoiselle, and added eighty-four new ones. Several months later, the same publishers republished this version in a grander format, again in two volumes, running more than nine hundred pages. Both editions included an elaborate dedication to Mademoiselle and a decorative frontispiece of an imaginary "gallery" hung with medallion portraits and surmounted with Mademoiselle's coat of arms. A copy in the grand format that apparently belonged to Mademoiselle survives at the Bibliothèque Nationale.

In 1663, without the collaboration of Barbin, Sercy produced yet another edition, retaining the 21 portraits from the original *Divers Portraits* but replacing a number of others, for a total of 104 portraits. This version of nearly eight hundred pages was also divided into two volumes, under the title *La Galerie des Peintures . . . ou Recueil des Portraits et Eloges en Vers Dédié à S.A.R. Mademoiselle.* A self-portrait by La Rochefoucauld was among those printed here for the first time.

All 152 portraits contained in these various editions were reprinted together with a number of unpublished portraits found in the Conrart papers at the Bibliothèque de l'Arsenal, by Edouard de Barthélemy in 1860 (Paris), under the title *La Galerie des Portraits de Mademoiselle de Montpensier.*

Barthélemy's edition is the last that has been published of the Sercy *Recueil/Galerie* in its entirety and is the most readily accessible printing of Mademoiselle's original fifty-nine portraits. But the small overlap between the *Divers Portraits* and the later Sercy-Barbin editions has made some scholars, notably Denise Mayer and Jacqueline Plantié, question the appropriateness and accuracy of tying these works together. The original *Divers Portraits*, with its modest fifty-nine portraits, was reprinted in the Wetstein edition of the *Mémoires* and in the Maestricht edition of 1776. Denise Mayer has also reprinted the seventeen portraits attributed to Mademoiselle, including the anonymous collective "Portrait des Précieuses," in her *Trois Etudes.*

The publishing history of these *Portraits* has been further troubled by a persistent misidentification with an anonymous work of a similar name, consisting of twenty-five individual and collective portraits of prominent members of the court and published in 1667 under the title *Pourtraits de la Cour Pour le Présent, c'est à dire, du Roy, des Princes, et des Ministres d'Etat et Autres.* It too seems to have made quite a sensation and was frequently reprinted. Félix Danjou reprinted it without attribution in *Archives Curieuses de l'Histoire de France*, second series, v. 8 (Paris, 1839). It was also translated into English as early as 1668 under the title *The Characters or Pourtraicts of the Present Court of France* (Thomas Palmer, London). Although the only mention of Mademoiselle in this work is as the subject of a very inferior portrait, a number of major libraries, including the British Library and the Library of Congress, confuse this work with the *Divers Portraits* and attribute it to Mademoiselle. The confusion is all the more surprising since the distinction between these works was pointed out in a widely used nineteenth-century reference work, Jacques-Charles Brunet's *Manuel du Librairie*.[5]

The *Relation de l'Ile Imaginaire* and *Histoire de la Princesse de Paphlagonie* were published anonymously in Bordeaux in a single volume in 1659 by Segrais on Mademoiselle's orders. The book was dedicated to Madame de Pontac, and only about a hundred copies were printed and distributed to Mademoiselle's friends. Neither the identity of the author nor those of the persons depicted under fanciful names were much of a secret. Several surviving copies have handwritten "keys" to the identities of these persons on flyleaves, and Segrais published one in his own *Mémoires* (1723). The *Relation* and the *Histoire* were reprinted in volume 2 of Segrais's *Oeuvres Diverses* (Amsterdam, 1723) and published separately in Paris by Prault in 1734; they were also included in the addenda to the Wetstein edition of Mademoiselle's *Mémoires* and in other eighteenth-century editions of the *Mémoires*. In 1788, C. G. Garnier included them in an anthology of travelers' tales published as *Voyages Imaginaires* (Amsterdam), v. 26. The last publication of these two small works seems to have been an 1805 printing in Paris by A. A. Renouard.[6]

Mademoiselle's exchange of letters with Madame de Motteville was first published in Cologne in 1667 under the title *Recueil des Pièces Nouvelles et Galantes*, and it was reprinted in the Wetstein edition of the *Mémoires*. In 1806 these letters were bundled with a few others between Mademoiselle and Bussy-Rabutin, her letter to the king requesting permission to marry Lauzun, and her self-portrait, and republished by Léopold Collin (Paris). A seventeenth-century manuscript copy of the correspondence between Mademoiselle and Motteville has recently been acquired by the Bibliothèque Nationale de France, N.A.F. 25670, and this includes a number of unpublished letters dating from 1661.[7]

Mademoiselle's letters to Bussy-Rabutin have also been published in the Lalanne edition of the *Correspondance* of Bussy-Rabutin (Paris, 1858–59).

Relatively few unpublished letters of Mademoiselle have survived in French archival deposits. Mademoiselle destroyed most of her correspondence for the early period of her life during her first exile at Saint-Fargeau and the rest, apparently, some time in the 1670s. A few short letters to Gaston and to her friends, notably to Madame de Pontac, written in the 1640s and 1650s, survive in the Collection Baluze at the Bibliothèque Nationale de France, as does some material on her quarrels with Gaston; miscellaneous letters are widely scattered in other collections at the Bibliothèque Nationale de France, the Ministère des Affaires Etrangères, and the Archives Nationales. These are listed in the Bibliography.

Mademoiselle corresponded regularly with her brother-in-law Cosimo III de Medici, and some letters survive in the Archivio di Stato, Archivio Mediceo, Florence. Emmanuel Pierre Rodocanachi published several of these in his biography of Marguerite-Louise d'Orléans (1902), and Patricia Ranum has graciously provided me with transcripts of those dating from the mid 1680s. These letters confirm that Mademoiselle liked her brother-in-law but thoroughly disapproved of Marguerite-Louise's return to France and subsequent behavior. Together with related letters from the Tuscan resident envoys at the French court found in the same series, they provide a glimpse of the frequent feuding that characterized Mademoiselle's relationship with her two surviving half sisters and her aunt Mademoiselle de Guise. Other letters from the late 1650s and early 1660s to her aunt Christine and her cousins of Savoy survive in the state archives in Turin.

Mademoiselle's first work, her *Histoire de Jeanne Lambert d'Herbigny, Marquise de Fouquerolles*—bound up with short pieces by Mesdames de Fiesque and Frontenac—was never reprinted after its initial small printing at Saint-Fargeau in 1653 and only a few copies have survived. One can be found at the Bibliothèque Nationale de France, and another at the Houghton Library, Harvard University. The existence of partial manuscript copies at the Bibliothèque de l'Arsenal in the Recueil Conrart suggests that it also circulated in this form within the circle of Mademoiselle's friends.

Mademoiselle's *Réflexions sur les Huit Béatitudes . . .* was published in 1685 (Paris) by Lambert Roulland. Although mentioned in several eighteenth-century reference works, no copy survived in any of the great French libraries, and it was forgotten until the beginning of this century, when Rodocanachi found the copy that Mademoiselle had sent to her brother-in-law Cosimo III in the Biblioteca Riccardiana, Florence. Rodocanachi reprinted it in 1903 under the title *Un Ouvrage de Piété Inconnu de la Grande Mademoiselle.*

Mademoiselle's *Réflexions . . . sur le Premier Livre de l'Imitation de Jésus-Christ* was published anonymously in 1694 as an addendum to a new translation of the *Imitation* by a Jansenist scholar, Nicolas Fontaine, and was reprinted in a second edition in 1722. Although attributed to

Mademoiselle in several eighteenth-century reference works, it was not until 1980 that Denise Mayer established Mademoiselle's authorship of this work.[8]

In addition to the *Portraits de la Cour* falsely attributed to Mademoiselle, about a dozen other apocryphal works attributed to Mademoiselle also survive; they are listed in the Bibliography for the convenience of the reader. These all date from the years of the Fronde (1649–53) and are a small portion of the thousands of such works known as "Mazarinades." Those concerning Mademoiselle consist of supposed "declarations" and "manifestos" from Mademoiselle to Gaston, to the queen, to the Archduke Leopold, to all "generous hearts," etc. One of these, called *Manifeste de Mademoiselle . . . à Son Altesse Royale* (Paris, 1652), is a justification by Mademoiselle of her decision to go to the rescue of Orléans. In it she regrets that the time of the Amazons had passed and that she had only "words" to put at the service of the princely cause. A literary scholar has recently cited this work with much approval in her study of Mademoiselle. Celeste Moreau, who catalogued the *Mazarinades* in the 1850s, expressed his surprise that the printer was allowed to "so stupidly abuse Mademoiselle's name." Anyone familiar with Mademoiselle's style can see at a glance that Moreau was right.[9]

 APPENDIX B

Mademoiselle's Fortune

LIKE THE FORTUNES OF THE OTHER GREAT ARISTOCRATIC FAM-
ilies of the period, the Montpensier fortune was rooted in widely scattered landed properties and in the revenues derived directly and indirectly from them: tenant and demesne revenues, various feudal dues and
levies, and other forms of indirect revenues from local commercial activities. Secondary sources of income included *rentes* derived from in-
vestments in government bonds, interest income from loans to individuals, and pensions and other income from estate settlements, royal gifts,
and so on. In addition to revenue-producing assets, the fortune of a great
family included the value of nonincome properties (e.g., a town house or
country houses without revenues) and personal possessions such as
jewelry, furniture, silver and gold table services, and books. Aristocratic

liabilities typically consisted of mortgages on landed properties, other obligations for borrowed money, often secured with pledges of future revenues, and sums owed to trade creditors, that is, the vendors who furnished luxury goods and services to aristocrats and their households.

Mademoiselle's most important inherited properties were found in the ancient Bourbon domains, with vast estates in the Bourbonnais, Auvergne, the Beaujolais, and Dombes, and secondary concentrations along the "historic" Loire (Champigny, Mézières-en-Brenne, Châtellerault) and in Lower Normandy (Mortain, Domfront, Auge). Additional holdings were found in La Puisaye/Burgundy (Saint-Fargeau), the Vendée (La Roche-sur-Yon), and Champagne. Available records, although fragmentary, suggest that Mademoiselle actively managed her properties, rounding out and rationalizing her estates with purchases of adjacent or complementary properties. Her most notable accomplishment here, the purchase of Eu, increased her annual income by at least 100,000 livres, with more than half of this sum derived from the sale of wood from its forests. At the end of her life, her successful pursuit of a share of her grandmother Guise's fortune brought her the great estate of Joinville in Champagne, as well as a large pension drawn on the Guises.

The division of Mademoiselle's property after her death and the destruction or disappearance of most of her financial records make it impossible to do a detailed study of her fortune—either by category, or even chronologically—analogous to the studies done of the fortunes of the Condés, the Contis, and the Orléans. Ironically, given Mademoiselle's pride in her business acumen, the most complete breakdown of her revenues available is that compiled by Gaston for the period of his guardianship (1627–50), and this is of little analytic value. His refusal to provide any accounting for the revenues from the Beaujolais and Dombes, together with his provision of only a partial accounting for her Norman revenues, understates her income by a very considerable margin and distorts the distribution of her revenues by category.

In 1626, at the time of Gaston's marriage to Mademoiselle's mother, his household officers estimated that the Montpensier revenues totaled 330,000 livres. Mademoiselle indicates in her *Mémoires* that her annual revenues as of 1662 were 500,000 livres, and from what can be gleaned from surviving records, this figure is unlikely to have changed substantially by the time of her death in 1693. The large increase over the 1626 figure can be attributed to her acquisition of Eu, to better management of her inherited properties, as evidenced by the surviving records of

Saint-Fargeau, and by the award of various pensions and settlements stemming from the many lawsuits to which she was a party, including 570,000 livres paid in irregular installments (1659–94) by the Richelieu heirs for the damage to Champigny, and small sums from Mademoiselle's stepmother. Although Mademoiselle's gifts to Lauzun diminished her revenues by 40,000 livres, the effect was partly offset almost simultaneously (1681) by liens of 26,000 livres on the Guise revenues. As noted earlier, in 1692 the princess obtained a judgment increasing this award to 35,000 livres and adding to it the estate of Joinville, which later passed to Philippe d'Orléans. Mademoiselle's fictitious sale of Eu and Dombes to the duc du Maine had no effect on her income, since she reserved the usufruct for herself, and the duke did not take possession of these great domains and their revenues until her death.

From surviving records, it is possible to identify specific sources for approximately 390,000 livres of Mademoiselle's revenues: 210,000 livres from Eu and Dombes; another 30,000 from Saint-Fargeau and Thiers, which she deeded to Lauzun; 80,000 from the balance of her estates left to Philippe d'Orléans; and at least 70,000 livres of income from *rentes* and pensions, most of which also fell to Philippe. Unlike her princely cousins, Mademoiselle did not enjoy large pensions provided by the Crown, nor, as is evident from these figures, did she derive a major portion of her income from nonlanded sources: at least 80 percent of her total income was derived from her landed estates, inclusive of the revenues from the sale of wood from Eu and other properties, notably Châtellerault and Saint-Fargeau.

Capitalizing these identifiable revenues at thirty times landed income and ten times other sources (per Jean-Pierre Labatut) provides an asset valuation of 10.3 million livres, of which at least 9.6 million can be attributed to her landed estates. To this must be added the value of two nonincome properties: Choisy, at 800,000 livres (cost basis); and her wing of the Luxembourg, at 600,000 livres (settlement basis); and also the gross proceeds from the auction after her death of her household furnishings and jewelry, 276,000 livres. We arrive at a total value of approximately 11,975,000 livres. But, if we assume that Mademoiselle's revenues aggregated 500,000 livres, as she states in her *Mémoires*, rather than the 390,000 livres we can identify, the final figure should be adjusted upward for the "missing" 110,000 livres of income. Since the sources are unknown, a conservative multiple of ten times for capitalization purposes would add another 1,100,000 livres to the estate, for a valuation of

13,075,000 livres. Mademoiselle's fortune would therefore range from 11,975,000 to 13,075,000 livres: a rounded average of 12,500,000 livres could be used as a working figure.

As an alternative and more conservative valuation technique for Mademoiselle's fortune, we might add the known purchase and sales prices of some of Mademoiselle's major estates—such as Eu and Saint-Fargeau—to the estimation by Nancy Barker of the value of Mademoiselle's landed estates inherited by Philippe d'Orléans (2.1 million livres) to arrive at a valuation of 8.2 million livres for the landed properties. After adjusting for *rentes* and pensions at the same multiple of ten, as well as for the nonincome properties and the personal possessions sold at auction, we arrive at an estimated total asset value of 10,975,000 livres. While admittedly crude, these two sets of calculation do establish an order of magnitude for Mademoiselle's fortune: 10,975,000 to 12,500,000 livres.

By comparison, Labatut has calculated that in the period 1693–1723, the average fortune of royal princes was 3 million livres, those of nonroyal dukes scarcely a million. With the exception of the Condés, whose landed properties alone have been valued at 19 million livres in the first decades of the eighteenth century, yielding an income of 900,000 livres, Mademoiselle may well have had the largest fortune (if not income) in the royal family. The Contis, for example, who shared in the Mazarin inheritance, had a landed fortune of perhaps 3.5 million livres in the 1690s, but a total income, derived largely from *rentes* and pensions, of 300,000 to 600,000 livres. Similarly, the Joyeuse fortune of Mademoiselle's grandmother Guise was estimated at 4.3 million livres just before her death in 1655, of which 1.8 million represented the value of landed estates.[1]

In her study of Philippe d'Orléans, Nancy Barker values his landed properties, excluding the Montpensier legacy, at a maximum of 4.5 million livres, with an annual income of about 200,000 livres. In some sense, this was the prince's basic fortune, since the rest of his enormous income, another 1.2 million livres, consisted of pensions received from the Crown, which were either greatly diminished or discontinued in succeeding generations. As noted above, Barker values the Montpensier estates left to Philippe at a maximum of 2.1 million livres, with an annual income of 80,000 livres. This inheritance, supplemented by the 60,000 livres of *rentes* that Mademoiselle also left to Philippe, was clearly a very significant augmentation of the Orléans family fortune, increasing its core revenues by 70 percent and the value of his estates by 50 percent, notwithstanding the debts that accompanied this legacy.[2]

As Barker notes, Philippe's joy at this magnificent inheritance was somewhat dampened by the accompanying debt level. Mademoiselle left behind 3.1 million livres of debt secured by mortgages on Eu, as well as unsecured debts, which probably exceeded 1 million livres. Since the deed of "sale" to Maine indemnified him against the mortgage debt, these obligations fell, contrary to normal legal principles and after some legal skirmishing, to her Orléans heirs. Servicing alone ate up 147,000 livres per annum at the outset, although Philippe was able to reduce the principal to 2.1 million livres and annual debt service to 100,000 livres by the time of his death. Payment, settlement, and litigation on the rest of Mademoiselle's debts continued almost to the Revolution.[3]

In his excellent study of the fortune of cardinal de Richelieu, Joseph Bergin distinguishes the *succession*, or estate value left by a great noble, from the "fortune" or net value after liabilities, asserting that from the point of view of heirs, the former was far more important than the latter, since liabilities accruing to such *successions* were complex, often took generations to settle, and were rarely a source of immediate anxiety. This concept is not very far from similar distinctions used in modern financial analysis. The calculations used above by Labatut et al. to calculate the size of various princely estates provide valuations on a "continuing enterprise" basis (to use the jargon of modern corporate finance), without consideration of accompanying liabilities. A "breakup" or liquidation valuation would differ from this by subtracting out the attached liabilities to arrive at a net value (for an owner/seller or heir). In Mademoiselle's case, this would mean reducing the estimated value range of 10.9 to 12.5 million livres by at least 4 million in liabilities, to arrive at a net valuation of 6.9 to 8.5 million livres, that is, the estimated net value *ultimately* transmitted to her various heirs. But as Bergin cautions, such calculations may overstate the impact of notional liabilities, since the passage of time, the ravages of inflation, and successful legal chicanery to stave off payment to creditors all inured to the benefit of heirs.

Even if we allow for an adjustment at the estimated level of liabilities, Mademoiselle's fortune was of exceptional magnitude by any measure of the time, and until the end she continued to live in splendor, attended by a retinue of noble attendants and trusted domestics, varying her time between her palatial residence of the Luxembourg, her estate at Choisy, and her princely domain of Eu. Even she may not have been aware of the extent of her holdings. In examining the book-length list of her estates provided by Gaston's accountants, one is struck by how many she neither visited in her long lifetime nor even mentions in her *Mémoires*.[4]

APPENDIX C

Genealogical
Tables

Henri IV, King of France, d. 1610, m. Marie de Medici, d. 1642

- **Louis XIII,** d. 1643, m. Anne of Austria, d. 1666
  - **Louis XIV,** d. 1715, m. Maria-Theresa of Spain, d. 1683
    - **Louis, Dauphin of France,** d. 1711
      - *illegitimate* Louis-Auguste, duc du Maine, d. 1736
  - **Philippe duc d'Orléans,** d. 1701, m. 1. Henrietta Stuart, d. 1670 2. Elizabeth-Charlotte of the Palatinate, d. 1722

- **Elisabeth,** d. 1644, m. Philip IV of Spain, d. 1665
  - **Maria-Theresa,** d. 1683, m. Louis XIV

- **Gaston, duc d'Orléans,** d. 1660, m. 1. Marie de Bourbon-Montpensier, d. 1627 2. Marguerite de Lorraine, d. 1672
  - (1) *Anne-Marie-Louise, duchesse de Montpensier, La Grande Mademoiselle (1627–1693)*
  - (2)
    - 1. Marguerite-Louise, d. 1721, m. Cosimo III de Medici
    - 2. Elisabeth, d. 1696, m. Louis-Joseph, duc de Guise, d. 1671
    - 3. Françoise-Madeleine, d. 1664, m. Charles-Emmanuel of Savoy

- **Christine,** d. 1663, m. Victor-Emmanuel, duke of Savoy, d. 1637
  - 1. Charles-Emmanuel, d. 1675, m. Françoise d'Orléans
  - 2. Marguerite, m. Ranuccio, duke of Parma
  - 4. Henrietta, m. Ferdinand, duke of Bavaria

- **Henrietta-Maria,** d. 1669, m. Charles I of England, d. 1649
  - 1. Charles II, d. 1685
  - 2. James II, d. 1701
  - 3. Mary, d. 1660, m. William, Prince of Orange
  - 3. Henrietta, d. 1670, m. Philippe, duc d'Orléans

- *illegitimate* **César, duc de Vendôme,** d. 1665, m. Françoise de Lorraine
  - 1. Louis, duc de Vendôme, d. 1669
  - 2. François, duc de Beaufort, d. 1669
  - 3. Elisabeth, d. 1664, m. Charles-Amadeus, duc de Nemours

Note: Persons not mentioned in the text have been omitted.

The Families of Bourbon-Condé and Bourbon-Soissons

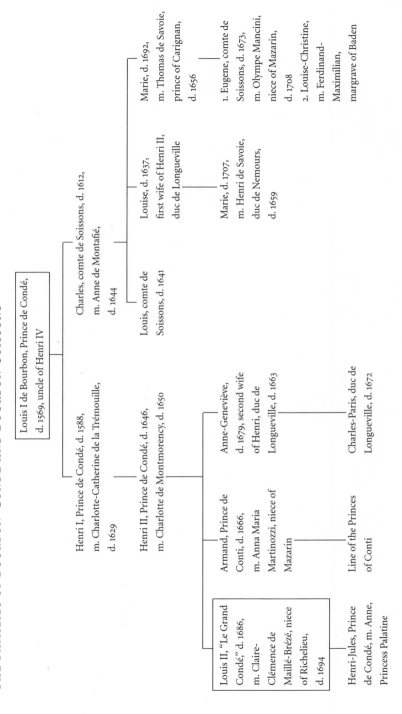

Louis I de Bourbon, Prince de Condé, d. 1569, uncle of Henri IV

Henri I, Prince de Condé, d. 1588, m. Charlotte-Catherine de la Trémouille, d. 1629

Henri II, Prince de Condé, d. 1646, m. Charlotte de Montmorency, d. 1650

Louis II, "Le Grand Condé," d. 1686, m. Claire-Clémence de Maillé-Brézé, niece of Richelieu, d. 1694

Henri-Jules, Prince de Condé, m. Anne, Princess Palatine

Armand, Prince de Conti, d. 1666, m. Anna Maria Martinozzi, niece of Mazarin

Line of the Princes of Conti

Anne-Geneviève, d. 1679, second wife of Henri, duc de Longueville, d. 1663

Charles-Paris, duc de Longueville, d. 1672

Charles, comte de Soissons, m. Anne de Montafié, d. 1644

Louis, comte de Soissons, d. 1641

Louise, d. 1637, first wife of Henri II, duc de Longueville

Marie, d. 1707, m. Henri de Savoie, duc de Nemours, d. 1659

Marie, d. 1692, m. Thomas de Savoie, prince of Carignan, d. 1656

1. Eugene, comte de Soissons, d. 1673, m. Olympe Mancini, niece of Mazarin, d. 1708

2. Louise-Christine, m. Ferdinand-Maximilian, margrave of Baden

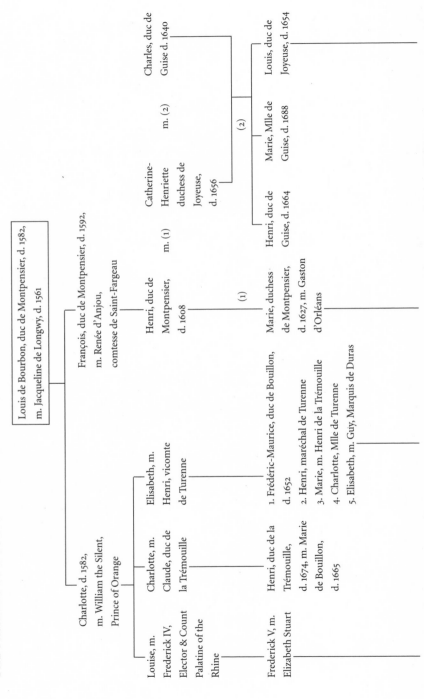

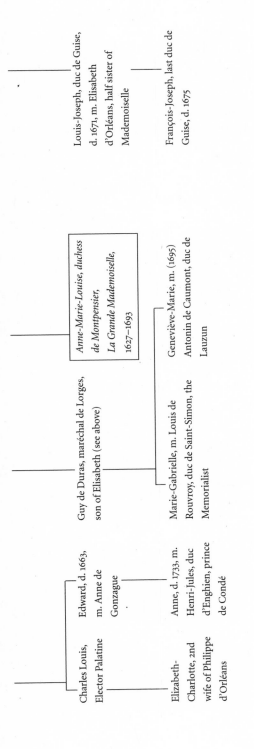

Charles Louis, Elector Palatine

Edward, d. 1663, m. Anne de Gonzague

Louis-Joseph, duc de Guise, d. 1671, m. Elisabeth d'Orléans, half sister of Mademoiselle

Guy de Duras, maréchal de Lorges, son of Elisabeth (see above)

Anne-Marie-Louise, duchess de Montpensier, *La Grande Mademoiselle*, 1627–1693

François-Joseph, last duc de Guise, d. 1675

Elizabeth-Charlotte, 2nd wife of Philippe d'Orléans

Anne, d. 1733, m. Henri-Jules, duc d'Enghien, prince de Condé

Marie-Gabrielle, m. Louis de Rouvroy, duc de Saint-Simon, the Memorialist

Geneviève-Marie, m. (1695) Antonin de Caumont, duc de Lauzun

Notes

INTRODUCTION

Epigraphs: Montpensier, self-portrait, in Denise Mayer, "Les Seize Portraits," *Trois Etudes d'après Ses Mémoires, Papers on French Seventeenth-Century Literature,* series Biblio 17–45 (Paris, 1989), 18–19; Jean Regnault de Segrais, *Oeuvres Diverses de Mr. de Segrais,* 1: *Mémoires/Anecdotes* (Amsterdam, 1723), 35.

1. Lois G. Schwoerer, *Lady Rachel Russell* (Baltimore, 1988), xviii.

2. Christian Bouyer, *La Grande Mademoiselle* (Paris, 1986), 12–13.

3. Robert Muchembled, *Popular Culture and Elite Culture in France, 1400–1750,* trans. Lydia Cochrane (Baton Rouge, La., 1985), 196–201, 221–30.

CHAPTER 1   THE DAUGHTER OF FRANCE

Epigraphs: *Mémoires de Mademoiselle de Montpensier,* ed. Adolphe Chéruel (Paris, 1858), 4: 83–84; Segrais, *Mémoires/Anecdotes,* 1: 33–34.

1. For a modern interpretation of this event and the connection to the Guises, see Arlette Jouanna, *Le Devoir de Révolte, 1559–1661* (Paris, 1989), 227–29; see also Georges Dethan, *La Vie de Gaston d'Orléans* (Paris, 1992), 53–60. For a traditional narrative, see Carl J. Burkhardt, *Richelieu and His Age: His Rise to Power* (London, 1967), 195–207. For an interpretation consistent with a general reappraisal of Louis XIII by more recent historians, see A. Lloyd Moote, *Louis XIII the Just* (Berkeley, 1989), 189–94; see also Orest Ranum, "Richelieu and the Great Nobility: Some Aspects of Modern Political Motives," *French Historical Studies* 3 (1963): 184–204.

Contemporaries were also wary of the role of the Guises in this marriage. See the so-called *Mémoires de Gaston, Duc d'Orléans*, attributed to Algay de Martignac, in *Nouvelle Collection des Mémoires Relatifs à l'Histoire de France*, ed. Joseph-François Michaud and Jean-Joseph Poujoulat (Paris, 1837–81), 23: 569. Georges Dethan argued in an article published in 1959 that the likely author was not Algay de Martignac, but probably Jean Lassere, another of Gaston's entourage. The article was reproduced in Dethan, *Gaston*, 369–72.

2. For Gaston's fortune, see *Mémoires de Gaston*, 570. While any attempt at capitalization of this income stream would be at best an approximation, one can arrive at a figure of twelve million livres by using the multiples provided by Jean-Pierre Labatut in *Les Ducs et Pairs de France au XVIIᵉ Siècle* (Paris, 1972), 258–59: thirty times for landed revenues, ten times for *pensions* and *rentes*. Per Labatut, the only comparable fortunes were those of Henri II de Condé, whose estate was valued at 14.6 million livres in 1651, an inheritance much swollen by the Montmorency properties that fell to the Condés in the 1630s and 1640s; of Richelieu, valued at 22.4 million livres; and of Mazarin, valued at 26 million livres. The fortunes of the two cardinal ministers included considerable revenues derived from ecclesiastical offices. For these calculations, see Labatut, *Les Ducs et Pairs*, 258–59, 262, 264. Labatut also estimates, 248, the average fortune of a prince of the blood in this period at 2.3 million livres.

For Gaston's household, see *Mémoires de Gaston*, 570; see also Eugene Griselle, *Les Maisons de la Grande Mademoiselle et de Gaston d'Orléans* (Paris, 1912), which lists the household of Gaston in 1627, 1–14, and that of the duchess d'Orléans, 15–17.

3. For Marie de Bourbon-Montpensier's revenues, see *Mémoires de Gaston*, 570. For a discussion of the Montpensier fortune, see Appendix B.

4. Dethan, *Gaston*, 64; *Mémoires de Gaston*, 571.

5. For the quotation, see Gédéon Tallemant des Réaux, *Historiettes*, ed. Antoine Adam (Paris, 1959), 1: 355. For the congratulations of courtiers, see *Mémoires de Gaston*, 571.

6. On these court titles, see Louis, duc de Saint-Simon, *Mémoires*, ed. Yves Coirault (Paris, 1983–88), 3: 428–43, esp. 435–37 on the title "Mademoiselle."

7. On the Tuileries and the Louvre in the first half of the seventeenth century, see Orest Ranum, *Paris in the Age of Absolutism* (New York, 1968), 69–72; Georges Lenôtre, *Les Tuileries* (Paris, 1933); Louis Hautecoeur, *Histoire de l'Architecture Classique en France* (Paris, 1943), 1: 513–30 passim; Hautecoeur, *Le Louvre et les Tuileries* (Paris, 1924); Louis Batiffol, *Le Louvre sous Henri IV et Louis XIII* (Paris, 1930); David

Thomson, *Renaissance Paris: Architecture and Growth 1475–1600* (Berkeley, 1984), 79–97, 165–75, 182–86; Ian Dunlop, *Royal Palaces of France* (London, 1985), 106–9, 210–13.

For a general introduction to Paris in this period, see Ranum, *Paris;* Hautecoeur, *Architecture Classique*; Hilary Ballon, *The Paris of Henri IV: Architecture and Urbanism* (New York, 1991); Emile Magne, *La Vie Quotidienne au Temps de Louis XIII* (Paris, 1942); and Anthony Sutcliffe, *Paris: An Architectural History* (New Haven, 1993), 8–47. Anthony Blunt, in *Art and Architecture in France* (New Haven, 1991), provides an overview of the arts of the period, including commentary on the contributions of Henri IV and Marie de Medici, as does Thomson, in *Renaissance Paris*.

8. Griselle, *Maisons*, provides Mademoiselle's household for 1630, 19–25, noting that there are fragmentary and partial listings from 1628. On the comparisons with the household of the sisters of Louis XIII, see *Mémoires de Mademoiselle de Montpensier*, ed. Adolphe Chéruel (Paris, 1858), 1: 3. Hereafter these will be cited as *MM*, with the appropriate volume (1 to 4). On the importance of these household appointments and their significance within the patronage/power networks of the period, see two articles by Sharon Kettering, "The Patronage Power of Early French Noblewomen," *Historical Journal* 32 (1989): 817–41; and "The Household Service of Early Modern French Noblewomen," *French Historical Studies* 20 (1997): 54–85.

9. On Madame de Saint-Georges, see *MM*, 1: 5–6; for Mademoiselle's excuses for her lack of foreign languages, *MM*, 3: 438. On Claire-Clémence de Maillé-Brézé's lack of education, see *MM*, 1: 51. For Fénelon's lament, see *De l'Education des Filles*, in *Oeuvres Complètes* (Paris, 1810), 6: 7. On Mademoiselle's grammar and handwriting, which has defied generations of archivists and scholars, see Chéruel's introduction, *MM*, 1: x–xi, and also his various notes in the body of the text. On Anne-Geneviève de Bourbon's lack of formal education as well, see Victor Cousin, *La Jeunesse de Madame de Longueville* (Paris, 1864), 20–24. Jean Garapon defines Mademoiselle's education as an exposure to the usages of society and to the fashionable literature of the period: "Mademoiselle de Montpensier dans Ses *Mémoires:* l'Exemple d'une Culture Princière," in *De l'Estoile à Saint-Simon, Recherche sur la Culture des Mémorialistes au Temps des Trois Premiers Rois Bourbons*, ed. Madeleine Bertaud and André Labertit (Paris, 1993), 93–107.

The general subject of women's education in this period is still relatively unexplored by modern scholars. See Philippe Ariès, *Centuries of Childhood*, trans. Robert Baldick (New York, 1962), 331–33; Maïté Albistur and Daniel Armogathe, *Histoire du Féminisme Français* (Paris, 1977), 1: 214–22; Roger Chartier, Marie-Madeleine Compère, and Dominique Julia, *L'Education en France du XVIᵉ et XVIIᵉ Siècles* (Paris, 1976); Georges Synders, *La Pédagogie en France aux XVIIᵉ et XVIIIᵉ Siècles* (Paris, 1965); Elfrieda Dubois, "The Education of Women in Seventeenth-Century France," *French Studies* 32 (1978): 1–19. See also Mark Motley, *Becoming a French Aristocrat: The Education of the Court Nobility, 1580–1715* (Princeton, 1990), esp. 18–67 on family and household education.

10. *MM*, 1: 5–6.

11. On the loss of her mother, see *MM*, 1: 2. On Madame de Guise, see *MM*, 1: 5–6.

12. *MM*, 1: 4–5.

13. On the Day of Dupes, see Burkhardt, *Richelieu*, 370–402. For a stimulating reinterpretation, see Moote, *Louis XIII*, 199–219. On the bonds between the king and Richelieu, see ibid., 155–74. See also Ruth Kleinman, *Anne d'Autriche* (Paris, 1993), 162–63, 178–79, for an analysis of Louis XIII's personality and his inconsistent behavior toward his family and his ministers. For Mademoiselle's lament on the loss of Marie de Medici, see *MM*, 1: 4–5.

14. *MM*, 1: 6. On Gaston's reaction to these events, see Dethan, *Gaston*, 81–84.

15. *Larousse Histoire de France Illustrée* (1925), 2: 9; Burkhardt, *Richelieu*, 196. See also the characterization of Gaston in Moote, *Louis XIII*, 192, and in Pierre Goubert, *Mazarin* (Paris, 1990), 111. On the reconsideration of aristocratic motives in contemporary historical work, see Jouanna, *Devoir*; J. Russell Major, *From Renaissance Monarchy to Absolute Monarchy* (Baltimore, 1994); and Moote, *Louis XIII*. See also the discussion of this issue in Dethan, *Gaston*, i–vii.

16. For the narrative, see Dethan, *Gaston*, 82–102 passim; Moote also notes the use Gaston and Marie de Medici made of the visible misery of the peasantry, which they attributed to Richelieu's policies, and their attempts to use the parlement of Paris as a forum for criticism of Richelieu in *Louis XIII*, 224–25.

17. *MM*, 1: 6–7.

18. *MM*, 1: 7.

19. *MM*, 1: 7–8. Dethan, in *Gaston*, 197, traces the rumor of a possible marriage between Anne of Austria and Gaston to a suggestion made to the king by Richelieu at the time of the conspiracy of Chalais. See also Moote, *Louis XIII*, 193, 280–81.

20. On the negotiations for Gaston's return to court, see *MM*, 1: 9–10; Dethan, *Gaston*, 101–6.

21. *MM*, 1: 9–10; Gaston made the same accusation, as did many other contemporaries. See *Mémoires de Gaston*, 599; Dethan, *Gaston*, 185–87. A more common form of misalliance in this period was that of a noblewoman, usually widowed, remarrying down the social scale. For the strains imposed on the social order by misalliances, see Gayle K. Brunelle, "Dangerous Liaisons: Mésalliance and Early Modern French Noblewomen," *French Historical Studies* 19 (1995): 75–103.

22. On the reunion between Mademoiselle and Gaston and on the ballet, see *MM*, 1: 10–11. The *ballet de cour*, a stylized and elaborate mixture of music, dancing, and theater, originated in the sixteenth century and was a mainstay of court amusements. Peter Burke, *The Fabrication of Louis XIV* (New Haven, 1992), notes the importance of these spectacles in the reign of Louis XIII as well as that of his son: see esp. 17, 45. See also Marie-Christine Moine, *Les Fêtes à la Cour du Roi Soleil* (Paris, 1984), 33–43; Margaret McGowan, *L'Art du Ballet de Cour en France, 1581–1643* (Paris, 1986); and Moote, *Louis XIII*, 267–68.

23. *MM*, 1: 12. For Gaston's reaction to Puylaurens's fate, see Dethan, *Gaston*, 163–69.

24. On the story of the assassination attempt at the time of Mademoiselle's baptism, see Jean François Paul de Gondi, Cardinal de Retz, *Mémoires*, 144–45, in *Oeuvres du Cardinal de Retz*, ed. Marie-Thérèse Hipp and Michel Pernot (Paris,

1984). On the conspiracy of Amiens, see Dethan, *Gaston*, 179–80; and Moote, *Louis XIII*, 251.

25. *MM*, 1: 15–16. On the interrogation of Anne of Austria, see Moote, *Louis XIII*, 280–81; Kleinman, *Anne d'Autriche*, 180–90.

26. Bibliothèque Nationale de France (hereafter BNF), Collection Baluze, v. 346, fol. 3: Mademoiselle to Gaston, August 26, 1637. This is one of the few surviving letters dating from Mademoiselle's childhood. The others are also found in the Collection Baluze.

27. For these anecdotes, see *MM*, 1: 16–32 passim. On the growth of the cult of Henri IV and its importance at the time of the Fronde, see Marcel Reinhard, *La Légende de Henri IV* (Saint-Brieuc, 1935), 31–39. For more recent work, see the colloquium by the Société d'Henri IV, *La Légende d'Henri IV*, ed. Pierre Tucoo-Chala and Paul Mironneau (Paris, 1995); see esp. Michel Magnien's contribution, "Les Sources Imprimées de la Légende de Henri IV," 21–43.

28. On the forced sale of Champigny to Richelieu, see Joseph Bergin, *Cardinal Richelieu: Power and the Pursuit of Wealth* (London, 1985), 129–31, 137, 282. See also *MM*, 1: 21–22; Tallemant des Réaux, *Historiettes*, 1: 251–52. On the indemnification by Gaston, see *MM*, 2: 359.

29. *MM*, 1: 27. On Urban's struggle with Richelieu over ecclesiastical benefices, which took place at about the same time as the sale of Champigny, see Bergin, *Richelieu*, 209–12. Tallemant des Réaux, in *Historiettes*, 1: 251–52, notes the refusal of the papacy to sanction the destruction of the chapel. Blunt, in *Art and Architecture*, 57–58, places the demolished château in the context of French Renaissance art; see also his remarks on the chapel, 103.

30. *MM*, 1: 22–23. On the presence of Madame d'Aiguillon as part of the scheme to marry her to Gaston, see Dethan, *Gaston*, 186–88. Mademoiselle's memory was at fault here; Richelieu's niece was still Madame de Combalet at the time of this excursion, and did not become duchess d'Aiguillon until 1638.

31. *MM*, 1: 23–25. On the château of Richelieu, see Blunt, *Art and Architecture*, 199–201; Hautecoeur, *Architecture Classique*, 1: 533–34.

32. *MM*, 1: 26–27.

33. *MM*, 1: 27. The original is "*la nature a refusé à ce lieu autant de grâce que l'art lui en donné.*" *L'art* in this context means the architectural skills involved in the design and construction of the château.

34. *MM*, 1: 27–28.

35. On Louison Roger, see *MM*, 1: 20–21. On Gaston's warm moments with his daughter at Tours and his ungallant comments about Anne of Austria, see *MM*, 1: 33–35.

36. *MM*, 1: 38.

37. For Richelieu's reluctance to let Mademoiselle stay with the queen, see *MM*, 1: 37–38. For Mademoiselle's description of court life and her assertion that Louis XIII tolerated the disparaging of Richelieu, see *MM*, 1: 40–41. See also the comments of Ruth Kleinman on the complicated relationship of Anne of Austria, Louis XIII, and Marie de Hautefort: *Anne d'Autriche*, 167–70.

38. *MM*, 1: 40–41.

39. *MM*, 1: 42–43.

40. *MM*, 1: 43–44.

41. For Mademoiselle's scorn of the Condé-Richelieu alliance by matrimony, see *MM*, 1: 49–50, and contrast her scorn for Condé "on his knees," 49, with her approval of Gaston's supposed refusal in 1634 to agree to a marriage with Madame d'Aiguillon as a condition of his return to court, 10.

42. *MM*, 1: 45–46.

43. On the social rivalries between the Condés and the Orléans-Soissons faction, see *MM*, 1: 44–45. On the Condés and Richelieu, see Jouanna, *Devoir*, 215–17. On the profit the Condés derived from the reversion of many of the Montmorency estates, see Labatut, *Ducs et Pairs*, 258–59.

44. On Gaston's ambiguous role during the final conspiracy by Soissons, see Dethan, *Gaston*, 191–92. See also *MM*, 1: 47.

45. *MM*, 1: 46–48.

46. For Anne of Austria's pleas to Richelieu, see Dethan, *Gaston*, 197, 201; *MM*, 1: 53; Kleinman, *Anne d'Autriche*, 208–9.

47. For Gaston's complicity in the conspiracy of Cinq-Mars, see Dethan, *Gaston*, 193–207 passim. See also the comments of Ruth Kleinman on the roles of Gaston and the queen, *Anne d'Autriche*, 226–34. Mademoiselle noted the dismissal of several commanders of Louis XIII's guards, including Tréville: *MM*, 1: 57. In a reign filled with ambiguous actions, few match those of the king at the inception of the Cinq-Mars conspiracy: see the comments in Moote, *Louis XIII*, 285–89. See also Philippe Erlanger, *Cinq-Mars* (Paris, 1962).

48. On Louis XIII's determination to exclude Gaston from any role in the regency of the child Louis XIV, see Dethan, *Gaston*, 209–11.

49. *MM*, 1: 54–55. For the temporary effects on Gaston's reputation among the high nobility, see Dethan, *Gaston*, 214.

50. For Mademoiselle's analysis of Richelieu's harshness in the wake of the Cinq-Mars affair, see *MM*, 1: 57. For her grudging tribute to Richelieu, see *MM*, 1: 58.

51. *MM*, 1: 58–59.

52. For Louis XIII's change of heart, see Dethan, *Gaston*, 206; see also *MM*, 1: 70–71. For the famous quotation of Mademoiselle's on Cinq-Mars and Thou, see *MM*, 1: 63.

53. For Gaston's attempts to soften Louis XIII, see Dethan, *Gaston*, 211–12. For the registration of the king's edict, see Olivier LeFèvre d'Ormesson, *Journal*, ed. Adolphe Chéruel (Paris, 1860–61), 1: 29–33. Chéruel reproduced this in *MM*, 1: app. 3, 373–78.

54. *MM*, 1: 64–66.

55. *MM*, 1: 73–74.

CHAPTER 2   A MOST ELIGIBLE PRINCESS

Epigraphs: *MM*, 1: 255; Segrais, *Mémoires/Anecdotes*, 1: 79–80.

1. *MM*, 1: 86.

2. Retz, *Mémoires*, 170. On breaking the king's will, see Kleinman, *Anne d'Au-*

triche, 257–64; and also Dethan, *Gaston*, 214–15. On the windfall to Gaston, see Dethan, *Gaston*, 256–57.

3. *MM*, 1: 76–81, 90; Françoise Bertaut, Mme de Motteville, *Mémoires*, in *Nouvelle Collection*, ed. Michaud and Poujoulat, 24: 56–59. Olivier d'Ormesson identifies the political factionalism at the heart of this quarrel: see Ormesson, *Journal*, 1: 89–95.

4. For Mademoiselle's criticism that power was again concentrated in the hands of a single minister, see *MM*, 1: 81–82. The theme occurs frequently in other aristocratic memoirs of the time. See Derek A. Watts, "La Notion de Patrie Chez les Mémorialistes d'avant la Fronde: Le Problème de la Traison," in *Les Valeurs Chez les Mémorialistes Français du XVIIᵉ Siècle avant la Fronde*, ed. Noémi Hepp and Jacques Hennequin (Moulins-lès-Metz, 1979), 195–209; and Watts, "Jugements sur la Cour," in *La Cour au Miroir des Mémorialistes, 1530–1682*, ed. Noémi Hepp (Paris, 1991), 123–33. For Mazarin's relations with the high nobility, see Richard Bonney, "Cardinal Mazarin and the Great Nobility during the Fronde," *English Historical Review* 96 (October 1981): 818–33; Sharon Kettering, "Patronage and Politics during the Fronde," *French Historical Studies* 14 (1986): 409–41. In the same issue, see Ellery Schalk, "Clientages, Elites, and Absolutism in 17ᵗʰ Century France," 442–48. Arlette Jouanna's *Devoir* offers a long perspective on the development and practice of aristocratic opposition to the crown.

5. On the *Cabale des Importants*, see Michel Pernod, *La Fronde* (Paris, 1994), 45–50; Kleinman, *Anne d'Autriche*, 303.

6. Dethan, *Gaston*, 247–59 passim.

7. Gaston had been a nominal co-commander at La Rochelle (1627–28) and in the campaign of 1636, but without any real authority.

8. On Freiburg, see Bernard Pujo, *Le Grand Condé* (Paris, 1995), 87–94.

9. On Mazarin's policy of encouraging the rivalry of the princely houses, see Chéruel's comments in *MM*, 1: 103–5 n. 4; Dethan, *Gaston*, 257; and the articles cited above in note 4.

10. *MM*, 1: 86–87.

11. *MM*, 1: 75.

12. *MM*, 1: 82–83.

13. Mademoiselle's self-portrait, written in 1657, is reprinted in Denise Mayer, *Mademoiselle de Montpensier: Trois Etudes d'après Ses Mémoires* (Paris, 1989), 16–20.

14. Jean Regnault de Segrais, *Mémoires/Anecdotes*, in *Oeuvres Diverses de M. de Segrais* (Amsterdam, 1723), 1: 35. On Madame de Fiesque, see *MM*, 1: 66–70, 72–73. See also Motteville, *Mémoires*, 156. Mademoiselle also saw La Rivière as a source of tension between herself and her father: see *MM*, 1: 87.

15. For Gaston's objection to the friendship with Elisabeth de Vendôme, see *MM*, 1: 86.

16. *MM*, 1: 94. On hanging the maps of Gaston's campaign, see BNF, Collection Baluze, v. 341, fols. 83–84: Mademoiselle to Léonard Goulas, May, n.d., 1644.

17. *MM*, 1: 94.

18. The last royal brother to have offspring was the brother of Charles VI, Louis,

duc d'Orléans (1370–1407), father of the poet-duke Charles d'Orléans (1394–1465) and of Jean, comte d'Angoulême (1404–1467). Through these sons, Louis was the ancestor of the last Valois kings of France.

19. Motteville, *Mémoires*, 83–84; Ormesson, *Journal*, 1: 232–37; and Nicolas Goulas, *Mémoires*, ed. Charles Constant (Paris, 1879), 2: 59–60.

20. Motteville, *Mémoires*, 84.

21. On Gaston's use of the title "royal highness," see Saint-Simon, *Mémoires*, 3: 440–41. Strictly speaking, after the death of Louis XIII, the designation "Monsieur" belonged to Philippe, the younger brother of Louis XIV. Because Philippe was a small boy, and Gaston had been called "Monsieur" for many years, Gaston's contemporaries continued to refer to him as "Monsieur." Mademoiselle, always correct in such matters, switched to "His Royal Highness" thereafter when she referred to Gaston.

22. Motteville, *Mémoires*, 84; Goulas, *Mémoires*, 2: 61–65. For Anne of Austria's growing exasperation with Mademoiselle, see Kleinman, *Anne d'Autriche*, 319–22.

23. *MM*, 1: 100.

24. Spain was initially a party to the negotiations (1644–48) that led to the Peace of Westphalia.

25. *MM*, 1: 106–10.

26. *MM*, 1: 110–15; Motteville, *Mémoires*, 90–91; Pujo, *Condé*, 97.

27. *MM*, 1: 132.

28. *MM*, 1: 132–33.

29. *MM*, 1: 129–33; Motteville, *Mémoires*, 91–95.

30. *MM*, 1: 126.

31. *MM*, 1: 126–27.

32. *MM*, 1: 127. Antonia Fraser, in *Royal Charles* (New York, 1979), 51, agrees that Henrietta Maria was the driving force in the courtship, which Charles pursued with a "kind of jolly gaucherie."

33. *MM*, 1: 138.

34. *MM*, 1: 138–40; quotation, 139.

35. *MM*, 1: 120.

36. *MM*, 1: 140, 142.

37. *MM*, 1: 142–43.

38. *MM*, 1: 145–47.

39. *MM*, 1: 158–60.

40. *MM*, 1: 120.

41. *MM*, 1: 191.

42. *MM*, 1: 258. See also her remark that Gaston often spoke fondly of the infanta: *MM*, 1: 213.

43. Ruth Kleinman notes that the regent and Mazarin suspected that Gaston was implicated in Saujon's communications with the enemy: Kleinman, *Anne d'Autriche*, 321.

44. *MM*, 1: 162.

45. *MM*, 1: 166.

46. *MM*, 1: 169. For Mademoiselle's account of Saujon's initiative and its aftermath, see *MM*, 1: 147–48, 155, 160–69.

47. Motteville, *Mémoires*, 155.

48. Motteville's account of the episode, in *Mémoires*, 154–56, is generally consistent with Mademoiselle's. She, too, notes that the issue reflected on Gaston's honor (*gloire*). For other accounts, see Goulas, *Mémoires*, 2: 283–86, who also faults Gaston for not following through on the Spanish and imperial marriage proposals; and Ormesson, *Journal*, 1: 487, who recorded the gossip that La Rivière had engineered a plot to discredit Mademoiselle in order to erode any support at court for Mademoiselle's request to obtain control of her own financial affairs. See also François Baudot de Dubuisson-Aubenay, *Journal des Guerres Civiles, 1648–1652*, ed. Gustave Saige (Paris, 1883–85), 1: 16, 21.

49. *MM*, 1: 175–79.

50. The Fronde is the subject of a voluminous and specialized literature. In addition to the other works cited in the bibliography, I have found the following especially useful: Adolphe Chéruel's classic *Histoire de France Pendant la Minorité de Louis XIV* (Paris, 1878–80) and his *Histoire de France sous Mazarin* (Paris, 1882); Ernst H. Kossman, *La Fronde* (Leiden, 1954); Hubert Méthivier, *La Fronde* (Paris, 1984); Pierre-Georges Lorris, *La Fronde* (Paris, 1961); A. Lloyd Moote, *The Revolt of the Judges: The Parlement of Paris and the Fronde 1643–1652* (Princeton, 1971); Michel Pernot, *La Fronde* (Paris, 1994); Orest Ranum, *The Fronde: A French Revolution 1648–1652* (New York, 1993). Richard Bonney's books provide a broad background to these events: *Political Change in France under Richelieu and Mazarin, 1624–1661* (Oxford, 1978) and *The King's Debts: Finance and Politics in France, 1589–1661* (Oxford, 1981). Arlette Jouanna, *Devoir*, and the articles cited above in note 4 offer insights into aristocratic factionalism and the ideological basis of revolt. Pierre Goubert, *Mazarin*; Bernard Pujo, *Le Grand Condé*; Kleinman, *Anne d'Autriche*; and Geoffrey Treasure, *Mazarin: The Crisis of Absolutism in France* (London, 1995) were also useful in my reconstruction of events.

51. On the theory of monarchical power during the minority of a king, see Jouanna, *Devoir*, 334–40; Pernod, *Fronde*, 11–18; Ranum, *Fronde*, 95–103.

52. *MM*, 1: 178.

53. Mademoiselle faulted the government for inconsistency, wavering between the alternatives of severity and leniency: *MM*, 1: 180.

54. *MM*, 1: 182–83.

55. For the Declaration of Rueil, October 1648, see Pernod, *Fronde*, 93–94; *MM*, 1: 193–94.

56. Pernod, *Fronde*, 94.

57. *MM*, 1: 194–97; quotation, 197.

58. *MM*, 1: 198–200.

59. *MM*, 1: 204–5.

60. *MM*, 1: 200–201.

61. *MM*, 1: 201.

62. For a narrative of the events from the defection of Conti, Longueville, and the others, to the Peace of Saint-Germain (or Rueil) in March 1649, see Pernod, *Fronde*, 100–141.

63. *MM*, 1: 209.

64. *MM*, 1: 208. The senior princess de Carignan, Marie de Bourbon (1606–1692), was a sister of Mademoiselle's first suitor, Louis de Bourbon, comte de Soissons.

65. *MM*, 1: 205–6.

66. *MM*, 1: 217–19.

67. On the discussions with Mademoiselle de Chevreuse, see *MM*, 1: 213–14; with La Rivière, see 219.

68. *MM*, 1: 220.

69. *MM*, 1: 221.

70. *MM*, 1: 223.

71. *MM*, 1: 223.

72. *MM*, 1: 224.

73. *MM*, 1: 224–26.

74. Goulas, *Mémoires*, 3: 114.

75. *MM*, 1: 232–33.

76. *MM*, 1: 235.

77. *MM*, 1: 235.

78. *MM*, 1: 236.

79. For the increasing strain between Condé and Mazarin in 1649, see Pernod, *Fronde*, 143–60; Goubert, *Mazarin*, 238–43; Pujo, *Condé*, 155–64.

80. *MM*, 1: 238.

81. *MM*, 1: 238–40.

82. *MM*, 1: 240.

CHAPTER 3 THE SECOND MAID OF ORLÉANS

Epigraphs: *MM*, 1: 363; Segrais, "On the Entry of Mademoiselle into the City of Orléans," in Tipping, *Segrais*, 203–5.

1. For the narrative, see Pernot, *Fronde*, 160–66.

2. On the uprising in Bordeaux, see Pernot, *Fronde*, 177–84; Dethan, *Gaston*, 271–74; Ranum, *Fronde*, 215–47. For Mademoiselle's actions, see *MM*, 1: 242–55.

3. *MM*, 1: 258–59.

4. Pernod, *Fronde*, 183–85; Dethan, *Gaston*, 273; *MM*, 1: 260–61.

5. Dethan, *Gaston*, 273–76; Pernod, *Fronde*, 184–85; *MM*, 1: 261–64. For the court's concern about Gaston's negotiations with the archduke, see *Lettres, Instructions, et Mémoires de Colbert*, ed. Pierre Clément (Paris, 1861–82), 1: 42–44: Colbert to LeTellier, September 17, 1650. Several apocryphal *Mazarinade* pamphlets purporting to be correspondence between Mademoiselle and the archduke were published in 1649. These are listed in the Bibliography.

6. *MM*, 1: 265–66.

7. *MM*, 1: 267.

8. *MM*, 1: 267–72.

9. *MM*, 1: 275–77, 281–85. Pernod, in *Fronde*, 183–84, citing a letter from Charles de Châteauneuf, the keeper of the Seals, argues that Gaston did consent to the transfer to Marcoussis and that the real issue was the further transfer of the princes to Le Havre; see also Dethan, *Gaston*, 280; Motteville, *Mémoires*, 354.

10. *MM*, 1: 282–83; and Pernod, *Fronde*, 192–95.

11. *MM*, 1: 284–85.

12. *MM*, 1: 285–87; Motteville, *Mémoires*, 357.

13. For the narrative, see Pernod, *Fronde*, 189–91.

14. For the events of December 1650–January 1651, see Pernod, *Fronde*, 192–97; Dethan, *Gaston*, 279–81.

15. *MM*, 1: 288–90.

16. For the terms of the treaty between the factions, see Pernod, *Fronde*, 196–97.

17. Motteville, *Mémoires*, 370; Marie de Longueville, duchess de Nemours, *Mémoires*, in *Nouvelle Collection*, ed. Michaud and Poujoulat, 23: 637.

18. *MM*, 1: 291–92. On the assemblies of noblemen and clergy, see Pernod, *Fronde*, 198; see also Jouanna, *Devoir*, 262–73.

19. Motteville, *Mémoires*, 373; Pernod, *Fronde*, 198.

20. *MM*, 1: 292.

21. *MM*, 1: 292–93. According to Motteville, the court at first tried to sway Gaston with an offer of marriage between the king and his second daughter, Marguerite-Louise. Subsequently, the court approached Mademoiselle with the offer for herself, if she could sway Gaston, and Mademoiselle refused. See Motteville, *Mémoires*, 365; see also Dubuisson-Aubenay, *Journal*, 2: 116.

22. *MM*, 1: 293–94, 296.

23. *MM*, 1: 297–300.

24. On the steps taken by Gaston to keep the king from fleeing the capital and on the proposals that he seize the regency, see Pernod, *Fronde*, 199. Motteville asserts that Gaston was first tempted to seize the regency at the time of the interview at Fontainebleau; and again, in February 1651 the court feared that Gaston, under Gondi's influence, would take "extreme" measures: see Motteville, *Mémoires*, 357, 378, 380. Mademoiselle, too, speaks of these "*grands desseins*": *MM*, 1: 301; as does the duchess de Nemours in her *Mémoires*, 640.

25. *MM*, 1: 301–2.

26. Motteville, *Mémoires*, 379–81; Pernod, *Fronde*, 199–200.

27. *MM*, 1: 302–3; Motteville, *Mémoires*, 382.

28. For Mazarin's interview with the princes, see Motteville, *Mémoires*, 381–82. Mademoiselle offers a fuller version, along with an account of her reconciliation with Condé: *MM*, 1: 303–5.

29. *MM*, 1: 308–9.

30. *MM*, 1: 249–50, 252–54, 269, 305. Some records of Saujon's mission survive in the Archives du Ministère des Affaires Etrangères, Correspondance Politique, Autriche, v. 17.

31. *MM*, 1: 320–33 passim.

32. On the initiative to secure Gaston's loyalty by a marriage of one of his daugh-

ters to Louis XIV, see the references in note 21 above. See also Kleinman, *Anne d'Autriche*, 434–35. On Louis's dislike of Mademoiselle, the reservations of Anne of Austria because of the age difference, and the preference for Marguerite-Louise, see *Lettres du Cardinal Mazarin*, ed. Jules Ravenel (Paris, 1836), 266: Mazarin to Bartet, September 12, 1651. Mademoiselle's code name in this correspondence was "Caprice."

33. Pernod, *Fronde*, 245–72; Pujo, *Condé*, 181–94.

34. *MM*, 1: 313–15.

35. On the Palatine's ambitions and her authorization to treat with Gaston and Mademoiselle, see Kleinman, *Anne d'Autriche*, 420–21, 434–35.

36. *MM*, 1: 315–16.

37. *MM*, 1: 322–24.

38. *MM*, 1: 329–31.

39. *MM*, 1: 330, 335. Mademoiselle is inconsistent about the amount demanded, stating it as 200,000 écus at one point (330), and 300,000 at another (335). For the steps Gaston took on the news of Mazarin's return to France in December 1651, see Pernod, *Fronde*, 283–85; Chéruel, *Mazarin*, 1: 69–71, 88–90, 96, 103–5.

40. *MM*, 1: 337–38, 341–42, 348.

41. Pernod, *Fronde*, 286–89; Chéruel, *Mazarin*, 1: 109–41.

42. *MM*, 1: 343–50. For Chéruel's comments that Mademoiselle was the dupe of a prearranged scenario, see Chéruel, *Mazarin*, 1: 141–44. Retz also noted the presence of Gaston's agents at Orléans and heaped ridicule on Mademoiselle's efforts: Retz, *Mémoires*, 800–803.

43. *MM*, 1: 350–51.

44. *MM*, 1: 349–55. On Gaston's fear of abandonment, see 352.

45. *MM*, 1: 356–60; quotation, 360. Chéruel, citing the correspondence of Fouquet-Croissy, established that the boatmen had been paid in advance for their enthusiasm: Chéruel, *Mazarin*, 1: 141, 144–45.

46. *MM*, 1: 361–63. Mademoiselle left another account of her activities during this period, including her actions at Orléans, in a short work entitled "Suite de l'Histoire de . . . Fouquerolles," in *Histoire . . . de Fouquerolles* (Saint-Fargeau, 1653), 178–97 passim. On this work, see below, chap. 4. See also François de Paul, marquis de Montglat, *Mémoires*, in *Collection des Mémoires Relatifs à l'Histoire de France*, ed. Claude B. Petitot et al. (Paris, 1820–29), 2d series, 50: 325–28; Dubuisson-Aubenay, *Journal*, 2: 188–91. Contemporary versions of these events can be found in the Mazarinade pamphlets listed in the "Apocryphal and Other Works . . ." section of the Bibliography.

47. For the text of Gaston's letter, see *MM*, 2: 16–17; for the text of Condé's letter, see *MM*, 2: 21.

48. *MM*, 2: 10–14.

49. For Mademoiselle's defense of Condé, see *MM*, 2: 30–31; for her comparison of princely intentions to the mysteries of faith, see *MM*, 2: 22. Mademoiselle actually used the expression *"le salut de la patrie."*

50. Pernod, *Fronde*, 290–92; Chéruel, *Mazarin*, 1: 161–65.

51. *MM*, 2: 45–53.

52. *MM* 2: 53–61. For Gondi's remarks, see Retz, *Mémoires*, 801. The memory of Joan of Arc enjoyed a revival in the seventeenth century. See the discussion and bibliographic references in Régine Pernoud and Marie-Véronique Clin, *Joan of Arc*, trans. Jeremy duQ. Adams (New York, 1998), 237, 242. Portions of Jean Chapelain's epic poem, *La Pucelle*, which was not published until 1656, had been disseminated in public recitations at the hôtel de Rambouillet as early as 1637 and was well known in salon circles. Comparisons with events of the Fronde were inevitable. See Emile Magne, *Voiture et les Années de Gloire de l'Hôtel de Rambouillet, 1635–1648* (Paris, 1912), 86–87. See also *Un Tournoi de Trois Pucelles en l'Honneur de Jeanne d'Arc: Lettres Inédites de Conrart, de Mlle de Scudéry, et de Mme du Moulin, 1646–1647*, ed. Edouard de Barthélemy and René Kerviler (Paris, 1878).

There were also numerous comparisons to the Age of the Amazons, another popular literary conceit of the period. See Micheline Cuénin, "Mademoiselle, une Amazone Impure," *Papers on French Seventeenth-Century Literature* 22 (1995): 25–36, on the pamphlet literature inspired by Mademoiselle's exploits at Orléans. See also Ian Maclean, *Woman Triumphant: Feminism in French Literature, 1610–1652* (Oxford, 1977), 209–32.

53. *MM*, 2: 67–68.

54. *MM*, 2: 56–57; Pernod, *Fronde*, 292–97.

55. *MM* 2: 73–76; Pernod, *Fronde*, 298–300.

56. For Mademoiselle's quarrel with her stepmother, see *MM*, 2: 81–82. For Mademoiselle's comments on her English relatives, see *MM* 2: 82–84. For Mazarin's negotiations with Lorraine, see Chéruel, *Mazarin*, 1: 183–89, 193–94; Pernod, *Fronde*, 298–300.

57. *MM*, 2: 89–90.

58. *MM*, 2: 90–92.

59. *MM*, 2: 93–97; Chéruel, *Mazarin*, 1: 216.

60. On Mademoiselle's encounters with the wounded, see *MM*, 2: 97–99; on her sleepless night after the battle, see 113.

61. *MM*, 2: 99–100.

62. For modern accounts of the battle, see Chéruel, *Mazarin*, 1: 208–18; Lorris, *Fronde*, 351–66; Pernod, *Fronde*, 301–4; Pujo, *Condé*, 207–9; Ranum, *Fronde*, 326–29. For contemporary accounts, see the sources cited in note 68 below.

63. *MM*, 2: 102, 104–5; for her plea to Condé, see 107.

64. *MM*, 2: 108–9.

65. *MM*, 2: 106; BNF, Collection Baluze, v. 208, fol. 59: Order of Gaston to Louvières, July 2, 1652. For Mademoiselle's surveillance of the royal army, see *MM*, 2: 109.

66. *MM*, 2: 109.

67. *MM*, 2: 111.

68. *MM*, 2: 114–15. Although Mademoiselle implies that she had left the Bastille before the firing began, virtually all of her contemporaries credit her with personally giving the commands. See, for example, Motteville, *Mémoires*, 438; Retz, *Mémoires*, 850; Dubuisson-Aubenay, *Journal*, 2: 246; Pierre Coste, *Histoire de . . . Condé*, in

Archives Curieuses de l'Histoire de France, ed. Félix Danjou, 2d series (Paris, 1839), 8: 171; and three sets of memoirs published in *Nouvelle Collection*, ed. Michaud and Poujoulat, v. 29: François, duc de la Rochefoucauld, *Mémoires*, 482; Jean Herault de Gourville, *Mémoires*, 508; and François de Paule, marquis de Montglat, *Mémoires*, 270–71. Another lively account of the battle can be found in the memoirs of the exiled James Stuart, duke of York, later James II, who served on Turenne's staff during the battle: *The Memoirs of James II: His Campaigns as Duke of York, 1652–1660*, ed. A. Lytton Sells (Bloomington, 1962), 82–96. See also the anonymous *Relation Véritable du Combat du Faubourg Saint-Antoine (July 1652)*, in *Archives Curieuses*, 2d series, 8: 258–83.

The famous remark of Mazarin's, "*Ce canon-là vient de tuer son mari*," is found in Voltaire, *Le Siècle de Louis XIV*, in *Oeuvres Complètes de Voltaire*, ed. Louis Moland (Paris, 1883–85), 14: 202. This work was first published in 1752, a century after the event in question, and Voltaire seems to have borrowed the account from Abraham Nicolas Amelot de la Houssaye (1634–1706), who treats the remark as a paraphrase and not a quotation. La Houssaye's memoirs were first published in 1722 and his source is not clear. See Amelot de la Houssaye, *Mémoires Historiques Politiques et Critiques* (Amsterdam, 1722), 1: 464. French authors usually cite the remark without attribution, and often insert a few additional vowels to create an Italian accent for the cardinal.

69. BNF, Nouv. Acq. Fr. 4815, fols. 195–98: Letter of Mademoiselle, July 3, 1652. The letter has no addressee, but it is bundled with two others addressed to Madame de Pontac, probably the intended recipient. The text of this letter includes a number of details, such as a list of the wounded Frondeurs, which are also found in the account of the battle in Mademoiselle's *Mémoires*, written a year later, suggesting that she used the letter as the basis for the later account. For her reflections on her role, see *MM*, 2: 112–13. The cross of St. Andrew, originally a badge of the dukes of Burgundy, was inherited by the Habsburgs and was carried by the Spanish troops brought back from the Lowlands by the duc de Nemours.

70. *MM*, 2: 112.

71. For the massacre at the Hôtel de Ville, see Chéruel, *Mazarin*, 1: 218–25; Pernod, *Fronde*, 304–6; Ranum, *Fronde*, 329–33.

72. *MM*, 2: 120–21.

73. *MM*, 2: 122–27; quotation on the "assassin," 124; quotation on Le Fèvre's resignation, 126.

74. *MM*, 2: 128.

75. *MM*, 2: 128.

76. *MM*, 2: 128. *Un coup de massue* is, literally, a blow with a mace.

77. *MM*, 2: 129–35.

78. *MM*, 2: 138–39.

79. On the very involved story of Mademoiselle and her regiments of cavalry and foot, see *MM*, 2: 142–44, 146–54, 157–58. Mademoiselle noted, 157, that her cavalry cost her 100,000 livres, whereas her two companies of foot were a bargain at 20,000

livres. For want of money to pay the troops, the army disintegrated rapidly; see Chéruel, *Mazarin*, 1: 235–39; and Pernod, *Fronde*, 309–13.

80. *MM*, 2: 154–56, 163; quotation, 155.

81. *MM*, 2: 173–76. For the negotiations in the late summer and fall of 1652, see Chéruel, *Mazarin*, 1: 240–49, 268–69, and 308–9; Pernod, *Fronde*, 311–12.

82. *MM*, 2: 179. Mademoiselle does not mention her unsuccessful attempt to spark a counterdemonstration at the Palais-Royal. See Chéruel, *Mazarin*, 1: 323–24, n. 2, citing the reports of various agents of Mazarin present at the scene, and 324.

83. For the final months of the Fronde in Paris, see Chéruel, *Mazarin*, 1: 283–357; Lorris, *Fronde*, 383–410; Pernod, *Fronde*, 314–34.

84. *MM*, 2: 191.

85. For Gaston's final negotiations with the court, see Chéruel, *Mazarin*, 1: 293–301; Pernod, *Fronde*, 312–21. Chéruel notes that Mademoiselle tried to get her father to threaten the municipal delegations treating with the court, but Gaston refused to do so, in *Mazarin*, 1: 344.

86. Lorris, *Fronde*, 407; Pernod, *Fronde*, 321. An amnesty covering all but a handful of the leading Frondeurs was included in Louis's declarations of October 22 at the *lit de justice* held at the Louvre.

87. *MM*, 2: 192–93.

88. *MM*, 2: 193–94.

89. *MM*, 2: 193–95.

90. *MM*, 2: 195–98.

91. *Lettres du Cardinal Mazarin*, ed. Adolphe Chéruel, Georges D'Avenel, et al. (Paris, 1889–1906), 5: 413: Mazarin to Le Tellier, October 19, 1652. Gaston was still in contact with the court; see Chéruel, *Mazarin*, 1: 347–49, 358–59, 367–69.

92. *MM*, 2: 204–5. Mademoiselle, Mesdames de Frontenac and Fiesque, and a number of other *Frondeuses* were formally banished from Paris on October 22. See Chéruel, *Mazarin*, 1: 362–63.

CHAPTER 4   THE PASTIMES OF THE PRINCESS AURÉLIE

Epigraphs: *MM*, 2: 243; Segrais, *Les Nouvelle Francaises*, 1: 15.

1. *MM*, 2: 201.

2. *MM*, 2: 204–5.

3. *Hollac, Holac,* and *Olac* were common mutilations of the German *Hohenlohe* in the correspondence of Mademoiselle and her contemporaries. The identification is made by Chéruel in *Lettres du Cardinal Mazarin*, ed. Chéruel et al., 5: 588 n. 2, and also by Georges D'Avenel in the same series, 7: 716 n. 3.

4. *MM*, 2: 209–13.

5. *MM*, 2: 214.

6. *MM*, 2: 217–18.

7. *MM*, 2: 218–19, 221–23.

8. *MM*, 2: 214–15.

9. *MM*, 2: 225–26.

10. *MM* 2: 271. For Mazarin's suspicions about Mademoiselle, see *Lettres du Cardinal Mazarin*, 5: 411–16: Mazarin to Le Tellier, October 19, 1652; 587–93: Mazarin to archbishop of Embrun, April 4, 1653.

11. *MM*, 2: 227–28.

12. *MM*, 2: 229–30.

13. *MM*, 2: 357. *Lettres de Madame de Sévigné*, ed. Emile Gérard-Gailly (Paris, 1953–63), 1: 113–14: Sévigné to Mademoiselle, October 30, 1656. An exchange of letters between Mademoiselle and the marquise d'Huxelles from January to May 1657 indicates that Mademoiselle was well informed on matters of interest in aristocratic society. These have been published in Edouard de Barthélemy, *La Marquise d'Huxelles et Ses Amis* (Paris, 1881), 36–41. The originals are found in BNF, Ms. Fr. 24984.

14. *MM*, 3: 8–9. Catherine d'Aspremont (1620–1684), called Mademoiselle de Vandy, was a protégé of the comtesse de Maure. Edouard de Barthélemy provides a biography of this lady in *Madame La Comtesse de Maure* (Paris, 1863), 211–52.

15. On Madame de Fiesque the younger (1619–1699), see Saint-Simon, *Mémoires*, 1: 651–52. On her patronage role with aspiring literati, see Wessie M. Tipping, *Jean Regnaud de Segrais: L'Homme et Son Oeuvre* (Paris, 1933), 24–43 passim.

16. *MM* 2: 265–68; quotation 266. Born in 1632, Madame de Frontenac lived until 1707 and was an acquaintance of Saint-Simon's. Saint-Simon confirms the poor relationship between the countess and her husband, who died in 1698. The joke at court was that Frontenac preferred the ice and snow of New France to his wife's company. See Saint-Simon, *Mémoires*, 1: 470–71 and 608–9; also 2: 858–59. Francis Parkman opens his classic *Count Frontenac and New France under Louis XIV* with an account of Mademoiselle's expedition to Orléans in 1652 in the company of Madame de Frontenac et al. For more background on both Frontenacs, see Parkman, *Frontenac* (Boston, 1925), 3–16, 477–80.

17. *MM*, 3: 16.

18. *MM*, 3: 17.

19. *MM*, 2: 241–42.

20. *MM*, 2: 243.

21. *MM*, 2: 308. On François LeVau, see François Bluche, *Dictionnaire du Grand Siècle* (Paris, 1990), 871–72.

22. Although the exterior of the château remains much as it was in Mademoiselle's time, the interior was heavily damaged in a great fire in 1752. Subsequent renovations by the later owners, the families of LePeletier and Ormesson, as well as the loss of records, pose considerable difficulties in attempting to reconstruct the interior of the château in Mademoiselle's time. For a recent attempt to do so, based on various archival records and on recent discoveries made in the course of the current restoration, see Claude Mignot, "Mademoiselle et Son Château de Saint-Fargeau," *Papers on French Seventeenth-Century Literature* 22 (1995): 91–101. Although Mignot cites among his sources the Archives of Saint-Fargeau preserved at the Archives Nationales (hereafter AN), series 90 AP, he does not seem to have consulted the very thorough inventory and physical description of Saint-Fargeau drawn up in 1714 by

Hugues Oudin de Masingil for the banker Antoine Crozat found in 90 AP 74, dossier "Mémoire de la Terre et Seigneurie du Comté de Saint-Fargeau." This includes maps of the parks and grounds, a description of the interior of the building, and financial information on the estate. The frame of reference is Saint-Fargeau in Mademoiselle's time. Unfortunately, a floor plan or drawing is not contained in the study. Mademoiselle's ordinary apartments are described and identified as her "summer apartments." Masingil also describes the theater, the *chambre des alliances* with its armorial bearings, the treasury which housed estate records and archives, and the "great chapel." I have found this material very useful in attempting to follow Mademoiselle's descriptions of the château and the work she had commissioned. A very simple floor plan of the building survives in the papers of the royal architect Robert Cotte: BNF, Cabinet des Etampes, Fonds Cotte, Va 449. The park was remodeled as an English romantic garden in 1808.

For additional background on the history of Saint-Fargeau, a number of older articles in regional publications are still of some use. See Etienne Chaillou des Barres, "Saint-Fargeau," *Annuaire Statistique de l'Yonne* (1839), 233–96; G. Cotteau and V. Petit, "Saint-Fargeau," *Annuaire/Yonne* (1858), 180–94; N. Dey, "Histoire de la Ville et du Comté de Saint-Fargeau," *Bulletin de la Société des Sciences Historiques et Naturelles de l'Yonne* (1848), 38–101, 296–348; Charles Moiset, "Mademoiselle de Montpensier à Saint-Fargeau," *Bulletin/Yonne* (1890), 469–78; and M. L. Montassier, "Séjour et Exil de Mademoiselle à Saint-Fargeau," *Bulletin/Yonne* (1927), 43–94. See also Etienne Chaillou des Barres, *Les Châteaux d'Ancy-le-Franc, de Saint-Fargeau, de Chastellux, et de Tanlay* (Paris, 1845), 43–129; Denise Mayer, "Mademoiselle de Montpensier et l'Architecture d'après ses Mémoires," *XVIIᵉ Siècle*, no. 118–119 (1978), 57–60; Anon., *Le Château de Saint-Fargeau et Son Histoire* (n.p., Editions Nivernaises, 1980).

23. *MM*, 2: 280. On the popularity of such galleries in the seventeenth century, see Hautecoeur, *Architecture Classique*, 1: 836–37.

24. *MM*, 2: 283–84.

25. On the theater and the troop of comedians, see *MM*, 2: 249–50, 275, 422. On the *Ballet de l'Eloquence*, see Charles Blanche, "Une Représentation au Théâtre de Saint-Fargeau," *Annuaire/Yonne* (1884), 223–32. For Mademoiselle's interests in music in general, including her relationship with Lully, see Catherine Massip, "Le Mécénat Musical de Mademoiselle," *Papers on French Seventeenth-Century Literature* 22 (1995): 79–90. See also Philippe Beaussant, *Lully: ou, le Musicien du Soleil* (Paris, 1992). For Mademoiselle's offhand reference to Lully, see *MM*, 3: 347–48. Charles Moiset, "Mademoiselle de Montpensier à Saint-Fargeau," *Bulletin/Yonne* (1890), 469–78, is still a useful overview of Mademoiselle's diversions at Saint-Fargeau.

26. *MM*, 2: 287–88.

27. *MM*, 2: 297.

28. *MM*, 2: 242.

29. *MM*, 2: 250.

30. For the visit to Champigny, see *MM*, 2: 277; on the tribute of the marquis de

Sourdis, see *MM*, 2: 275. The accounts of Mademoiselle's visits to the Loire are scattered throughout this section of her *Mémoires*, but are largely found in *MM*, 2: 239–56 passim, and *MM*, 3: 2–54 passim.

31. On Charny, see *MM*, 2: 275–76, 281, 384; *MM*, 3: 57–58.

32. *MM*, 2: 240–41.

33. *MM*, 2: 249.

34. *MM*, 2: 249, 258–61.

35. *MM*, 2: 259–60.

36. *MM*, 2: 248.

37. *MM*, 1: 1–2.

38. Louis de Préfontaine (d. 1700) was the brother of Guillaume LeRoi, abbé de Haute-Fontaine (1610–1684), a canon of Notre Dame and a prominent Jansenist. Later in life, Préfontaine became active in Jansenist circles and left behind a correspondence with another important Jansenist, Germain Vuillart, who had been a pupil of his brother. See *Lettres de Germain Vuillart Ami de Port-Royal à M. Louis de Préfontaine, 1694–1700*, ed. Ruth Clark (Geneva, 1951). On the death of the senior Fiesque, and Mademoiselle's strong reaction, see *MM*, 2: 288–90.

39. The original is "*elle cousinait.*" Saint-Simon, *Mémoires*, 1: 52. Although the sense is clear, there is no exact English equivalent. Bayle St. John offers, "She interested herself much in those who were related to her . . . ," and Lucy Norton, "She claimed kinship with . . ." See *Memoirs of Louis XIV and the Regency by the Duke of Saint-Simon*, ed. Bayle St. John (New York, 1901), 1: 42; *Saint-Simon at Versailles*, ed. Lucy Norton (London, 1958), 11.

40. *MM*, 2: 308–10; quotations, 310.

41. For speculation on the origins of Mademoiselle's newfound literary pastimes, see the general intellectual portrait of Mademoiselle in Jean Garapon, *La Grande Mademoiselle Mémorialiste* (Geneva, 1989), 20–29; and two more recent articles by Garapon: "Mademoiselle de Montpensier dans Ses *Mémoires*: l'Exemple d'une Culture Princière," in *De L'Estoile à Saint-Simon, Recherche sur la Culture des Mémorialistes au Temps des Trois Premiers Rois Bourbons*, ed. Madeleine Bertaud and André Labertit (Paris, 1993), 93–107; and "Mademoiselle à Saint-Fargeau: la Découverte de l'Ecriture," *Papers on French Seventeenth-Century Literature* 22 (1995): 37–47. See also Tipping, *Segrais*, 53; and Eglal Henein, "Mademoiselle de Montpensier à la Recherche du Temps Perdu," *Papers on French Seventeenth-Century Literature* 6 (1976–77): 45–46. In his memoirs, Segrais recalls reading Tasso and Homer to Mademoiselle while out driving: *Mémoires/Anecdotes*, 1: 136–37.

42. On Segrais, there is a consensus that his work is of some importance in the transition from the traditional genre of the heroic fantasy of the traditional *roman* to the more realistic *nouvelle* in French literature. Unfortunately, the most extensive studies of Segrais remain Tipping's doctoral thesis cited above and an even older biography, Léon Brédif, *Segrais: Sa Vie et Ses Oeuvres* (Paris, 1863). A recent monograph by Denise Godwin, *Les Nouvelles Françaises . . . une Conception Romanesque Ambivalente* (Paris, 1983), contains a good bibliography on available materials through the date of publication, 105–14. See also Roger Guichemerre's introduction

to his new and well-annotated edition of Segrais's *Les Nouvelles Françaises, ou, Les Divertissements de la Princesse Aurélie* (Paris, 1990–92), 1: vii–xiv. Segrais is also remembered as a collaborator of Madame de La Fayette. See Roger Duchêne, *Madame de La Fayette: La Romancière aux Cent Bras* (Paris, 1988). Mademoiselle later tried, unsuccessfully, to obtain a pension for Segrais from the king. See Colbert, *Lettres*, 5: 509: Mademoiselle to Colbert, August 5, 1665.

43. Segrais, *Sur l'entrée de Mademoiselle dans la Ville d'Orléans*. Tipping notes that two copies of this chanson survive at the Bibliothèque Mazarine and prints the text in *Segrais*, 203–5.

44. Mademoiselle first mentions Segrais as a witness to a quarrel with Madame de Fiesque on New Year's Day, 1657..See *MM*, 3: 2.

45. *MM*, 2: 243.

46. *Nouvelles Françaises*, ed. Guichemerre, 1: 9, 11.

47. *Nouvelles Françaises*, 1: 16–17.

48. *Nouvelles Françaises*, 1: 10.

49. The six are identified in Tipping, *Segrais*, 112. Guichemerre, in his edition of the *Nouvelles Françaises*, 1: 8, notes that the identification is found in the copy of the first edition at the Bibliothèque Nationale. The ladies' qualities are discussed in the text of the *Nouvelles*, 1: 12–15. In a later article, Guichemerre asserts that the work is a thinly disguised account of life at Saint-Fargeau and of the personalities of Mademoiselle and her close circle of friends. See Guichemerre, "La Grande Mademoiselle et *Les Nouvelles Françaises* de Segrais," *Papers on French Seventeenth-Century Literature* 22 (1995): 49–54.

50. Tipping, *Segrais*, 122, notes the obvious attempt by Segrais to imitate Marguerite d'Angoulême's *Heptaméron* with the *hexaméron* of stories by the princess Aurélie and her ladies. Tipping does not mention the tie between Mademoiselle and Marguerite d'Angoulême, Henri IV's maternal grandmother, which is alluded to in the text of the *Nouvelles Françaises*. When Silerite mentions the "tales of the queen of Navarre," Aurélie calls them "my grandmother's stories," a pun in context but also an allusion to Mademoiselle's descent: see *Nouvelles Françaises*, 1: 22.

51. For the identification of Mademoiselle, Condé, and Charles Stuart, see Tipping, *Segrais*, 128. For the text of the story, see *Nouvelles Françaises*, 2: 383–475. The dynastic boast that the French royal house was "*la première du monde*" is found on 458.

52. *MM*, 2: 216.

53. The *Histoire de Jeanne Lambert d'Herbigny, Marquise de Fouquerolles*, also known as *Vie de Fouquerolles* (Saint-Fargeau, 1653) includes the *Suite*, a *Manifesto*, and several other satirical pieces by members of Mademoiselle's entourage. Some of these selections are clearly aimed at the court. For example, one called *L'Entrée de la Reine de la Lune en la Ville Capitale de Son Estat*, by Frontenac, seems to be a satire on the return of the court to Paris in 1652. Since the *Suite* includes accusations that the court was responsible for keeping Gaston and Mademoiselle apart, it presumably was written after Mademoiselle's arrival at Saint-Fargeau. The original printing was very limited. Only two or three copies have survived in public collections, including one

at the Bibliothèque Nationale de France. Handwritten copies of fragments of the work survive in the Recueil Conrart at the Bibliothèque de l'Arsenal. Ms. 5421, Conrart v. 12, contains the *Histoire*; Ms. 5426, v. 17, contains the *Suite*, the *Manifesto*, and other pieces. These handwritten fragments suggest that the work may have had a wider audience among Mademoiselle's friends in Paris than might otherwise be assumed. On the details of the secret publication at Saint-Fargeau, see *MM*, 2: 243–44.

54. *MM*, 1: 178. See also *MM*, 2: 30–31, for Mademoiselle's allusion to the activities of Henri IV and Henri I de Condé during the civil wars of the previous century.

55. *MM*, 3: 54. See also note 41 above, for Segrais's account of reading Tasso and Homer to Mademoiselle.

56. Pierre-Daniel Huet, *Mémoires*, ed. Charles Nisard (Paris, 1853), 123–24.

57. *MM*, 2: 280–81. The Béthune collection of more than two thousand volumes, plus other papers, engravings, etc., eventually came to rest at the Bibliothèque Nationale de France. See Léopold Delisle, *Le Cabinet des Manuscrits de la Bibliothèque Imperiale* (Paris, 1868), 1: 266–70.

58. See Reinhard, *Légende*, 40–41.

59. The *Mémoires* of Marguerite de Valois have been published in *Nouvelle Collection*, ed. Michaud and Poujoulat, 10: 401–53. The initial publication in 1628–29 by Mauléon de Granier does not seem to have made the sensational impression occasioned by the edition of 1649. The work was frequently reprinted thereafter in the remaining decades of the seventeenth century.

60. *MM*, 2: 248. On Marguerite de Valois's Parisian residence built in 1606 on the site of the present Ecole des Beaux-Arts, see Hautecoeur, *Architecture Classique*, 1: 549.

61. *MM*, 2: 248.

62. *MM*, 2: 424.

63. *MM*, 2: 248. Mademoiselle's surviving autograph manuscript has no evidence of corrections; perhaps Préfontaine prepared a corrected text that has been lost. During the French Revolution, the first archivist to catalogue and examine the manuscript, a M. Bellissent, complained about Mademoiselle's terrible handwriting and added that he had used the printed editions (based on the Harlay Ms.) for guidance in reading the manuscript. See his comments in BNF, Ms. Fr. 6698, fols. 1–5.

64. On the complicated interaction of Mademoiselle and Segrais during their years at Saint-Fargeau, see Tipping, *Segrais*, 50–54, 71–74, who sees Segrais as a tactful editor of Mademoiselle's *Mémoires*; Brédif, *Segrais*, 41, 169–78, 316, who sees no influence of Segrais on Mademoiselle's *Mémoires*; Garapon, *Mémorialiste*, 30–35, who argues strongly that there are strong stylistic differences between the *Mémoires* of Mademoiselle and the language of a later work, the *Divers Portraits*, which clearly show Segrais's influence and therefore concludes that the *Mémoires* are solely Mademoiselle's works. See also Marc Fumaroli, who sees significant stylistic and conceptual convergences between the *Mémoires* and the *Nouvelles Françaises* and calls Mademoiselle the collaborator of Segrais in the preparation of this second work, in "Les Mémoires du XVIIe Siècle au Carrefour des Genres," *XVIIe Siècle*, no. 94–95 (1971):

32–33. Denise Mayer, in her essay "Architecture," simply asserts that Mademoiselle was the author of the *Nouvelles* "under Segrais's signature," 97 n. 7.

65. Reinhard, *Légende*, 31–33, notes that during the Fronde, Henri's image as a conciliator respectful of parlement was appropriated by the opposition to criticize the contemporary royal government.

66. See Garapon, *Mémorialiste*, 48–51.

67. AN, 90 AP 28: Letters Patent December 7, 1650, concerning the emancipation of [Anne-] Marie-Louise d'Orléans and extract of the registers of parlement December 9, 1659 (printed pamphlet). See also Dubuisson-Aubenay, *Journal*, 1: 347. For Mademoiselle's admiration of the infanta and the grand duchess, see *MM*, 2: 251–52.

68. *MM*, 2: 367–68. The Archives of Saint-Fargeau, although incomplete for the period of Mademoiselle's ownership, offer ample proof that, at least with respect to Saint-Fargeau, Mademoiselle paid a great deal of attention to detail. Financial records are scattered in AN, 90 AP, côtes 28, 75, 79, 89, and 91. The 1714 study by Hugues de Masingil in 90 AP 74, cited above in note 26, contains a great deal of information about Mademoiselle's administration of the property, improvements, additional purchases of surrounding properties, and revenues.

69. Goulas, *Mémoires*, 2: 255–56.

70. Motteville, *Mémoires*, 158.

71. *MM*, 2: 349; see also 351.

72. Mademoiselle's half sisters, the daughters of Gaston and Marguerite d'Orléans were children at the time of these events: Marguerite-Louise (1645–1721), called Mademoiselle d'Orléans, later grand duchess of Tuscany; Elisabeth (1646–1696), called Mademoiselle d'Alençon, later duchess de Guise; Françoise-Madeleine (1648–1664), called Mademoiselle de Valois, later duchess of Savoy; and Marie-Anne (1652–1656), called Mademoiselle de Chartres. An infant son, Jean-Gaston, duc de Valois (1650–1652), died during the Fronde.

73. *MM*, 2: 366.

74. *MM*, 2: 395–96.

75. *MM*, 2: 366, 395–96.

76. *MM*, 2: 444.

77. *MM*, 2: 238–39, 244–45.

78. *MM*, 2: 255–56. For Embrun's account, see his letter to Mazarin, March 31, 1653, in *MM*, app. 2, 505–12. See also *Lettres du Cardinal Mazarin*, 5: 587–93: Mazarin to Embrun, April 4, 1653.

79. *MM*, 2: 273–74.

80. *MM*, 2: 293.

81. *MM* 2: 293–94. The calculations of Gaston's officers and the various legal arguments to support his position are contained in a series of memoranda and other documents, most without dates, preserved in BNF, Collection Baluze, v. 344, fols. 97–138. The net calculation of a shortfall of approximately 2,080,000 livres of expenses over revenues is found in an untitled "La Recette . . . La Dépense" memorandum, fols. 122–27v. This same memorandum also contains the flat refusal to account for the revenues of the Dombes and Beaujolais, and only a partial accounting for the

Norman revenues, fol. 123. Other pieces contain various proposed corrections, possibly as a result of questions raised by Mademoiselle's advisers or by the arbitrators. Among these are a memorandum attributed to Choisy detailing the origins of the various debts that encumbered Mademoiselle's properties, fols. 97–98; a series of questions and answers to justify Gaston's actions, fols. 99–101; and a draft of the eventual accord between Gaston and Mademoiselle, dated April 27, 1655, which summarizes Gaston's legal claims to residual rights to pensions, usufructs, etc., fols. 108–12v.

These should be used in conjunction with the set of accounts for the years 1627–50 provided by Gaston to the parlement of Paris as part of this transaction and conserved at the Bibliothèque de l'Arsenal, as Ms. 4211. Nearly 320 folio pages, it is bound together with copies of the royal decrees of 1627 and other instruments that formed the legal basis for his guardianship. Unfortunately, none of Gaston's calculations can be verified, since the account books and records for the various estates do not survive. Their value is further limited by the important omissions for the Dombes, Beaujolais, and Normandy already noted. It is clear that Gaston was prepared to defend himself vigorously, and it is hard to agree with Georges Dethan's dismissal of the whole episode as needless and due to foolish chicanery on Mademoiselle's part, in Dethan, *Gaston*, 313–14.

82. *MM*, 2: 295.

83. *MM*, 2: 255.

84. *MM*, 2: 296–97.

85. *MM*, 2: 327–29.

86. *MM*, 2: 330–31.

87. *MM*, 2: 331–33. A number of letters from Mademoiselle to either Gaston or his secretary Léonard Goulas for this period are found in BN, Nouv. Acq. Fr. 6207. These are dated by day and month, with the year omitted, but clearly date from 1654–55. These letters are consistent with Mademoiselle's account of her attempts to move the arbitration forward. See, for example, fols. 6–8: Mademoiselle to Gaston, February 26 [1655]; and fols. 13–15: same to same, March 10 [1655].

88. *MM*, 2: 341–43.

89. *MM*, 2: 343–45.

90. *MM*, 2: 345–46. Mademoiselle's summary is somewhat at variance with the surviving documentation on points of detail, but the overall result is as she states. Mademoiselle was required to recognize certain residual rights of Gaston to revenues from her estates, and she was forced to acknowledge that on a net basis she owed Gaston money. In consideration of Mademoiselle's assuming various debts and after ratifying various actions taken during her minority, Gaston agrees to waive the amounts due to him. See BNF, Collection Baluze, v. 344, fols. 108–12v, draft April 27, 1655; and AN, Minutier Central, CXV, 129, Transaction between Gaston and Mademoiselle, May 13, 1655.

91. *MM*, 2: 346–47.

92. *MM*, 2: 349.

93. *MM*, 2: 347–50.

94. *MM*, 2: 350–52.

95. *MM*, 2: 356.

96. *MM*, 2: 355–56.

97. *MM*, 2: 367.

98. *MM*, 2: 359–60. A copy of the decree of the parlement of Paris awarding Champigny to Mademoiselle is found in AN, 300 API 93.

99. *MM*, 2: 360.

100. *MM*, 2: 360–64.

101. *MM*, 2: 325.

102. Aumale, *Condé*, 6: 667–69: Condé to Mademoiselle, March 6, 1655, in response to a February letter from Mademoiselle (exact date not stated).

103. *MM*, 2: 374–76.

104. Aumale, *Condé*, 6: 353.

105. The French is *créature*, *MM*, 2: 473. For the special meaning of this word in seventeenth-century France in the context of patron and clientage roles, see Sharon Kettering's study *Patron, Brokers, and Clients in Seventeenth-Century France* (Oxford, 1986), and also her "Forum: Fidelity and Clientage. Patronage and Politics during the Fronde," *French Historical Studies* 14 (1986): 409–41; and the commentary by Ellery Schalk, 442–48. See also Orest Ranum's remarks on the term in his *Richelieu*, 27–44. For a bibliographic introduction to the subject and a critique of its conceptual limitations, see Kristen B. Neuschel, *Word of Honor: Interpreting Noble Culture in Sixteenth-Century France* (Ithaca, 1989), 1–25.

106. *MM*, 2: 473–74.

107. Aumale, *Condé*, 6: 669–70: Condé to the Comte d'Auteuil, August 10, 1657.

108. *Lettres du Cardinal Mazarin*, 7: 716: Mazarin to Béthune, May 14, 1657.

109. *MM*, 2: 386.

110. *MM*, 2: 386–97 passim. See also the exchange of letters, 403–14.

111. *MM*, 2: 390–91, 392–93.

112. *MM*, 2: 395. See also *Lettres du Cardinal Mazarin*, 7: 658–59: Mazarin to Béthune, August 3, 1656.

113. Records of the king's intervention survive for the period January to September 1656: BNF, Ms. Fr. 4233, fols. 283–313v. These include copies of letters from Louis to Gaston and to Mademoiselle, and other correspondence involving Michel LeTellier, Pierre Séguier, and Gaston's officials. It is very evident that Louis wished to avoid more public acrimony within the royal family. The interview between Séguier and Mademoiselle mentioned in her *Mémoires* was approved by the king and was probably intended only as a pacifying gesture: see fols. 309v–311: Mademoiselle to Louis XIV, August 29, 1656; fols. 311v–312: Louis XIV to Mademoiselle, September 2, 1656; fols. 313–313v: LeTellier to Choisy, September 2, 1656. For Mademoiselle's narrative, see *MM*, 2: 452–53, 454–55.

114. *MM*, 2: 488.

115. *MM*, 3: 42.

116. *MM*, 3: 27. Mazarin offered to pay the damages himself, but never kept his promise: see *MM*, 3: 38; Bergin, *Richelieu*, 282–83.

117. *MM*, 3: 55.

118. *MM*, 2: 336.

119. BNF, Collection Baluze, v. 346, fols. 12–13: Mademoiselle to Gaston, May 12, 1657. For the reaction, see *MM*, 3: 47.

120. *MM*, 3: 59–62.

121. *MM*, 3: 62.

122. *MM*, 3: 79.

123. *MM*, 3: 78–79. Mazarin had followed the reconciliation closely; see *Lettres du Cardinal Mazarin*, 7: 716: Mazarin to Béthune, May 14, 1657; 725: Mazarin to Béthune, June 2, 1657; 740: Mazarin to Gaston, June 27, 1657.

124. *MM*, 2: 385–86.

125. *MM*, 2: 429–30, 433–40 passim.

126. *MM*, 2: 455.

127. *MM*, 2: 456–57.

128. *MM*, 2: 459.

129. *MM*, 2: 460.

130. *MM*, 2: 456–62.

131. *MM*, 2: 478–81.

132. *MM*, 3: 162.

133. The priest who heard the victim's last confession left an eyewitness account of the "execution." See N. LeBel, "Relation de la Mort du Marquis de Monaldeschi, le 6 novembre 1657," in *Archives Curieuses*, 2d series, 8: 287–97. For French reaction, see *MM*, 3: 190; Motteville, *Mémoires*, 462.

134. *MM*, 3: 188–90.

CHAPTER 5   A MUSE AT THE COURT OF APOLLO

Epigraphs: Montpensier, *Lettres*, 30: Montpensier to Motteville, n.d.; Segrais, *Mémoires/Anecdotes*, 1: 137.

1. Sévigné, *Lettres*, 1: 115: Sévigné to La Fayette, July 24, 1657.

2. *MM*, 3: 80.

3. *MM*, 3: 80.

4. *MM*, 3: 76.

5. *MM*, 3: 83.

6. *MM*, 3: 85–91 passim.

7. *MM*, 3: 84.

8. *MM*, 3: 94.

9. *MM*, 3: 96.

10. *MM*, 3: 98–111 passim.

11. *MM*, 3: 112.

12. *MM*, 3: 112–13.

13. *MM*, 3: 119.

14. *MM*, 3: 121. Although Louis is mentioned a number of times in the first part of Mademoiselle's *Mémoires*, usually as a silent companion to the then regent Anne of Austria, this is the first time that he actually appears as a *personnage* in her *Mémoires*.

15. *MM*, 3: 121–22.

16. *MM*, 3: 124.

17. *MM*, 3: 124–26, 131.

18. *MM*, 3: 128–29.

19. *MM*, 3: 127–28. For a modern interpretation of Philippe's character and behavior during the early decades of his brother's reign, see Nancy Nichols Barker, *Brother to the Sun King* (Baltimore, 1989), 11–65; see also Philippe Erlanger, *Monsieur: Frère de Louis XIV* (Paris, 1953), 34–48.

20. *MM*, 3: 132–34. On the young Louis XIV, see François Bluche, *Louis XIV*, trans. Mark Greengrass (New York, 1990), 71–91; and John B. Wolf, *Louis XIV* (New York, 1968), 56–95.

21. *MM*, 3: 130–31.

22. *MM*, 3: 156.

23. *MM*, 3: 142.

24. *MM*, 3: 143–57 passim.

25. *MM*, 3: 166–73 passim.

26. *MM*, 3: 128.

27. *MM*, 3: 173.

28. *MM*, 3: 173–76; see also Denise Mayer, "l'Architecture," in *Trois Etudes*, 99–101.

29. *MM*, 3: 177.

30. *MM*, 3: 176. Members of minor royal houses domiciled in France were accorded the style of "foreign princes" for purposes of court ceremonials. The most prominent of these persons belonged to branches of the families of Lorraine, Savoy, Gonzaga, and the Palatinate. As any reader of Saint-Simon knows, the pretensions of these families caused endless quarrels over precedence, a problem compounded by the fact that all members of these princely families, not simply the heads of branches, claimed this status. A number of great French families, not to be outdone, insisted on the same status of "foreign prince" under various genealogical pretexts. These included the La Tour d'Auvergne, the Rohans, and the La Trémouilles.

31. *MM*, 3: 187–88.

32. *MM*, 3: 200–208 passim, on these balls and ballets. For the importance of the *ballet de cour* as a political statement, see Peter Burke, *The Fabrication of Louis XIV* (New Haven, 1994), 17, 45, 185–87. See also Burke, "The Courtier," in *Renaissance Characters*, ed. Eugenio Garin, trans. Lydia Cochrane (Chicago, 1991), 106–7; Marie-Christine Moine, *Les Fêtes à la Cour du Roi Soleil, 1653–1715* (Paris, 1984), 33–42; Margaret McGowan, *L'Art du Ballet de Cour en France, 1581–1643* (Paris, 1986); and McGowan, "La Fonction des Fêtes dans la Vie de Cour au XVIIᵉ Siècle," in *La Cour au Miroir des Mémorialistes, 1530–1682*, ed. Noémi Hepp (Paris, 1991), 27–41.

33. *MM*, 3: 205–7.

34. *MM*, 3: 212–15.

35. *MM*, 3: 228–30.

36. *MM*, 3: 235–38.

37. See *MM*, 3: 243–47. Mademoiselle's grandmother Catherine-Henriette de Joyeuse, duchess de Guise, had died in February 1656, leaving all of her Joyeuse

properties to her Guise descendants. Mademoiselle brought suit to recover part of this inheritance, based on the terms of Catherine-Henriette's marriage contract with her first husband, Mademoiselle's grandfather Henri, duc de Montpensier. For a statement of her claims, see BNF, Nouv. Acq. Fr. 6207, fols. 77–81: Mademoiselle to Achille d'Harlay, July 22, 1656. A copy of the decree of the parlement of Paris dated March 28, 1681, awarding Mademoiselle a pension drawn on the Guise estate is found in AN, 300 API 93. After the death of Mademoiselle de Guise in 1688, Mademoiselle and the Condés reopened litigation to recover the remainder of the Guise properties. On this, see chap. 7 and Appendix B.

38. *MM*, 3: 239.

39. *MM*, 3: 251–52.

40. *MM*, 3: 250.

41. *MM*, 3: 253. On the king's nearly fatal illness, see Bluche, *Louis XIV*, 74–76; Wolf, *Louis XIV*, 96–98.

42. *MM*, 3: 253.

43. *MM*, 3: 252.

44. *MM*, 3: 254.

45. *MM*, 3: 255.

46. "Portrait de Monsieur," in Denise Mayer, "Les Seize Portraits Littéraires de Mlle de Montpensier," *Trois Etudes*, 60–62. Notwithstanding the title, Mayer reprints here seventeen portraits that she attributes to Mademoiselle, inclusive of a collective portrait of the *Précieuses* not previously identified as Mademoiselle's work.

47. "Portrait de Monsieur le Prince," in Mayer, "Portraits," *Trois Etudes*, 74–77.

48. "Portrait du Roi," in Mayer, "Portraits," *Trois Etudes*, 67–69.

49. *MM*, 3: 181.

50. "Portrait de Mademoiselle," in Mayer, "Portraits," *Trois Etudes*, 16–20.

51. The preface has been reprinted in Mayer, "Portraits," *Trois Etudes*, 14. For Segrais's version of events, see Segrais, *Mémoires/Anecdotes*, in *Oeuvres Diverses*, 1: 171–73; see also *MM*, 3: 181, 187. The original *Divers Portraits* was republished in the 1735 Dutch edition of Mademoiselle's *Mémoires*. The last full printing of all of the portraits found in the *Divers Portraits* and the Sercy/Barbin *Recueil/Galerie* series was edited by Edouard de Barthélemy under the title *La Galerie des Portraits de Mlle de Montpensier* (Paris, 1860). For the origins of the *Divers Portraits* and a description of the bound volumes that Mademoiselle had secretly printed, see three important articles by Denise Mayer: "Recueils de Portraits Littéraires Attribués à la Grande Mademoiselle," *Bulletin du Bibliophile* (1970): 136–74; "Les Seize Portraits," in *Trois Etudes*, esp. 79–81; and "Les *Divers Portraits* de Mademoiselle de Montpensier," *Médecine de France* 213 (1970): 43–50.

In the article in *Bulletin du Bibliophile* cited above, Mayer criticizes Barthélemy's editorial and scholarly apparatus and his failure to distinguish with sufficient precision the textual variations of the different editions of these works. Mayer's critique is seconded by a recent exhaustive study of the portrait literary genre by Jacqueline Plantié, *La Mode du Portrait Littéraire en France, 1641–1681* (Paris, 1994), 193–204, 677–82. See also Renate Baader, *Dames de Lettres (1649–1698) . . . Mlle de Scudéry,*

Mlle de Montpensier (Stuttgart, 1986); and Jean Lafond, "Mademoiselle et les *Divers Portraits*," *Papers on French Seventeenth-Century Literature* 22 (1995): 55–63. For additional references and discussion, see chap. 8, note 26, and Appendix A.

52. Compare Mademoiselle's description of Madame d'Epernon, in *MM*, 3: 239–43, with her "Portrait de Mme la Duchesse d'Epernon," in Mayer, "Portraits," *Trois Etudes*, 35–37. See also the comments of Plantié, *Portrait Littéraire*, 208–9, 617–58 passim.

53. Renate Baader, *Dames de Lettres*, 160–62; the discrepancy is due to differing opinions on the authorship of several portraits. Both Baader and Plantié accord Mademoiselle an important place in the development and dissemination of this literary genre. For the links between Mademoiselle's work and the use of the portrait in the novels of Scudéry, see the essays in *Les Trois Scudéry: Actes du Colloque du Havre* (1991), ed. Alain Niderst (Paris, 1993). See the comments as well of Dirk Van der Cruysse, *Le Portrait dans les Mémoires du Duc de Saint-Simon* (Paris, 1971), 28–43; and Malina Stefanovska, "A Monumental Triptych: Saint-Simon's *Parallèle des Trois Premiers Rois Bourbons*," *French Historical Studies* 19 (1996): 928–33.

54. On the trip to Lyons, see Bluche, *Louis XIV*, 84–85; and Wolf, *Louis XIV*, 99–105.

55. *MM*, 3: 314.

56. *MM*, 3: 325.

57. *MM*, 3: 323.

58. *MM*, 3: 324.

59. *MM*, 3: 325.

60. *MM*, 3: 330–32.

61. The building, known as the "Maison de Mademoiselle," is still standing, although it was significantly altered in the nineteenth century. See Mayer, "l'Architecture," in *Trois Etudes*, 103–4.

62. *MM*, 3: 337–44.

63. *MM*, 3: 340.

64. *MM*, 3: 340–43. See also the preface to the printed version, addressed to Madame de Pontac, in Segrais, *Oeuvres Diverses*, 2: 182–84. Louise de Pontac was the sister of François-Auguste de Thou, who was executed in 1642 for his part in the conspiracy of Cinq-Mars. Mademoiselle became a close friend of Madame de Pontac's during her stay in Bordeaux in 1650. See Chéruel's biographical note in *MM*, 1: 273.

65. *Relation de l'Ile Imaginaire*, in Segrais, *Oeuvres Diverses*, 2: 187–237. This work is sometimes referred to as the *Relation de l'Ile Invisible* and was published under this title in the 1735 and 1746 editions of Mademoiselle's *Mémoires*. The confusion may stem from the fact that Huet gave it this title in his *Mémoires*, and the error was picked up in the preface to Segrais's *Oeuvres Diverses*, 1: xxi–xxiv.

66. *MM*, 3: 380.

67. *MM*, 3: 380–81.

68. Segrais, *Mémoires/Anecdotes*, in *Oeuvres Diverses*, 1: 218–21. The entire work, *Histoire de la Princesse de Paphlagonie*, is published in Segrais, *Oeuvres Diverses*,

2: 238–303. Citations immediately following to this work will be abbreviated as *Paphlagonie*.

69. *Paphlagonie*, 246–47.

70. *Paphlagonie*, 281.

71. *Paphlagonie*, 282.

72. *Paphlagonie*, 283–84.

73. *Paphlagonie*, 302–3.

74. For the reactions of Mademoiselle de Scudéry and of Madame de Sablé, see Bibliothèque de l'Arsenal, Ms. 5420, Recueil Conrart, v. 11, fol. 79: Sablé to Maure, July n.d., 1660; and fols. 80–82: Scudéry to Maure, n.d. [probably also July 1660]. For the publication of these works, see *MM*, 3: 380–81; Segrais, *Mémoires/Anecdotes*, 1: 170–71, and the introduction by the Dutch editors of Segrais, 1: xx–xxiv. For the tradition that Paphlagonie was aimed at *Le Grand Cyrus* and that Scudéry replied with her *Célinte*, see the comments of Jean Garapon, "Tradition et Nouveauté dans *Célinte*," in *Les Trois Scudéry*, 497–505.

Although the ties between Mademoiselle de Montpensier and the Scudéry family were sometimes strained by the supposed rivalry between their respective salon circles, Mademoiselle by and large remained on friendly terms with Georges de Scudéry. Georges de Scudéry's work *Almahide*, published in segments in 1660–63, was dedicated to Mademoiselle, and Mademoiselle was godmother to Scudéry's son in 1662 in a baptismal ceremony at the Luxembourg. See Alan Niderst, "Georges et Marie-Madeleine de Scudéry," in *Les Trois Scudéry*, 62.

Roger Duchêne notes some interesting connections between *Paphlagonie*, the *Divers Portraits*, and the *Nouvelles Françaises*, and their significance in the development of the modern novel. See Duchêne, "Vers la *Princesse de Clèves*: de la *Princesse de Paphlagonie* à l'*Histoire Amoureuse des Gaules*," *Papers on French Seventeenth-Century Literature* 22 (1995): 65–77.

75. *MM*, 3: 370.

76. *MM*, 3: 383.

77. *MM*, 3: 384.

78. *MM*, 3: 398.

79. *MM*, 3: 397–401.

80. *MM*, 3: 403. Nostradamus is also cited in the last paragraphs of the *Ile Imaginaire* in Segrais, *Oeuvres Diverses*, 2: 237.

81. *MM*, 3: 438.

82. *MM*, 3: 439–41.

83. *MM*, 3: 435.

84. *MM*, 3: 435–36.

85. *MM*, 3: 408–9. For Condé's frigid reception, see Pujo, *Condé*, 260–61.

86. *MM*, 3: 413.

87. *MM*, 3: 408.

88. *MM*, 3: 414–15.

89. *MM*, 3: 375–77.

90. *MM*, 3: 376–77.

91. *MM*, 3: 391–95.

92. *MM*, 3: 409–13.

93. *MM*, 3: 414–17.

94. *MM*, 3: 428. For Gaston's last years, see Dethan, *Gaston*, 310–25.

95. *MM*, 3: 422.

96. *MM*, 3: 423–24.

97. *MM*, 3: 424.

98. *MM*, 3: 424.

99. *MM*, 3: 449. For the political history and for secondary accounts of the wedding, see Bluche, *Louis XIV*, 86–91; Wolf, *Louis XIV*, 114–24.

100. *MM*, 3: 455.

101. *MM*, 3: 455.

102. *MM*, 3: 457.

103. *MM*, 3: 458–61. Many of these details are also found in Vandy's correspondence, and it is likely that Mademoiselle had copies of Vandy's letters available at the time she composed her own account. See Bibliothèque de l'Arsenal, Ms. 5420, Recueil Conrart, v. 11, fols. 1279–80: Vandy to Comtesse de Maure, June 4, 1660.

104. *MM*, 3: 461–65.

105. *MM*, 3: 471. Other interesting accounts of this ceremony are found in Bibliothèque de l'Arsenal, Ms. 5420, Recueil Conrart, v. 11, fols. 1243–46: Vandy to Comtesse de Maure, June 8/13, 1660; and fol. 1281: Motteville to Madame de Montausier, June 4, 1660.

106. *MM*, 3: 477–78. Vandy's letter to Maure, June 8/13, cited in note 105, provides more details. See also Mathieu Montreuil, *Relation . . . du Marriage du Roi* (1660), in *Archives Curieuses*, 2d series, 8: 303–29.

107. *MM*, 3: 254.

108. *MM*, 3: 217–18, 230–31, 278–79, 391–95, 410–13. See also Motteville, *Mémoires*, 473.

109. On her "indifference," see *MM*, 3: 387–89, 391.

110. *MM*, 3: 424.

111. *MM*, 3: 453–54.

112. Four letters, two by Mademoiselle and two by Madame de Motteville, were first published at Cologne in 1667 in a volume entitled *Recueil de Pièces Nouvelles et Galantes*. See Chéruel's comments, in *MM*, 3: 454 n. 2. For the subsequent publishing history, see Appendix A. The Bibliothèque Nationale de France has recently acquired a late seventeenth-century manuscript copy of the correspondence, Nouv. Acq. Fr. 25670, which includes a further exchange of letters in 1661 on the same subject, apparently spurred by the rumor of a match between Mademoiselle and prince Charles de Lorraine. These are very similar in tone to the published letters. As far as I can determine, these letters have never been published, although a notation in the manuscript indicates that Monmerqué examined the volume in 1842. This correspondence is bound with a small *roman*, *Histoire de la Princesse Adamirze*, and a cover letter by Motteville, dated 1664, to Mademoiselle at Eu.

113. *Lettres de Montpensier*, 8: Montpensier to Motteville, May 14, 1660.

114. *Lettres de Montpensier*, 3–14: Montpensier to Motteville, May 14, 1660.

115. *Lettres de Montpensier*, 22: Motteville to Montpensier, n.d.

116. *Lettres de Montpensier*, 22–23: Motteville to Montpensier, n.d.

117. *Lettres de Montpensier*, 15–25: Motteville to Montpensier, n.d.

118. *Lettres de Montpensier*, 30: Montpensier to Motteville, n.d.

119. *Lettres de Montpensier*, 30: Montpensier to Motteville, n.d.

120. *Lettres de Montpensier*, 40: Motteville to Montpensier, n.d.

121. *Lettres de Montpensier*, 51: Motteville to Montpensier, n.d.

122. *Lettres de Montpensier*, 53: Motteville to Montpensier, n.d.

123. *MM*, 3: 453–54. For the debate about women and political power in the aftermath of the Fronde, see Natalie Z. Davis, "Women in Politics," in Davis and Arlette Farge, *A History of Women in the West* (Cambridge, 1993), 3: 167–83; and Ian Maclean, *Woman Triumphant*, 64–87. Maclean also deals directly with the Motteville-Montpensier correspondence, which he sets at the extreme edge of views on marriage espoused in some contemporary circles; see 88–118, esp. 115–16. See also Madeleine Bertaud, "En Marge de leurs Mémoires, une Correspondance entre Mlle de Montpensier et Mme de Motteville," *Travaux de Littérature*, no. 3 (1990): 278–95.

CHAPTER 6   THE TRIUMPH OF VENUS

Epigraphs: *MM*, 4: 249; Bussy-Rabutin, *Correspondance*, 1: 356: Bussy-Rabutin to the Comte de Tavannes, January 10, 1671; Segrais, quoting Guilloire, in *Mémoires/ Anecdotes*, 1: 119.

1. *MM*, 3: 489; see also Archives du Ministère des Affaires Etrangères, Mémoires et Documents, France, vol. 292, fols. 320–22: Mademoiselle to Mazarin, June 30, 1660.

2. Archives Nationales, 300 API 93: "Contrat Fait entre les Commissaires du Roi . . . Mme la Duchesse d'Orléans . . . Mademoiselle d'Orléans de Montpensier," September 19, 1665. Mademoiselle renounced several small claims against Gaston's estate in exchange for the arrangements at the Luxembourg. On these quarrels with her stepmother and later with her sister Elisabeth, duchess de Guise, see *MM*, 3: 488; *MM*, 4: 16, 19, 373. It is generally assumed that the decor of Mademoiselle's apartments at the Luxembourg was much as it had been in the time of Marie de Medici, as were the gardens. See Denise Mayer, "l'Architecture," in *Trois Etudes*, 101–2; and *Marie de Médicis et le Palais du Luxembourg*, ed. Marie-Noëlle Baudouin-Matuszek (Paris, 1991), 170–223.

3. *MM*, 3: 499. See also Dethan, *Gaston*, 418 n. 201.

4. *MM*, 3: 500.

5. *MM*, 3: 423.

6. *MM*, 3: 490.

7. *MM*, 3: 490, 497–98. The abbé François de Choisy, the son of Madame de Choisy and Gaston's chancellor Jean de Choisy, also left a record of these assemblies. See *Mémoires de l'Abbé de Choisy*, ed. Georges Mongrédien (Paris, 1966), 83–84, 280.

8. Choisy, *Mémoires*, 280. For Marguerite-Louise, see Emmanuel Pierre Rodocanachi, *Les Infortunes d'une Petite-Fille d'Henri IV: Marguerite d'Orléans, Grande*

Duchesse de Toscane (Paris, ca. 1902). Mademoiselle and Condé had served as god-parents to Marguerite-Louise in June 1651: see Dubuisson-Aubenay, *Journal*, 2: 78.

9. *MM*, 3: 490–91.

10. *MM*, 3: 496.

11. *MM*, 3: 496.

12. *MM*, 3: 491.

13. *MM*, 3: 423.

14. *MM*, 3: 500–501, an allusion to Christine de Lorraine (1565–1636), the consort of Ferdinand I de Medici.

15. *MM*, 3: 491.

16. *MM*, 3: 503, on "merrymaking"; 506, on Mazarin's death.

17. *MM*, 3: 510.

18. *MM*, 3: 507–9.

19. *MM*, 3: 509–10; quotation, 510.

20. *MM*, 3: 500.

21. *MM*, 3: 498.

22. *MM*, 3: 504–5. The "daughter of France" to whom Mademoiselle alludes is Catherine de Bourbon (1559–1604), the sister of Henri IV, whose husband Henri, duc de Bar, became duke of Lorraine in 1608.

23. *MM*, 3: 512.

24. *MM*, 3: 513.

25. *MM*, 3: 513.

26. *MM*, 3: 514–15.

27. *MM*, 3: 516–17.

28. *MM*, 3: 518.

29. *MM*, 3: 519.

30. *MM*, 3: 519–22. François de Choisy gives a very different version of events, stating that Mademoiselle was interested in the prince, but he fell in love with the beautiful young Marguerite-Louise. A jealous Mademoiselle then forced her sister to marry the Tuscan heir. See Choisy, *Mémoires*, 83–84, 280–81.

31. *MM*, 3: 570–71. For the duke's fear, first expressed at the meeting at Lyons in 1658, that Mademoiselle was too old for childbearing, see chap. 5, and also Motteville, *Mémoires*, 463. According to Amelot de la Houssaye, Mademoiselle's dismissal of the duke as "worthless" (*dappoco*) infuriated her aunt Christine and doomed any chances Mademoiselle may have had for a Savoy marriage: see Amelot de la Houssaye, *Mémoires*, 1: 455–56.

32. *MM*, 3: 581.

33. *MM*, 3: 578. For Mademoiselle's encounter with Condé, see *MM*, 4: 4–5.

34. *MM*, 4: 4–5.

35. On the Condé ambitions in Poland, see Pujo, *Condé*, 265–74 passim, 280–81.

36. *MM*, 4: 44–46. The king actually provided a dowry of 300,000 livres. For a copy of the marriage contract, dated May 15, 1667, see BNF, Mélanges de Colbert, v. 15, fols. 583–89.

37. For the exchange of letters with Motteville, see BNF, Nouv. Acq. Fr. 25670, fols. 22v–29v. Only the third in the series of letters is dated, fols. 26v–28v: Mademoiselle to Motteville, August 21, 1661. From the context, the entire exchange can probably be dated June–August 1661. For the quotation from Mademoiselle's *Mémoires*, see *MM*, 3: 501.

38. *MM*, 3: 495–96; quotation, 496.

39. Countess of Derby to Madame de la Trémouille, n.d., quoted in Julia Cartwright, *Madame: A Life of Henrietta, Daughter of Charles I and Duchess of Orléans* (New York, 1901), 66. Lady Derby was Charlotte de la Trémouille, sister of Henri, duc de Thouars (1599–1674), and a cousin of Mademoiselle's.

40. *MM*, 3: 504.

41. *MM*, 3: 533–38. Charlotte de Bourbon-Montpensier (d. 1582), formerly abbess of Jouarre, became the third wife of William the Silent in 1574. The descendants of the couple in Mademoiselle's lifetime included the dukes of Bouillon (Turenne's family); the La Trémouilles; and the family of the Electors Palatine of the Rhine. Ironically, given Mademoiselle's feelings, these were among her closest kin on the Montpensier side. According to Amelot de la Houssaye, Mademoiselle used to refer to Charlotte de Bourbon as "La Grande Mère Abbesse," a pun on her great-aunt's dual vocation. See Amelot de la Houssaye, *Mémoires*, 1: 463. Mademoiselle's Montpensier ancestors and Turenne's family had disputed title to the principality of Sedan, and Mademoiselle amused herself with the idea of reopening a lawsuit: see Valentin Conrart to Félibien, August 9, 1647, printed in René Kerviler and Edouard de Barthélemy, *Valentin Conrart* (Paris, 1881), 368–69; see also Jean Bérenger, *Turenne* (Paris, 1987), 29–35.

42. *MM*, 3: 538–39. For Louis XIV's policy, see *Louis XIV, Mémoires for the Instruction of the Dauphin*, ed. Paul Sonnino (New York, 1970), 26–27, 45–46, 98, 116, 244–45; see also Louis XIV to Estrades, August 25, 1661, in Louis XIV, *Lettres Particulières*, ed. Philippe de Grouvelle (Paris, 1806), 5: 46–50. For Turenne's role, see Bérenger, *Turenne*, 348–52.

43. *MM*, 3: 539.

44. *MM*, 3: 541.

45. *MM* 3: 543.

46. *MM*, 3: 543–44.

47. *MM*, 3: 543–44. While the date of Mademoiselle's letter to Charny is not stated, by late May 1662 it had fallen into the hands of Louis XIV's ambassador in Spain, Georges de la Feuillade, archbishop of Embrun, who forwarded it to the king. See *Archives de la Bastille*, ed. François Ravaisson (Paris, 1866–84), 3: 297: Louis XIV to Embrun, May 28, 1662; 304: same to same, August 20, 1662. Mademoiselle's letter to Charny predates the marriage of Charles II to Catherine de Braganza, which took place at Portsmouth on May 31, 1662. Although there is no evidence of an earlier marriage by proxy, the English began to refer to Catherine as their queen immediately after the engagement was announced in May 1661, and Mademoiselle probably took her lead from this. See Fraser, *Royal Charles*, 204–6.

48. Bussy-Rabutin put some importance on the intercepted letter to Charny in his explanation of her disgrace: Bussy-Rabutin, *Mémoires*, 2: 131.

49. *MM*, 3: 545–46.

50. *MM*, 3: 547.

51. *MM*, 3: 553.

52. *MM*, 3: 562–63.

53. *MM*, 3: 557–58. For the entirety of these revelations, see *MM*, 3: 552–62.

54. *MM*, 3: 563.

55. Bussy-Rabutin, *Mémoires*, 2: 141. Mademoiselle told Bussy-Rabutin that she believed her correspondence was intercepted and read by royal spies, in same, 134–35. Mademoiselle mentions that many of her friends wrote frequently with news of Paris and the court, but she burned all of these letters: *MM*, 3: 571.

56. *MM*, 3: 572–73.

57. *MM*, 3: 573–74.

58. The county of Eu was to remain a major property of the French royal family into the twentieth century. Although the surviving records are voluminous, most, unfortunately, postdate Mademoiselle. For Eu's history and rank in the peerage of France, see BNF, Mélanges de Colbert, v. 15, fols. 576–81: "Note sur le Comté d'Eu," n.d. (about 1670). For a description of the county of Eu at the time of Mademoiselle's death, see Archives Nationales, Fonds de Dreux, 300 APII 14: "Etat de la Consistance du Comté d'Eu Dressé après le Décès de la Duchesse de Montpensier 1 juillet 1693." Financial records for Eu in Mademoiselle's time are scattered in a number of côtes in the Fonds de Dreux, which are cited in the Bibliography.

For Mademoiselle's account of her interest in the château and the work she commissioned, see *MM*, 3: 324–25, 576. An early nineteenth-century document preserved in 300 APII 14 provides additional details: "Comté d'Eu Procès-Verbaux de Prise de Possession 14 novembre 1814." Denise Mayer notes that no documentation survives to date the stages of Mademoiselle's work: see Mayer, "l'Architecture," in *Trois Etudes*, 104–7. The château, which is now a museum, underwent major renovations in the eighteenth and nineteenth centuries, and the interior was badly damaged in a fire in 1902; consequently, very little remains today from the time of Mademoiselle. For a general background for this and later periods, see the papers on Eu published as *Mélanges Dédiés à Mme la Comtesse de Paris*, ed. Martine Bailleux-Delbecq (Luneray, 1992), which includes an interesting presentation by Bailleux-Delbecq on the glassware industry in the district, 17–28.

59. *MM*, 3: 525.

60. Bussy-Rabutin, *Mémoires*, 2: 147–48: Mademoiselle to Bussy-Rabutin, November 28, 1663; *MM*, 3: 576.

61. *MM*, 3: 576.

62. *MM*, 3: 577–81.

63. *MM*, 3: 583.

64. *MM*, 3: 583. See Louis XIV, *Lettres Particulières*, 186–87: Louis XIV to Mademoiselle, May 27, 1664. The comte d'Estrades also seems to have interceded on

Mademoiselle's behalf; she wrote to thank him. See BNF, Collection Clairambault, v. 581, fols. 91–93: Mademoiselle to Estrades, July 7, 1664.

65. *MM*, 3: 583–84.

66. *MM*, 3: 584–85; *MM*, 4: 5.

67. *MM*, 4: 4–5.

68. *MM*, 4: 3–4.

69. *MM*, 4: 4.

70. *MM*, 4: 4, 8.

71. Ormesson, *Journal*, 2: 148.

72. *MM*, 4: 4. See also the correspondence of Condé with Marie-Louise de Gon-zague, queen of Poland, in *Le Grand Condé et le Duc d'Enghien: Lettres Inédites sur la Cour de Louis XIV*, ed. Emile Magne (Paris, 1920), 32–35: Condé to Marie-Louise, June 3, 1664; 38–39: same to same, June 17, 1664; 115: same to same, December 14, 1664; 120: same to same, December 26, 1664. Louis's efforts and excuses can be found in Louis XIV, *Lettres Particulières*, 201: Louis to Mademoiselle, July 12, 1664; 235–36: same to same, September 2, 1664.

73. *MM*, 3: 581–82.

74. *MM*, 4: 74.

75. *MM*, 4: 75.

76. *MM*, 4: 13.

77. *MM*, 4: 13–14, and also 15.

78. *MM*, 4: 18–19.

79. *MM*, 4: 20.

80. *MM*, 4: 23.

81. *MM*, 4: 23–24.

82. *MM*, 4: 24.

83. *MM*, 4: 24.

84. *MM*, 4: 26.

85. *MM*, 4: 27.

86. *MM*, 4: 27.

87. For the entirety of this scene, see *MM*, 4: 22–28. Mademoiselle's account should be compared with Motteville, *Mémoires*, 559–72; see also Kleinman, *Anne d'Autriche*, 500–508.

88. The standard biography of Lauzun remains that of Auguste-Armand, duc de La Force, *Lauzun: Un Courtier du Grand Roi* (Paris, 1913). A collateral descendant of Lauzun, La Force made good use of archival sources and documents and family papers for his portrayal of Lauzun. He covers Lauzun's early life, summarized here, in 1–25. Lauzun's contemporaries were fascinated by his meteoric rise and fall and by his extraordinary personality. Saint-Simon, who became Lauzun's brother-in-law in 1695 and saw him almost daily in the years thereafter, has left a long and brilliant portrait of the man, on which La Force and others have drawn heavily: see Saint-Simon, *Mémoires*, 9: 619–45. Jean de La Bruyère has left a much shorter but penetrat-ing characterization in his *Les Caractères ou Moeurs de ce Siècle* (1691) under the name of "Stratton": see *Oeuvres de La Bruyère*, ed. Gustave Servois (Paris, 1865), 1: 335–36. A

recent new biography by Jean-Christian Petitfils, *Lauzun, ou, l'Insolente Séduction* (Paris, 1987), adds little not found in the older work by La Force. For an English language biography, see Mary Sandars, *Lauzun: Courtier and Adventurer* (London, 1908).

89. La Force, *Lauzun*, 5.

90. *MM*, 3: 355.

91. For Lauzun's physical appearance, see Saint-Simon, *Mémoires*, 9: 620; *MM*, 4: 249; La Force, *Lauzun*, 38.

92. Saint-Simon, *Mémoires*, 9: 620–21, 635, 638–39. See also Bussy-Rabutin, *Mémoires*, 2: 231. Bussy-Rabutin mentions (265) that Mademoiselle wanted to visit him at the Bastille, but was refused permission.

93. Saint-Simon, *Mémoires*, 9: 625–26; La Force, *Lauzun*, 18–20. The text of Louis XIV's letter explaining the incident is printed in *Archives de la Bastille*, 3: 14–18: Louis XIV to comte d'Estrades, May 19, 1666.

94. Saint-Simon, *Mémoires*, 9: 624. Lauzun was allied with Turenne and Lorges in opposition to the military reforms championed by Louvois: see André Corvisier, *Louvois* (Paris, 1983), 156. Technically, the minister of war until 1677 was Louvois's father, Michel Le Tellier. In practice, as his father's deputy with the right of succession, Louvois normally performed the duties of this office.

95. Saint-Simon, *Mémoires*, 9: 624–25. See also *MM*, 4: 70–73.

96. *MM*, 4: 393–94.

97. *MM*, 3: 478. Mademoiselle's account of Lauzun's behavior at the king's wedding was written in 1677, in the second part of her *Mémoires*. The earlier mention of Lauzun during the carnival season of 1659 occurs in the first portion of the *Mémoires* and was therefore written much earlier, around 1660: see *MM*, 3: 355.

98. *MM*, 3: 542.

99. *MM*, 3: 551. On Mademoiselle's faulty memory in describing Lauzun's emblem, see La Force, *Lauzun*, 13. For the political significance of the carousel of 1662, see Peter Burke, *The Fabrication of Louis XIV* (New Haven, 1992), 65–66; and Moine, *Les Fêtes*, 21–32. As noted by Burke and Moine, this spectacle was commemorated in a magnificent book of engravings published in 1670 under the title *Festiva ad Capita*, with a text by Charles Perrault. Mademoiselle mentions that she took great delight in this volume: *MM*, 3: 551.

100. *MM*, 4: 38–41.

101. *MM*, 4: 41.

102. See, for example, the remarks in *MM*, 4: 53, 68, 79.

103. *MM*, 4: 73. For her version of the episode with Louvois, see 70–73.

104. *MM*, 4: 73.

105. *MM*, 4: 80, 85.

106. Segrais, *Mémoires/Anecdotes*, 1: 121.

107. *MM*, 4: 92.

108. *MM*, 4: 92.

109. *MM*, 4: 92. Mademoiselle's quotation in its entirety comprises lines 1221–34 from Corneille's *La Suite du Menteur*, IV, i.

110. *MM*, 4: 95.

111. *MM*, 4: 92, 94.

112. Contemporaries were quick to see the connection. In a famous letter quoted at the end of this chapter, Madame de Sévigné noted that the news of Mademoiselle's engagement would "fill Madame de Rohan and Madame d'Hauterive with joy." The two women she named were daughters of dukes who had contracted well-publicized misalliances. See Sévigné, *Lettres*, 1: 181: Sévigné to Coulanges, December 15, 1670. A recent study suggests that the high nobility were tolerant of great noblemen marrying down the social scale, but strongly disapproved of marriages between daughters of great houses and lesser men. See Emmanuel LeRoy-Ladurie and Jean-François Fitou, *Saint-Simon: ou, le Système de la Cour* (Paris, 1997), 274–94. See also Gayle K. Brunelle, "Dangerous Liaisons: Mésalliance and Early Modern French Noblewomen," *French Historical Studies* 19 (1995): 75–103.

The interplay of public and private authority, specifically the patriarchal nature of the seventeenth-century family and the extension of that image to models of the social hierarchy has been the subject of much discussion in the last several decades, as has the related subject of marriage in this context. For some basic material, see David Hunt, *Parents and Children in History: The Psychology of Family Life in Early Modern France* (London, 1970); Jean Louis Flandrin, *Familles: Parenté, Maison, Sexualité dans l'Ancienne Société* (Paris, 1984); Sarah Hanley, "Engendering the State: Family Formation and State Building in Early Modern France, *French Historical Studies* 16 (1989): 4–27; Robert Muchembled, *Popular Culture and Elite Culture in France, 1400–1750*, trans. Lydia Cochrane (Baton Rouge, La., 1985); Claude Dulong, *L'Amour au XVIIe Siècle* (Paris, 1969); P. C. Timbal, "L'Esprit du Droit Privé au XVIIe Siècle," *XVIIe Siècle* 58–59 (1963): 30–39. See also Merry E. Wiesner, *Women and Gender in Early Modern Europe* (New York, 1993), 239–55. Wiesner's survey of the literature on this subject, 255–58, provides an excellent guide to further reading.

113. *MM*, 4: 94.

114. *MM*, 4: 99.

115. *MM*, 4: 97–99.

116. *MM*, 4: 100–101.

117. *MM*, 4: 106.

118. *MM*, 4: 107.

119. *MM*, 4: 108.

120. *MM*, 4: 114–16.

121. *MM*, 4: 116.

122. *MM*, 4: 120.

123. *MM*, 4: 105.

124. On the Longueville candidacy, see *MM*, 4: 104–5, 124, 137. See also Segrais, *Mémoires/Anecdotes*, 1: 142–43.

125. *MM*, 4: 132–33, 137.

126. *MM*, 4: 138–39.

127. *MM*, 4: 140–41; quotation, 140.

128. *MM*, 4: 143.

129. *MM*, 4: 144. From a description of the symptoms, it is likely that Henrietta died from acute peritonitis. See Barker, *Brother to the Sun King*, 113–18.

130. *MM*, 4: 146.

131. *MM*, 4: 143–48. The other classic account is that of Madame de La Fayette. See her *Histoire de Madame Henriette d'Angleterre*, in *Oeuvres Complètes*, ed. Roger Duchêne (Paris, 1990), 481–90. Duchêne notes that there is now some question among literary scholars about the attribution of this famous biography to La Fayette: see 433–36.

132. *MM*, 4: 148.

133. *MM*, 4: 148–50; quotation, 150.

134. *MM*, 4: 155, 158–59.

135. *MM*, 4: 161.

136. *MM*, 4: 162–64.

137. On the arrest of Philippe de Lorraine and its sequel, see Barker, *Brother to the Sun King*, 100–109.

138. Barker, *Brother to the Sun King*, 121–23.

139. *MM*, 4: 101–2.

140. *MM*, 4: 165–66. See also Mademoiselle's disparaging comments on a "regime" of favorites such as that of Philippe de Lorraine: *MM*, 4: 157.

141. *MM*, 4: 167–69; quotation, 167.

142. *MM*, 4: 169–70.

143. *MM*, 4: 151; quotation, 148.

144. *MM*, 4: 155.

145. *MM*, 4: 156.

146. *MM*, 4: 156–58.

147. *MM*, 4: 165, 167.

148. *MM*, 4: 167.

149. *MM*, 4: 169.

150. *MM*, 4: 171–73.

151. *MM*, 4: 174. These documents do not survive. Mademoiselle notes that she burned all of her correspondence with Lauzun: see *MM*, 4: 185.

152. *MM*, 4: 174–75.

153. *MM*, 4: 175–76.

154. *MM*, 4: 177–80.

155. *MM*, 4: 183.

156. *MM*, 4: 184–85.

157. *MM*, 4: 185.

158. *MM*, 4: 186.

159. *MM*, 4: 186–88.

160. *MM*, 4: 188–89.

161. *MM*, 4: 189–90. I have very loosely translated *ambition* here as "false pride." This is closer to Mademoiselle's meaning than a more literal translation. The entire sentence reads: "*Je ne trouve rien de blessé en cette affaire que mon ambition.*"

162. *MM*, 4: 190–91.

163. *MM*, 4: 191.

164. *MM*, 4: 201.

165. *MM*, 4: 193.

166. *MM*, 4: 205.

167. *MM*, 4: 207.

168. *MM*, 4: 211–13.

169. *MM*, 4: 207.

170. Sévigné, *Lettres*, 1: 181–82: Sévigné to Coulanges, December 15, 1670.

CHAPTER 7   THE MASK OF APOLLO AND THE END OF ILLUSIONS

Epigraphs: Bussy-Rabutin, *Correspondance*, 2: 353: Mademoiselle to Bussy-Rabutin, May 31, 1674; La Fayette, quoting Mademoiselle, in *Mémoires de la Cour de France*, 757; Bussy-Rabutin, *Correspondance*, 6: 209: Bussy-Rabutin to Sévigné and Corbinelli, February 2, 1689.

1. *MM*, 4: 217.

2. *MM*, 4: 208.

3. *MM*, 4: 183.

4. *MM*, 4: 225–26.

5. Sévigné, *Lettres*, 1: 183: Sévigné to Coulanges, December 19, 1670. Sévigné mistakenly included Saint-Fargeau, Châtellerault, and Eu, while the initial donation consisted of Montpensier and Dombes: see *MM*, 4: 225. The donation of Eu was delayed because of legal formalities: see below, note 117. Saint-Simon mistakenly included the duchy of Aumale, but this actually belonged at that time to the family of Savoie-Nemours: Saint-Simon, *Mémoires*, 9: 630. Choisy also erred here, stating that Guilloire delayed the gift of Dombes, but that Montpensier and Eu were signed over: Choisy, *Mémoires*, 282.

6. *MM*, 4: 204–11.

7. Contemporary observers had a great deal of trouble sorting out the motives of the principal players in this story. To cite a few examples, Choisy saw Lauzun as a schemer; La Fare as a man of low character taking advantage of the princess's weakness; La Bruyère as "an enigma"; Sévigné as an actor who played his part well. Choisy, *Mémoires*, 281; La Fare, *Mémoires*, in Michaud and Poujoulat, *Nouvelle Collection*, 32: 269–70; La Bruyère, "Stratton," in *Les Caractères*, 1: 336; and Sévigné, *Lettres*, 1: 184: Sévigné to Grignan, December 24, 1670. The popular view of Lauzun as the consummate gambler playing for high stakes is found in the pamphlet *Les Amours de Mademoiselle* (see note 87).

A number of observers believed that Mademoiselle was motivated in part by a desire to please the king by bestowing her hand on Louis's male favorite. Segrais was especially emphatic in asserting that Mademoiselle had never loved Lauzun but chose him in order to curry favor with the king, as was Philippe's second wife, Elisabeth-Charlotte, Princess Palatine. See La Fare, *Mémoires*, 269–70; Segrais, *Mémoires/Anecdotes*, 1: 34, 143; *Madame Palatine: Lettres Françaises*, ed. Dirk Van der Cruysse (Paris, 1989), 193: Elisabeth-Charlotte to Sophia of Hanover, September 27, 1702.

Others concluded that the king, wishing to make Lauzun's fortune, had secretly encouraged, if not forced, Mademoiselle to propose the marriage, an accusation levied by Philippe d'Orléans to the king's face and denied by Mademoiselle. There is no reason to doubt the sincerity of Louis's distress at this accusation, as reported by Mademoiselle and as noted in his Letter to the Ambassadors. The Savoyard resident at court, Thomas de Saint-Maurice, also reported the king's displeasure at this rumor, although, initially, he also suspected the king of some hidden motive for permitting such a misalliance. See *MM*, 4: 204–5 and 211–12 for Philippe's accusations; Louis's Letter in *MM*, 4: app. 9, 626, and his remarks to Mademoiselle on these accusations, *MM*, 4: 233–34. For Saint-Maurice's reports, see Saint-Maurice, *Lettres sur la Cour de France*, ed. Jean LeMoine (Paris, 1910), 1: 522: December 17, 1670; and 526: December 19, 1670.

Without commenting on the king's role, Ormesson speculated that the proposed marriage stemmed from a political alliance between Colbert and Montespan at the expense of Louvois. See Ormesson, *Journal*, 2: 605. Mademoiselle's account, written some years later, was intended to refute the suggestions that she was motivated in any way by the wishes of the king to make Lauzun's fortune, or that she had been deceived by Lauzun, or that her proposal had anything to do with the Colbert-Louvois rivalry.

8. For Philippe's remarks, see Ormesson, *Journal*, 2: 603. For Philippe's personal reasons to resent Lauzun, see Claude Dulong, *L'Amour au XVIIe Siècle* (Paris, 1969), 211, 227–28. For the queen's position, see *MM*, 4: 204–9 passim.

9. Quotation, *MM*, 4: 219. On the opposition of Gaston's widow, supported by the rest of the Guise and Lorraine families, see also Ormesson, *Journal*, 2: 604; and Saint-Maurice, *Lettres*, 1: 537: December 26, 1670.

10. Mademoiselle commented harshly on the opposition of the Condés. See *MM*, 4: 235, 373. For other accounts of the opposition to the marriage, see Ormesson, *Journal*, 2: 603–5; Saint-Maurice, *Lettres*, 1: 514–25: December 17, 1670; and 525–31: December 19, 1670. For Condé's threat to shoot Lauzun, see La Fare, *Mémoires*, 269–71. La Fare also credits the future Madame de Maintenon with persuading Montespan to oppose the marriage, while Choisy tells the same story but attributes this action to Marie de Bourbon-Soissons, princesse de Carignan: see Choisy, *Mémoires*, 282. For other details, see Saint-Simon, *Mémoires*, 9: 625; Sévigné, *Lettres*, 1: 182–83: Sévigné to Coulanges, December 19, 1670; and *Archives de la Bastille*, 3: 95–96: Don Miguel de Iturrieta, Spanish chargé d'affaires, to Don Diego de la Torre, December 21, 1670.

11. *MM*, 4: 94, 97. A contemporary study of the Montpensier lineage to identify Mademoiselle's possible heirs is found in BNF, Collection Clairambault, v. 634–35, fols. 140–58, "Discours sur les Héritiers de Mademoiselle." The major "natural heirs" were all people Mademoiselle disliked, including the La Tour d'Auvergne family, the family of the Elector Palatine of the Rhine, and various branches of the house of Lorraine.

12. *MM*, 4: 162.

13. *MM*, 4: 383.

14. *MM*, 4: 205–6.

15. Sévigné, *Lettres*, 1: 185–86: Sévigné to Coulanges, December 31, 1671. Olivier d'Ormesson was a friend of the Rabutin family and hence of Madame de Sévigné. His account of the reaction to the announcement, cited above, and his own evident dismay suggest the widespread opposition to such a marriage in parlementary and "official" circles. For other indignant reactions to the announcement of Mademoiselle's engagement, see BNF, Collection Clairambault, v. 500, fols. 433–60, which contains many denunciations of Lauzun and the proposed marriage; and Clairambault, v. 634–35, fols. 112–32, which contains several significant pieces including a "Mémoire des Sentiments de Plusieurs Grands des Etats du Royaume," fols. 120–32, which argued that nobles, clergy, and commoners were united in their opposition to the misalliance. Copies of these materials and others of the same type are widespread in major French archives, attesting to the high level of interest in this subject. For example, a duplicate of the "Mémoire . . . Réponse" cited below, note 16, is found in BNF, Ms. Fr. 20625; and Ms. Fr. 6046 contains copies of the *Amours de Mademoiselle . . . et Lauzun*, of Louis XIV's Letter to the Ambassadors, and satirical material on the engagement.

16. On the standing of the Caumont family, as well as an attack on the Lorraines, see *MM*, 4: 213–15, including Chéruel's n. 1, 213–14; and *MM*, 4: app. 8, 558–62. Montausier's delegation cited a list of precedents of French princesses marrying simple noblemen. The list was widely circulated and helped fuel the controversy about the engagement, and Louis XIV actually mentions it in his Letter to the Ambassadors: see *MM*, 4: Chéruel's n. 1, 215–16, and Louis's Letter, in *MM*, 4: app. 9, 625. A copy of the memoir and a response dismissing the precedents is found in BNF, Collection Clairambault, fols. 114–19: "Mémoire pour Justifier le Mariage de Mademoiselle . . . Réponse au Mémoire." A companion piece, fols. 120–32, "Mémoire des Sentiments . . . des Plusieurs Grands," cited in note 15, is scornful of any comparison between the Caumonts and the princely family of Guise-Lorraine into which Mademoiselle's sister Elisabeth had married.

17. Saint-Maurice, *Lettres*, 1: 514: December 17, 1670.

18. Ormesson states that during her interview with the king, Mademoiselle accused Michel Le Tellier, Louvois's father, of opposing the marriage, and Saint-Maurice made the same report, saying that she named both Le Tellier and Louvois. Saint-Simon also noted that Lauzun was considered to be a friend of Colbert's as well as an enemy of Louvois's. In her account of her interview with the king, Mademoiselle does not mention any accusation directed against Le Tellier or Louvois, although she later accused the two of hostility to Lauzun: see *MM*, 4: 388. Elsewhere in her account of the preparation for the wedding, she noted that Colbert had taken responsibility for the contractual arrangements and other formalities involved: see *MM*, 4: 222, 232; Ormesson, *Journal*, 2: 605; Saint-Maurice, *Lettres*, 1: 538: December 26, 1671; and Saint-Simon, *Mémoires*, 9: 621.

19. *MM*, 4: 207.

20. Segrais, *Mémoires/Anecdotes*, 1: 119.

21. *MM*, 4: 205, 207.

22. *MM*, 4: 218, 220.

23. *MM*, 4: 218 (Rochefort), 220 (Guitry), 221–23 (Montausier). Montausier used the phrase "crowned head to crowned head," "*couronne à couronne,*" which seems to have stuck as a description of Lauzun's attitude. The phrase is often attributed to Madame de Caylus, who used it years later in her account of the abortive engagement: Caylus, *Souvenirs,* in *Nouvelle Collection,* ed. Michaud and Poujoulat, 32: 491.

24. *MM*, 4: 224; Sévigné, *Lettres,* 1: 185–86: Sévigné to Coulanges, December 31, 1670.

25. *MM*, 4: 228–29.

26. *MM*, 4: 231–32.

27. *MM*, 4: 232–33.

28. *MM*, 4: 233.

29. *MM*, 4: 233–36. See also note 18.

30. Choisy, *Mémoires,* 283.

31. *MM*, 4: 238–39.

32. Louis XIV's Letter is printed in *MM,* 4: app. 9, 624–27. The letter was drafted by the minister for foreign affairs, Hugues de Lionne, who acted in such haste that unsigned copies were sent to the embassies abroad. See *Archives de la Bastille,* 3: 95: Lionne to Pomponne, December 19, 1670. According to Choisy, Louis offered Lauzun the rank of maréchal of France on this occasion, but Lauzun declined. From a letter of Madame de Sévigné, this offer occurred in February 1671. Choisy, *Mémoires,* 283; Sévigné, *Lettres,* 1: 209: Sévigné to Grignan, February 27, 1671.

33. Sévigné, *Lettres,* 1: 184–85: Sévigné to Coulanges, December 24, 1670. See also Ormesson, *Journal,* 2: 604; Saint-Maurice, *Lettres,* 1: 537–38: December 26, 1670.

34. *MM*, 4: app. 9, 624–27.

35. Sévigné, *Lettres,* 1: 186: Sévigné to Coulanges, December 31, 1670.

36. For Bussy-Rabutin's initial raillery and his subsequent change of heart, see Bussy-Rabutin, *Correspondance,* 1: 356: Bussy-Rabutin to Tavannes, January 10, 1671; 361–62: Madame de Scudéry to Bussy-Rabutin, January 21, 1671; 366–67: Bussy-Rabutin to Scudéry, January 29, 1671. Madame de Scudéry, Marie-Madeleine de Martinvast, was the wife of Georges de Scudéry and the sister-in-law of the famous *Précieuse* Madeleine de Scudéry, to whom this exchange of letters is sometimes mistakenly attributed.

37. *MM*, 4: 240–47 passim. Madame de Sévigné does not even hint of any discordant emotions during her visits to Mademoiselle: Sévigné, *Lettres,* 1: 186: Sévigné to Coulanges, December 24, 1670.

38. *MM*, 4: 246.

39. *MM*, 4: 247–48.

40. *MM*, 4: 251; for various instances of her public distress, see 248–53.

41. *MM*, 4: 252.

42. *MM*, 4: 253.

43. *MM*, 4: 257–58.

44. *MM*, 4: 261–63. Amelot de la Houssaye confirms the story in *Mémoires Historiques,* 1: 466.

45. Sévigné, *Lettres*, 1: 241–42: Sévigné to Grignan, April 1, 1671.

46. *MM*, 4: 265.

47. Sévigné, *Lettres*, 1: 245: Sévigné to Grignan, April 3, 1671.

48. *MM*, 4: 263, 267.

49. For the dismissals of Guilloire and Segrais, see *MM*, 4: 257–58, 261–67. See also Sévigné, *Lettres*, 1: 232: Sévigné to Grignan, March 20, 1671; 241: same to same, April 1, 1671; 245: same to same, April 3, 1671. See also Saint-Maurice who also mentions the dismissal of the chambermaid in *Lettres*, 2: 36–38: March 20, 1671. For the dismissal of her confessor, see *MM*, 4: 272–75. Segrais denied that he had publicly opposed the marriage, adding that he was not of sufficient standing to speak directly to Mademoiselle, although he credits Guilloire with such a confrontation. For his own dismissal and that of Madelon, the chambermaid, see Segrais, *Mémoires/Anecdotes*, 1: 118–21. See also his comments on 103.

50. *MM*, 4: 275–76.

51. *MM*, 4: 275–308 passim.

52. Bussy-Rabutin, *Correspondance*, 1: 384–87: Madame de Scudéry to Bussy-Rabutin, March 6, 1671.

53. *MM*, 4: 242–43.

54. Saint-Maurice, *Lettres*, 1: 536: December 26, 1670; Segrais, *Mémoires/Anecdotes*, 1: 120; La Force, *Lauzun*, 66–67.

55. Choisy, *Mémoires*, 283; Sévigné, *Lettres*, 1: 209: Sévigné to Grignan, February 27, 1671. For the timing of this offer to Lauzun, see note 32.

56. *MM*, 4: 266.

57. *MM*, 4: 275–76.

58. Bussy-Rabutin, *Correspondance*, 1: 387: Bussy-Rabutin to Madame de Scudéry, March 13, 1671; Saint-Simon, *Mémoires*, 9: 642.

59. See La Force, *Lauzun*, 67–68 and 148, and his later *La Vie Amoureuse de la Grande Mademoiselle* (Paris, 1927), 2: 60, 108–23, 154–55. La Force's arguments rested largely on the secret correspondence between Barrail and Lauzun in 1681, which suggests that the two were not yet married. He also cites Lauzun's fears that Mademoiselle might marry another and her anxieties about his intentions, as well as passages in Mademoiselle's *Mémoires* to support the conclusion that the marriage occurred in the period 1682–84, after Lauzun's release from prison.

The Barrail correspondence, now on deposit with the La Force family papers at the Archives Nationales, series 353 AP, côte 25, is discussed in note 123 below. Taken as a whole, it can be used to sustain La Force's argument. Since these are Barrail's letters to Lauzun, however, one might also conclude that Lauzun may have chosen not to confide such a secret to Barrail, and that Lauzun feared that an earlier, secret marriage would simply go unacknowledged by the king.

Most modern biographers of Mademoiselle have followed La Force's lead. See, for example, Amiguet, *Une Princesse*, 402; Bouyer, *La Grande Mademoiselle*, 236–37; Ducasse, *La Grande Mademoiselle*, 227–29, 236; Dulong, *L'Amour*, 244; Melchior-Bonnet, *La Grande Mademoiselle*, 317–18; Sackville-West, *Daughter of France*, 315–17. Claude Dulong, who agrees that such a marriage did not take place until the 1680s, suggests that Lauzun might have been arrested to prevent a secret marriage and was imprisoned for a long enough time to make sure that Mademoiselle was beyond the childbearing age. See Dulong, *L'Amour*, 239–40.

While some contemporaries of Mademoiselle suggested that they had wed in the period 1670–71, there are none who place it in the later period preferred by modern writers. Both La Fare and Voltaire believed that the two were married in 1671 and that the discovery of this disobedience led to Lauzun's arrest. Saint-Maurice also reported these rumors, while Baron Spanheim, the envoy of Brandenburg, wrote in 1690 that he believed Lauzun and the princess had already married at the time of his arrest. See La Fare, *Mémoires*, 270–71; Voltaire, *Siècle de Louis XIV*, in *Oeuvres*, 14: 449; Saint-Maurice, *Lettres*, 2: 201–3: December 4, 1671; Ezéchiel Spanheim, *Relation de la Cour de France* (1690), ed. Charles Schefer (Paris, 1882), 83. An earlier reference by Spanheim to the secret marriage (35) does not suggest a time frame. Several other contemporaries assert their belief in such a marriage but are silent on the timing. For example, see Saint-Simon, *Mémoires*, 9: 642; and the *Mémoires* of the maréchal de Berwick, in *Nouvelle Collection*, ed. Michaud and Poujoulat, 32: 332. Barine, in *Louis XIV et La Grande Mademoiselle*, 316–20, argues strenuously from a close reading of the text of Mademoiselle's *Mémoires* that the two were probably married in the spring of 1671. She is supported in this position only by Sandars, *Lauzun: Courtier and Adventurer*, 1: 329–34.

60. Choisy believed that they never married, while Segrais argued that Mademoiselle would never have dared to dismiss her personal maid if she had married Lauzun: the implication is that the maid would have avenged herself by speaking out. It did not occur to Segrais that the dismissal might have been a prelude to a marriage, with Mademoiselle replacing an untrustworthy servant to facilitate matters. See Choisy, *Mémoires*, 284; Segrais, *Mémoires/Anecdotes*, 1: 120–21.

Among modern authors, Michel Le Moël and Jean-Christian Petitfils, citing a denial by Lauzun late in life, are almost alone in believing that a marriage did not take place. See Le Moël, *La Grande Mademoiselle*, 177–78; Petitfils, *Lauzun*, 134, 238–39. There are several problems with this denial, supposedly made to Madame de Fallari, a mistress of the regent, Philippe II d'Orléans. The Orléans family were sensitive on the subject of Lauzun and Mademoiselle, and the denial may have been an attempt of the old courtier to appease the regent. Given Lauzun's bizarre behavior and character, which Saint-Simon chronicles well into Lauzun's last years, one wonders how much reliance can be placed on this supposed denial. It is also at variance with Lauzun's behavior at the time of Mademoiselle's death, when he openly wore mourning as if he was a bereaved spouse. The best person to testify to a secret marriage is Saint-Simon, who became Lauzun's brother-in-law in 1695, and who was allowed to see the Barrail correspondence of 1681 (see Saint-Simon, *Mémoires*, 1: 686). He states flatly that Lauzun and Mademoiselle had been secretly married, without, as mentioned earlier, stating when this had occurred: Saint-Simon, *Mémoires*, 9: 642. Francis Steegmuller took no position on this question in *Grand Mademoiselle*, 298–99.

61. *MM*, 4: 279.

62. *MM*, 4: 284–85.

63. *MM*, 4: 307.

64. See, for example, *MM*, 4: 267, 281. For Charles II's offer to help, see 281–82.

65. *MM*, 4: 307–9.

66. *MM*, 4: 307.

67. *MM*, 4: 308.

68. *MM*, 4: 309.

69. Sévigné, *Lettres*, 1: 425: Sévigné to Guitaut, December 2, 1671.

70. Sévigné, *Lettres*, 1: 434: Sévigné to Grignan, December 23, 1671.

71. La Fare, who was close to the Condés, believed that Lauzun was arrested because the king discovered that he had secretly married Mademoiselle. La Fare's *Mémoires* were first published in 1716, and it is possible that Voltaire derived this from La Fare. Saint-Maurice also reported this rumor to the duke of Savoy. See La Fare, *Mémoires*, 270–71; Voltaire, *Siècle de Louis XIV*, in *Oeuvres*, 14: 449; Saint-Maurice, *Lettres*, 2: 201: December 4, 1671.

72. The comte d'Ayen's report about the false rumors of Lauzun's arrest mentioned in *MM*, 4: 307, immediately precedes Mademoiselle's comment that stories continued to circulate in Paris of a secret marriage. Mademoiselle may be indirectly providing an explanation of Lauzun's subsequent arrest, which occurred shortly after Ayen's false report.

73. Saint-Simon, *Mémoires*, 9: 627.

74. Sévigné, *Lettres*, 1: 453: Sévigné to Grignan, January 13, 1672. These scenes between Lauzun and Montespan were widely reported in court circles, and Mademoiselle admitted to a belated knowledge of these as well. See *MM*, 4: 389; Choisy, *Mémoires*, 283; Segrais, *Mémoires/Anecdotes*, 1: 138–39; Saint-Simon, *Mémoires*, 9: 627; Saint-Maurice, *Lettres*, 2: 201–3: December 4, 1671.

75. Saint-Maurice, *Lettres*, 2: 203: December 4, 1671; and 223: January 15, 1672.

76. Sévigné, *Lettres*, 1: 434: Sévigné to Grignan, December 23, 1671. In the final part of her *Mémoires*, written in the late 1680s, Mademoiselle speaks openly of the hostility between Lauzun and the father-son ministerial team of Michel Le Tellier and Louvois, a fact that she does not mention in the account she wrote a decade earlier of the opposition to her marriage. See *MM*, 4: 388. Saint-Simon also ascribed Lauzun's fall to an alliance between Montespan and Louvois: *Mémoires*, 9: 627.

77. Sévigné, *Lettres*, 1: 435: Sévigné to Grignan, December 23, 1671.

78. Nerli's dispatch (December 1671) is quoted extensively in La Force, *Lauzun*, 94–96.

79. Saint-Simon, *Mémoires*, 9: 627; see also Saint-Maurice, *Lettres*, 2: 192–96: November 27, 1671.

80. Sévigné, *Lettres*, 1: 434: Sévigné to Grignan, December 23, 1671.

81. The details of Lauzun's harsh captivity can be reconstructed from the extensive correspondence between Louvois and Saint-Mars that survives in the Archives Nationales and the Archives du Ministère de la Guerre. The instructions of Louvois and occasional pieces of correspondence by Le Tellier, Colbert, or some other high official to Saint-Mars are preserved in AN, K120 A. Although Louvois denied any personal

responsibility for the harshness of Lauzun's treatment, the files contain innumerable letters of approval and encouragement to Saint-Mars. For the prohibition against outside communications or news, see Louvois to Saint-Mars, no. 93, November 26, 1671; no. 105, April 5, 1672; no. 114, October 2, 1672; and no. 146, January 27, 1674. For concerns about clandestine communication, see same to same, no. 134, May 6, 1673; and no. 177, March 18, 1677. This last letter from Louvois and a subsequent one, no. 217, September 24, 1677, remind Saint-Mars that Lauzun is not to have any information at all about Mademoiselle. A fair sampling of this correspondence and of Saint-Mars's reports have been printed in *Archives de la Bastille*, v. 3. For Saint-Mars's promise to keep Lauzun *in pace*, see 104: Saint-Mars to Louvois, December 9, 1671.

82. Sévigné, *Lettres*, 1: 451: Sévigné to Grignan, January 6, 1672. According to Saint-Mars, Lauzun himself coined the bon mot, a fitting rejoinder to Saint-Mars's own *in pace*: see *Archives de la Bastille*, 3: 106: Saint-Mars to Louvois, December 22, 1671. There is a lengthy correspondence on Lauzun's refusal to resign his offices in AN, K120 A, for the period April 1672 to April 1673 and again for 1675.

83. *MM*, 4: 311–12. For Mademoiselle's letter to Bussy-Rabutin, see Bussy-Rabutin, *Correspondance*, 2: 353: May 31, 1674.

84. *MM*, 4: 311.

85. *MM*, 4: 312–13, 318–20.

86. *MM*, 4: 323–24. For the sensation caused by the examination of Lauzun's papers, see Sévigné, *Lettres*, 1: 435–36: Sévigné to Grignan, December 23, 1671.

87. Chéruel has printed *Les Amours de Mademoiselle et de M. de Lauzun*, which included a copy of Louis's Letter to the Ambassadors, in *MM*, 4: app. 9, 566–627. Mademoiselle's affair with Lauzun became a staple of the sensationalist literature about the court of France printed in Germany, Holland, and the Spanish Netherlands. The *Amours* went through a number of printings in the 1670s in Holland and Germany and survives in multiple copies at the Bibliothèque Nationale (including Huet's copy) and at the Bibliothèque de l'Arsenal. On its popularity among contemporaries, see Antoine Adam, *Grandeur and Illusion: French Literature and Society, 1600–1715*, trans. Herbert Tint (London, 1972), 61. A copy of *L'Aigle, le Moineau, et le Perroquet* is found in BNF, Collection Clairambault, v. 634–35, fols. 112–13.

88. *MM*, 4: 328–29.

89. *MM*, 4: 367–68. See also Louis XIV, *Lettres Particulières*, 524–25: Louis XIV to Mademoiselle, May 27, 1674; 550–51: same to same, May 19, 1676, in which Louis expresses his sorrow at Mademoiselle's "troubled spirit."

90. *MM*, 4: 342–43.

91. *MM*, 4: 390. Mademoiselle spells the surname "Barail." La Force, in *Lauzun*, prefers "Barrail," while Coirault, in his edition of Saint-Simon, uses another alternative, "Barrailh."

92. *MM*, 4: 326–28.

93. *MM*, 4: 325–26; see also Sévigné, *Lettres*, 1: 510: Sévigné to Grignan, April 6, 1672.

94. *MM*, 4: 326 and 370–71.

95. See Mademoiselle's sour comment on Condé's victory at Seneffe in August

1674: *MM*, 4: 369. Mademoiselle's comment is found in the last part of her *Mémoires* and was therefore written at the end of the 1680s. A surviving letter from Mademoiselle to Condé congratulating him suggests that she managed to hide her true feelings. See Mademoiselle to Condé, August 17, 1674, in Aumale, *Princes de Condé*, 7: 535.

96. *MM*, 4: 372–75.

97. *MM*, 4: 350.

98. *MM*, 4: 351–53; see also Rodocanachi, *Les Infortunes*, 148–237.

99. *MM*, 4: 376–79.

100. *MM*, 4: 329.

101. *MM*, 4: 369–70.

102. Sévigné, *Lettres*, 2: 53: Sévigné to Grignan, March 8, 1676. The text of Lauzun's letter is printed in La Force, *La Vie Amoureuse*, 2: 91–94.

103. *MM*, 4: 379–80. Louis's letter of May 19, 1676, cited in note 89, may have been intended as an indirect response.

104. For Louvois's furious inquiries after the attempted escape, see *Archives de la Bastille*, 3: 186–88: Louvois to Saint-Mars, March 2, 1676; and same to same, March 9, 1676. For Louvois's fear of a clandestine correspondence between Mademoiselle and Lauzun, see AN, K120 A: Louvois to Saint-Mars, March 18, 1676.

105. At the very end of the second part of her *Mémoires*, Mademoiselle alludes to the king's departure for the field, which can be dated to mid-April 1676. See *MM*, 4: 381, with Chéruel's notes 2 and 3.

106. Chéruel, in *MM*, 4: 381 n. 3, suggests that the second part of the *Mémoires* was written entirely in 1677, rather than simply begun in August 1677, as Mademoiselle indicates: see *MM*, 3: 370. Mademoiselle broke off the narrative with the events of 1676, when Lauzun's failed escape and the cold response of Louis to her plea for some amelioration of his punishment probably made her despair of his eventual release. There was some improvement in Lauzun's treatment in the years after 1677, which were followed by the negotiations of 1680 and 1681. Mademoiselle might have put down her pen to work toward Lauzun's release. This would suggest a time frame of August 1677 to early 1680 for the writing of the second section. While taking no position on the likely date when Mademoiselle ceased writing the second part of her *Mémoires*, Jean Garapon also concludes that Mademoiselle stopped because she believed Lauzun's situation was hopeless and she was too discouraged to continue. See Garapon, *La Grande Mademoiselle Mémorialiste*, 55–56. This question is discussed at greater length in chap. 8.

107. BNF, Ms. Clairambault, v. 501, fols. 225–32, and v. 634–35, fols. 133–39, contain duplicate copies of an account of these family interviews, apparently written by the *notaire* present, a M. Isarn. The account has been published in *Archives de la Bastille*, 3: 197–204. It circulated in aristocratic circles and may have embarrassed Louvois into permitting Lauzun a few liberties. See AN, K120 A, no. 221: Louvois to Saint-Mars, November 1, 1677, in which Louvois orders Saint-Mars to let Lauzun exercise on the ramparts and authorizes social contact between Lauzun and his fellow prisoner Fouquet.

108. *MM*, 4: 391.

109. *MM*, 4: 397.

110. *MM*, 4: 415–16. For the authorization for Barrail to see Lauzun, see AN, K120 A, no. 296: Louvois to Saint-Mars, February 7, 1680.

111. *MM*, 4: 405–12.

112. *MM*, 4: 420–21.

113. *MM*, 4: 422.

114. *MM*, 4: 422–23.

115. *MM*, 4: 423.

116. *MM*, 4: 424.

117. Mademoiselle had intended to bestow Eu on Lauzun at the time the marriage contracts were signed in 1670. The transaction was not completed because the requirements of local Norman law mandated a fictitious sale rather than a donation. The transaction was completed after Lauzun's arrest, with Madame de Nogent acting on behalf of her brother as the "purchaser." See *MM*, 4: 426. A similar fictitious sale was required when Mademoiselle deeded Eu to the duc du Maine in 1681, as detailed below in note 119.

118. *MM*, 4: 426.

119. *MM*, 4: 426–27; see also Louis's remarks to Mademoiselle: *MM*, 4: 438. Copies of the documents required for the fictitious sale of Eu to the child duc du Maine for 1.6 million livres are found in the Fonds de Dreux, AN 300 APII 14: "Vente du Comté d'Eu," February 2, 1681. Copies of the documentation for the gift of Dombes are found in 300 API 93: "Donation entre Vifs," February 2, 1681. In both cases, Montespan, who had never been legally acknowledged as the mother of Maine, was authorized to sign on behalf of the child.

120. *MM*, 4: 439.

121. *MM*, 4: 442–43. See also AN, K120 A, no. 324: Louvois to Saint-Mars, February 28, 1681.

122. *MM*, 4: 443–45. The order of release is found in AN, K120 A, no. 327: Louis XIV to Saint-Mars, April 16, 1681.

123. The secret correspondence between Barrail and Lauzun dealing with compensation to Lauzun for the renunciation of his "rights" to the properties Mademoiselle had deeded to the duc du Maine extends from February 1681 to February 1682. The surviving portion consists entirely of reports by Barrail to Lauzun of his discussions with Colbert, Montespan, Mademoiselle et al. on this subject. Lauzun's instructions and replies to Barrail, which are alluded to in the Barrail letters, have not survived. This correspondence came into the possession of Lauzun's La Force relatives at some later date and remained in the family archives. The scholarly duke Auguste-Armand de La Force made use of these documents in his *Lauzun* (1912) and in his *La Vie Amoureuse de la Grande Mademoiselle*, published in 1927.

The deposit of the La Force family archives at the Archives Nationales in recent years has made these letters available to other scholars for the first time. The Barrail letters, a few letters from Lauzun to Louvois, and other materials concerning Lauzun are found in the La Force papers, series 353 AP, côte 25. In addition to the original letters from Barrail, the deposit includes a modern transcription, probably prepared by Auguste-Armand de La Force. Saint-Simon may have been the last nonfamily member to read these letters before their deposit at the Archives Nationales. For his comments, see Saint-Simon, *Mémoires*, 1: 686–87.

124. This account is drawn largely from the Barrail reports to Lauzun found in the Archives La Force, AN, 353 AP 25. The key letters, listed by date, are April 13, 1681; two undated letters, probably also April or early May 1681, pp. 62–70 and 88–91 in the transcription copies; August 19, 1681; August 28, 1681; September 28, 1681; September 30, 1681; undated, probably late September 1681, pp. 99–103 in the transcription copy; October 11, 1681; October 20, 1681; October 25, 1681; November 2, 1681. Mademoiselle's account of this transaction is extremely abbreviated, and only picks up with the final months of the negotiations: *MM*, 4: 450–54. Without the Barrail letters, none of the details of the involvement of Colbert, the king, and Montespan, nor of the pressure placed on Mademoiselle to compensate Lauzun, would be known.

125. *MM*, 4: 451–52. There is an ambiguity in the text. On 452, Mademoiselle lists the income from Saint-Fargeau as 22,000 livres, provides no income for the barony of Thiers, and 10,000 livres of income drawn on the salt tax (*gabelle*) in Languedoc. In the following paragraph on the same page she totals the income as 40,000 livres, implying that the income for Thiers should have been listed as 8,000 livres, and Chéruel mentions (n. 1) that older editions inserted this figure for Thiers in the text. Barrail's letter to Lauzun dated October 20, 1681, assigned a revenue of 7,500 livres to Thiers, and 18,000 to Saint-Fargeau: AN, 353 AP 25, October 20, 1681. What is really striking is how well-informed Barrail was about Mademoiselle's finances. According to Masingil's survey, the revenues of Saint-Fargeau had dropped from an average of about 24,000 livres per annum in the period 1672–78 to about 18,500 livres in the period 1679–84. See Masingil, "Etat . . . Saint-Fargeau" in AN, 90 AP 74.

While Mademoiselle's recollection is that Lauzun demanded an income of 100,000 livres from her, the maximum figure in the Barrail-Lauzun correspondence is 50,000. For Louis's orders to Colbert, see Colbert, *Lettres*, 6: 356–57: Louis XIV to Colbert, October 5, 1681. Copies of the deeds of gift to Lauzun, signed at Choisy October 29, 1681, can be found in the Archives de Saint-Fargeau, AN, 90 AP 28, with other copies in 90 AP 74.

126. *MM*, 4: 453. As indicated in his letter of October 5, 1681, to Colbert (see note 125), Louis was especially anxious to complete the formalities of the gift of Dombes to the duc du Maine. A decree of March 1682 ratified the gift, and this was registered with the parlement of Dijon in May 1682 and with that of Dombes in June 1682. See the Fonds de Dreux, AN, 300 AP 93, "Donation entre Vifs . . . Dombes."

127. *MM*, 4: 447–48.

128. *MM*, 4: 450.

129. *MM*, 4: 455.

130. *MM*, 4: 455. For Barrail's embarrassment, see Archives La Force, AN, 353 AP 25: June 1, 1681; August 1, 1681; August 19, 1681; October 25, 1681; and February 2, 1682.

131. *MM*, 4: 455–56.

132. *MM*, 4: 457–59; quotation, 459.

133. *MM*, 4: 458–59.

134. *MM*, 4: 461–62; see n. 1 by Chéruel on the original text struck out by Mademoiselle.

135. *MM*, 4: 460–63.

136. *MM*, 4: 479–80.

137. *MM*, 4: 495.

138. *MM*, 4: 466, 470, 480.

139. *MM*, 4: 466–68. La Force, *La Grande Mademoiselle*, 149–50, offers a corrected figure of 550,000 livres. A good part of the difference may be prior payments made by the duc de Luxembourg to Lauzun's property managers during his captivity as part of the 400,000 livres due Lauzun for his commission as captain of the guard.

140. *MM*, 4: 485.

141. See Mayer, "l'Architecture," in *Trois Etudes*, 108; La Force, *Lauzun*, 150.

142. Saint-Simon, *Mémoires*, 9: 642.

143. *MM*, 4: 484–86. Lauzun received a letter from his mother chiding him for his behavior toward Mademoiselle. The letter, dated October 8, 1682, is quoted in La Force, *La Grande Mademoiselle*, 163–65.

144. *MM*, 4: 464–65, 473–74.

145. *MM*, 4: 475–76.

146. *MM*, 4: 437. For a description of the château and its contents, see *MM*, 4: 427–28. See also Mayer, "l'Architecture," in *Trois Etudes*, 108–11; Hautecoeur, *Architecture Classique*, 2: 644–45. B. Chamchine, *Le Château de Choisy* (Paris, 1910), 5–28. Chamchine adds (22 n. 2) that several portraits of Mademoiselle holding a miniature of Gaston have survived, including the one by Le Bourguignon reproduced in this book.

147. *MM*, 4: 437–38.

148. *MM*, 4: 461, 480–81.

149. *MM*, 4: 482.

150. *MM*, 4: 481, 505. Saint-Simon called Lauzun a very lucky gambler: Saint-Simon, *Mémoires*, 9: 632.

151. *MM*, 4: 494–95. At that time the Ile Saint-Louis was known as the Ile Notre-Dame.

152. *MM*, 4: 467–68.

153. *MM*, 4: 494.

154. *MM*, 4: 495–96.

155. *MM*, 4: 464.

156. *MM*, 4: 478–79.

157. *MM*, 4: 490.

158. *MM*, 4: 464.

159. *MM*, 4: 469–70; see Lauzun's earlier comments as well: *MM*, 4: 466–67.

160. *MM* 4: 470, 482.

161. *MM*, 4: 474, 476–79, 514–16; quotation, 479.

162. *MM*, 4: 507–9; for Montespan's exasperation, see 512–13.

163. *MM*, 4: 509–10.

164. *MM*, 4: 529, recounts one incident; see also La Fayette, *Cour de France*, 757–

58; and Dangeau, *Journal*, 2: 78–79, December 11, 1687, which relates that Lauzun asked Philippe d'Orléans to intercede, but Mademoiselle refused to have anything to do with the "ingrate." See also Sévigné, *Lettres*, 3: 313: Sévigné to Grignan, January 10, 1689.

165. Bussy-Rabutin, *Correspondance*, 6: 209: Bussy-Rabutin to Sévigné, February 2, 1689.

166. The confirmation of her award required more litigation against her former allies, the Condés and the duchess of Hanover. The voluminous records on these claims are scattered throughout the Fonds de Dreux. See AN, 300 API, côtes 93, 97–107, and 921.

167. *MM*, 4: 536. From an allusion in Mademoiselle's text to a victory by the maréchal de Luxembourg that occurred in July 1690, Chéruel dates the final pages of the *Mémoires* to that year. See *MM*, 4: 528 n. 2.

168. Sévigné, *Lettres*, 3: 292: Sévigné to Grignan, December 27, 1688.

169. For the story of the rescue of the Stuarts, see La Force, *Lauzun*, 157–72. For Lauzun's triumphant return see Dangeau, *Journal*, 2: 235–36, December 23, 1688; La Fayette, *Cour de France*, 757–70 passim; Saint-Simon, *Mémoires*, 9: 633; and the letters of Sévigné cited in note 170. For La Bruyère's quotation, see "Stratton," in *Les Caractères*, 335–36.

170. For Mademoiselle's anger at Lauzun's rehabilitation, see Sévigné, *Lettres*, 3: 292: Sévigné to Grignan, December 27, 1688; 328, same to same, January 24, 1689; 343, February 7, 1689; La Fayette, *Cour de France*, 757. After presenting Lauzun with the garter, James II called on Mademoiselle to smooth things over: see Dangeau, *Journal*, 3: 338, February 25, 1689; La Fayette, *Cour de France*, 770; Sévigné, *Lettres*, 3: 359: Sévigné to Grignan, February 25, 1689; 363–64, same to same, February 28, 1689. Saint-Simon observed that Lauzun never reestablished any intimacy with the king, and that he was well aware of his ambiguous position: Saint-Simon, *Mémoires*, 9: 634–35

171. As mentioned earlier, Mademoiselle's former steward, Louis de Préfontaine, was prominent in later life in Jansenist circles. In June 1657, Mademoiselle paid a visit to Port-Royal des Champs and indicated in her *Mémoires* that she found the life of that convent "edifying." See *MM*, 3: 67–75. When she wrote her *Ile Imaginaire* in 1658, Mademoiselle made flattering references to Jansenist industriousness. Denise Mayer has discussed the possibility of some Jansenist influence on Mademoiselle in "Mademoiselle et la Vie Spirituelle," in *Trois Etudes*, 163–65 and 176–77. But Mademoiselle tells us in the *Imitation*, xii–xiii, that she considered the writings of Teresa of Avila second only to those of the Scriptures, and that if she had had a religious vocation, she would have entered the Carmelites, xii–xiii, lxvi.

172. Emmanuel Pierre Rodocanachi rediscovered this work in the archives of Florence and republished it as *Un Ouvrage de Piété Inconnu de la Grande Mademoiselle* (Paris, 1903). For background, see Rodocanachi's introduction, i–xix. For additional discussion of Mademoiselle's religious works, see also Denise Mayer, "Deux Ouvrages de Piété de la Grande Mademoiselle," *Bulletin du Bibliophile*, no. 2 (1980): 170–84.

173. Mademoiselle, *Réflexions sur les Huit Béatitudes*, 63; see also 2.

174. For the publishing history, see Appendix A, and the article by Denise Mayer cited in note 172.

175. Mademoiselle, *Réflexions . . . Imitation*, xii–xiii.

176. Mademoiselle, *Réflexions . . . Imitation*, xxiv. The translation is somewhat free. In the original, Mademoiselle uses the phrase "*des comédiens qui représentions un rôle sur le théâtre.*" In this period, the word *comédien* often meant simply "actor," and I have so translated it.

177. Sévigné used the designation "la grande Mademoiselle" in her famous letter of December 15, 1670, and again in a letter dated January 12, 1674, to distinguish her from Philippe's daughter Marie-Louise (1662–1689), later queen of Spain. The usage seems to have become common by the time Dangeau began writing his *Journal*, which begins in 1684. The title "Mademoiselle" was used after 1679 to refer to Philippe's youngest daughter, Elisabeth-Charlotte (1676–1744), later duchess of Lorraine. Sévigné's usage of the term "la grande Mademoiselle" would thus seem to suggest a meaning of "the senior" or "the elder." Both Saint-Simon and Baron Spanheim, the envoy of the margrave of Brandenburg, believed the title derived from Mlle de Montpensier's height. See Sévigné, *Lettres*, 1: 181–82: Sévigné to Coulanges, December 15, 1670; 380: Sévigné to Grignan, January 12, 1674; Saint-Simon, *Mémoires*, 3: 435–36; and Spanheim, *Relation*, 70–71.

178. Dangeau, *Journal*, 4: 237, February 19, 1693.

179. Dangeau, *Journal*, 4: 259–60, April 6, 1693. There is a final note of ambiguity here. In the late seventeenth century, it was considered an act of piety for dying persons to refuse visits from loved ones, to keep the mind on salvation and the next world. Madame de Sévigné, as is well known, refused to see her daughter Grignan on her deathbed, and La Rochefoucauld refused to see his beloved Madame de La Fayette. See Duchêne, *Madame de Lafayette*, 372.

180. On the vigil of Philippe d'Orléans and Elisabeth-Charlotte, see Saint-Simon, *Mémoires*, 1: 52. The explosion of an urn containing her entrails marred Mademoiselle's funeral rites. See Saint-Simon, *Mémoires*, 1: 52–54. The original of the will, naming Archille d'Harlay as executor is found in AN, Minutier Central, XCVIII, 818, February 27, 1685. A copy of the will, inventories of her personal property, and incomplete records of the legacy are found in the Fonds de Dreux, 300 API 93, "Succession Montpensier," and 300 AP I 921, "Successions Montpensier et Guise."

181. On Lauzun appearing in full mourning, see Saint-Simon, *Mémoires*, 1: 53 and 9: 642; Dangeau, *Journal*, 4: 262, April 7/8, 1693; *Madame*, ed. Stevenson, 112: Madame to Duchess of Hanover, April 9, 1693. Elisabeth-Charlotte also called Lauzun a "wicked and ungrateful wretch." In 1714 Lauzun sold Saint-Fargeau to the financier Antoine Crozat, who in turn resold it scarcely a year later to the LePeletier family. See Archives de Saint-Fargeau, AN, 90 AP 28 and 90 AP 74.

CHAPTER 8   THE MUSE'S LAMENT

Epigraphs: *MM*, 4: 351; Mademoiselle, *Réflexions . . . Imitation*, xii–xiii.

1. Arvède Barine's two works, *La Jeunesse de La Grande Mademoiselle* (Paris, 1909)

and *Louis XIV et La Grande Mademoiselle* (Paris, 1912), are still very useful. Barine had limited access to the archives of the Orléans family, at that time not yet available to researchers. Philippe Amiguet's *Une Princesse à l'Ecole du Cid* (Paris, 1957) is the most serious attempt to date to integrate Mademoiselle's literary and historical *personnages*. Surprisingly, three recent but somewhat narrowly written studies do not: Christian Bouyer, *La Grande Mademoiselle* (Paris, 1986); Bernardine Melchior-Bonnet, *La Grande Mademoiselle Héroïne et Amoureuse* (Paris, 1985); and Michel Le Moël, *La Grande Mademoiselle* (Paris, 1994).

The literature on French seventeenth-century memoirs has grown exponentially in the last two decades. It is impossible to cite all of the articles and books that I have found useful in evaluating Mademoiselle's works (see the Bibliography). Some of the most interesting material is found in papers originating in colloquia organized by the Centre de Philologie et de Littératures Romanes at the University of Strasbourg in the period 1979–95. Works in this series include: *Les Valeurs chez les Mémorialistes du XVIIe Siècle avant la Fronde*, ed. Noémi Hepp and Jacques Hennequin (Paris, 1979); *La Cour au Miroir des Mémorialistes*, ed. Noémi Hepp (Paris, 1991); *De L'Estoile à Saint-Simon, Recherche sur la Culture des Mémorialistes au Temps des Trois Premiers Rois Bourbons*, ed. Madeleine Bertaud and André Labertit (Paris, 1993); *Le Genre des Mémoires, Essai de Définition*, ed. Madeleine Bertaud and François-Xavier Cuche (Paris, 1995).

In addition, I have found especially stimulating Marc Fumaroli's classic "Les Mémoires du XVIIe Siècle au Carrefour des Genres en Prose," *XVIIe Siècle*, no. 94–95 (1971): 7–37, notably his comments on Mademoiselle (32–33). The entirety of this issue of *XVIIe Siècle*, edited by Yves Coirault, is dedicated to "Mémoires et Création Littéraire," and should be consulted by the serious student of this topic. See also Fumaroli, "Mémoires et Histoire," in *Les Valeurs*, ed. Hepp and Hennequin, 21–45. Marie-Thérèse Hipp, *Mythes et Réalités: Enquête sur le Roman et les Mémoires* (Paris, 1976), has long been recognized as a major contribution. See also Emmanuèle Lesne (-Jaffro)'s excellent *La Poétique des Mémoires (1650–1685)* (Paris, 1996), which integrates much contemporary literary criticism on seventeenth-century memoirs, and should be read as an excellent, updated source on current approaches to the subject.

2. On the changes in style in the course of the seventeenth century, see Dewald, *Aristocratic Experience*, and Motley, *Becoming a French Aristocrat*.

3. *MM*, 1: 2. Emmanuèle Lesne-Jaffro cites the passage at the head of this chapter ("I often digress . . .") as proof that Mademoiselle intended her *Mémoires* to see the light of day, notwithstanding her frequent disclaimers to the contrary: Lesne-Jaffro, "Les Mémoires et Leurs Destinaires," in *Le Genre des Mémoires*, ed. Bertaud and Cuche, 34–35.

4. The circulation within aristocratic circles of manuscript copies of memoirs and other literary works by aristocratic authors was a common practice in the century. See the comments of Frédéric Briot, "Du Dessein des Mémorialistes," in *Le Genre des Mémoires*, 185–86; and of Hubert Carrier, "Pourquoi Ecrit-on des Mémoires au XVIIe Siècle," also in *Le Genre des Mémoires*, 143–44. In the same collection, Madeleine Cuénin argues that Mademoiselle intended that her *Mémoires* be circulated

and read within the narrow circle of her friends and never expected them to be published. In support of this argument, she cites the care the princess took to entrust a copy to Harlay as proof of the intent to circulate them only within a circle of intimates. See Cuénin, "Les Mémoires Féminins du XVIIᵉ Siècle," in *Le Genre des Mémoires*, 101–2. In the same publication, as noted above, Emmanuèle Lesne-Jaffro insists on Mademoiselle's awareness that her audience would someday extend to a more remote posterity. See Lesne-Jaffro "Les Mémoires et Leurs Destinaires," 34–35 and 43.

That Mademoiselle gave a copy to Harlay strongly suggests that she wanted the *Mémoires* to survive, and probably assumed that eventually they would be published. It is also possible that at least the early sections were known and circulated in her lifetime: for example, her account of the Fronde, the voyage to the south of France for Louis XIV's wedding, etc. The portions concerning Lauzun probably remained hidden until after her death. For a discussion of the manuscript history, see Appendix A.

5. Voltaire, *Oeuvres Complètes*, 32: *Le Sottisier*, 594; and 14: *Siècle de Louis XIV*, 109. See also his letter dated April 1729 to Thieriot commenting on the 1728 edition of the *Mémoires*, in 33: *Correspondance*, 193–94.

6. Saint-Simon, *Mémoires*, 8: 625; see also Coirault's note in 1: 1184.

7. Sainte-Beuve, *Causeries* (1851), 524–25. A footnote in this edition comments on the Chéruel edition and adds that it restores Mademoiselle to her "*incorrection naturelle.*" It is not clear whether this is a comment by Sainte-Beuve or by a later editor.

8. Chéruel foreword, *MM*, 1: v–ix; Gabrielle Verdier, "Mademoiselle de Montpensier et le Plaisir du Texte," *Papers on French Seventeenth-Century Literature* 10, no. 18 (1983): 12; Derek A. Watts, "Self-Portrayal in Seventeenth-Century French Memoirs," *Australian Journal of French Studies* 12, no. 3 (1975): 278. As will be noted below, both of these commentators do appreciate many other qualities they find in the pages of Mademoiselle.

9. Lesne (-Jaffro), *La Poétique des Mémoires 1650–1685*, 376. Madeleine Cuénin notes the paucity of memoirs by women of this period when contrasted with the profusion of contemporary male authors. See her comparison of the works of Madame de la Guette, the duchess de Nemours, Motteville, and Mademoiselle, "Les Mémoires Féminins du XVIIᵉ Siècle," 99–109. Cuénin, who has also published a modern edition of Nemours's *Mémoires* (1990), does not share my opinion of that author. See also Françoise Watson, "Le Moi et l'Histoire dans les Mémoires de Mme de Motteville, Mme de la Guette, et Mlle de Montpensier," *Papers on French Seventeenth-Century Literature* 17 (1991): 141–56.

10. See Merry Wiesner, *Women and Gender in Early Modern Europe* (Cambridge, 1995), 241–55. See also Natalie Z. Davis, "Women in Politics," in Davis and Farge, *Women in the West*, 3: 167–83, and esp. 179–80; Flandrin, *Familles*, 117–36 passim; Muchembled, *Popular Culture*, 198, 226–28; Sarah Hanley, "Engendering the State: Family Formation and State Building in Early Modern France," *French Historical Studies* 16 (1989): 4–27; Jacques Hennequin, "La Paternité chez Quelques Mémori-

alistes," in *Les Valeurs chez les Mémorialistes du XVIIᵉ Siècle avant la Fronde*, 289–305; and see also the exchange among colloquium participants, "Valeurs Poursuivies et Conflits de Valeurs," in *Les Valeurs*, 269–85.

11. Faith Beasley, *Revising Memory: Women's Fiction and Memoirs in Seventeenth-Century France* (New York, 1990), 80. See below for a further discussion of Beasley's interpretation of Mademoiselle's works. A number of the essays in *Le Genre des Mémoires* deal with the issue of classification. See especially the comments of Jean Garapon, "Les Mémoires du XVIIᵉ Siècle, Nébuleuses de Genres," 259–71, and Jean Mesnard, "Conclusion: Les Mémoires comme Genre," 361–71."

12. *MM*, 2: 248. Jean Garapon argues that the "intermediate stage" of the *Mémoires*, covering Mademoiselle's dispute with Gaston and her reconciliation with the court, was probably written after Mademoiselle's return to court in 1657 and was finished in the early part of 1660. This framework corresponds to the departure of the court for the south of France in the spring of 1659. Garapon does not offer any explanation for why Mademoiselle stopped, other than her own assertion, written in 1677, that the distractions of the court kept her otherwise engaged. See Garapon, *La Grande Mademoiselle Mémorialiste*, 49–51.

13. See Ian Maclean, *Woman Triumphant*, 25–63, 64–87, and Davis, "Women in Politics," 3: 179–80.

14. On the popularity of *Les Amours*, see Antoine Adam, *Grandeur and Illusion: French Literature and Society, 1600–1715*, trans. Herbert Tint (London, 1972), 61. There can be no doubt that it was read by many of Mademoiselle's friends and acquaintances: one of the copies preserved at the Bibliothèque Nationale de France once belonged to the learned Huet: BN, LN 27/14733.

15. For Mademoiselle's remarks on Spanish princesses, see *MM*, 3: 385–86. On Lauzun, then known as the marquis de Puyguilhem, see *MM*, 3: 478; for the use of Corneille, *MM*, 4: 92.

16. *Les Amours* was reprinted in virtually all of the editions of Mademoiselle's *Mémoires* after 1735. Chéruel reprinted it in *MM*, 4: app. 9, 566–627.

17. *MM*, 4: 92.

18. See Verdier, "Le Plaisir du Texte," *Papers on French Seventeenth-Century Literature* 10, no. 18 (1983): 20.

19. Although the conflict is not resolved in the *Mémoires*, it may have been in life, as indicated by the two religious tracts attributed to Mademoiselle and written after the abandonment of the *Mémoires*. See Denise Mayer, "Deux Ouvrages de Piété de la Grande Mademoiselle," *Bulletin du Bibliophile* (1980): 170–83. Mademoiselle's religious interests, including her fascination with convent life and a momentary interest in Port-Royal, are in need of a thorough modern study. See the discussion in Mayer's "Mademoiselle et la Vie Spirituelle," *Trois Etudes*, 124–25, 163–65, and 176–77. See the interesting observations of Madeleine Bertaud in "En Marge de Leurs Mémoires: une Correspondance entre Mademoiselle de Montpensier et Madame de Motteville," *Travaux de Littérature* 3 (1990): 287–89; Jean Garapon, *La Grande Mademoiselle Mémorialiste*, 169–73; and also his "Les Mémorialistes et le Réel: l'exemple du Cardinal de Retz et Mlle de Montpensier," *Littératures Classiques*, no. 11 (1989): 187;

see also Philippe Ariès, "Pourquoi écrit-on des Mémoires" in *Les Valeurs*, 19; and Fumaroli, "Mémoires et Histoire," 34.

20. Verdier suggests that Mademoiselle tried to create a second identity out of her mother's side of the family, and that the rehabilitation of Saint-Fargeau, the attention to her maternal genealogies, etc., are indications of the search for a second identity. See Verdier, "Le Plaisir du Texte," *Papers on French Seventeenth-Century Literature* 10, no. 18 (1983): 22. Her arguments are seconded in Patricia F. Cholakian, "A House of Her Own: Marginality and Dissidence in the Memoirs of La Grande Mademoiselle," *Prose Studies* 9 (1986): 5. Again, while the idea is intriguing, especially when coupled with Mademoiselle's musings on female rulers and the possibility of a female-dominated society (e.g., Motteville correspondence, *Paphlagonie*, etc.), it should not be pushed too far. One could argue that this was simply a stage on the road to self-discovery, and that a later stage is signaled by Mademoiselle's purchase of Eu and her later building of Choisy as monuments to her sense of self. And if Saint-Fargeau was the link to her mother's memory, bestowing it on Lauzun seems almost unfilial.

21. *MM*, 4: 99. Consistent with her general argument, Cholakian makes much of the uniqueness of this situation, with Lauzun taking the Montpensier name, in "House of Her Own," 12–13. One should be careful not to confuse the assumption of a new title with a change of patronymic. Had Lauzun kept Mademoiselle's gifts, he would have been styled "M. le duc de Montpensier," although his family name would have remained Caumont, in the same way that an English peer can be referred to by his title, for example "Marlborough," while retaining his family name, "Churchill," for other purposes. In seventeenth-century France, such changes of style were not unusual in aristocratic circles when a nobleman married an heiress of higher rank or of great wealth. In Mademoiselle's lifetime, Henri de Chabot was pleased to be rebaptized as the "duc de Rohan," and a branch of the Savoy family used the title of "comte de Soissons" by virtue of the marriage of the Bourbon-Soissons heiress into that family; Turenne's family of La Tour were happy to be known by the Bouillon titles that fell to them by marriage. It was the size of Mademoiselle's fortune and the family tie to the king that dazzled Lauzun's contemporaries. See Saint-Simon's comment that Lauzun's return to grace after 1688 was nothing compared to what would have been his position after "a public marriage with Mademoiselle, the donation of all her immense wealth, and the title and rank of duc de Montpensier, peer [of France]. What a monstrous elevation, and with children from such a marriage, there would have been nothing beyond his reach, and who can say where he would have ended up?" Saint-Simon, *Mémoires*, 8: 634.

22. See Beasley's comments on the letters in *Revising Memory*, 50–51; and also Garapon, *Mémorialiste*, 284–85; and Madeleine Bertaud, "Une Correspondance . . . Montpensier et Motteville," *Travaux de Littérature* 3 (1990): 277–95.

23. Fumaroli, "Les Mémoires," 32–33.

24. Garapon, *La Grande Mademoiselle Mémorialiste*, 233. For Mademoiselle's self-portrayal, see her *Vie de Fouquerolles* (1653), 8–9, 42, as well as her sharp and unflattering characterization of Madame de Fouquerolles, 8. Marie-Thérèse Hipp is one of the few critics to note the importance of *Fouquerolles* as a prelude to the *Mémoires*.

See Hipp, *Mythes et Réalités*, 241, 307. See also Garapon, "Mademoiselle à Saint-Fargeau," 41–42.

25. On the use of the portrait within other genres, such as the memoir, see Lesne (-Jaffro), *Poétique*, 115–60, esp. 115–22 on Mademoiselle; and Jacqueline Plantié, *La Mode du Portrait Littéraire en France, 1641–1681* (Paris, 1994), 617–58. Citing Mademoiselle's portrait of Condé's son the duc d'Enghien in the *Mémoires*, Madeleine Cuénin also pays tribute to Mademoiselle's skill with this literary weapon, which she believes merits a comparison to Saint-Simon. See Cuénin, "Mémoires Féminins," 104.

26. A perceptive reader will recognize the similarity to Saint-Simon's description of Lauzun: Saint-Simon, *Mémoires*, 8: 620, 642–43. On the portrait as a literary device and its seventeenth-century origins, Plantié's *La Mode du Portrait Littéraire en France* is likely to remain the standard reference work for some time. See also Dirk Van der Cruysse, *Le Portrait dans les Mémoires du Duc de Saint-Simon* (Paris, 1971), 25–47; Renate Baader, *Dames de Lettres* (Stuttgart, 1986), 159–82; Beasley, *Revising Memory*, 49; and Beasley, "Rescripting Historical Discourse: Literary Portraits by Women," *Papers on French Seventeenth-Century Literature* 14, no. 27 (1987): 517–35; Watts, "Self-Portrayal," 263–85; and Jean LaFond, "Mademoiselle et les *Divers Portraits*," *Papers on French Seventeenth-Century Literature* 22 (1995): 55–63.

Consistent with her view that the *Mémoires* are part of an "alternative view of history," in the article cited above Beasley has argued the same for the *Divers Portraits*, seeing them as written primarily by women and about women and as similar to the *galerie des portraits* found in La Fayette's *Princesse de Clèves* (without, however, noting the tie through Segrais). One can counter that some of Mademoiselle's most striking portraits are of men: notably, those of Louis XIV and of Condé. Renate Baader, with less of an ideological edge, has also noted the predominance of portraits of women and by women in the *Divers Portraits*. See Baader, *Dames de Lettres*, 157–82.

27. Garapon, *La Grande Mademoiselle Mémorialiste*, 251.

28. For Mademoiselle's overall connections to the world of the literary salons, see the following by Jean Garapon: "Les Mémoires, Nébuleuses de Genres," in *Le Genre des Mémoires*, 268–70; "Mademoiselle à Saint-Fargeau," 37–47; and "Mademoiselle de Montpensier dans ses *Mémoires*: L'Exemple d'une Culture Princière," in *De L'Estoile à Saint-Simon*, 93–107. The ties between Mademoiselle and Madame de la Fayette have yet to be fully explored. See Faith Beasley's comparison of the *Divers Portraits* and the portraits in the *Princesse de Clèves*: "Rescripting Historical Discourse," *Papers on French Seventeenth-Century Literature* 14 (1987): 517–35; and her comments in *Revising Memory*, 49. See also Baader, *Dames de Lettres*, 140–51; Roger Duchêne, *Madame de Lafayette*, 142–47 and 157–59; and Duchêne, "Vers *la Princesse de Clèves*: de la *Princesse de Paphlagonie à l'Histoire Amoureuse des Gaules*," *Papers on French Seventeenth-Century Literature* 22 (1995): 65–77. As mentioned in note 26, the personal link, through Segrais, is not mentioned by Beasley. It is especially intriguing that La Fayette's first major work, *La Princesse de Montpensier*, makes use of Mademoiselle's ancestors and is set at Champigny. Duchêne repeats the story that Made-

moiselle was told by Segrais that La Fayette's work originated in archival sources found at Champigny. See Duchêne, *Madame de Lafayette*, 198–207.

29. See Garapon, "Les Mémorialistes et le Réel," 187; and Cholakian, "A House of Her Own," 12–13.

30. On Mademoiselle and Corneille, in addition to the above, see Garapon, *La Grande Mademoiselle Mémorialiste*, 27–29, 127–59 passim; Lesne (-Jaffro), *Poétique*, 191–211; and Bertaud, "Une Correspondance," 281. See also Amiguet, *Princesse*, 441–43. On the tradition linking the brawl and the Molière play, see Amiguet, *Princesse*, 411; and Baader, *Dames de Lettres*, 140. On Cotin's links to Mademoiselle, see Adam, *Histoire . . . Littérature Française*, 3: 163–65; and René Bray, *La Préciosité et les Précieuses* (Paris, 1968), 211. The performance of *Tartuffe* in 1669 was at a wedding reception given by Mademoiselle in honor of one of her ladies, Marie-Claire de Créqui, and the groom, Guy-Henry de Chabot, comte de Jarnac. See *MM*, 4: 74.

31. Beasley, *Revising Memory*, 58–60, 91–128; see esp. 111–12 for the contention that Mademoiselle was concerned that women would be excluded from "official" versions of history. Beasley's perspective suggests a line of argument that might well be developed further. Her study of Mademoiselle and her arguments are marred, however, by her insistence that Mademoiselle's *Mémoires* are largely ignored or treated with reservations by literary scholars because of the difficulty of categorizing them as memoir, autobiography, etc. The difficulty of a simple characterization is evident to any reader of the *Mémoires*, but scholars have hardly ignored the issue. The collective study cited here with some frequency, *Les Valeurs* (1979), deals extensively with the problem and the evolution of genres of prose in the seventeenth century, as do Marie-Thérèse Hipp in her excellent *Mythes et Réalités* (1976), and Fumaroli in "Les Mémoires au Carrefour des Genres" (1971). Since the appearance of *Revising Memory* (1990), the subject has also been treated in *La Cour au Miroir* (1991) and *Le Genre des Mémoires* (1995). It is surprising that Beasley, who stresses the personal element as a distinguishing characteristic of the women's view of history, spends no time on Mademoiselle's relationship with Gaston, clearly the most significant one in her life. Mademoiselle's mistrust of conventional authority, her disillusionment with those around her, and her appreciation of the hidden motives and agenda of others all stem from her stormy relationship with Gaston.

While it is also true that certain themes are consistent throughout the *Mémoires*, there is considerable change and development over time. Beasley does not deal with the editorial issues raised by the production of the work in at least three distinct parts, widely separated by the events of an adventurous life. By contrast, as noted above, Gabrielle Verdier, who shares much of Beasley's point of view, is sensitive to the "triggering" of each portion of the *Mémoires* by a specific betrayal at the hands of a man: Gaston in abusing Mademoiselle's property, Louis in retracting his permission to marry, Lauzun in spurning her love. See Verdier, "Le Plaisir du Texte," 20. Jean Garapon emphasizes the movement in time to explain the shift in the structure of the work from a conventional memoir to a proto-autobiography in *La Grande Mademoiselle Mémorialiste*, 233. See his comments as well in "Les Mémoires, Nébuleuses de Genres," 267–71.

32. Watts, "Jugements sur la Cour," in *La Cour au Miroir*, 131; Marie-Thérèse Hipp, *Mythes et Réalités*, 58; Louise Godard de Donville, "L'art de Plaire chez les Dames de la Cour," *La Cour au Miroir*, 151.

33. Claude Dulong has called them "un des plus savoureux et plus précieux documents du XVIIᵉ siècle" in *L'Amour au XVIIᵉ Siècle*, 207; see also Derek Watts, "Self-Portrayal," 278, and the comments of Lesne in "La Question du Genre des Mémoires," in *La Cour au Miroir*, 193–205. In her recent *Poétique*, Lesne concludes that "Mlle de Montpensier succeeds in narrating a real life, but one lived like a novel (*roman*), so well that the dimension of reality proper to the genre of memoir recedes from view and is lost" (17).

34. Madeleine Bertaud, "Louis XIII Vue par Quelques Mémorialistes," in *La Cour au Miroir*, 86; Margaret McGowan, "La Function des Fêtes dans la Vie de Cour au XVIIᵉ Siècle," in *La Cour au Miroir*, 38–39.

35. Jonathan Dewald, "Politics and Personalities in Seventeenth-Century France," *French Historical Studies* 16, no. 4 (1990): 899.

36. Garapon, *La Grande Mademoiselle Mémorialiste*, 173.

37. Self-portrait by Mademoiselle, in Mayer, "Portraits," 19–20.

APPENDIX A   MADEMOISELLE'S WRITINGS

1. For the publishing history of the *Mémoires* see Emile Bourgeois and Louis André, *Les Sources de l'Histoire de France* (Paris, 1913), 12: 112–14. See also the *Catalogue des Livres Imprimés de la Bibliothèque Nationale* (Paris, 1933), 116: cols. 707–12; British Museum, *General Catalogue of Printed Books* (London, 1965), 5: cols. 739–40, and the *National Union Catalogue: Pre-1956 Imprints* (Chicago, 1969), 392: 534–36. See also the summaries by Bernardine Melchior-Bonnet, *La Grande Mademoiselle*, 343; and by Christian Bouyer in the 1985 Fayard reprint of the Chéruel edition of the *Mémoires*, 1: 15–16. For Petitot's lament, see his *Collection*, 40: 366. On the soundness of Chéruel's edition, see Garapon, in *La Grande Mademoiselle Mémorialiste*, 15 n. 16. Joseph C. Evans provides a very useful comparison of the Petitot and Chéruel editions, in effect comparisons of the Harlay and autograph manuscripts: "Versions of the *Mémoires* of Mademoiselle de Montpensier (1627–1693)," *Romance Notes* 7 (1966): 161–64. See also the comments of Patricia Cholakian cited below, note 4.

2. The Bibliothèque Nationale de France has four manuscript copies of the *Mémoires*. The Harlay manuscript, Ms. Fr. 19588–92, originally belonged to Achille III de Harlay, the executor of Mademoiselle's will. An examination of the manuscript is quite suggestive of Mademoiselle's view of its sensitivity: the first three volumes are clearly in the handwriting of a professional copyist secretary. The last two, which correspond to the second and third parts of the *Mémoires*, dealing with the *affaire Lauzun*, are in a variety of handwritings, none of which seem to be professional. More than likely, Mademoiselle did not trust the discretion of any paid copyist, but confided the task of copying to members of her close circle. Eventually, the manuscript passed from the Harlay family to Louis-Germain de Chauvelin, and thereafter to the library of the abbey of Saint-Germain-des-Prés. In 1795–96, the abbey library was confiscated and transferred to the Bibliothèque Nationale. As noted several

times, the Harlay manuscript has long been identified as the source of the Wetstein edition of Mademoiselle's *Mémoires*, which was the standard until superseded by Chéruel's great work.

A second copy, Ms. Fr. 4154–56, belonged to Gros de Boze, the secretary of the Académie des Inscriptions. In 1728, Boze included this manuscript in an exchange with the old Bibliothèque Royale for duplicate printed books from the collection of the royal library. This copy seems to be very close in text to the third manuscript copy, Ms. Fr. 4157–60, called the Lancelot Ms., which passed into the royal library in 1733. A note in Ms. Fr. 4157 indicates that the Lancelot Ms. is a 1721 copy of the original, "which belongs to the duc du Maine."

This last note is particularly intriguing, because the manuscript whose history is least well known is that in Mademoiselle's own hand, Ms. Fr. 6698–99. Records at the Bibliothèque Nationale de France indicate that this precious original found its way to the Bibliothèque Nationale during the Revolution, sometime in the early to mid 1790s. Its prior whereabouts is not certain, although conceivably it entered the royal collections at an earlier date, since many manuscripts in the royal collection were not recorded or catalogued prior to the Revolutionary period. This manuscript was originally kept unbound and boxed, and at some point the estimated 82 folio pages containing the text up to 1649 were lost or destroyed. Assuming the notation on the Lancelot manuscript is correct, this autograph copy may have passed after Mademoiselle's death to the duc du Maine. It is possible that the original was kept at Eu, which Maine took possession of after Mademoiselle's death. Presumably, the manuscript remained within the royal family before coming to rest in the Bibliothèque Nationale. In the introduction to his edition of the *Mémoires*, Petitot noted that the Lancelot and Boze Mss. seem to be copies of the autograph version, 40: 365–66. See also Chéruel's introduction to his 1858 edition, v–xi, and Jean Garapon's brief comment in *La Grande Mademoiselle Mémorialiste*, 15 n. 16.

For more information on the manuscript copies preserved at the Bibliothèque Nationale, see the printed *Catalogue Général des Manuscrits Français de la Bibliothèque Nationale* under the respective Ms. numbers listed above. See also Leopold Delisle, *Le Cabinet des Manuscrits de la Bibliothèque Imperiale*, 1: 374, 378–79; 2: 100–103. According to records maintained at the Bibliothèque Nationale, at least five other manuscript copies of the *Mémoires* were sold at auction during the eighteenth century. One of these had belonged to the Bourbon-Conti family, while another had been in the library of the comte de Toulouse at Rambouillet. For much of this information, I am indebted to M. François Avril and Mme Nicole Morfin of the Département des Manuscrits of the Bibliothèque Nationale de France.

The manuscript copy in the British Library, Egerton Ms.1679, acquired in 1856 from an estate sale in Paris, is a copy in four different handwritings, missing some of the later portions of the text, which is believed to resemble that of the 1746 edition published in London and Paris. This would suggest it is a copy of the Harlay Ms., but no one has ever examined this text in depth. See the *Catalogue of the Egerton MSS.*, 848–49. In 1867, a French scholar, Gustave Masson, did a cursory examination of the Egerton Ms. and noted some interesting differences between it and Chéruel's recently published version. His findings were summarized in the *Annuaire/Bulletin de la Société de l'Histoire de France* (1867): 139–43. I have also benefited from communications on this manuscript from Dr. Frances Harris of the British Library staff.

The manuscript that belonged to Saint-Simon is still in the Archives of the Ministère des Affaires Etrangères, series Mémoires et Documents: France, vols. 70–74. For information on this manuscript, I am indebted to M. Louis Amigues of the staff of the Archives. See also Armand Baschet, *Le Duc de Saint-Simon, Son Cabinet et l'Histoire de Ses Manuscrits* (Paris, 1874).

3. On the composition of the *Mémoires*, see Garapon, *La Grande Mademoiselle Mémorialiste*, 219–22. Garapon argues, quite reasonably, that Mademoiselle had access to copies of her correspondence, possibly a journal or diary of events, and other materials to help her, which have now been lost. See also his comments on Mademoiselle's development as a writer in three articles, "Les Mémoires du XVIIᵉ Siècle, Nébuleuses de Genres," 268–70; "Mademoiselle à Saint-Fargeau: la Découverte de l'Ecriture," 37–47; and "Mademoiselle de Montpensier dans ses *Mémoires*: L'Exemple d'une Culture Princière," 93–107.

The Cholakian editorial comment cited below, note 4, about a handwritten correction by Mademoiselle in the Harlay manuscript is especially intriguing, given the known variations between the texts. Mademoiselle's unpublished letter, July 3, 1652, is found in BNF, Nouv. Acq. Fr. 4815, fols. 195–197v. The originals of Mademoiselle de Vandy's letters are found in the Recueil Conrart at the Bibliothèque de l'Arsenal, Ms. 5420, vol. 11, fols. 1243–46 and 1279–80. They have been published in Edouard de Barthélemy, *Comtesse de Maure* (Paris, 1863), 240–50; and in Victor Cousin, *Madame de Sablé* (Paris, 1859), 496–503.

4. As an interesting example of textual problems, Patricia F. Cholakian has found a correction in Mademoiselle's hand of the Harlay Ms., and, by an examination of the autograph manuscript, has also detected that the princess began with one explanation of her interest in Lauzun, a desire to deny her inheritance to her greedy relatives, and then substituted another, destiny or divine providence, backed up by a quotation from Corneille. See Cholakian, "A House of Her Own," 12–13, on the change of explanation, and her footnote, 18 n. 28, on the handwritten correction by Mademoiselle in the Harlay text.

5. For the complicated publishing history of the *Divers Portraits* and the *Recueil/Galerie*, the indispensable guide is Jacqueline Plantié's encyclopedic *La Mode du Portrait Littéraire en France, 1641–1681* (Paris, 1994), which includes a guide to manuscript deposits of the portraits, 774–78. Plantié argues that the *Divers Portraits* and the Sercy-Barbin *Recueil* should be considered separate, even competing collections, in spite of the use of some of the portraits from the *Divers Portraits* in the Sercy-Barbin editions. On the *Divers Portraits*, see *La Mode*, 185–248, and on the *Recueil*, see 248–90. In support of her argument, Plantié further argues that the traditional publishing chronology of these works flies in the face of common sense and that the *Divers Portraits* may even have appeared after the *Recueil*: see 196–97. Plantié is very critical of Barthélemy's scholarship (677–82), and provides a comprehensive list of all of the portraits published in the *Divers Portraits* and the *Recueil* editions (737–72).

Plantié's work is a worthwhile expansion of Denise Mayer's earlier efforts. Mayer, in "Recueils de Portraits Littéraires Attribués à la Grande Mademoiselle," *Bulletin du Bibliophile* 20 (1970): 136–74, reviews and corrects much of the earlier literature on the subject. She provides excellent physical descriptions of the various editions and repeats Bourgeois and André's warning not to confuse these publications with the apocryphal *Pourtraits de la Cour*. See also the catalogues of the Bibliothèque Nationale de France, the British Library, and the National Union Catalogue cited above; Bourgeois and André, *Les Sources de l'Histoire de France* (Paris, 1923), 13: 13; Renate Baader, *Dames de Lettres (1649–1698) . . . Mlle de Scudéry, Mlle de Montpensier* (Stuttgart, 1986); Edouard de Barthélemy's introduction to his edition of the *Galerie des Portraits de Mademoiselle de Montpensier* (Paris, 1860), i–iv; Jacques-Charles Brunet, *Manuel du Libraire* (Paris, 1861), 2: 770; Victor Cousin, *Madame de Sablé* (Paris, 1859), 79–82 n. 1; Anon. [Guyot de Villeneuve], "Trois Recueils de Portraits Publiés en 1659," *Bulletin du Bibliophile* (1889): 447–53; F. Lachèvre, "La Galerie des Portraits de Mlle de Montpensier," *Revue Biblio-Iconographique* (1903): 18–30, which takes issue with much of the preceding article; F. Lachèvre, *Bibliographie des Recueils Collectifs*, 2: 106–12, and 3: 7; Alain Girard, *Repertoire des Livres Imprimés en France au XVIIᵉ Siècle* (Paris, 1985), 13: 139; Jules Le Petit, *Bibliographie des Principales Editions Originales d'Ecrivains Français du XVᵉ au XVIIIᵉ Siècle* (Paris, 1888), 217–19; Denise Mayer, "Les Seize Portraits Littéraires de Mlle de Montpensier," in *Mademoiselle de Montpensier: Trois Etudes d'Après ses Mémoires* (Paris, 1989); and Mayer's earlier article, "Les *Divers Portraits* de Mlle de Montpensier," *Médecine de France* 213 (1970): 43–50; Jean Lafond, "Mademoiselle et les *Divers Portraits*," *Papers on French Seventeenth-Century Literature* 22 (1995): 55–63.

In his own *Mémoires*, Segrais insists that only thirty copies of the *Divers Portraits* were printed at Caen in 1659. He adds that there were a hundred portraits in this edition, forty of which were by Mademoiselle: see Segrais, *Mémoires / Anecdotes* 1: 171. Given the inaccuracy of most of this statement, it is hard to accept his mention of thirty copies. A surviving copy of the *Divers Portraits* at the Bibliothèque Nationale de France (Res. Lb. 37.187.a) bears a handwritten note from the eighteenth century stating that in 1718 Huet had told a friend that there were only sixty copies printed of this work. There are two other copies of this edition at the Bibliothèque: one with Huet's arms, and the other apparently Mademoiselle's own copy. On the work known as *Les Pourtraits de la Cour*, see Bourgeois and André, *Les Sources*, 13: 13–14; and also Brunet, *Manuel du Libraire* 2: 770.

6. On the *Relation de l'Ile Imaginaire* and the *Histoire de la Princesse de Paphlagonie*, again see the printed catalogues cited above of the Bibliothèque Nationale de France, the British Library, and the National Union Catalogue. Two copies preserved at the Bibliothèque Nationale have handwritten "keys"; one of these belonged to a minor literary figure, Charlotte-Rose de Caumont de la Force. See Le Petit, *Editions Originales*, 215–16; see also the comments of Segrais's editors in the 1723 edition of the *Mémoires / Anecdotes*, 1: xxi–xxiv, and of Segrais, 170–71; see Huet, *Mémoires*, 124–25.

7. Mademoiselle's exchange of letters with Motteville is mentioned by Mademoi-

selle in her *Mémoires*, ed. Chéruel, 3: 454. As with so many of the other works cited above, they were reprinted in the Wetstein editions of the *Mémoires* of Mademoiselle. The last independent edition seems to have been that of Collin in 1806. A few excerpts were also published in the Petitot and Monmarqué *Collection des Mémoires* (2d series) in the introduction to Motteville's *Mémoires*, 36: 301. For the publishing history, see Bourgeois and André, *Les Sources*, 12: 312. For the unpublished correspondence between Mademoiselle and Motteville, see Bibliothèque Nationale de France, N.A.F. 25670. My thanks to M. François Avril, who brought this manuscript to my attention.

8. On Mademoiselle's two pious works, see Denise Mayer, "Deux Ouvrages de Piété de la Grande Mademoiselle," *Bulletin du Bibliophile* (1980): 170–84; Mayer, "Mademoiselle de Montpensier et la Vie Spirituelle," in *Trois Etudes*, 117–81; and Emmanuel Pierre Rodocanachi, ed., *Un Ouvrage de Piété de la Grande Mademoiselle* (Paris, 1903), i–xix.

9. On the various apocryphal works attributed to Mademoiselle, see the listing in the catalogue of the Bibliothèque Nationale de France cited above. Other than the *Pourtraits de la Cour* discussed in note 5, most of these date from the time of the Fronde and are clearly crude political propaganda and satire. See the comments of Celestin Moreau on the *Manifestes* attributed to Mademoiselle in *Bibliographie des Mazarinades* (Paris, 1850–51), 2: entries 2364 and 2365; see also Robert O. Lindsay and John Neu, *Mazarinades: A Checklist of Copies in Major Collections in the United States* (Metuchen, N.J., 1972). Faith Beasley cites the "Manifeste de Mademoiselle . . . à S.A.R." (1652) in her *Revising Memory: Women's Fiction and Memoirs in Seventeenth-Century France* (New Brunswick, 1990), 72–73. I find this troubling. Mademoiselle mentions all of her published works in her *Mémoires*, except for her religious writings, the first of which was published anonymously, and the second written after she broke off the text of the *Mémoires*. She was also proud of her behavior during the Fronde. It would stand to reason that if this manifesto or any of the other Mazarinades attributed to her were authentic, she would have acknowledged them. I am unaware of any other scholar who credits Mademoiselle with these apocrypha, and Beasley does not address the issue of attribution.

APPENDIX B   MADEMOISELLE'S FORTUNE

1. For capitalization purposes, I have used throughout Labatut's formula of estimating noble fortunes by capitalizing landed revenues by a multiple of thirty times and *rentes* by a multiple of ten times, and then adjusting the total with the addition of other forms of property: see Labatut, *Ducs et Pairs de France*, for his valuation of the Condé fortune at 14.6 million livres in 1651 using this technique, 258–59; on the comparative fortunes of princes and peers, see 248; and on the Joyeuse fortune of Madame de Guise, 264. Katia Béguin, in *Les Princes de Condé* (Paris, 1999), has recalculated the Condé fortune to be 16.5 million livres in 1651 (53). For more on the Condé fortune, see Daniel Roche, "La Fortune . . . des Princes de Condé," *Revue d'Histoire Moderne et Contemporaine* 14 (1967): 217–43, which includes an estimate of 19 million livres of landed property alone at the beginning of the eighteenth cen-

tury (234). In the same journal, see François Mougel, "La Fortune des Princes de Bourbon-Conty 1655–1791," 16 (1971): 30–49, and 37 for an estimate of the landed portion of that fortune in the 1690s. The wide variation in Mougel's revenue estimate is due to a lack of detailed records for the period.

2. See Nancy N. Barker, *Brother to the Sun King*, 175–98 passim. Barker's calculation of the maximum capital value of the landed property left by Mademoiselle to Philippe, 2.1 million livres (189), yields slightly less than a calculation using Labatut's formula (2.4 million livres), but the results are close enough to justify its use in an attempt to consistently rely on her valuation of the Orléans fortune. I should note one small error in Baker: she includes the duchy of Aumale as part of Mademoiselle's forced donation to the duc du Maine (178). The error stems from a passage in Saint-Simon. In fact, Maine purchased Aumale from the family of Savoie-Nemours in 1685.

3. On Mademoiselle's debts, see Fonds de Dreux, 300 AP I 93, 761, and 921. The Orléans family also had to settle claims put forward by various collateral heirs, chiefly members of German princely families and the Condés, who could trace a line of descent from the marriage of William the Silent and Charlotte de Montpensier, Mademoiselle's great aunt. These can be followed in 300 AP I 93 and 921.

4. For Bergin's distinction between *succession* ("estate") value and "fortune," see his *Cardinal Richelieu: Power and the Pursuit of Wealth* (1985), 245–46. Bergin's extraordinary study in depth of the Richelieu fortune also underscores the conceptual difficulties and assumptions required in this kind of exercise: see 243–92 passim.

As mentioned earlier, Mademoiselle's financial records are woefully incomplete. Most glaringly, there is no simple listing of Mademoiselle's revenues and their sources, nor even of her estates at any time after Gaston's tutelage, although records do survive on the auction of her furniture and jewelry, as do partial lists of her creditors, etc. To cite a typical example of an important omission, there is no record in Mademoiselle's papers of the final Richelieu settlement, 364,000 livres awarded after appeals in 1659 and paid irregularly with interest through 1694, for a total of 570,000 livres. The records do survive in the Richelieu papers: see Bergin, *Richelieu*, 282–83.

The most useful files for Mademoiselle's fortune are those found in the Fonds de Dreux, which include notes on the issues surrounding Mademoiselle's legacy to the Orléans family and claims by various creditors and collateral heirs. Since Eu later passed to the Orléans through the marriage of the heiress of the Bourbon-Penthièvre line to the future Philippe Egalité, the Fonds de Dreux also contains extensive material on that magnificent property. But the financial records for Mademoiselle's period have been lost. To estimate the revenues from Eu, I have used surviving records in the Fonds for the period just before her purchase of the estate from the Guises, and figures from the time of the duc du Maine which are consistent with the earlier figures. For the second, asset-based calculation of Mademoiselle's fortune, I have valued Eu at its purchase price from the Guises, 2.55 million livres.

For the Dombes, I have also used Maine's revenue records found in the Fonds de Dreux. For asset-based calculations, I have used a valuation found there of 3 million livres at the time of Mademoiselle's death. This is consistent with its estimated ordinary revenues of 80,000 to 100,000 livres. Dombes was sold to the Crown in 1762 for about 17 million livres: given inflation, the passage of time, and the separate value of the sovereign rights ceded in that transaction, this sum seems inappropriate for our purposes here. Other records preserved in the Fonds de Dreux bear on the income derived by the Orléans from Mademoiselle's legacy, her share in the Guise inheritance, and the 600,000 livres value placed on her interest in the Luxembourg.

On these matters, see: Archives Nationales, Fonds de Dreux, Series 300 AP I 93, Papiers de Mlle de Montpensier; 300 AP I 921, Successions Montpensier et Guise; 300 AP I 440, Beaujolais et Dombes, comptes 1562–1813; 300 AP I 746, Inventaire après décès de Monsieur, 1701; 300 AP I 761, Succession du Régent; 300 AP II 2A, Eu, titres et papiers; 300 AP II 14 and 15, Comté d'Eu ; 300 AP II 104, Eu, acquisitions; 300 AP II 239 and 240, Eu, comptes.

Masingil's study of the revenues of Saint-Fargeau, found in the archives of that duchy, AN, 90 AP 28, establish the variation in revenues from that property during the entirety of Mademoiselle's ownership as well as that of Lauzun. It also serves as a way of verifying the figures used in the Barrail-Lauzun correspondence, AN, Archives de La Force, 353AP 25. This correspondence provides some useful revenue estimates for the various properties Mademoiselle considered as possible gifts to Lauzun, including Saint-Fargeau, Thiers, Châtellerault, and Brosses, as well as information on Mademoiselle's income from *rentes* and pensions. The sales price of Saint-Fargeau in 1714, 500,000 livres, is used for asset valuation calculations above.

Dangeau estimates that Choisy cost Mademoiselle 800,000 livres, a figure accepted by Chamchine, and used here for valuation purposes. See Dangeau, *Journal*, 4: 260; Chamchine, *Choisy*, 827. At the time of Gaston's marriage to Marie de Montpensier, his officials estimated her income at 330,000 livres: see *Mémoires de Gaston*, 570. For Mademoiselle's estimate of her income at 500,000 livres in the 1660s see *MM*, 3: 537. For the *comptes de tutelle* assembled by Gaston, see Arsenal Ms. 4211 and BNF Baluze, v. 344, fols. 97–138. Gaston's refusal to account for Mademoiselle's revenues in the Dombes and the Beaujolais, and the partial accounting of her Norman revenues make his calculations of little real use. With these exclusions, Mademoiselle's revenues were calculated by Gaston's officials at an aggregate 1.9 million livres for the twenty-four years of Gaston's stewardship: an average of 102,000 livres per annum. For the same period, his expenditures on Mademoiselle's behalf are supposed to have totaled about 3.9 million livres. One might speculate that this second figure comes somewhat closer to aggregate revenues than that put forward by his officials. Because the available evidence is limited and ambiguous, certain assumptions were necessary to make the calculations above. Another researcher might well arrive at different totals, but that Mademoiselle's fortune still ranked among the most important in France at the time of her death cannot be doubted.

Bibliography

Manuscript Versions of Mademoiselle's *Mémoires*

Bibliothèque Nationale de France
    Ms. Fr. 6698–99. Autograph Version.
    Ms. Fr. 19588–92. Ms. Harlay.
    Ms. Fr. 4154–56. Ms. Boze.
    Ms. Fr. 4157–60. Ms. Lancelot.

Archives du Ministère des Affaires Etrangères
    Series *Mémoires et Documents, France*, vols. 70–74. Ms. copy from library of
        Saint-Simon.

British Library
    Ms. Egerton 1679.
    Note: While I have examined the manuscript copies at the Bibliothèque Nationale

de France and have corresponded with archivists at the British Library and the Ministère des Affaires Etrangères about their respective copies, I have relied in this study on Chéruel's edition of the *Mémoires*, which is largely based on Ms. Fr. 6698–99, and I have also used the Petitot edition, which is based on Ms. Fr. 19588–92. I have examined the early printed editions listed below for textual comparison purposes. See Appendix A for a discussion of these manuscripts and editions.

Other Unpublished Materials

Archives du Ministère des Affaires Etrangères
> Series *Mémoires et Documents, France*: vols. 292 and 1876. Several miscellaneous letters by Mademoiselle.
> Series *Correspondance Politique, Autriche*, v. 17. Saujon Mission (1650).

Archives Nationales
> Archives de Saint-Fargeau. Series 90 AP. Property and Estate Records; Inventories; Estate Plans.
> Archives La Force. Series 353 AP 25. Lauzun-Barrail Correspondence 1681; Lauzun-Louvois Correspondence 1680–84; Miscellaneous Lauzun papers.
> Fonds de Dreux. Series 300 AP I 93, Papers of Mademoiselle de Montpensier; 300 AP I 440, Beaujolais et Dombes, accounts 1562–1813; 300 AP I 746 and 747, *Inventaire après décès* of Philippe d'Orléans, 1701; 300 AP I 761, *Succession du Régent*; 300 AP I 904, Papers and property records of the duc du Maine and family; 300 AP I 921, *Successions Montpensier et Guise*; 300 AP II 2A, Eu, property records and documents; 300 AP II 14 and 15, Eu, property records and documents; 300 AP II 104, Eu, acquisitions; 300 AP II 239, 240, Eu, accounts.
> Minutier Central: XCVIII 818, Mademoiselle's Testament, February 27, 1685; CXV 129, Transaction with Gaston d'Orléans, May 13, 1655.
> Series K 120A. Louvois–Saint-Mars Correspondence on Lauzun's Imprisonment 1671–80.
> Series Z 1A 523. Montpensier Household, 1652–93.

Archivio di Stato, Florence
> Series Mediceo del Principato. Nos. 4767, 4783, 4784, 4785, 4816, 4820, 6265: Correspondence of Florentine residents, Paris, 1672–88. Nos. 4783 and 4785: Letters of Mademoiselle 1685–87. Transcriptions courtesy of Patricia Ranum.

Bibliothèque de l'Arsenal
> Ms. 4211. *Comptes de Tutelle* of Mademoiselle 1627–50.
> Ms. 5418, Recueil Conrart, v. 9. Various literary portraits.
> Ms. 5420, Recueil Conrart, v. 11. Letters of Vandy, Maure, Motteville, Sablé. Draft Portrait of Vandy by Mademoiselle.
> Ms. 5421, Recueil Conrart, v. 12. *Histoire de . . . Fouquerolles* (incomplete Ms.).
> Ms. 5422, Recueil Conrart, v. 13. Letter of Mademoiselle to abbé Charles Cotin. 1660.
> Ms. 5426, Recueil Conrart, v. 17. Addenda from the *Vie de Fouquerolles: Suite de*

l'Histoire de la Marquise de Fouquerolles; Le Manifeste de Mademoiselle; Stances sur le Manifeste; La Réponse de la Marquise au Manifeste; Mémoires et Relations de la Guerre de Paris, 1652. Various literary portraits.

Bibliothèque Nationale de France

Ms. Fr. 4233. Correspondence of Louis XIV and His Ministers on the Dispute between Mademoiselle and Gaston d'Orléans, 1656.

Ms. Fr. 24984. Letters of Mademoiselle to Mme d'Huxelles, 1657.

Nouv. Acq. Fr. 4815. Letters of Mademoiselle, June and July 1652.

Nouv. Acq. Fr. 6207. Letters of Mademoiselle to Léonard Goulas and Gaston d'Orléans dealing with the *comptes de tutelle.* Undated, but apparently 1654–55.

Nouv. Acq. Fr. 25670. Correspondence Montpensier-Motteville, 1660–61, bound with *Histoire de la Princesse Adamirze.* Late 17th Century Ms. Copy.

Collection Baluze, v. 208. Order to fire on the Royal Army. Gaston d'Orléans, July 3, 1652.

Collection Baluze, v. 217. Testament of Mademoiselle, February 27, 1685.

Collection Baluze, v. 341. Letters of Mademoiselle to Gaston d'Orléans et al., undated, but from the period of her exile at Saint-Fargeau, 1652–57.

Collection Baluze, v. 344. Memoranda and papers on the *comptes de tutelle* prepared by Gaston d'Orléans's staff, 1655.

Collection Baluze, v. 346. Letters of Mademoiselle to Gaston d'Orléans and Léonard Goulas, 1634–59.

Ms. Clairambault, vols. 491, 500, 501, 581, 634–35. Miscellaneous papers, letters, and documents concerning Mademoiselle, Lauzun, Gaston d'Orléans, Mademoiselle's stepmother and half sisters, and Mademoiselle's collateral heirs.

Cinq Cents de Colbert, v. 54. Mademoiselle's Household, 1652.

Cinq Cents de Colbert, v. 142. Pompes Funèbres de Mademoiselle, 1693.

Mélanges de Colbert, v. 15. Note on the Comté d'Eu.

Mélanges de Colbert, vols. 109 and 109 *bis.* Montpensier Letters, 1662.

Mélanges de Colbert, v. 176 *bis.* Montpensier Letters, 1670.

Cabinet des Estampes. Fonds Robert Cotte. Va 439. Plans of Choisy; Va 449: Plan of Saint-Fargeau.

The Morgan Library, New York

Letter of Mademoiselle to Colbert, August 17, 1669; Letter of Mademoiselle to Marie Christine, duchess of Savoy, August 19, 1650.

The Montpensier Manuscript (devotional treatises which may have been owned by Mademoiselle).

Editions of Mademoiselle's Works

Histoire de Jeanne Lambert d'Herbigny, Marquise de Fouquerolles. Saint-Fargeau, 1653.

Lettres de Mademoiselle de Montpensier, de Mesdames de Motteville, Montmorency, de Mademoiselle du Pré, et de Madame la Marquise de Lambert, ed. Léopold Collin. Paris, 1806.

La Galerie des Portraits de Mademoiselle de Montpensier, ed. Edouard de Barthélemy. Paris, 1860.

Mémoires, ed. Christian Bouyer. 2 vols., Paris, 1985 (reissue of the text established by Chéruel).

Mémoires, ed. Adolphe Chéruel. 4 vols., Paris, 1858–59.

Mémoires, in *Nouvelle Collection des Mémoires pour servir à l'Histoire de France*, ed. Joseph-François Michaud and Jean-Joseph Poujoulat, 3d series, v. 4. Paris, 1838. Reprinted in *Nouvelle Collection des Mémoires Relatifs à l'Histoire de France*, ed. Joseph-François Michaud and Jean-Joseph Poujoulat, v. 28. Paris, 1857.

Mémoires, in *Collection des Mémoires Relatifs à l'Histoire de France*, ed. Claude B. Petitot et al., 2d series, v. 40–43. Paris, 1824.

Mémoires. First edition, incomplete. 1 vol., Paris, 1718.

Mémoires. Second (first complete) edition. 6 vols., chez Le Breton, Paris, 1728.

Mémoires. Third edition. 4 vols., chez J. F. Bernard, Amsterdam, 1730.

Mémoires de Mademoiselle de Montpensier, fille de Gaston d'Orléans . . . et Divers Ouvrages Très Curieux, ed. J. Wetstein and G. Smith. 8 vols., Amsterdam, 1735.

The Memoirs of La Grande Mademoiselle, trans. Grace Hart Seely. New York, 1928.

Histoire de la Princesse de Paphlagonie, and *Relation de l'Ile Imaginaire*, in Segrais, *Oeuvres Diverses de Mr. de Segrais*, v. 2. Amsterdam, 1723.

Réflexions sur les Huit Béatitudes du Sermon de Jésus-Christ sur la Montagne (1685), in *Un Ouvrage de Piété Inconnu de la Grande Mademoiselle*, ed. Emmanuel Pierre Rodocanachi. Paris, 1903.

Réflexions Morales et Chrétiennes, sur le Premier Livre de l'Imitation de Jésus-Christ, in *De l'Imitation de Jésus-Christ*, ed. Nicolas Fontaine. First edition, Paris, 1694; second edition, Paris, 1722.

Apocryphal and Other Works Concerning Mademoiselle

Les Amours de S. A. R. Mademoiselle Souveraine de Dombes avec M. le Comte de Lauzun. Cologne, 1672.

Advertissement pour Mademoiselle à l'Archiduc Léopold. Mazarinade, Paris, 1649.

Les Généreux Sentiments de Mademoiselle exprimés à M. le Duc d'Orléans. Mazarinade, Paris, 1652.

Harangue Fait à Mademoiselle à son Arrivée en la Maison de Ville d'Orléans. Mazarinade, Paris, 1652.

Lettre de l'Archiduc Léopold envoyée à Mademoiselle pour traiter la Paix. Mazarinade, Paris, 1649.

Seconde Lettre de l'Archiduc Léopold à Mademoiselle. Mazarinade, Paris, 1649.

Lettre de Mademoiselle à l'Archiduc Léopold. Mazarinade, Paris, 1652.

Lettre d'une Bourgeoise de la Paroisse de Saint Eustache présentée à Mademoiselle. Mazarinade, Paris, 1649.

Lettre du Duc de Lorraine à Mademoiselle. Mazarinade, Paris, 1652.

Lettre d'un Prince généreux à Mademoiselle. Mazarinade, Paris, 1649.

Lettre de Mademoiselle escrite à Son Altesse Royale. Mazarinade, Paris, 1652.

Lettre de Mademoiselle d'Orléans . . . à la Reine. Mazarinade, Paris, 1649.

Le Manifeste de Mademoiselle présenté à Son Altesse Royale. Mazarinade, Paris, 1652.

Le Manifeste de Mademoiselle présenté aux coeurs généreux. Mazarinade, Paris, 1652.

Relation générale . . . dans la ville d'Orléans. Mazarinade, Paris, 1652.

Remerciement des Parisiens à Mademoiselle pour avoir procuré la Paix. Mazarinade, Paris, 1649.

Réponse de Mademoiselle à l'Archiduc Léopold. Mazarinade, Paris, 1649.

Réponse véritable de Mademoiselle à la lettre supposée de l'Archiduc Léopold. Mazarinade, Paris, 1649.

Très Humbles Remonstrances à Mademoiselle et aux Messieurs son Conseil par la Noblesse et le Tiers-Etat de Son Duché de Montpensier sur la Pauvreté du Peuple. Mazarinade, Paris, 1650.

Les Pourtraits de la Cour pour le Présent, c'est à dire, du Roy, des Princes, et des Ministres d'Etat. Cologne, 1667.

Les Pourtraits de la Cour . . . in *Archives Curieuses de l' Histoire de France*, ed. Félix Danjou, 2d series, v. 8. Paris, 1839.

The Characters or Pourtraicts of the Present Court of France . . . made English by J. B. Gent. London, 1668 (translation of *Les Pourtraits*).

Contemporary Memoirs, Works, and Printed Sources

Archives de la Bastille, ed. François Ravaisson. 16 vols., Paris, 1866–83.

Berwick, James Fitzjames, maréchal de. *Mémoires*, in *Nouvelle Collection des Mémoires Relatifs à l'Histoire de France*, ed. Joseph-François Michaud and Jean-Joseph Poujoulat, v. 32. Paris, 1857.

Bussy-Rabutin, Roger de. *Correspondance*, ed. Ludovic Lalanne. 6 vols., Paris, 1858–59.

——. *Mémoires*, ed. Ludovic Lalanne. 2 vols., Paris, 1857.

Caylus, Marthe-Marguerite de Villette, marquise de. *Souvenirs*, in *Nouvelle Collection*, ed. Joseph-François Michaud and Jean-Joseph Poujoulat, v. 32. Paris, 1857.

Choisy, François de. *Mémoires pour servir à l'Histoire de Louis XIV*, ed. Georges Mongrédien. Paris, 1966.

Colbert, Jean-Baptiste. *Lettres, Instructions, et Mémoires de Colbert*, ed. Pierre Clément. 7 vols., Paris, 1861–82.

Condé, Louis de Bourbon, prince de, and Enghien, Henri-Jules de Bourbon, duc d'. *Lettres Inédites à Marie-Louise de Gonzague, Reine de Pologne, sur la Cour de Louis XIV (1660–1667)*, ed. Emile Magne. Paris, 1920.

Conrart, Valentin. *Mémoires*, in *Collection des Mémoires Relatifs à l'Histoire de France*, ed. Claude B. Petitot et al., 2d series, v. 48. Paris, 1825.

——. *Un Tournoi de Trois Pucelles en l'Honneur de Jeanne d'Arc: Lettres Inédites de Conrart, de Mlle de Scudéry, et de Mme du Moulin (1646–1647)*, ed. Edouard de Barthélemy and René Kerviler. Paris, 1878.

Coste, Pierre. *Histoire de Louis de Bourbon . . . Prince du Sang* [Condé], in *Archives Curieuses de l'Histoire de France*, ed. Félix Danjou, 2d series, v. 8. Paris, 1839.

Dangeau, Philippe de Courcillon, marquis de. *Journal*, ed. Félix Feuillet de Conches. 19 vols., Paris, 1854–60.

Dubuisson-Aubenay, François Baudot, seigneur de. *Journal des Guerres Civiles 1648–1652*, ed. Gustave Saige. 2 vols., Paris, 1883–85.

Fénelon, François de Salignac de la Mothe-. *De l'Education des Femmes*, in *Oeuvres Complètes de Fénelon*, v. 6. 10 vols., Paris, 1810.

Goulas, Nicolas. *Mémoires*, ed. Charles Constant. 3 vols., Paris, 1879–82.

Herault de Gourville, Jean. *Mémoires*, in *Nouvelle Collection*, ed. Joseph-François Michaud and Jean-Joseph Poujoulat, v. 29. Paris, 1857.

Huet, Daniel. *Mémoires*, trans. Charles Nisard. Paris, 1853.

La Bruyère, Jean de. *Oeuvres*, ed. Gustave Servois. 3 vols., Paris, 1865.

La Fare, Charles-Auguste, marquis de. *Mémoires et Réflexions*, in *Nouvelle Collection*, ed. Joseph-François Michaud and Jean-Joseph Poujoulat, v. 32. Paris, 1857.

La Fayette, Marie Madeleine de la Vergne, comtesse de. *Oeuvres Complètes*, ed. Roger Duchêne. Paris, 1990.

La Houssaye, Abraham Nicolas Amelot de. *Mémoires Historiques, Politiques, Critiques*. 2 vols., Amsterdam, 1722.

La Rochefoucauld, François, duc de. *Mémoires*, in *Nouvelle Collection*, ed. Joseph-François Michaud and Jean-Joseph Poujoulat, v. 29. Paris, 1857.

LeBel, N. *Relation de la Mort du Marquis de Monaldeschi le 6 Novembre 1657*, in *Archives Curieuses*, ed. Félix Danjou, 2d series, v. 8. Paris, 1839.

Louis XIV. *Lettres Particulières*, in *Oeuvres de Louis XIV*, ed. Philippe de Grouvelle, v. 5. Paris, 1806.

———. *Mémoires for the Instruction of the Dauphin*, ed. and trans. Paul Sonnino. New York, 1970.

Mazarin, Jules Cardinal. *Lettres du Cardinal Mazarin*, ed. Adolphe Chéruel et al. 9 vols., Paris, 1889–1906.

———. *Lettres du Cardinal Mazarin (1651–1652)*, ed. Jules Ravenel. Paris, 1836.

Montglat, François de Paule, marquis de. *Mémoires*, in *Collection*, ed. Claude B. Petitot et al., 2d series, v. 49–51. Paris, 1825.

Montreuil, Mathieu. *Lettre . . . Contenant une Relation . . . du Marriage du Roy (1660)*, in *Archives Curieuses*, ed. Félix Danjou, 2d series, v. 8. Paris, 1839.

Motteville, Françoise Bertaut, Madame de. *Mémoires*, in *Nouvelle Collection*, ed. Joseph-François Michaud and Jean-Joseph Poujoulat, v. 24. Paris, 1857.

Nani, Giovanni Battista di. *Historia della Republica Veneta*. 2 vols., Venice, 1679.

Nemours, Marie d'Orléans-Longueville, duchesse de. *Mémoires*, in *Nouvelle Collection*, ed. Joseph-François Michaud and Jean-Joseph Poujoulat, v. 23. Paris, 1857.

Orléans, Elisabeth-Charlotte, Princess Palatine, duchesse d'. *The Letters of Madame*, trans. Gertrude Scott Stevenson. London, 1924.

———. *Lettres Françaises*, ed. Dirk Van der Cruysse. Paris, 1989.

Orléans, Gaston de France, duc d'. *Mémoires (1608–1636)*, attributed to Algay de Martignac, in *Nouvelle Collection*, ed. Joseph-François Michaud and Jean-Joseph Poujoulat, v. 23. Paris, 1857.

Ormesson, Olivier Lefèvre d'. *Journal*, ed. Adolphe Chéruel. 2 vols., Paris, 1860–61.

Relation Véritable du Combat du Faubourg Saint-Antoine (1652) [Anon.], in *Archives Curieuses*, ed. Félix Danjou, 2d series, v. 8. Paris, 1839.

Retz, Jean-François de Gondi, cardinal de. *Mémoires*, in *Oeuvres du Cardinal de Retz*, ed. Marie-Thérèse Hipp and Michel Pernot. Paris, 1984.

Saint-Maurice, Thomas-François Chabod, marquis de. *Lettres sur la Cour de Louis XIV*, ed. Jean LeMoine. 2 vols., Paris, 1910.

Saint-Simon, Louis, duc de. *Mémoires*, ed. Yves Coirault. 8 vols., Paris, 1983–88.

Segrais, Jean Regnault de. *Les Nouvelles Françaises ou Les Divertissements de la Princesse Aurélie*, ed. Roger Guichemerre. 2 vols., Paris, 1990–92.

——. *Oeuvres Diverses de Mr. de Segrais*, v. 1: *Mémoires/Anecdotes*; v. 2: *Eglogues . . . Princesse de Paphlagonie . . . Relation de l'Ile Imaginaire*. Amsterdam, 1723.

Sévigné, Marie de Rabutin-Chantal, marquise de. *Lettres*, ed. Emile Gérard-Gailly. 3 vols., Paris, 1953–63.

Spanheim, Ezéchiel. *Relation de la Cour de France (1690)*, ed. Charles Schefer. Paris, 1882.

Tallemant des Réaux, Gédéon. *Historiettes*, ed. Antoine Adam. 2 vols., Paris, 1959.

Valois, Marguerite de. *Mémoires*, in *Nouvelle Collection*, ed. Joseph-François Michaud and Jean-Joseph Poujoulat, v. 10. Paris, 1881.

Voltaire (François-Marie Arouet). *Le Siècle de Louis XIV*, in *Oeuvres Complètes de Voltaire*, ed. Louis Moland., v. 14 and 15. Paris, 1883–85.

——. *Correspondance*, in *Oeuvres Complètes*, v. 33. Paris, 1885.

——. *Le Sottisier*, in *Oeuvres Complètes*, v. 32. Paris, 1885.

Vuillart, Germain. *Lettres de Germain Vuillart, Ami de Port-Royal, à M. Louis de Préfontaine*, ed. Ruth Clark. Geneva, 1951.

York, James Stuart, duke of [James II of England]. *The Memoirs of James II: His Campaigns as Duke of York, 1652–1660*, ed. A. Lytton Sells. Bloomington, Ind., 1962.

Studies of La Grande Mademoiselle

Amiguet, Philippe. *Une Princesse à l'Ecole du Cid: La Grande Mademoiselle et Son Siècle d'après Ses Mémoires*. Paris, 1957.

Baader, Renate. *Dames de Lettres: Autorinnen des Preziösen, Hocharistokratischen und "Modernen" Salons (1649–1698): Mlle de Scudéry, Mlle de Montpensier, Mme d'Aulnoy*. Stuttgart, 1986.

Barine, Arvède [Cécile Vincens, pseud.]. *La Jeunesse de la Grande Mademoiselle*. Paris, 1909.

——. *Louis XIV et la Grande Mademoiselle*. Paris, 1912.

Beasley, Faith E. "Rescripting Historical Discourse: Literary Portraits by Women." *Papers on French Seventeenth-Century Literature* 14 (1987): 517–35.

——. *Revising Memory: Women's Fiction and Memoirs in Seventeenth-Century France*. New Brunswick, N.J., 1990.

Bertaud, Madeleine. "En Marge de leurs Mémoires: Une Correspondance entre Mlle de Montpensier et Madame de Motteville." *Travaux de Littérature* 3 (1990): 278–95.

——. "Louis XIII Vu par Quelques Mémorialistes." In *La Cour au Miroir des Mémorialistes 1530–1682*, ed. Noémi Hepp, 77–87. Colloque, Université de Strasbourg, no. 31. Paris, 1991.

Blanche, Charles. "Une Répresentation au Théâtre de Saint-Fargeau." *Annuaire Historique du Département de l'Yonne* 48 (1884): 223–32.

Bourgeois, Emile, and Louis André. *Les Sources de l'Histoire de France.* Paris, 1913 (v. 12), 1923 (v. 13). V. 12, no. 801: "*Mémoires* de Mademoiselle," 112–14; no. 1116: "*Lettres* Montpensier/Motteville," 312. V. 13: nos. 1303 and 1304, "*Divers Portraits*" and "*Portraits de la Cour*," 13–14; no. 1819, "Oraison funèbre" and "Les Amours," 309–10.

Bouyer, Christian. *La Grande Mademoiselle.* Paris, 1986.

Bradley, John William. *The Montpensier Manuscript: Four Devotional Treatises Written for Anne-Marie-Louise d'Orléans, Called La Grande Mademoiselle.* London, 1905.

Cholakian, Patricia Francis. "A House of Her Own: Marginality and Dissidence in the *Mémoires* of La Grande Mademoiselle (1627–1693)." *Prose Studies* 9 (1986): 3–20.

Cuénin, Micheline. "Mademoiselle, une Amazone impure?" *Papers on French Seventeenth-Century Literature* 22 (1995): 25–36.

Doolittle, James. "A Royal Diversion: Mademoiselle and Lauzun." *L'Esprit Créateur* 2, no. 11 (1971): 123–40.

Ducasse, André. *La Grande Mademoiselle: la plus riche Héritière d'Europe 1627–1693.* Paris, 1937.

Duchêne, Roger. "Vers *la Princesse de Clèves*: de la *Princesse de Paphlagonie* à *l'Histoire Amoureuse des Gaules*." *Papers on French Seventeenth-Century Literature* 22 (1995): 65–77.

Evans, Joseph C. "Versions of the *Mémoires* of Mademoiselle de Montpensier." *Romance Notes* 7, no. 2 (1966): 161–64.

Freudmann, Felix R. "Deux Lettres Inédites de la Grande Mademoiselle." *XVIIᵉ Siècle*, no. 45 (1959): 314–23.

Garapon, Jean. *La Grande Mademoiselle Mémorialiste: une Autobiographie dans le Temps.* Geneva, 1989.

——. "Mademoiselle à Saint-Fargeau: la Découverte de l'Ecriture." *Papers on French Seventeenth-Century Literature* 22 (1995): 37–47.

——. "Mademoiselle de Montpensier dans ses *Mémoires*: l'exemple d'une Culture Princière." In *De L'Estoile à Saint-Simon, Recherche sur la Culture des Mémorialistes au Temps des Trois Premiers Rois Bourbons*, ed. Madeleine Bertaud and André Labertit, 93–107. Colloque, Université de Strasbourg, no. 43. Paris, 1993.

——. "Les Mémorialistes et le Réel: l'exemple du Cardinal de Retz et de Mademoiselle de Montpensier." *Littératures Classiques*, no. 11 (1989): 181–89.

Glaserman, Rose Huguette. *Etude sur la Grande Mademoiselle.* Ann Arbor, Mich., 1981.

Goldin, Jeanne. "Métalangage de l'Autoportrait dans les Recueils de Mademoiselle de Montpensier." In *Storiografia della Critica Francese nel Seicento*, ed. Enea Balmas, 267–85. Bari, 1986.

Guichemerre, Roger. "La Grande Mademoiselle et les *Nouvelles Françaises* de Segrais." *Papers on French Seventeenth-Century Literature* 22 (1995): 49–54.

Guyot de Villeneuve. "Note sur Trois Recueils de Portraits Publiés en 1659." *Bulletin du Bibliophile* (1889): 447–53.

Henein, Eglal. "Mademoiselle de Montpensier à la Recherche du Temps Perdu." *Papers on French Seventeenth-Century Literature* 6 (1976–77): 38–52.

Lachèvre, Frédéric. "La Galerie des Portraits de Mlle de Montpensier." *Revue Biblio-Iconographique* (1903): 18–30.

Lafond, Jean. "Mademoiselle et les *Divers Portraits.*" *Papers on French Seventeenth-Century Literature* 22 (1995): 55–63.

La Force, Auguste-Armand, duc de. *La Vie Amoureuse de la Grande Mademoiselle.* 2 vols., Paris, 1927.

Le Moël, Michel. *La Grande Mademoiselle.* Paris, 1994.

——. "Mademoiselle et Paris." *Papers on French Seventeenth-Century Literature* 22 (1995): 15–24.

Le Petit, Jules. "Ouvrages de Mlle de Montpensier." In *Bibliographie des Principales Editions Originales d'Ecrivains Français du XVᵉ au XVIIIᵉ Siècle*, 215–20. Paris, 1888.

Lesne, Emmanuèle. *La Poétique des Mémoires 1650–1685.* Paris, 1986.

Lesne-Jaffro, Emmanuèle. "La Question du Genre des Mémoires chez l'abbé Arnauld, Bussy-Rabutin, et Mademoiselle de Montpensier." In *La Cour au Miroir*, ed. Noémi Hepp, 193–205.

Massip, Catherine. "Le Mécénat Musical de Mademoiselle." *Papers on French Seventeenth-Century Literature* 22 (1995): 79–90.

Masson, Gustave, and Gustave Servois. Untitled Report on the Ms. Egerton 1679. *Annuaire/Bulletin de la Société de l'Histoire de France* (1867): 139–43.

Mayer, Denise. "Deux Ouvrages de Piété de La Grande Mademoiselle." *Bulletin du Bibliophile* (1980): 170–83.

——. "Les *Divers Portraits* de Mademoiselle de Montpensier." *Médecine de France* 213 (1970): 43–50, 60.

——. "Mademoiselle de Montpensier et l'Architecture d'après ses *Mémoires.*" *XVIIᵉ Siècle*, nos. 118–19 (1978): 57–71.

——. *Mademoiselle de Montpensier: Trois Etudes d'après Ses Mémoires. Papers on French Seventeenth-Century Literature*, series Biblio 17–45. Paris, 1989.

——. "Recueils de Portraits Littéraires Attribués à la Grande Mademoiselle." *Bulletin du Bibliophile* (1970): 136–74.

Melchior-Bonnet, Bernardine. *La Grande Mademoiselle: Héroïne et Amoureuse.* Paris, 1985.

Mignot, Claude. "Mademoiselle et son château de Saint-Fargeau." *Papers on French Seventeenth-Century Literature* 22 (1995): 91–101.

Moiset, Charles. "Mademoiselle de Montpensier à Saint-Fargeau." *Bulletin de la Société des Sciences Historiques et Naturelles de l'Yonne* 44 (1890): 469–78.

Montassier, Louis. "Mademoiselle de Montpensier: Séjour et Exil à Saint-Fargeau." *Bulletin/Yonne* 81 (1927): 43–94.

Sackville-West, Vita. *Daughter of France: The Life of La Grande Mademoiselle.* New York, 1959.

Sainte-Beuve, Charles-Augustin. "La Grande Mademoiselle." In *Les Causeries du Lundi*, v. 3, March 24, 1851. Paris, 1851.

Steegmuller, Francis. *The Grand Mademoiselle*. New York, 1956.

Thierry, Felicien. "Mouvement Littéraire dans la Bourgogne-Auxerroise . . . Mlle de Montpensier à Saint-Fargeau." *Annuaire/Yonne* 24 (1860): 3–18.

Verdier, Gabrielle. "Mademoiselle de Montpensier et le Plaisir du Texte." *Papers on French Seventeenth-Century Literature* 10, no. 18 (1983): 11–33.

Watson, Françoise. "Le Moi et l'Histoire dans les Mémoires de Mme de Motteville, Mme de la Guette, et Mlle de Montpensier." *Papers on French Seventeenth-Century Literature* 18 (1991): 141–56.

Watts, Derek A. "Jugements sur la Cour chez Retz et Quelques Contemporains." In *La Cour au Miroir*, ed. Noémi Hepp, 123–33.

General Secondary Works

Abraham, Claude Kurt. *Gaston d'Orléans et Sa Cour: Etude Littéraire*. Chapel Hill, N.C., 1963.

Adam, Antoine. *Grandeur and Illusion: French Literature and Society, 1600–1717*, trans. Herbert Tint. London, 1972.

———. *Histoire de la Littérature Française au XVIIᵉ Siècle*. 5 vols., Paris, 1962–68.

Albister, Maïté, and Daniel Armogathe. *Histoire du Féminisme Français*, v. 1: *Du Moyen Age à la Révolution*. Paris, 1977.

Ariès, Philippe. *Centuries of Childhood*, trans. Robert Baldick. New York, 1960.

———. "Pourquoi Écrit-on des Mémoires." In *Les Valeurs chez les Mémorialistes Français du XVIIᵉ Siècle avant la Fronde*, ed. Noémi Hepp and Jacques Hennequin, 13–20. Colloque, Université de Strasbourg, no. 22. Moulins-les-Metz, 1979.

Ariès, Philippe, and Georges Duby, eds. *A History of Private Life*, v. 3: *Passions of the Renaissance*, trans. Arthur Goldhammer. Cambridge, Mass., 1989.

Aumale, Henri d'Orléans, duc d'. *Histoire des Princes de Condé*. 7 vols., Paris, 1885–92.

Bailleux-Delbecq, Martine, et al. *Mélanges Dédiés à la Comtesse de Paris*. Luneray, 1992.

Baldner, R. "The *Nouvelles Françaises* of Segrais." *Modern Language Quarterly* 18 (1957): 199–205.

Barker, Nancy Nichols. *Brother to the Sun King: Philippe Duke of Orléans*. Baltimore, 1989.

Barthélemy, Edouard de. *Madame la Comtesse de Maure: Sa Vie et Sa Correspondance*. Paris, 1863.

———. *La Marquise d'Huxelles et Ses Amis*. Paris, 1881.

Batiffol, Louis. *Le Louvre sous Henri IV et Louis XIII*. Paris, 1930.

Baudouin-Matuszek, Marie Noëlle, ed. *Marie de Médicis et le Palais du Luxembourg*. Paris, 1991.

Beaussant, Philippe. *Lully: ou, Le Musicien du Soleil*. Paris, 1992.

Béguin, Katia. *Les Princes de Condé: Rebelles, Courtisans, et Mécènes dans la France du Grand Siècle*. Paris, 1999.

Berenger, Jean. *Turenne*. Paris, 1987.

Bergin, Joseph. *Cardinal Richelieu: Power and the Pursuit of Wealth*. New Haven, 1985.

Bertaud, Madeleine, and François-Xavier Cuche. *Le Genre des Mémoires, Essai de Définition*. Colloque, Université de Strasbourg, no. 44. Paris, 1995.

Bertaud, Madeleine, and André Labertit. *De L'Estoile à Saint-Simon, Recherche sur la Culture des Mémorialistes au Temps des Trois Premiers Rois Bourbons*. Colloque, Université de Strasbourg, no. 43. Paris, 1993.

Bluche, François. *Louis XIV*, trans. Mark Greengrass. New York, 1990.

Blunt, Anthony. *Art and Architecture in France, 1500–1700*. London, 1991.

Bonney, Richard. "Cardinal Mazarin and the Great Nobility during the Fronde." *English Historical Review* 96, no. 381 (1981): 818–33.

———. *The King's Debts, Finance, and Politics in France, 1589–1661*. Oxford, 1981.

———. *Political Change in France under Richelieu and Mazarin, 1624–1661*. Oxford, 1978.

Boyer, Christian. *Gaston d'Orléans (1608–1660)*. Paris, 1999.

Bray, René. *La Préciosité et les Précieux de Thibaut de Champagne à Jean Giraudoux*. Paris, 1968.

Brédif, Léon. *Segrais: Sa Vie et Ses Oeuvres*. Paris, 1863.

Briot, Frédéric. "Du Dessein des Mémorialistes: La Seconde Vie." In *Le Genre des Mémoires*, ed. Madeleine Bertaud and François-Xavier Cuche, 183–91.

Broglie, Gabriel de. *L'Orléanisme: La Ressource Libérale de la France*. Paris, 1981.

Brunelle, Gayle K. "Dangerous Liaisons: Mésalliance and Early Modern French Noblewomen." *French Historical Studies* 19, no. 1 (1995): 75–103.

Brunet, Jacques-Charles. *Manuel du Libraire*. 7 vols., Paris, 1861.

Burckhardt, Carl J. *Richelieu and His Age: His Rise to Power*, trans. Edwin Muir and Willa Muir. London, 1967.

Burke, Peter. "The Courtier." In *Renaissance Characters*, ed. Eugenio Garin, trans. Lydia Cochrane, 98–122. Chicago, 1991.

———. *The Fabrication of Louis XIV*. New Haven, 1994.

Carrier, Hubert. "Pourquoi Ecrit-on des Mémoires au XVIIᵉ Siècle? L'exemple des Mémorialistes de la Fronde." In *Le Genre des Mémoires*, ed. Madeleine Bertaud and François-Xavier Cuche, 137–51.

———. *La Presse de la Fronde 1648–1653*. 2 vols., Geneva, 1989–91.

Chaillou des Barres, Etienne. *Les Châteaux d'Ancy-le-Franc, de Saint-Fargeau, de Chastellux, et de Tanlay*. Paris, 1845.

———. "Saint-Fargeau." *Annuaire/Yonne* 3 (1839): 233–96.

Chamchine, B——. *Le Château de Choisy*. Paris, 1910.

Chapco, Ellen J. "Historical Versimilitude and Literary Creation: The Rise of the *Petit Roman* in 17ᵗʰ Century France;" and Bruno Neveu, "Commentary," *Proceedings of the Twelfth Annual Meeting of the Western Society for French History* (1984): 50–57, 67–69.

Chartier, Roger, Marie-Madeleine Compère, and Dominique Julia. *L'Education en France du XVIᵉ et XVIIᵉ Siècles*. Paris, 1976.

Le Château de Saint-Fargeau. [Anon.] Editions Nivernaises, 1980.

Chaussinand-Nogaret, Guy, et al. *Histoire des Elites en France du XVIe au XXe Siècle*. Paris, 1991.

Chéruel, Adolphe. *Histoire de France sous le Ministère de Mazarin*. 3 vols., Paris, 1882.

———. *Histoire de France sous la Minorité de Louis XIV*. 4 vols., Paris, 1879.

Coirault, Yves, et al. "Mémoires et Création Littéraire." *XVIIe Siècle*, nos. 94–95 (1971).

Corvisier, André. *Louvois*. Paris, 1983.

Cotteau, G., and V. Petit. "Saint-Fargeau." *Annuaire/Yonne* 22 (1858): 180–94.

Cousin, Victor. *La Jeunesse de Madame de Longueville*. Paris, 1864.

———. *Madame de Sablé*. Paris, 1859.

———. *La Société Française au XVIIe Siècle*. 2 vols., Paris, 1886.

Cuénin, Micheline. "Les Mémoires Féminins du XVIIe Siècle, Disparités et Convergences." In *Le Genre des Mémoires*, ed. Madeleine Bertaud and François-Xavier Cuche, 99–109.

Davis, Natalie Zemon. *Society and Culture in Early Modern France*. Stanford, 1975.

———. "Women in Politics." In *A History of Women in the West*, ed. Davis and Arlette Farge, 3: 167–83. Cambridge, Mass., 1993.

DeJean, Joan. "Amazones et Femmes de Lettres: Pouvoirs Politiques et Littéraires à l'Âge Classique." In *Femmes et Pouvoirs sous l'Ancien Régime*, ed. Danielle Haase Dubosc and Eliane Viennot, 153–71. Paris, 1991.

Delisle, Léopold. *Le Cabinet des Manuscrits de la Bibliothèque Imperiale*. 3 vols., Paris, 1868.

Desprat, Jean-Paul. *Les Bâtards d'Henri IV: l'Epopée des Vendômes 1594–1727*. Paris, 1994.

Dethan, Georges. *Gaston d'Orléans, Conspirateur et Prince Charmant*. Paris, 1959.

———. *Mazarin, Un Homme de Paix à l'Age Baroque (1602–1661)*. Paris, 1981.

———. *Paris au Temps de Louis XIV, 1660–1715*. Paris, 1990.

———. *La Vie de Gaston d'Orléans*. Paris, 1992.

Dewald, Jonathan. *Aristocratic Experience and the Origins of Modern Culture: France, 1570–1715*. Berkeley, 1993.

———. "Politics and Personality in Seventeenth-Century France." *French Historical Studies* 16, no. 4 (1990): 893–908.

Dey, N. "Histoire de la Ville et Comté de Saint-Fargeau." *Bulletin/Yonne* 12 (1858): 38–101, 297–348.

Dubois, Elfreida. "The Education of Women in Seventeenth-Century France." *French Studies* 32 (1978): 1–19.

Duchêne, Roger. *Madame de La Fayette: La Romancière aux Cent Bras*. Paris, 1988.

———. *Madame de Sévigné et la Lettre d'Amour*. Paris, 1970.

Dulong, Claude. *L'Amour au XVIIe Siècle*. Paris, 1969.

———. *Anne d'Autriche, Mère de Louis XIV*. Paris, 1980.

———. *La Fortune de Mazarin*. Paris, 1990.

———. "From Conversation to Creation." In *A History of Women in the West*, ed. Natalie Zemon Davis and Arlette Farge, 3: 395–419.

——. *La Vie Quotidienne des Femmes au Grand Siècle*. Paris, 1984.

Dumont, François. "La Royauté Française et Monarchie Absolue au XVIIe Siècle." *XVIIe Siècle*, nos. 58–59 (1963): 4–29.

Dunlop, Ian. *Royal Palaces of France*. London, 1985.

Elias, Norbert. *La Société de Cour*, trans. Pierre Kamnitzer and Jeanne Etore. Paris, 1985.

Erlanger, Philippe. *Cinq-Mars*. Paris, 1962.

——. *Monsieur: Frère de Louis XIV*. Paris, 1953.

Evans, Margaret T. "Gaston, Richelieu, and the Publicists: Lèse-Majesté vs. Reason of Monarchy." *Proceedings of the Twelfth Annual Meeting of the Western Society for French History* (1984): 33–69.

Flandrin, Jean-Louis. *Familles: Parenté, Maison, Sexualité dans l'Ancien Régime*. Paris, 1984.

Foisil, Madeleine. *La Vie Quotidienne au Temps de Louis XIII*. Paris, 1992.

Fumaroli, Marc. "Les Mémoires du XVIIe Siècle au Carrefour des Genres en Prose." *XVIIe Siècle*, nos. 94–95 (1971): 7–37.

——. "Mémoires et Histoire: Le Dilemme de l'Historiographie Humaniste au XVIe Siècle." In *Les Valeurs*, ed. Noémi Hepp and Jacques Hennequin, 21–45.

Garapon, Jean. "Les Mémoires du XVIIe Siècle, Nebuleuses de Genre." In *Le Genre des Mémoires*, ed. Madeleine Bertaud and François-Xavier Cuche, 259–71.

Gibson, Wendy. *Women in Seventeenth-Century France*. New York, 1989.

Girard, Alain. *Répertoire des Livres Imprimés en France au XVIIe Siècle*, v. 13. Baden, 1985.

Godwin, Denise. *Les Nouvelles Françaises; ou, Les Divertissements de la Princesse Aurélie de Segrais: Une Conception Romanesque Ambivalente*. Paris, 1983.

Goldsmith, Elizabeth. *Exclusive Conversations: The Art of Interaction in Seventeenth-Century France*. Philadelphia, 1988.

Goubert, Pierre. *Louis XIV and Twenty Million Frenchmen*, trans. Anne Carter. New York, 1970.

Griselle, Eugène. *Maisons de la Grande Mademoiselle et de Gaston d'Orléans son Père*. Paris, 1912.

Hanley, Sarah. "Engendering the State: Family Formation and State Building in Early Modern France." *French Historical Studies* 16, no. 1 (1989): 4–27.

Hartha, Erica. "The Ideological Value of the Portrait in 17th Century France." *L'Esprit Créateur* 21 (1981): 15–25.

Hautecoeur, Louis. *Histoire de l'Architecture Classique en France*. 2 vols., Paris, 1943.

——. *Le Louvre et Les Tuileries*. 2 vols., Paris, 1924.

Hennequin, Jacques. "La Paternité chez Quelques Mémorialistes: Pères et Fils dans les Mémoires." In *Les Valeurs*, ed. Noémi Hepp and Jacques Hennequin, 289–305.

Hepp, Noémi, ed. *La Cour au Miroir des Mémorialistes 1530–1682*. Colloque, Université de Strasbourg, no. 31. Paris, 1991.

Hepp, Noémi, and Jacques Hennequin, eds. *Les Valeurs chez les Mémorialistes Français du XVIIe Siècle avant la Fronde*. Colloque, Université de Strasbourg, no. 22. Moulins-les-Metz, 1979.

Hipp, Marie-Thérèse. *Mythes et Réalités: Enquête sur le Roman et les Mémoires (1660–1700)*. Paris, 1976.

Hunt, David. *Parents and Children in History: The Psychology of Family Life in Early Modern France*. New York, 1970.

Isherwood, Robert. *Music in the Service of the King*. Ithaca, N.Y., 1973.

Jouanna, Arlette. *Le Devoir de Révolte: La Noblesse Française et la Gestation de l'Etat Moderne 1559–1661*. Paris, 1989.

Jouhaud, Christian. *Mazarinades: La Fronde des Mots*. Paris, 1985.

Kerviler, René, and Edouard de Barthélemy. *Valentin Conrart: Premier Secrétaire Perpétuel de l'Académie Française*. Paris, 1881.

Kettering, Sharon. "The Household Service of Early Modern French Noblewomen." *French Historical Studies* 20, no. 1 (1997): 54–85.

———. "Patronage and Politics during the Fronde." *French Historical Studies* 14, no. 3 (1986): 409–41.

———. "The Patronage Power of Early French Noblewomen." *The Historical Journal* 32 (1989): 817–41.

———. *Patrons, Brokers, and Clients in Seventeenth-Century France*. Oxford, 1986.

Kleinman, Ruth. *Anne d'Autriche*, trans. Ania Ciechanowska. Paris, 1993.

Krajewska, Barbara. *Mythes et Découvertes: Le Salon Littéraire de Madame de Rambouillet dans les Lettres de Contemporains*. Papers on French Seventeenth-Century Literature, series Biblio 17–52. Paris, 1990.

Labatut, Jeanne-Pierre. *Les Ducs et Pairs de France au XVIIᵉ Siècle*. Paris, 1972.

La Chesnaye-Dubois, François-Alexandre, et al. *Dictionnaire de la Noblesse*. 19 vols., Paris, 1863–76.

La Force, Auguste-Armand, duc de. *Lauzun: Un Courtisan du Grand Roi*. Paris, 1913.

———. *Louis XIV et Sa Cour*. Paris, 1956.

LeRoy-Ladurie, Emmanuel, and Jean-François Fitou. *Saint-Simon; ou, Le Système de la Cour*. Paris, 1997.

Lesne, Emmanuèle. *La Poétique des Mémoires 1650–1685*. Paris, 1996.

Lesne-Jaffro, Emmanuèle. "Les Mémoires et Leurs Destinaires dans la Seconde Moitié du XVIIᵉ Siècle." In *Le Genre des Mémoires*, ed. Madeleine Bertaud and François-Xavier Cuche, 28–43.

Lindsay, Robert O., and John Neu. *Mazarinades: A Checklist of Copies in Major Collections in the United States*. Metuchen, N.J., 1972.

Lorris, Pierre-Georges. *La Fronde*. Paris, 1961.

Lossky, Andrew. *Louis XIV and the French Monarchy*. New Brunswick, N.J., 1994.

Lougee, Carolyn C. *Le Paradis des Femmes: Salons and Social Stratification in Seventeenth-Century France*. Princeton, 1976.

Maclean, Ian. *Woman Triumphant: Feminism in French Literature, 1610–1652*. Oxford, 1977.

Magne, Emile. *La Vie Quotidienne au Temps de Louis XIII*. Paris, 1942.

———. *Voiture et l'Hôtel de Rambouillet: Les Origines 1597–1635*. Paris, 1929.

———. *Voiture et les Années de Gloire de l'Hôtel de Rambouillet 1635–1648*. Paris, 1912.

Major, J. Russell. *From Renaissance Monarchy to Absolute Monarchy: French Kings, Nobles, and Estates*. Baltimore, 1994.

——. "The Revolt of 1620: A Study of Ties of Fidelity." *French Historical Studies* 14 (1986): 391–408.

Maland, David. *Culture and Society in Seventeenth-Century France*. New York, 1970.

Mandrou, Robert. *Louis XIV en Son Temps*. Paris, 1973.

Marvick, Elizabeth Wirth. *Louis XIII: The Making of a King*. New Haven, 1986.

——. "Psychobiography and the Early Modern French Court: Notes on Method with Some Examples." *French Historical Studies* 19 (1996): 943–65.

McGowan, Margaret. *L'Art du Ballet de Cour en France 1581–1643*. Paris, 1986.

——. "La Fonction des Fêtes dans la Vie de Cour au XVIIe Siècle." In *La Cour au Miroir*, ed. Noémi Hepp, 27–41.

Méthivier, Hubert. *La Fronde*. Paris, 1984.

Mignet, François. *Négotiations Relatives à la Succession d'Espagne sous Louis XIV*. 4 vols., Paris, 1835.

Miller, John. *Bourbon and Stuart: Kings and Kingship in France and England in the Sevententh Century*. New York, 1987.

Mironneau, Paul, and Pierre Tucoo-Chala, eds. *La Légende d'Henri IV: Colloque du 25 Novembre 1994 au Palais du Luxembourg (Société d'Henri IV)*. Biarritz, 1995.

Moine, Marie-Christine. *Les Fêtes à la Cour du Roi Soleil*. Paris, 1984.

Mongrédien, Georges. *Le Grand Condé*. Paris, 1959.

——. *La Vie de Société aux XVIIe et XVIIIe Siècles*. Paris, 1950.

Moote, A. Lloyd. *Louis XIII the Just*. Berkeley, 1991.

——. *The Revolt of the Judges: The Parlement of Paris and the Fronde, 1643–1652*. Princeton, 1971.

Moote, A. Lloyd, and Jo Burr Margadant, eds. *French Historical Studies, Special Issue: Biography* 19, no. 4 (1996).

Moreau, Célestin. *Bibliographie des Mazarinades*. 3 vols., Paris, 1850–51.

Morlet-Chantalat, Chantal, and Micheline Cuénin. "Châteaux et Romans au XVIIe Siècle." *XVIIe Siècle*, nos. 118–19 (1978): 101–23.

Motley, Mark. *Becoming a French Aristocrat: The Education of the Court Nobility, 1580–1715*. Princeton, 1990.

Mougel, François. "La Fortune des Princes de Bourbon-Conty 1655–1791." *Revue d'Histoire Moderne et Contemporaine* 16 (1971): 30–49.

Muchembled, Robert. *Popular Culture and Elite Culture in France, 1400–1750*, trans. Lydia Cochrane. Baton Rouge, La., 1985.

Mueller, Marlies. "The Taming of the Amazon: The Changing Image of the Woman Warrior in *Ancien Régime* Fiction." *Papers on French Seventeenth-Century Literature* 22 (1995): 199–232.

Niderst, Alain, et al. *Les Trois Scudéry: Actes du Colloque du Havre*. Paris, 1991.

Orieux, Jean. *Bussy-Rabutin: Le Libertin Galant-Homme*. Paris, 1958.

Parkman, Francis. *Count Frontenac and New France under Louis XIV*. Boston, 1925.

Pernod, Michel. *La Fronde*. Paris, 1994.

Petitfils, Jean-Christian. *Lauzun; ou, l'Insolente Séduction.* Paris, 1987.

Plantié, Jacqueline. *La Mode du Portrait Littéraire en France 1641–1681.* Paris, 1994.

Pujo, Bernard. *Le Grand Condé.* Paris, 1995.

Ranum, Orest. *Artisans of Glory: Writers and Historical Thought in Seventeenth-Century France.* Chapel Hill, N.C., 1980.

———. *The Fronde.* New York, 1993.

———. *Paris in the Age of Absolutism.* New York, 1968.

———. *Richelieu and the Councillors of Louis XIII.* Oxford, 1963.

———. "Richelieu and the Great Nobility: Some Aspects of Early Modern Political Motives." *French Historical Studies* 3, no. 2 (1963): 184–204.

Reinhard, Marcel. *La Légende de Henri IV.* Saint-Brieuc, 1935.

Richardt, Aimé. *Colbert et le Colbertisme.* Paris, 1997.

Roche, Daniel. "La Fortune . . . des Princes de Condé." *Revue d'Histoire Moderne et Contemporaine* 14 (1967): 217–43.

Rodocanachi, Emannuel Pierre. *Les Infortunes d'une Petite-Fille d'Henri IV: Marguerite d'Orléans, Grande Duchesse de Toscane 1645–1721.* Paris, 1902.

Sandars, Mary I. *Lauzun: Courtier and Adventurer.* 2 vols., London, 1908.

Schalk, Ellery. "Clientages, Elites, and Absolutism in 17th Century France." *French Historical Studies* 14, no. 3 (1986): 442–48.

Solnon, Jean-François. *La Cour de France.* Paris, 1987.

Stefanovska, Malina. "A Monumental Triptych: Saint-Simon's *Parallèle des Trois Premiers Rois Bourbons.*" *French Historical Studies* 19, no. 4 (1996): 928–33.

Stegmann, André. "Le Roi, La Loi, Le Moi." In *Les Valeurs*, ed. Noémi Hepp and Jacques Hennequin, 170–93.

Sutcliffe, Anthony. *Paris: An Architectural History.* New Haven, 1993.

Synders, Georges. *La Pédagogie en France aux XVIIᵉ et XVIIIᵉ Siècles.* Paris, 1965.

Thomson, David. *Renaissance Paris: Architecture and Growth, 1475–1600.* Berkeley, 1984.

Timbal, P. C. "L'Esprit du Droit Privé au XVIIᵉ Siècle." *XVIIᵉ Siècle*, nos. 58–59 (1963): 30–39.

Tipping, Wessie M. *Jean Regnaud de Segrais: L'Homme et Son Oeuvre.* Paris, 1933.

Treasure, Geoffrey. *Mazarin: The Crisis of Absolutism in France.* London, 1997.

Van der Cruysse, Dirk. *Le Portrait dans les "Mémoires" du Duc de Saint-Simon.* Paris, 1971.

Van Kerrebrouck, Patrick. *La Maison de Bourbon 1256–1987.* Villeneuve d'Ascq, 1987.

Walsh, James E. *Mazarinades: A Catalogue of the Collection . . . in the Houghton Library, Harvard University.* Boston, 1976.

Walton, Guy. *Louis XIV's Versailles.* Chicago, 1986.

Watts, Derek A. "La Notion de Patrie Chez les Mémorialistes d'avant la Fronde: Le Problème de la Trahison." In *Les Valeurs*, ed. Noémi Hepp and Jacques Hennequin, 195–209.

———. "Self-Portrayal in Seventeenth-Century French Memoirs." *Australian Journal of French Studies* 12 (1975): 263–85.

Wolf, John B. *Louis XIV.* New York, 1968.

Index

Library of Congress Cataloging-in-Publication Data

Pitts, Vincent J. (Vincent Joseph), 1947–
    La Grande Mademoiselle at the Court of France: 1627–1693/ Vincent J. Pitts.
        p.   cm.
    Includes bibliographical references and index.
    ISBN 0-8018-6466-6 (alk. paper)
    1. Montpensier, Anne-Marie-Louise d'Orléans, duchesse de, 1627–1693.
2. France—Court and courtiers—History—17th century.   3. France—History—
Louis XIV, 1643–1715.   I. Title.
DC130.M8 P58 2000
944'.03'092—dc21   00-008266